FOOD IN
SUB-SAHARAN
AFRICA

D0141175

· FOOD IN AFRICA SERIES ·

Series Editor: *Art Hansen*
  Center for African Studies
  University of Florida
  Gainesville, Florida

• Africa's Agrarian Crisis: The Roots of Famine •
Stephen K. Commins, Michael F. Lofchie, and Rhys Payne, editors

• Food in Sub-Saharan Africa •
Art Hansen and Della E. McMillan, editors

FOOD IN SUB-SAHARAN AFRICA

edited by
Art Hansen and Della E. McMillan

Lynne Rienner Publishers, Inc. • Boulder, Colorado

Figure 3.5 reprinted with permission from John M. Pritchard.
1979. *Africa: A Study Geography for Advanced Students*. Revised
metric edition. London: Longman Inc. P. 65.

Figure 6.10 reprinted with permission from John M. Pritchard. 1979.
Africa: A Study Geography for Advanced Students. Revised metric
edition. London: Longman Inc. P. 64.

Published in the United States of America in 1986 by
Lynne Rienner Publishers Inc.
948 North Street, Suite 8, Boulder, Colorado 80302

©1986 by Lynne Rienner Publishers, Inc. All rights reserved

Library of Congress Cataloging-in-Publication Data

Main entry under title:

Food in Sub-Saharan Africa.

    Includes bibliographies and index.
    1. Food supply—Africa, Sub-Saharan—Addresses,
essays, lectures. 2. Nutrition policy—Africa, Sub-
Saharan—Addresses, essays, lectures. 3. Agriculture—
Africa, Sub-Saharan—Addresses, essays, lectures.
I. Hansen, Art. II. McMillan, Della E.
HD9017.S82F66   1986   338.1′9′67   85-28260
ISBN 0-931477-59-X
ISBN 0-931477-58-1 (pbk.)

Casebound edition distributed outside of North and South America and Japan by
Frances Pinter (Publishers) Ltd, 25 Floral Street,
London WC2E 9DS England   UK ISBN 0-86187-598-2

Printed and bound in the United States of America

Contents

Tables and Figures

• TABLES •

xi

• FIGURES •

Preface

The idea for this book grew out of a recognized need at the University of Florida for faculty and students to have a better understanding of the perspectives of their colleagues in other disciplines who were involved in the same overseas development projects or who were conducting research on related problems, often in the same Third World countries. Although there was a confluence of goals—usually related to increasing the food production and income of small farmers—there were wide differences in the assessments of priorities and in disciplinary acquisition of the necessary skills and experiences needed for the design of sound policies and programs.

In 1977 various faculty members began to explore ways to strengthen interdisciplinary dialogue on development issues. One of the outcomes of this effort was an informal lunch seminar—Social, Agricultural, and Food Scientists Working Group—in which faculty and graduate students from different disciplines met on a weekly basis to discuss research interests and opportunities and to present research results and theoretical models dealing with Third World agriculture. This group became interested in a mode of research called farming systems research, and some of these people became involved in establishing at Florida one of the first formal programs for university-level training in farming systems research and extension. Another outcome was a conscientious effort on the part of the university's Center for African Studies to develop research, teaching, and public events on African agriculture. The center established a Food in Africa Program to encourage and coordinate these activities.

In 1983 the Center for African Studies began an annual spring seminar on African food issues. Faculty were invited to present survey papers dealing with some of the critical food issues of concern to their own discipline, the evolution of this disciplinary concern over time, and their estimation of future research directions. Important topics, pertinent interested disciplines, experts in various fields, and critical readings were identified through this seminar, and then served as the basis for the present book.

We encourage readers who have comments, suggestions, or questions to send them to the Food in Africa Program, Center for African Studies, 470 Grinter Hall, University of Florida, Gainesville, FL 32611.

We would like to thank a number of people who have contributed directly to the production of the book. R. Hunt Davis, Jr., director of the Center for African Studies at the University of Florida, has been an invaluable force behind the development of interdisciplinary studies in general and the development of the Food in Africa Program and this book in particular; we extend him a special note of thanks for his steady support throughout the entire project. Our publisher, Lynne Rienner, and her staff have been very encouraging and helpful. Paul Monaghan has performed his job of verifying the chapter citations and bibliography with enthusiasm and precision. Paul R. Stayert and Randy Pearsall deserve recognition for the excellent maps and figures. Carol Lauriault and Robin Sumner of the Center for African Studies should be thanked for the tables and general administrative assistance. We would also like to thank Akim Hansen, Anita Spring, and David Wilson for their support. We have learned a great deal.

Art Hansen
Della E. McMillan

FOOD IN SUB-SAHARAN AFRICA

·1·

Overview: Food in Sub-Saharan Africa

DELLA E. McMILLAN
ART HANSEN

Africans are experiencing a series of short-term and long-term food crises. Short-term crises are more evident to foreign observers and the news media than long-term ones, but the two types of crises are fundamentally linked in Sub-Saharan Africa. Short-term, or acute, crises are characterized by the sudden appearance somewhere in Africa of large numbers of starving people or people weakened by undernutrition who, consequently, are dying of diseases and exposure. Quite often these sufferers are also embroiled in a war or fleeing as refugees or as drought-driven migrants. Examples of acute crises during the past two decades include the Biafran famine of the late 1960s, the Sahelian and Ethiopian drought and famine of the late 1960s and early 1970s, wars and refugees in many countries (Angola, Chad, Ethiopia, Uganda, and Zimbabwe, among others), and the Ethiopian and Sahelian drought and famine in the mid-1980s. Sometimes the onset of an acute crisis is more gradual than the sudden realization or recognition of the crisis by observers might imply. A recent instance is the 1984 Ethiopian famine with its accompanying exodus into Sudan of hundreds of thousands of people. Although official reports had anticipated this disaster for some time, the crisis burst almost unheralded into the U.S. public consciousness with a single television special in October 1984.

The long-term, or chronic, food crises are less dramatic, less immediate, and less obvious to the casual observer. They are characterized by gradual—over a period of years or decades—changes and trends in economic or ecological factors or relationships. In the beginning these trends are merely worrisome, but their continuation threatens the stability and existence of the societies and economies because the systems are obviously failing to cope. These chronic crises starve national and local food systems by depleting reserves that would otherwise be available to individuals, families, villages, and countries to help improve living standards or, at least, to serve as buffers from the effects of acute crises. Examples of chronic crises include decreasing food production per capita, desertification, de-

1

forestation, increasing foreign debt, and increased importation of staple foods.

Acute crises often seem to be independent of these long-term trends; identifiable and immediate events are seen as sufficient to cause the acute crises. A war begins in the Ogaden between Somalia and Ethiopia, then hundreds of thousands of refugees appear—a recognizable rapid cause and effect. The same occurs with wars in Chad and Mozambique. The rains fail for one or two years in northern Ethiopia or the West African Sahel, and people are driven by drought to cluster around the capital cities and towns and even to flee to Sudan, Cameroon, and Nigeria in search of food—immediate cause and effect. Famine of drought and famine of war are both acute crises. Yet the severity of the popular responses, the deaths and dislocations, and the inadequacy of national food systems to cope with acute crises are directly linked with the more deeply rooted long-term crises. The linkage of acute and chronic crises is often overlooked and many observers naively believe that the acute crises are the only crises. As Robert MacNamera recently noted, "Ironically this avalanche of compassion for the open and visible suffering of the victims of famine—genuine as it is—has tended to obscure the more fundamental problems not only of the Sahelian zone itself, but of much of Sub-Saharan Africa as a whole" (1985:12).

Although the rains may begin in northern Ethiopia, the food crisis is not over. Even if the Eritrean war were over; the Tigrean and Ogaden regions, Angola, Chad, and Mozambique peaceful; all of the parties to the conflicts satisfied; and all of the refugees repatriated; the food problems in Africa would continue. Spaceship Earth has sprung a leak in Africa. The relationships of population, food production, natural resources, reserve capital, and political and technical expertise still spell disaster. The lifeboat is riding very low in the water, and the next wave—a war, drought, locusts, disease—will sweep more people away.

Africa's population is growing faster than that of any other continent. With its current annual growth rate of approximately 3.0 percent, the population will double in approximately twenty-three years. Agriculture is the single largest employer of this population. Sixty-three percent of Africa's economically active labor force were still engaged in agriculture in 1984. This percentage has been steadily decreasing over the years as more people move to towns and cities or as those remaining in the rural areas become involved in nonagricultural work. In many African countries—particularly the poorer ones with less industry, mining, and other off-farm sources of employment—80 percent or more of the labor force remains devoted to agriculture (see Table 1.1). Even though the percentage of the labor force in agriculture is slowly decreasing, the rapid increase in the total size of the population means that the total number of workers relying directly on agriculture for their living will increase in the years to come. This statistic does not include, of course, the additional noneconomically active people (young children, the sick and aged) who also rely directly on agriculture for their livelihood.

Although this book focuses on problems and problemsolving, we must not forget that the vast majority of African farmers continue to be productive. Food production has actually increased over the years in most Sub-Saharan African countries, as shown by the index of food production (see Table 1.1). This index is based on each country's domestic production of food during the 1974–1976 period. The average annual production during these years is the baseline for comparison and has been given the value of 100; the index shows the relationship of 1984 food production to that earlier period. A few countries have not maintained the level of food production that they attained almost ten years ago, although a few others have made significant increases. The real measure of self-sufficiency is not in food production per se but in production per capita. Comparing these statistics (see Table 1.1) shows that many countries have not managed to maintain or improve their production per capita. Many countries have failed to keep up with their increase in population, which is a primary reason for the increase in food imports. On the other hand, imports (and the reasons for imports) may have caused the poor performance of the agricultural sector (see Asante and Lemarchand in this book).

Food production is obviously an essential element of the food crises, but wealthy countries can afford to purchase the food they need. Unfortunately, Sub-Saharan African countries are not wealthy and have already accumulated large external debts, especially in relation to their Gross National Products, so food imports are not a satisfactory long-term solution. These statistics are disheartening, and they reveal some of the systemic weaknesses and long-term trends that further diminish the stability and integrity of Africa's food systems.

• AN INTEGRATED UNDERSTANDING •

How do we address these fundamental problems, and how may we better understand the relationship between Africa's acute and chronic food crises? The complexity of the problems and linkages demands a multifaceted and interdisciplinary approach that is able to probe deeply into or work intensively with individual factors and relationships without losing sight of how these pieces fit together. Unfortunately, such an approach is rarely, if ever, encountered. The usual research and development approaches to food issues in Africa and elsewhere are specialized, compartmentalized, and not integrated. National planning, research, and development units are often in separate ministries and work independently, without any coordination. Agricultural research and extension units are not only administratively separate but often opposed and competitive, rather than cooperative.

Foreign aid is similarly fragmented. Emergency relief for acute crises is zealously guarded to prevent its use for long-term development. Development assistance is packaged in projects, each of which is usually focused on one locale, aspect, or level and restricted to one recipient unit or ministry. The multiplicity of projects and donors commonly overwhelms the administrative ability of the developing country and actually diminishes the effectiveness of the small number of skilled, experienced administrators who are a critical and limited resource.

Research scientists based in universities are similarly uncoordinated in their research efforts. Each discipline generally carries out its work independently of

TABLE 1.1. Crisis Indicators for Sub-Saharan African Countries

Region and Country	1984 Population (millions)	1984 Labor in Agriculture (percentage)	1984 Index of Food Production (1974-1976=100)	1984 Index of Food Production per Capita (1974-1976=100)	1983 Ratio of External Dept to GNPb (percentage)
West Africa (17)					
Benin	3.9	44	131	103	59
Burkina Faso	6.8	79	110	90	38
Cape Verde	0.3	54	--	--	--
Chad	4.9	80	107	88	44
Gambia	0.6	76	82	68	--
Ghana	13.0	48	96	72	28
Guinea	5.3	78	109	90	69
Guinea-Bissau	0.9	80	122	89	--
Ivory Coast	9.5	77	150	107	79
Liberia	2.1	67	116	86	72
Mali	7.8	85	123	99	89
Mauritania	1.8	81	122	95	158
Niger	5.9	85	130	103	49
Nigeria	92.0	50	128	95	18
Senegal	6.4	72	85	64	61
Sierra Leone	3.5	62	98	84	35
Togo	2.8	66	113	89	114
Northeast Africa (4)					
Djibouti	0.4	--	--	--	--
Ethiopia	35.4	77	110	90	26
Somalia	5.4	78	110	64	62
Sudan	20.9	75	106	81	78
Central Africa (7)					
Cameroon	9.5	79	101	81	27
Central Afr. Rep.	2.5	85	113	92	33
Congo	1.7	31	116	93	76
Equatorial Guinea	0.4	72	--	--	--

Country					
Gabon	1.1	74	119	104	--
Sao Tome, Principe	0.1	--	--	--	--
Zaire	32.1	72	123	95	92
East Africa (6)					
Burundi	4.5	81	103	86	26
Kenya	19.8	76	112	77	43
Rwanda	5.9	87	139	103	14
Seychelles	0.1	--	--	--	--
Tanzania	21.7	79	128	94	59
Uganda	15.2	79	122	90	18
Southern Africa (14)					
Angola	8.5	55	104	79	--
Botswana	1.0	77	84	61	--
Comoros	0.4	62	--	--	23
Lesotho	1.5	81	90	72	52
Madagascar	9.7	80	115	90	55
Malawi	6.8	81	128	97	--
Mauritius	1.0	26	96	81	--
Mozambique	13.7	60	98	70	--
Namibia	1.5	46	90	70	--
Reunion	0.6	25	128	111	--
South Africa	31.6	27	101	81	--
Swaziland	0.6	69	147	113	84
Zambia	6.4	64	98	74	28
Zimbabwe	8.5	57	92	67	--
Total Africa	536.9	63	116	88	52

Sources: 1984 statistics are from the 1984 FAO Production Yearbook, Food and Agriculture Organization, Rome, and 1983 statistics are from the World Development Report 1985 published by Oxford University Press for the World Bank.

a Labor represents the economically active sector of the population.
b GNP means the Gross National Product.

the others. This isolation of the disciplines is continued by the tradition of academic departmentalization within the university system that educates professionals. Agricultural scientists focus on technical dimensions of crop and animal production and specialize in particular species. Their work is further subdivided by a traditional separation into breeding and genetics, soil fertility, crop production and management, animal husbandry, and control of diseases, insects, weeds, and nematodes. Meteorologists, foresters, ecologists, and wildlife biologists investigate the weather and the state of natural resources, often in isolation from the agricultural scientists. Social scientists study socioeconomic dimensions of production and distribution of products and income, including varying sociopolitical access to productive resources, as well as pricing, marketing, and other national policy issues. Food scientists and nutritionists concentrate on processing, storage, and the real "bottom line"—food consumption and the quantitative and qualitative adequacy of supplies. Seldom do these disciplines interact in any sustained manner to address the complexities of African food issues, a tendency that is also evident in most textbooks and even edited reference books on African or Third World food and development topics. A notable exception is the multidisciplinary volume, *The Politics of Natural Disaster: The Case of the Sahel Drought* (Glantz 1976).

Although disciplinary specialization is an essential element of agricultural research, it is associated with the loss of the integrated (generalist or interdisciplinary) capacity to see how specialized diagnoses and proposed solutions interrelate with one another, as well as with the wider ecological, socioeconomic, and political context in which the production, distribution, and consumption of food take place. This book offers an integrated multidisciplinary perspective on African food issues. In its entirety, the volume is a message about the complexity of contemporary food issues and about how different disciplines fit together to offer insights and to provide useful information. Fifteen disciplines are represented here from the natural, production, and social sciences. Almost all of the authors have worked in Africa and are continuing to work there; all are concerned with Africa's people, with what lies behind the current events and acute emergencies, with the Africa that seldom or never makes the news. This type of broad, interdisciplinary perspective is important for anyone involved in teaching, administration, or research on African food issues who wants a vantage point for seeing the interrelationships among domains of expertise and policy concern.

• OUTLINE OF THE BOOK •

Although the entire book is an integrated statement, it is divided into five parts, and different readers may be most interested in using various parts or chapters as introductions to unfamiliar data, areas, or perspectives. Each of the five parts of the book may be used as a separate set of readings to complement a reader's current expertise or as supplemental readings in university courses. All of the contributing authors have written in a manner intelligible to people in other disciplines and to nonacademics, i.e., jargon has been minimized or eliminated. In addition to the usual scholarly citations in the text, each author has also suggested a short list of articles and books that are readily accessible for those readers who are new to the material or perspective presented in that chapter; a list is appended to each chapter. References that are cited in the text are collected into a common bibliography at the end of the book.

In the four chapters that constitute the first part, political scientists and economists provide a general overview at the level of policy and also compare theoretical and disciplinary perspectives. S.K.B. Asante introduces the concept of food policy, and four levels (global, continental, regional, and national) of policy responses to food crises are discussed. He considers the overevaluation of national currency exchange rates to be the most devastating national policy in terms of depressing agricultural production.

René Lemarchand examines the political economy of food, beginning with the effects of colonial policies. Various interpretations of the peasant mode of production are contrasted, and the ideological differences between supposedly socialist and supposedly capitalist states appear less important than the forms of smallholder social organization, the elite manipulation of their market advantage, and external constraints.

John Staatz and Carl Eicher describe the theoretical evolution since 1950 of development economics, focusing on the changing perception of agriculture and the interplay between theory and experience. From the 1950s to the 1960s, the emphasis was on investment in industry; agriculture was viewed as a passive cow to be milked and smallholder labor was viewed as a free good. African leaders and other Third World leaders based their countries' development on these theories and were disappointed by the results—the need to develop agriculture became more apparent. As the authors trace this evolution, we realize how much these theories have influenced the direction that many Third World governments followed in the design of policies and investment priorities.

Sara Berry begins her review of the social science literature on food in Africa with a much-needed reminder about the weakness of the data on which discussions of food crises are based (including the data in Table 1.1). She examines a broad range of sociopolitical, socioeconomic, and ecological studies, then clarifies the major directions and perspectives in this diverse body of knowledge.

The second part contains five chapters written by historians, anthropologists, and a meteorologist to provide an introduction to Africa for readers who are unfamiliar with the continent, its resources, climate, and people. The heterogeneity of Africa, the existence and relevance of historical patterns in climate and politics, and the importance of socioeconomic factors are revealed in these chapters. Charles Guthrie emphasizes a number of dimensions of the African environment— size, political regions, climatic and vegetation patterns, and agricultural systems—thereby demonstrating the heterogeneity and diversity of Sub-Saharan Africa. Population growth and distribution and economic patterns are described, as is the importance of ethnicity, language, and religion to individual and group identity. Africa is seen to be sociopolitically dynamic.

Sharon Nicholson describes long-term climatic fluctuations in Sub-Saharan Africa, providing an important time depth for recent drought periods. Her fascinating data reveal that droughts are "an inherent characteristic of the environment"; they must be seen as normal events that recur at irregular intervals and must be included in development planning and policy decisions. Daniel McGee points out that the existence of natural resources is only one dimension; another dimension is the technology that people choose to use to exploit these resources. He outlines four basic land-use systems or subsistence strategies—agriculture, herding, fishing, and hunting and gathering—each has been associated with characteristic ways to organize people and their labor.

The "ways of feeling, believing, and behaving" that are indigenous to Sub-Saharan Africa are defined and described by Ronald Cohen. Although contemporary African societies are complex and contain many features that are not traditional in Africa, married and family life and larger sociopolitical relationships continue to be strongly influenced by indigenous principles and patterns. Agricultural and socioeconomic development programs are usually based on the individual or the household, but it is naive to assume that these behave entirely according to Western economic principles and to ignore their embeddedness in traditional social formations. R. Hunt Davis, Jr. examines in depth a controversial topic alluded to by many other contributors: the importance of the colonial experiences as causes of contemporary food crises. He places the colonial period in a longer historical context, documenting the precolonial origins of cash cropping and discussing the postcolonial continuation of many colonial policies.

The third part gives readers from the socioeconomic and policy sciences an opportunity to appreciate the empirical and analytical concerns of technical scientists. Four chapters cover a wide range of technical issues dealing with food production. The contributors, representing the disciplines of soil science, agronomy, horticulture, agricultural economics, animal science, anthropology, and dairy science, point out that there are many technical problems that have not yet been solved. Hugh Popenoe addresses the soil types found in Africa and the interaction of soils, plants, climate, and management. Soil fertility and erosion are major concerns, as are policy questions dealing with self-sustainability, industrial inputs, and the advantages of smaller versus larger farms. Clifton Hiebsch and Stephen O'Hair clarify the nutritional characteristics, geographic distribution, and production requirements and constraints of the major food crops, both by category (cereal grains, farinaceous, and legume grains) and by individual species. James Simpson and Robert McDowell describe the economic and nutritional importance of domestic livestock and their byproducts, as well as the production systems and constraints found in Africa. Michael McGlothlen, Paul Goldsmith, and Charles Fox discuss the most underrated sources of food in Africa—undomesticated animals and plants. They document the importance of these food sources, the need for additional research, and the integration of this information into national food planning and development.

The four chapters in the fourth part of this book rectify another common imbalance in discussions of African food and famine. All too often the only issue discussed is production; the critical importance of distribution, storage, preparation, consumption patterns, and nutritional needs are ignored. Robert P. Bates begins this section by examining postharvest considerations as one element in the food chain. Olivia Webley points out the importance of fuelwood in converting crop and animal products into food, and she clarifies the relationship between deforestation and food crises. One of the editors addresses questions of intra- and interhousehold distributions. Many observers consider farmers to be organized in self-sufficient households, so that the only distributional concern is how to move their surplus food to the cities. Based on her research in Burkina Faso, Della McMillan details the complexity and social embeddedness of the ways that rural people gain access to productive resources, especially land and labor, and to the food that is produced. She also questions the usefulness of the household concept as a basis for development planning because of intrahousehold and suprahousehold decisionmaking and distribution patterns. A discussion by Patricia Wagner on human nutritional needs and the relationship of nutrition, diet, health, and performance follows.

In the final four chapters in the fifth part, ways in which Africans and international development agencies are working toward solutions to food crises are addressed. Donald Plucknett, Nigel Smith, and Robert Herdt describe the evolution and work of the international agricultural research centers, important resources in themselves and designed to support and encourage strong national research and extension programs. Louise Fresco and Susan Poats define and discuss farming systems research and extension, an innovative approach to understanding the problems confronting African farmers and to establishing effective working relationships among farmers and research and extension staffs. This approach provides a methodology for more practical research and more integrated research and extension. Anita Spring presents another way in which a better understanding of the socioeconomic characteristics of African agriculture will contribute to more effective policies and development programs. Women are extremely important in African agriculture, both as laborers and as decisionmakers; yet research and development are guided by mistaken Western beliefs about "the farmer and his wife," which serve to block women's access to information and other resources that would help women increase their effectiveness as farmers.

A discussion by Robert Browne and Robert Cummings completes the book by returning to the level of national and international policy that was the subject of the first chapters. In this final chapter, as in others throughout the book, the clear message is that Africans and African initiatives are the bases for progress. Africa has problems, both acute and chronic, and these problems must be addressed by Africans in order for any meaningful policies to be formulated and implemented. The Lagos Plan of Action is a long-range plan agreed to by the African heads of state to restructure African economies. Browne and Cummings compare the plan to the World Bank's program, as described in the 1981 Berg Report, which addresses more immediate concerns.

The problems and constraints that Africans confront are difficult and intricately interrelated. We hope that this book illuminates that there are no simple solutions nor facile understandings.

·2·

Food as a Focus of National and Regional Policies in Contemporary Africa

S. K. B. ASANTE

The disappointing performance of Africa's food and agricultural sector, resulting in what is now termed a continental African food crisis, has continued to occupy the attention of the international community, African governments, policymakers, and academics during the 1970s and 1980s. Concern over the magnitude and complexity of this crisis has evoked policy responses and declarations at four levels. At the global level, the 1974 United Nations (UN) World Food Conference was entrusted with developing ways and means whereby the international community, as a whole, could take specific action to resolve the world food problem within the broad context of development and international cooperation. The conference produced an impressive declaration on the eradication of hunger and malnutrition (UN 1975:64). At the continental level, collective African policy within the framework of the Organization of African Unity (OAU) is articulated in the very first substantial chapter of the 1980 *Lagos Plan of Action*, the 1984 Harare Declaration of the Food and Agriculture Organization (FAO) and the Addis Ababa OAU Declaration, and the 1985 OAU Declaration "Africa's Priority Program for Economic Recovery, 1986-1990" (OAU 1981, 1984, 1985; FAO 1984). At the African regional level, groups such as the Economic Community of West African States (ECOWAS) express their responses to the crisis in their respective food and agricultural programs; at the national level, responses to the crises are stressed in the development plans of individual African countries.

This four-pronged policy response reflects the magnitude of Africa's food problem. The problem is even more alarming when it is considered that Sub-Saharan Africa is the only region in the world where per capita food production has declined during the past two decades. Food self-sufficiency ratios had dropped from 98 percent in the 1960s to around 86 percent by 1980, implying that, on the average, each African had 12 percent less home grown food in 1980 than twenty years earlier (Economic Commission for Africa 1983:8; World Bank 1984:10–11). This disappointing performance in agriculture and in food production reflects a very serious situation because this sector, the mainstay in most African economies, makes the single largest contribution (40 to 60 percent) to the gross domestic product and provides over 50 percent of the export earnings of most African countries (Hinderink and Sterkenberg 1983:1). Although this contribution varies among countries, it remains, in most countries, the single most important generator of overall economic growth and any sustained future development, including the supply of capital, raw materials, and labor for industrialization. Hence the food question is inextricably entwined with the general problems of agriculture and economic development in Africa, and no government can afford to ignore the social and political disruptions caused by food production failures on this scale.

Not surprisingly, the causes and remedies of Africa's agrarian malaise have been the subject of wide-ranging debate among experts and policymakers. This debate has, in turn, given rise to a series of such crucial and challenging questions as the following: How did Africa's food situation come to be in such a thoroughly disturbing and perilous state? What are the root causes of food deficits of this magnitude? Why has food proved to be so intractable a problem? Why has the "temporary" resort to food imports become a permanent feature of Africa's food trade? How have African governments intervened in the food and agricultural sector? Put differently, what policies have been adopted at both national and regional levels to deal with the problem? What are the components or objectives of these policies? Finally, what prospect for solving the crisis do these policies offer?

These questions cannot be conclusively answered here. To throw light on some of them, this chapter focuses attention primarily on the key issue of national and regional food policies of African countries since independence. Because regional approaches to food problems in Africa are a relatively recent phenomenon, national policies receive wider coverage and emphasis. Before considering these policies, it seems appropriate to set the stage with a brief review of the concept of food policy, its rationale, scope, and objectives.

· THE CONCEPT OF FOOD POLICY ·

Food policy (variously termed national food plan, national food strategy, national food security scheme, or national agriculture and nutrition plan) at its core constitutes an integrative policy approach to food production, distribution, and consumption, encompassing the broad economic and social policies and reforms that affect the wider distribution of income and people's access to food. In other words, this is a policy which, as a recent World Bank publication puts it, encompasses the collective efforts of governments to "influence the decision making environment of food producers, food consumers, and food marketing agents in order to further social objectives" (Timmer et al. 1983:9). Generally, this policy serves as a mechanism to give institutional expression to the priority for food and the elimination of hunger, transcending the sometimes sharp, sectoral demarcations in national decisionmaking.

Food policy is first and foremost a political act. It is political to the extent that it is aimed primarily at placing (or replacing) a country's food and nutrition problems, along with other aspects of development, on a scale of priorities—at the top of the list if necessary. It is also a political act because the strategy is not just one more policy document. Food policy must be designed and presented to mobilize promotion for the policy not only in the administration, but also, and most importantly, among the first to be concerned—the peasants or food producers themselves. Therefore, it is important to get the rural population as involved in the design and implementation of food policy as possible. Food policy has to define and plan the implementation of measures that give national producers, including fishermen and herdsmen, the economic and social incentives and the security they need to go beyond subsistence farming and help meet the needs of the country as a whole. Basically, food policy should involve the rural world in a development process that will be self-sustaining in the long run.

National food policy in most societies is designed to achieve four basic objectives: efficient growth in the food and agricultural sectors, job creation, a decent, minimum standard-of-living, and security against famine or extreme food shortages (Timmer et al. 1983:14–15). The emphasis placed on each objective varies by country and over time; the importance of each objective reflects the contribution of each to a nation's health and welfare and, implicitly, to its political stability. From this perspective, understanding the causes of Africa's food problem should lead to better policy.

Amaryta Sen has succinctly remarked, "There is, indeed, no such thing as an apolitical food problem" (Sen 1982:459). Regardless of the variety of perspectives permeating the literature, it is increasingly apparent that the poor performance of African agriculture cannot be attributed to physical constraints or infrastructural defects. The key to Africa's agrarian malaise seems to lie ultimately in government policies over the years. Agricultural, food, and other rural policies set by governments are crucially important in creating incentives and in shaping the economic environment within which food producers operate. Given much needed incentives and realistic policy directives, physical and biological constraints are not factors that farmers are unable to transcend (Bates 1981:2; Tarrant 1980:45). Theodore Schultz has gone as far as to argue that "incentives to guide and reward farmers are a critical component" in food production. And, once there "are investment opportunities and efficient incentives, farmers will turn sand into gold" (Schultz 1964:5). Although this may seem a little oversimplified, the significance of Schultz's argument may hardly be disputed. Undoubtedly, it is the "complex web of interrelationships between Africa's agricultural markets and government policies" that, more than anything else, has created the present agrarian malaise (Scarlett 1981:175). Markets and government policies have not received much attention in the literature, probably because they are complex and because pronouncements concerning them are more "politically volatile" than are evaluations of technical and physical problems (Scarlett 1981:175). But it is precisely within this more controversial arena that understanding of Africa's food problems must be sought and future research areas and policy reforms must be identified.

· THE POLITICS OF ECONOMIC INTERVENTION ·

The food problem in Africa has deeper historical roots than are usually appreciated. (For details about these roots see Davis in this volume.) Food was not a priority area for capital investment during the entire colonial period (Eicher 1982:157–58; Tandon 1981:86–88; E. Hansen 1981:103–105; Dinham and Hines 1984:17–20). Land, labor, and other resources of the colonies were diverted away from food and into the production of industrial raw materials. Infrastructural developments that took place in Sub-Saharan Africa during this period, and for almost fifteen years after independence, were mainly to service the production, transportation, and marketing of industrial crops; after independence, developments also included the creation of import substitution industries (Tandon 1981:88). Throughout this period, little attention was paid to investments in human capital, i.e., the training of African agricultural scientists and managers, or to research on food crops or to strengthening internal market linkages. Research on export crops was more intensive and generally more productive. Virtually all the peasants—practically the whole population—were "left pretty much to their own devices to feed themselves" (Tandon 1981:88). There was no food policy or organization to encourage food production.

Colonial agricultural policy—indeed, the inherited structure of most economies as a whole—has not been appreciably altered by the successive African elites. Since independence, the agricultural strategies of almost all African countries, especially regarding the food subsector, have been generally laissez faire: They have allowed the status quo to prevail (Dittch 1981:53). It is not suggested that African governments have not intervened in agriculture. On the contrary, they have intervened extensively and have exhibited a wide range of diversity in the extent of government intervention in food systems. Despite differences in policy choice and priorities, African countries have stressed the great importance of agriculture both in their official pronouncements and in their development plans. These plans, in almost identical terms, acknowledge the overriding need to increase and diversify agricultural output, to achieve self-sufficiency in food supply, and to raise rural income and living standards (Hinderink and Sterkenberg 1983:6). Although such stated policies for increasing food production reflect a growing commitment to the agricultural sector, the implementation of these policies is often thwarted, inter alia, by changing government priorities and developmental deficiencies.

Another common factor worth stressing is related to the general approach of African governments to the agricultural sector. Whereas the approach of developed countries to agriculture may be called "the integrative view," which sees this sector as more or less an equal partner with industry and other sectors of society, in the Third World and in Africa in particular, the approach to agriculture may be called "the exploitative view." This perspective does not accept the agricultural sector as an equal partner with other sectors of development. Rather, it sees this sector as a subservient one to be exploited for urban industrialization (Clute 1982:1–2). As Robert H. Bates observed:

> To secure revenues to promote industry, African states seek taxes from agriculture. By maintaining a sheltered industrial order, they generate economic benefits for elites, as well as resources for winning the political backing of influential groups in the urban centers. To safeguard their urban-industrial base, they seek low-cost food. This aim therefore leads them to intervene in markets and to attempt to depress the level of farm prices (Bates 1981:120).

Leaders and governments throughout Africa, whether civilian or military, capitalist or socialist, generally view agriculture as a backward sector that should be exploited and controlled in order to provide agricultural surpluses, taxes and labor, and to finance structural change and industrial/urban development. There exists, therefore, a striking similarity between the colonial policy that exploited the resources of colonial territories to develop the metropolis and the national policy that now exploits the resources of the countryside to develop the urban cities. This is reflected in various aspects of agricultural and food policies adopted by African governments since attaining independence.

Public Investment in Agriculture

Allocation of public investments to the food and agricultural sector merits special attention in any discussion of national food policy in Africa as this underscores the low priority assigned to this sector over the years. A recent review of government expenditure policy by the Economic Commission for Africa (ECA) concluded that African governments "have not been backing up their avowed food self-sufficiency objectives by increased allocation of public resources" (ECA 1984). This is reinforced by the FAO's "Interim Report on Constraints on Food Production," which shows the extent to which expenditures of African governments on agriculture from domestic resources have tended to decline in real terms (FAO 1983a). Intercountry comparisons are not easy to come by, owing to definitional, data, and measurement problems. However, in the 1970s around 10 percent or less of planned development expenditure was allocated to the agricultural sectors in Kenya and Mali, as compared with 31 percent in India during the first five-year-plan in 1951 and 20 percent of the much larger absolute investment in the subsequent three plans (Lele 1984:440). By way of contrast, in both Ghana and Nigeria the commitment to agricultural development has been merely verbal. Ghana allocated a mere 7 percent of public investments to the agricultural sector during 1974–1976. Nigeria's Second (1970–1974) and Third (1975–1979) Development Plans showed a distinct industrial bias. In the latter plan, less than 6 percent of total expenditure, recurrent and capital, was reserved for agriculture, despite professed belief in its important role (Hinderink and Sterkenberg 1983:6–8).

This relative neglect of agriculture has resulted in little research on food crops, weakly staffed extension services for food farming, and inadequate investments in farm-to-market transportation. Many areas of potentially significant surpluses remain cut off from urban consumers and, hence, producers have no incentive to produce in surplus of family and social needs. In addition, the emphasis on exports (the cash-crop syndrome) inherited from the colonial era has meant that the meager public investment allocated to agriculture goes into the development of the export sector. Overwhelming emphasis on this sector adversely affects food production. The case of tobacco as a cash crop in Tanzania is illustrative of the adverse impact of the cash-crop syndrome on the food-production sector. The success of the Tanzanian government's special program in the 1970s to encourage the growing of tobacco in Mpanda resulted in rapid decline in local maize production from 1,110 tons in 1969–1970 to 131 tons in 1974–1975, while tobacco production increased from 184 tons to 310 tons. Mpanda thus became dependent on imports of maize (U.S. Department of Agriculture 1981:165, as cited in Clute 1982:10–11). A significant feature of the cash-crop syndrome is the willingness of African governments to undercut the interests of food producers in order to promote cash cropping. Rather than harnessing the traditional agricultural system as a tool in development, government policies have often been exploitative and antitraditional. Nowhere is this more clearly demonstrated than in pricing policies.

Pricing Policy

Keeping food prices low is a standard government technique generally accepted by observers as the fundamental cause of the continent-wide problem of food deficits. Unlike many countries in Asia where there are guaranteed floor prices for farm produce, in most African countries producer prices for domestic food products are not guaranteed. In Indonesia promotion of rice output is complemented and strengthened by the government rice pricing policy, which guarantees the farmer a minimum price for his product while also taking into consideration the limited purchasing power of the consumers at large (Amat 1982:145). In most African countries, food pricing policies are consumer-oriented. Prices are fixed at a low level that favors consumers, mostly urban consumers, and deters producers from increasing their efforts. Policy motivations have been more political than economic, reflecting the expediency of responding to urban elites who are more visible even if less numerous than rural farmers. Low food prices are a means of maintaining the support of the urban masses whose violent demonstrations and riots, often against rising food prices, can provide the catalyst for a coup d'etat. The April 1979 rice riots in Monrovia led to the ousting of the Tolbert regime in Liberia in 1980 (Asante 1984); the April 1985 demonstrations in Khartoum culminated in the overthrow of the government of President Gaafar el-Nimeiry of Sudan.

Due to the vulnerability of governments to urban pressure, food imports are subsidized to keep prices low, and domestic food prices are reduced through the operation of government-controlled marketing institutions and the manipulation of trade policies. Bates noted that:

> agricultural policy is devised to cope with political problems whose immediate origins lie outside of the agricultural sector. Pricing policy finds its origins in the struggle between urban interests and their governments; and in the political reconciliation of that struggle, it is the rural producers who bear the costs; they are the ones who bear the burden of policies designed to lower the price of food (Bates 1981:35).

The mirror image of urban pressure for cheap food is production stagnation, or unsatisfactory performance in the agricultural sector. Agricultural pricing policies of African governments tend to have an adverse impact on the gap between rural and urban incomes and on incentives to produce food. They also affect the ability of governments to establish and maintain food reserves, and they disturb employment opportunities in farming, processing, and rural industries (Eicher and Baker 1982:59).

Of all the governmental policies which have had a negative impact upon the agricultural sector, none has had more devastating consequences than the general tendency of African governments to overvalue the exchange rates of their currencies. This practice has set in motion a whole set of "powerful disincentives to agricultural growth" to which the Berg Report of the World Bank, *Accelerated Development in Sub-Saharan Africa: An Agenda for Action,* has drawn attention in recent years (World Bank 1981:24–27). Overvalued currencies have made food imports artificially cheap in relation to domestic production, and price policies have often been criticized for failing to stimulate domestic production. These two factors, together with a marked shift in consumer tastes in favor of "new" foods that are not well suited to domestic production such as bread, and in some cases rice, have led to a growing dependence on imports to satisfy the demands of politically powerful groups. Food aid, through which population groups may have been introduced to nontraditional foods, has at times contributed to this shift in consumer preferences. In some cases, imported farm inputs such as tools, machinery, and agrochemicals have been made more expensive or restricted in their supply in order to protect infant, domestic industries; in some cases, the incentive for farmers to produce a surplus for sale has been reduced by the limited availability of imported consumer goods, once again to protect domestic industries. The operation of government-controlled marketing agencies is another policy constraint adversely affecting food production.

State Marketing Boards

Marketing boards, or parastatal institutions, in many countries have grown into monopolies controlling agricultural input and output as well as marketing and processing. These boards operate as a means of controlling trade, regulating prices, enforcing grading standards, and directing operations within national borders. They have incurred added costs to the consumer, reduced returns to the producer, and also stifled initiatives to keep costs down and provide improved services. These parastatals appear to lack the purchasing networks, pricing policies, and other means needed to secure large quantities of foodstuffs relative to consumption needs (Nicholson and Esseks 1978:694). Colin Leys cited the case of Kenya's Maize and Produce Marketing Board, which proved itself unequal to the responsibilities entrusted to it during the drought periods of 1965 and 1970–1971; Lynn Scarlett stressed the tendency of marketing boards to encourage black market sales and impede the operation of market signals regarding supply and demand (Leys 1974:106–107; Scarlett 1981:181). The widespread appearance of state farms, the government-directed cooperatives, and the so-called green revolution have not improved the food production situation.

State Farms and Crash Programs

State farms and crash programs proliferated in the past two decades as means of promoting agricultural production by pooling rural resources, introducing farming inputs and techniques, and improving rural incomes. Evidence suggests that none has realized its objectives (Delancey 1980:109–122; Gusau 1981:19–22; Clute 1982:12). Barry Munslow recently studied Mozambique's huge investments in the state farm sector that failed to produce the hoped-for bumper harvests (Munslow 1984:211). Ghana launched state farms in the 1960s with a total work force of 20,800 and a budgetary allocation of approximately 90 percent of the total agricultural development budget; they were a gigantic failure. The Agricultural Development Corporation, which managed most of the 135 state farms, accumulated a loss of $4 million by 1964, $7 million by 1965, and over $9 million by 1966 (Bates 1981:46–47; Dittch 1981:54). State, community, and cooperative farms and settlements are often inappropriate, expensive, and not directed at the productive forces in the economy—the peasant farmers. Large-scale schemes divert attention and cash from the underlying problems of rural poverty and inadequate infrastructure, which affect the majority of Africa's farming population. A classic example of this process in Zambia was illustrated by Barbara Dinham and Colin Hines (Dinham and Hines 1984:146–147). Crash programs such as Nigeria's "Operation Feed the Nation" or Ghana's "Operation Feed Yourself" are launched with great fanfare and end in "crash failure" (E. Hansen 1981:99–115).

In theory, the small farmer is the cornerstone and major beneficiary of the various crash programs. In practice, however, there is a distinct bias against the smallholder sector, comprising over 90 percent of all producers, because of a widespread belief among planners and policymakers that peasant farmers cannot achieve the desired overall increases in output and keep pace with population growth. Instead of tackling the underlying causes of the problems facing peasant farmers—low farm prices and poor marketing, storage, and distribution systems—many African governments choose to initiate crash programs that are not based on an analytical understanding of the problems at hand. These programs have great emotional and political appeal, especially if cast in a rhetoric for mass consumption that oversimplifies complex problems. Yet food problems are extraordinarily complicated, and politically expedient short-term interventions frequently have devastating long-term consequences. The greater the short-term pressures to implement a program, the greater the probability that the program will have effects just opposite to those intended. Crash programs tend to crash.

Although the small farmer is neglected, public food production schemes tend to confer benefits on and promote the fortunes of a few privileged farmers. Ghana's "Operation Feed Yourself," launched in February 1972, promoted the rise of a wealthy "farmer" class of military men and high-ranking bureaucrats and their business friends who owned large-scale enterprises. In contrast, the smallholder sector was discriminated against and suffered heavily from the increasingly unfavorable food pricing policy and many other aspects of the program. Yet experience in Malawi, Kenya, Zimbabwe, and other countries demonstrates that smallholders respond to economic incentives with significant production increases if they have access to markets, services, and improved cultivation technology (Williams 1983:24).

State farms are established to produce food as well as other agricultural products; however, evidence shows that food is seldom a priority. The cash-crop syndrome still dominates. Emmanuel Hansen analyzed the case of Ghana's state farms and found that they devoted only 40 percent of acreage to food crops and paid serious attention only to rice and maize (E. Hansen 1981:107). Similarly, despite public declarations to the contrary, the priority of Ghana's "Operation Feed Yourself" was still on export and industrial crops. Moreover, although Ghana's state farms in the 1960s consumed a significant proportion of the public agricultural budget, they nonetheless supplied a small fraction of the total market. John Dadson showed that they provided less than two percent of the total marketed output of most commodities (Dadson 1970, as cited in Bates 1981:49).

The emphasis on large-scale, capitalized, and mechanized farms since the mid-1970s introduces a more serious problem to Africa's food production policies. The scarcity of high-quality management and imported inputs has led to an increased dependence on foreign expertise and diverse foreign involvement in capital-intensive food production in many African countries, notably Benin, Ethiopia, Ghana, Kenya, Nigeria, Mozambique, Sudan, Tanzania, and Togo. Hence, transnational agribusiness has been brought into the domestic food sector in Africa (Dinham and Hines 1984:144). In Nigeria, for example, transnational corporations are invited to participate in large-scale food production envisaged in the Green Revolution launched in 1981. The Nigerian Enterprises Promotion Act was amended in 1981 to encourage private, foreign investment in agriculture to as much as 60 percent of the equity (Hinderink and Sterkenberg 1983:91). Africa may be moving towards deepening dependency in the food sector. Against this background, the regional approach based on the strategy of collective self-reliance, as espoused in both the *Lagos Plan of Action* and the July 1978 FAO Regional Food Plan for Africa, merits special attention (OAU 1981: FAO 1978b:ii–ix).

· THE REGIONAL APPROACH ·

The 1974 world food crisis and its severe impact on Africa have strengthened interest in regional approaches to the food problem. Hence, the regional integration schemes established in Africa since then have each devoted special attention to food. Among these regional schemes is ECOWAS, which was established in Lagos in May 1975 to bring together sixteen West African countries. Besides ECOWAS there are the nine-member Southern African Development Coordination Conference (SADCC), which was formally inaugurated in Lusaka, Zambia, in April 1980; the Preferential Trade Area for Eastern and Southern African States (PTA), which was also concluded in Lusaka in December 1981 by nine out of the potential eighteen states; and the Economic Community of the States of Central Africa (CEEAC), established in Libreville, Gabon, in October 1983.

In response to the target of self-sufficiency in food production contained in the *Lagos Plan of Action,* ECOWAS adopted in May 1980 an elaborate agricultural program comprising four sectors. In order of priority these sectors are: food crops, livestock, fisheries, and forestry. The main program objectives are to fight the serious subregional food problems, improve rural incomes and living conditions, and provide necessary inputs to the community's industrial program. The 1982 ECOWAS summit in Cotonou, Benin, reinforced this program by adopting the ECOWAS Agricultural Development Strategy, a blueprint for agricultural development in the subregion. This was given a further impetus by the May 1983 Conakry, Guinea, ECOWAS meeting and, especially, by the November 1984 ECOWAS Heads of State and Government summit in Lome, Togo, which, in an important resolution on economic recovery in West Africa, adopted measures to rationalize regional production so as to achieve food self-sufficiency (ECOWAS 1984).

The question that poses itself is this: To what extent have the West African countries attempted to transform the food policies and programs of ECOWAS from a political slogan into a framework for policy and action? Although ECOWAS began initiating food strategies in 1980, the Community has not implemented any of its food policies, and no conscious effort has been made at the regional level to link recognition of problems with the measures and resources required for their solution (Asante 1985).

Although PTA, which was finally launched in Harare in July 1984, has not yet advanced much beyond ratification of its treaty, SADCC seems to have made some substantial progress towards implementing its projects for "enhancing the productivity of the land on a permanent basis, and towards national and regional food policies" (SADCC 1984:9). The SADCC food security program includes three main objectives: (1) satisfying the basic need for food for the region's population, and progressively improving food supplies to all the people, irrespective of their specific economic situation or their position in society; (2) achieving national self-sufficiency in food supplies in order to free the region from constraints imposed by the present situation of external dependence; and (3) eliminating the periodic food crises in the region that have catastrophic social consequences and reinforce dependency and underdevelopment (Mafeje 1985).

Given the region's present stage of development, SADCC's economic strategy aims to reinforce national and regional production capacity. Particular attention focuses on the following: regionally producing and distributing seeds; reproducing livestock; producing tools, agricultural equipment, agrochemicals, and other inputs; and improving infrastructure necessary for input distribution at national and regional levels. The second aim is to improve systems for delivery, conservation, processing, and storage of food. SADCC has initiated policies for the prevention of food crises. These involve five main elements: implementing an early-warning system, preventing plagues and diseases, creating regional food security reserves, creating seed stocks for basic food crops, and, finally, establishing regional mechanisms to coordinate external support in times of emergency (Asante 1986). On the whole, SADCC is much more advanced in implementing its regional food policies than any of the other existing African regional integration schemes. It has made detailed studies of regional food marketing and a regional resources information system, and is coordinating its technical assistance program for agrarian issues.

Nevertheless, African regional schemes have not been as dynamic and progressive in adopting and implementing regional food policies as have been those schemes in other developing areas such as Asia. By the mid-1970s, for example, the Association of Southeast Asian Nations (ASEAN) had agreed to establish an emergency food supply facility known as the ASEAN Food Security Reserve. Because the international community has failed to establish such a facility at the global level, although the United Nations World Food Conference in Rome in 1974 recommended establishing one, such a facility organized by ASEAN represents a particularly innovative step towards international food security (Hanpongpandh 1982:281–306). Are the African regional schemes able to learn from the ASEAN experience?

· POLICY REFORMS ·

Evidence suggests that food policies in contemporary Africa, at both the national and regional levels, have not been designed to deal effectively with the issues of food production, rural-employment generation, domestic-food price formation, and efficient storage, transportation, and processing. A thorough reform of policies toward agriculture in Africa is long overdue. Policy change is required in the area of public-investment allocations to agriculture. Government inputs into agriculture and rural development are extremely low, rarely designed to assist the traditional farmer, and tend to favor so-called modern schemes such as state farms, cooperatives, and large-scale mechanized farms, which have not been viable or productive. There is a need to allocate adequate resources to support agricultural production at all levels, especially because a higher government priority to agriculture is a requirement for more assistance from the international community.

Whereas there is indiscriminate government intervention in some policy areas, others are neglected, namely agricultural research, extension networks, development of trained manpower, and establishment of effective institutions and delivery systems to assist in distribution and marketing. Food policies will not be successfully implemented over the long term unless adequate institutions and trained manpower are available to monitor and oversee policy implementation. Lack of sufficient manpower and institutions has often been the bottleneck in slowing down the implementation process. Any program, no matter how beautifully designed, is only as good as the ability to make it work in the field. Increased attention to training, public management, and sustained institutional support are, therefore, top priorities.

An option for policy change that is likely to offer the highest returns in a relatively short time is an incentive policy package that combines establishment of improved incentive systems through more remunerative producer prices, more efficient marketing systems, and sufficient and timely supplies of inputs and consumer goods. In this regard, pricing policy merits special attention. Effective price policy is the most essential element in a program to increase agricultural production. There is no substitute for positive price incentives to the agricultural sector based on long-term opportunity costs (Timmer et al. 1983:290). The first element of an agricultural policy, therefore, is to fix guaranteed agricultural prices and set up a system that ensures that the peasant farmer will, in fact, obtain these prices. Such an incentive policy package would probably contribute more to domestic food self-reliance than an infusion of crash food production projects that risk faltering in the absence of sound policies.

The need to strengthen the fragile subsistence sector may not be overemphasized. Too often in the past the needs of the subsistence farmer have been overlooked by policymakers. Yet the peasant farmer is, and will remain, the principal participant in any agricultural policy and the principal organizer of the rural sector. The development of smallholder agriculture is therefore essential. Because of its share in national output and total employment, this subsector holds the key to agricultural and overall progress. Increasingly, it is being recognized that African smallholders respond to economic opportunities and, given the right incentives and income generating opportunities, he and she are quite prepared to change and modernize (Pallangyo and Odero-Ogwel, in press).

Policy change is also required at the regional level. There are a number of important activities in support of food and agricultural development that lend themselves to easier forms of cooperation at the regional level. These include the development of regional natural resources such as river basins, transfer of technology, food storage, marketing, agricultural research and training, and investment and finance. Regional schemes offer considerable potential for action to increase food production through intergovernmental organizations for land-and-water–resources development, particularly where lakes and river basins transcend national boundaries. Priority attention is needed by regional organizations to assist national governments to strengthen and adapt their production structures. Above all, African regional planners should learn from recent experiences of the Caribbean Community and Common Market (CARICOM). This regional scheme created the Caribbean Food Corporation to implement a regional food plan aimed specifically at stemming the trend of the large and rapidly growing regional food import bill, which rocketed to $500 million in 1974. The plan will mobilize funds and technical and managerial skills from within and without the region to promote, finance, and implement agricultural production schemes (Axline 1979:165–166).

• SUMMARY •

Governmental policies during the colonial period and since national independence have contributed to the current African food crisis. The colonial tradition of exploiting the agricultural sector, especially the small farmers and their families who comprise the majority of the population in most African countries, continued after African elites replaced Europeans and continues even today. As John Staatz and Carl Eicher point out in another chapter, this exploitation agreed with the formerly prevailing idea that developing countries should emphasize industrialization by taxing agriculture. The traditional agricultural sector would provide capital from taxation, labor from the underemployed rural population, and raw materials from its production to fuel industrial growth.

Even after the errors of this approach became evident and world food crises appeared, contemporary African governments did not adopt adequate and realistic policies for food production, marketing, and consumption. All or almost all African countries stress the importance of the agricultural sector in public pronouncements and official development plans, but per capita production continues to decline because effective action is not taken. Some countries and regional organizations have now devised food policies to encourage self-sufficiency and promote domestic production, but this political act antagonizes important political actors, particularly the urban elites and masses who desire artificially low food prices and continued reliance on imports. Pricing policies and currency exchange rates provide disincentives to farmers, but favor the urban minority. State farms and other large-scale schemes receive the scarce managerial time and development funding that smallholder agriculture needs. Undue emphasis is still given to export crops for the world market, and too little emphasis is given to food for Africa.

• SUGGESTED FURTHER READINGS •

Asante, S. K. B. 1986. *The Political Economy of Regionalism in Africa: A Decade of the Economic Community of West African States (ECOWAS)*. New York: Praeger.

Balaam, David N., and Michael J. Casey, eds. 1981. *Food Politics: The Regional Conflict*. Totowa, New Jersey: Allanheld, Osmun Publishers.

Bates, Robert H. 1981. *Markets and States in Tropical Africa: The Political Basis of Agricultural Policies*. Berkeley, California: University of California Press.

Clute, Robert E. 1982. The Role of Agriculture in African Development. *African Studies Review* 25:4:1–20.

Delancey, Mark W. 1980. Cameroon National Food Policies and Organizations: The Green Revolution and Structural Proliferation. *Journal of African Studies* 7:2:109–122.

Hansen, Emmanuel. 1981. Public Policy and the Food Question in Ghana. *African Development* 6:3:99–115.

Nicholson, N. K., and John D. Esseks. 1978. The Politics of Food Scarcities in Developing Countries. *International Organization* 32:3:679–719.

OAU (Organization of African Unity). 1985. Africa's Priority Programme for Economic Recovery, 1986-1990. Adopted by the Heads of State and Government of the Organization of African Unity at its 21st Ordinary Session, held in Addis Ababa, Ethopia, 18–20 July 1985. Addis Adaba: African Heads of Government, Declaration No. 1.

Sen, Amaryta. 1982. The Food Problem: Theory and Practice. *Third World Quarterly* 4:3.

·3·

The Political Economy
of Food Issues

RENÉ LEMARCHAND

Africa's famine has entered the American consciousness as a dramatic media event; it has yet to enter the U.S. consciousness as a political event. Behind the agonies of hundreds of thousands of Africans dying of starvation lies more than a natural catastrophe of unprecedented severity. Humanitarian concern for, and public awareness of, this massive affliction have yet to be accompanied by a clear understanding of the tragic incapacity of African governments to cope with food scarcities. Even where climatic and environmental perturbations are most painfully evident, as in the Sahel, a reasonable case may be made that African hunger has as much to do with political conditions as with weather conditions.

The magnitude of Africa's food crisis is well established. Africa is the only continent where food output per capita has declined over the last two decades. With a population growth of approximately 3 percent per annum, recorded per capita agricultural production declined by 1.5 percent annually in the 1970s and early 1980s. Precisely when grain prices are going up and African currency reserves are shrinking, the demand for food imports is increasing dramatically. A total of approximately 150 million Africans are directly threatened by famine and malnutrition. In the Sudan alone, 10 million are said to be at risk of starvation. According to UNICEF estimates, the number of Sudanese children dying each year of malnutrition now reaches 750,000 (as compared with 200,000 in "normal" years!). The statistics for Chad and Ethiopia are equally alarming. Not just people but entire communities and ways of life are faced with extinction.

What remains open to debate are the underlying causes and implications of the crisis. The devastating effects of natural calamities cannot be overlooked any more than the severe physical constraints of the African environment; yet these factors alone are not enough to explain the existence of a "continent-wide agricultural breakdown" (Lofchie and Commins 1984:2). The constraints of the international economy, the deterioration of Africa's terms of trade, the setting of wrong sectoral priorities, and inept agricultural policies have all had a powerful multiplier

25

effect on the adversities of nature. In brief, the basic questions that lie in the background of the current food crisis—how much food to grow, what kinds of food, at what cost, by what means, by whom and for whom—are preeminently political questions.

The following pages explore the relationship between food and politics from the three-dimensional perspective of local, national, and international arenas. The first dimension involves a critical look at the so-called peasant mode of production as a key dimension of the social environment of African states. The second brings into focus the ongoing debate about the relative merits or demerits of socialist versus capitalist experiments. The third draws attention to external constraints arising from the international parameters within which food policies are formulated and put into practice. In looking at these dimensions of analysis we proceed on the assumption that the relationship between politics and agricultural output is a reciprocal one. Just as political choices have a decisive bearing on the structure and volume of food production, the resulting patterns of agricultural production, distribution, and consumption are bound to affect the way in which power and wealth are distributed in society.

· THE ROOTS OF ECONOMIC VULNERABILITY: THE LEGACY OF COLONIAL RULE ·

The issue of the relationship between food and politics did not arise with independence; it lies at the heart of the policy choices made by European powers in their attempt to cushion the costs of their political hegemony and maximize the returns on their capital investments. Fiscal autonomy, the key corollary of colonial rule, presupposed a taxable income, and both in turn came to depend on the ability of the colonial state to bring about the so-called mise en valeur, or development of human and economic resources. In a way that few of its advocates anticipated, the imperative of mise en valeur has had a determining impact on the structure of African agricultural economies.

To blame African hunger on the perverse effects of colonial rule seems scarcely compatible with the statistical evidence available. At the time of independence in the 1960s, Africa produced roughly 95 percent of its food requirements. Today virtually every African state, with the exception of South Africa and Zimbabwe, must import food. Statistics alone do not tell the full story, however, and they may be made to tell very different stories. A closer examination of the colonial record provides ample proof of food crises originating not just from adverse climatic conditions but also from policy decisions that, directly or indirectly, profoundly undermined the viability of indigenous food systems. Clearly, the benefits derived from the development of new productive forces and infrastructures must be assessed against the human and environmental costs involved, including "the loss of life, the loss of reliable and nutritious sources of food, and, more generally, the loss of many skills with which the inhabitants had learnt to turn their harsh environment to their advantage" (Coulson 1982:32).

Among the several areas of economic vulnerability created by colonial rule, none has been more potentially damaging to African food systems than the decline of peasant commodity production under the combined pressures of cash cropping and industrial capitalism. The introduction of cash crops proved the quickest way to meet the revenue-generating needs of the nascent colonial state. Only by subjecting African peasants to stringent fiscal obligations could the state generate enough cash to pay its own way into the avenues of colonization. Compulsory cultivation of cash crops thus became the standard policy through which African peasants were forced to earn a taxable income. Though implemented on different scales and with varying degrees of severity, this policy lies at the root of what Michael Lofchie referred to a decade ago as "Africa's agrarian paradox": "A continent unable to produce sufficient food to provide the majority of its citizens with even a barely minimal diet has been able to record sharp increases in its annual production of agricultural goods destined for external markets" (Lofchie 1975:554). While the priority given to cash crops by the European colonizer is still very much in evidence in most African states,[1] so also are the discriminating effects of pricing and marketing policies. Just as the prices paid to producers of food crops remain abysmally low compared to the prices fetched by export crops, the highly skewed distribution of marketing and storage facilities, agricultural extension services, and technological inputs tend to put the food-producing sectors at a striking disadvantage.

Critically related to the decline of indigenous food crops was the development of mining and industrial activities; both made increasingly heavy demands on African labor while creating a situation in which "the wages paid to men who worked on the mine were subsidized by the rural areas" (Seidman 1977:414). In Zimbabwe (formerly Southern Rhodesia), Zambia (formerly Northern Rhodesia), and Zaire (formerly Congo), the expansion of labor recruitment networks into the rural sectors led to massive migrations of African peasants into the mining areas. Through the enforcement of discriminatory policies against the marketing of African produce, additional pressures were applied on the rural sectors to insure a regular flow of cheap labor. By keeping the prices paid to African producers at an artificially low level, entry into the wage labor force of industrial capitalism became the only alternative to starvation. Where European commercial farming was allowed to develop, as in Zambia and Zimbabwe, further steps were taken to reduce the competitiveness of African agriculture, for example, "through the subsidy and encouragement given to settler-farmers, through capturing of the African grain market, and by refusing to exchange cash in return for African produce" (Riddell 1978:6). Illustrative of the effects of such policies on African agriculture was the situation prevailing in the Rhodesian (Zambian) Copperbelt in 1911:

> The whole country is in a state of starvation, and we are a long way from the next season's harvest. The village people are in a miserable state, and for the time being are subsisting on roots and anything edible they can find in the bush. In many of

the villages all one sees are a few old women and children. The men have disappeared (Perring 1979:20).

In sum, the involvement of the colonial state in the expansion of industrial capitalism, first as a labor-recruiting agency, then as a price-setting authority, and ultimately as the ally of European settlers, must be seen as the central factor behind the decline and dislocations suffered by African food systems.

Bolstered by the full panoply of colonial policies and land regulations, the spread of European settlement resulted in massive alienations of agricultural land in states such as Kenya, Zambia, and Zimbabwe, thus posing additional threats to African commodity producers. By far the most serious threat to African agriculture stemmed from the need for a cheap labor supply to bring the European estates into the sphere of capitalist production. This meant that "the settler had to compete against alternative uses of African labor in commodity production as well as subsistence agriculture" (Berman and Lonsdale 1980:62). To improve the competitiveness of European commercial farming, African "reserves" were created in both Kenya and Zimbabwe in which land was set aside for the sole use of African producers, but with the ultimate intention of converting them into vast reservoirs of agricultural labor. As the population pressure on the reserves increased, and as local production barely reached subsistence levels, more and more Africans were driven into wage labor. As R. C. Riddell noted, "cheap labor supplies from the reserves could only be forthcoming 'voluntarily' if reserve farming was carried out at, or better, below subsistence levels and if the reserves were reasonably full" (Riddell 1978:7). As a result, major distortions in the structure of rural economies were created, with a commercial farming sector heavily dependent on a continuing influx of cheap labor that coexisted side by side with a subsistence sector in which population pressures and land hunger combined to perpetuate rural poverty. These distortions are still visible today in both Kenya and Zimbabwe. In neither state is there much room for an "uncaptured peasantry," to use Goran Hyden's phrase (1980). The key fact, whose roots lie in the history of European settlement, is that the respective peasantries are at a serious competitive disadvantage, politically and financially, relative to medium- and large-scale commercial farms owned by the state or private enterprise, and the peasantries are unable to act as a significant countervailing force.

Just as there are important connections between colonial policies and the multiplicity of issues associated with the land problem, both are in turn intimately related to the dynamics of political protest in colonial Africa. The drastic restructuring of African rural economies under the impact of the colonial state, and most importantly through the commercialization of agriculture, holds crucial implications for an understanding of anticolonial rural protest. From tax-payers' revolts in nineteenth century Ghana to the Mau-Mau Emergency in Kenya, from the rural radicalism of the Bataka Association in Uganda to the Pende revolt in the Belgian Congo, the grievances generated by the commercialization of agriculture emerge as the dominant theme of anticolonial rural-based protest movements (Bates 1979).

This is not the place for a sustained inquiry into the history of these pro-tonationalist manifestations. What needs to be stressed is that colonial authorities have often responded to these threats by instituting land reforms, which in turn created the conditions for new forms of social conflict. A case in point is the Swynnerton Plan, devised as a political counterweight to the Mau-Mau insurgency. Intended to provide the basis for the emergence of a sizable rural African middle class enjoying access to individual freehold titles, the Swynnerton Plan ended up creating a very different type of social pyramid, characterized by a substantial concentration of landholdings among individuals with access to off-farm cash income. As Angelique Haugerud has ably demonstrated, "land is being accumulated not necessarily for agricultural development but to hold for speculative purposes, for sons' future inheritance, and to increase one's borrowing power for loans on the security of title deeds" (Haugerud 1983:84). In Kenya, as in many other parts of Africa, land reform has done relatively little to alter existing patterns of rural inequality. The reasons for this lack of effect lie in part in the questionable priorities set by urban elites in the allocation of land and agricultural technology, and in part in the patterns of articulation between local peasant communities and the wider political frameworks within which they are encapsulated.

• THE VIEW FROM BELOW: THE PEASANT MODE OF PRODUCTION REEXAMINED •

Is the "peasant mode of production" a short-hand formula for an economy in which affective ties, based on kinship, are so prevalent as to enable peasant communities to effectively resist the assaults of the state? Or does it incorporate a nascent class conflict between rural capitalists and peasant producers? These questions lie at the heart of the ongoing debate among Africanists about the relevance of the mode of production in historical and contemporary analysis. Although no definitive answer has yet emerged from the exchange, there is nonetheless a widespread agreement about the centrality of the peasant mode (however defined) in the structuring of rural communities. Where opinions differ is in the extent to which the peasant mode may be said to effectively block state intervention or, alternatively, to facilitate its penetration into the fabric of rural communities. At the root of this dissent lie radically different conceptions of the types of normative orientations and articulations associated with peasant modes of production.

The case for looking at African peasantries as "uncaptured," i.e., as basically resistant to state pressures, is nowhere more forcefully argued than by Goran Hyden (1980) in his classic study of villagization (ujamaa) in Tanzania. The "economy of affection," according to Hyden, incorporates a logic of social solidarity that departs fundamentally from that of capitalism or socialism:

> In the economy of affection, economic action is . . . embedded in a range of social considerations that allow for redistribution of opportunities and benefits in a

manner which is impossible where modern capitalism or socialism prevails and formalized state action dominates the process of redistribution (Hyden 1980:19).

Unlike capitalism or socialism, the economy of affection "is primarily concerned with problems of reproduction rather than production" (Hyden 1980:18). The profit motive is conspicuously absent from such economies; social solidarity provides the basic mechanisms through which resources are redistributed among members of the community. The implications are two-fold. On the one hand, the economy of affection offers peasant communities enough autonomy and self-reliance to evade the encroachments of the state. On the other hand, because it serves as a survival mechanism in conditions of relative scarcity, "it dampens the revolutionary potential of the peasants" (Hyden 1980:192).

On both counts there are major reservations about the Hyden thesis. For one thing, the line of demarcation between the economy of affection and the market economy is not as easily traced as the foregoing might suggest. Marxist analysts are basically correct in stressing the transitional character of the peasant mode of production, and, in some instances, its tendency "more and more to become mere aspects of the capitalist mode of production" (Leys 1975:172). The least that may be said is that the economy of affection, as articulated by Hyden, is far too static a concept to provide meaningful analytic leverage. Just as one may conceptualize this economy in very different ways, shown by comparing Hyden's characterization with the more sophisticated and contrasting efforts of James Scott (1976) and Samuel Popkin (1979), one may also visualize fundamental differences in the extent to which Africans have in fact remained uncaptured by the advances of rural capitalism. In addition, how far the economy of affection acts as a disincentive to revolutionary upheavals is by no means self-evident.[2] The susceptibility of African peasants to radical protest is well established, and where rural protest failed to materialize, the reasons may not lie exclusively with the dampening effects of affection.

Whereas Hyden tends to reduce African modes of production to a single affective denominator, contemporary Marxist analysts look at these realities through a variety of analytic lenses. Nothing like a consistent definition of the peasant mode of production emerges from the work of people such as Claude Meillassoux, Emmanuel Terray, Catherine Coquery-Vidrovitch, Gervase Clarence-Smith, or Martin Klein.[3] This lack of consistency, in a sense, reflects a greater sensitivity to the historical particularities of African peasantries as well as to their different modes of incorporation in wider capitalist economies. These authors call attention to the classic distinction between the forces of production and the relations of production. The first of these concepts throws into relief the extremely low level of technology available to most African societies, the forbidding constraints of the environment, the rudimentary character of the division of labor, and ultimately the Sisyphean task of harnessing these extraordinarily feeble and fragmented forces to a cohesive organizational framework. This is particularly true of attempts to convert African peasants into socialist producers. As one observer noted: "The idea that a disciplined vanguard party could force the course of history and get socialism now, whatever the level of development of the forces of production, led people to ignore or trivialize the vital question of economic productivity" (Clarence-Smith 1985:20).

The question of the relations of production, on the other hand, directs attention to a range of possible links between peasant communities and the state. Although state-peasant relations are implicitly defined in the terms commonly used to designate land-tenure systems, to categorize African peasants in terms of smallholders, communal farmers, tenants, and squatters leaves out a crucial variable in defining relations of production: the role of the state or its agents in providing access to land resources, technology, labor, and credit facilities. It is the state in Zimbabwe that defines the status of "legitimate squatter," i.e., "genuine and deserving illegal occupants"—a category that includes "those who moved on to vacant commercial farms during the war, farm workers who lost their jobs when owners abandoned their farms, and returning refugees" (Cheater 1983:79). It is the state in Rwanda that allocates plots to the bénéficiaires (recipients of land) in newly settled areas (Lemarchand 1982). It is the state in Tanzania that makes it possible for rich peasants (the so-called kulaks) to have access to conveniently located plots, extension services, and technology (Hyden 1980). It is the state in Kenya that organizes and regulates land registration and consolidation, and it is the state that enables certain privileged recipients to secure loans and import licenses from the Industrial and Commercial Development Corporation (ICDC), thereby allowing the accumulation of large holdings in a few private hands (Haugerud 1983).

In this context the "state" involves specific actors, more often than not politicians and bureaucrats who trade (sometimes literally) on their access to strategic resources, including land and credit, to build rural clienteles. The result in many instances has been to force relations of production into highly politicized and personalized circuits of exchange, in which aid is given (or withdrawn) as an unplanned and sometimes unproductive benefit.

This state of affairs is consistent with the mechanisms of internal dependency generally subsumed under the rubric of "political clientelism," a phenomenon that fragments peasant communities along vertical lines, facilitates the control of a patron class, concentrates resources in relatively few hands, and ultimately contributes to the reproduction of rural inequalities (Lemarchand 1981). Whether rural clientelism operates within the context of marketing cooperatives, ujamaa villages, paysannats (settlement schemes), individual land holdings, or commercial farms, the evidence points to its ubiquity as a relation of production. Despite important variations in the balance of exchange between rural clients and their patrons, the basis of the extensive literature dealing with clientelistic phenomena in East and Central Africa, there is every reason to believe that the overall impact of local hierarchies has been to severely compromise the equity goals of rural development schemes, to lower productivity, and to shift peasant activities away from food production to export crops.

This last point is central to the argument advanced by Robert Bates in his analysis of how markets have been manipulated by political elites to maximize the extraction of export commodities from agrarian societies. Though argued from the perspective of class-based collective actions, the Bates thesis is fully compatible with a clientelistic view of rural poverty. In the system that he so convincingly describes, "the losers are those who are not located in positions of access to (scarce resources) and who nonetheless must purchase imported goods;" the beneficiaries, on the other hand, are the members of the patron class who "become enormously powerful because they control the allocation of a scarce and valuable resource" (Bates 1984:235), in this case, foreign exchange. His argument is that market manipulation creates the very conditions that force peasants out of market circuits and into the subsistence economy. We shall return to the Bates thesis. Note that, insofar as one may generalize from his analysis, it raises some obvious questions about the pertinence of capitalist and socialist models for evaluating the performance of African states.

• SOCIALIST VERSUS CAPITALIST MODELS: AN INTERIM ASSESSMENT •

Assessing the respective contributions of agrarian socialism and capitalism to the current food crisis is risky: some may even be tempted to dismiss the exercise as pointless. Each of these labels covers a wide range of policies and experiments. Because of their holistic connotations, the labels fail to convey an appropriate picture of the changes that have taken place over time in the formulation and implementation of these policies. Nor are the labels particularly helpful in describing such notoriously hybrid cases as Zimbabwe, Rwanda, and Mali. Further complicating the task of analysis is the incidence of factors and circumstances (civil wars, liberation struggles, refugee problems, and so on) that have had a direct impact on the agricultural performance of African states, regardless of their commitment to socialist or capitalist models. Finally, the absence of clear-cut correlations between ideological preferences and agricultural production (see Table 3.1) raises the question of whether socialist or capitalist options have anything to do with the seeds of famine.

Although these are serious reasons to exercise caution, available evidence suggests the following broad generalizations: (1) The egregious failure of socialist experiments in countries such as Tanzania, Mozambique, Ethiopia, and Angola is traceable not just to political crises and external attempts at destabilization but to certain fundamental shortcomings in the strategies associated with agrarian socialism. (2) Capitalist models show a very mixed track record, ranging from poor (Nigeria) to disastrous (Zaire), and seldom anywhere has rural capitalism generated a pattern of self-sustaining growth. Even though the reasons for this outcome are varied and complex, in Zaire and Nigeria the plundering of state resources for personal enrichment emerges as the most plausible explanation for the failure of capitalist strategies. (3) The deficiencies discernible in the socialist and

TABLE 3.1. Classification of Sub-Saharan Africa According to Agricultural Production Performance, 1961-1981

Total Agricultural Production[a]	Increase > 105	Stagnant > 95-≤ 105	Decrease ≤ 95
Strong Increase > 130	Swaziland (152,142)		
Increase > 105-≤ 130	Burundi (111,111) Cameroun (127,120) Ivory Coast (116,112) Malawi (127,119) Rwanda (128,127)		
Stagnant > 95-< 105	Botswana (102,112) Sudan (99,112)	Central African R. (99,101) Gabon (101,101) Sierra Leone (99,99) Zambia (100,101)	Kenya (99,91) Liberia (104,90)
Decrease > 80-< 95			Chad (82,81) Congo (85,84) Ethiopia (85,84) Ghana (83,83) Guinea (92,89) Lesotho (87,94) Mali (91,88) Mozambique (81,85) Niger (82,82) Nigeria (87,88) Somalia (85,85) Tanzania (90,93) Upper Volta (95,93) Zaire (90,91)
Strong Decrease ≤ 80		Zimbabwe (75,99)	Angola (70,94) Gambia (79,79) Mauritania (74,74) Namibia (77,77) Senegal (71,70) Uganda (76,90)

Source: J. Hinderink and J.J. Sterkenburg. 1983. Agricultural Policy and Production in Africa: The Aims, the Methods and the Means. Journal of Modern African Studies XII:1:2.

[a]The figures in brackets give the index for total agricultural production per capita followed by the index for food production per capita. They are based on 5-yearly averages for the period 1976-1980, in comparison with the base period of 1961-65 = 100.

capitalist modes of development have been further aggravated by the manipulation of markets by the political class, resulting in a drastic decline of material incentives available to the food-producing sectors. At this level the effect of ideological options on peasant behavior appears far less decisive than the inability of the state to generate minimally attractive pricing policies and other incentives to encourage the production of food crops.

Agrarian socialism presupposes a major shift in the relationships between the state and the peasantry, a shift from what is usually described as an exploitative relationship to one in which, over time, self-reliant village communities will come into being, obviate the need for state intervention, and hence eliminate a major source of capitalist exploitation. In Julius Nyerere's formulation:

> Most of our farming will be done by groups of people who live as a community and work as a community. . . . The activities of the village, and the type of production they undertake, as well as the distribution of crops and other goods they produce will all be determined by the village members themselves (Nyerere 1975).

The contrast between Nyerere's vision and the stark realities of Tanzanian socialism requires little elaboration. In both Tanzania and Mozambique, "villagization" policies have resulted in a catastrophic decline in agricultural output, making both countries more dependent than ever on outside aid.

The failure of villagization policies reflects a number of fundamental contradictions between the assumptions and exigencies of agrarian socialism, on the one hand, and the cultural and political parameters of state intervention, on the other. Between the official view of precapitalist African societies as inherently predisposed to endorse socialist ideas and the sociocultural realities of the Tanzanian setting exists a chasm of such proportions that it was only bridged by the application of coercive measures. Forced villagization emerged as the only alternative to voluntarism. Forcing the peasants to join registered communal villages on command went hand in hand with the bureaucratization of village communities; thus, an "authoritarian, managerial approach" (Hyden 1980:106) was substituted for the principles of self-reliance and decentralized decisionmaking. At this point yet another contradiction emerged, involving the relations of rural cooperatives to the state. Initially viewed as a crucial element in the elaboration of rural redistribution strategies, and therefore as a necessary complement of villagization, the cooperatives were eventually seen as a major obstacle between the state and the village communities and, indeed, as a threat to state supremacy. The elimination of voluntary cooperatives and their replacement by state-run marketing boards and trading corporations spelled the abandonment of the single most important operative principle in Nyerere's dream of bringing together "people who live as a community and work as a community."

Though carried through on a lesser scale, villagization in Mozambique ran into much of the same kinds of problems, including resistance to state intervention and bureaucratic rule, but with an additional calamitous consequence—by forcing people into villages the state unwittingly turned villagers into recruits for the Mozambican National Resistance (MNR). Where the case of Mozambique differs from that of Tanzania is in the heavy investments made in the state-farm sector, officially viewed as "the quickest way of responding to food needs because of the size of the areas they cover, their rational organization of human and material resources, and the immediate availability of machinery" (Hanlon 1984:100).

The state farms, as it turned out, proved the quickest way to disaster, which is why priority is now being given to cooperatives and family farms. The failure of state farms may be attributed in part to the dramatic lack of managerial and technical skills required to run such large-scale farming units (covering 350,000 square miles in 1981) and in part to the total breakdown of distributive networks caused by the massive flight of Portuguese traders after national independence. The sudden evaporation of consumer commodities from the rural markets led to a situation in which "peasants had huge amounts of money in their hands and nothing to spend it on" (Hanlon 1984:111). In the absence of consumer commodities, a barter system quickly supplanted the official marketing networks, pushing the Mozambican economy into the most primitive type of exchange and eventually prompting the Central Committee of the National Liberation Front of Mozambique (FRELIMO) to recognize the need "to re-establish the market economy" (Hanlon 1984:111)—an appropriate epitaph to the Mozambican version of agrarian socialism.

The cases of Tanzania and Mozambique sound like horror stories, but the examples of Zaire and, in a qualified sense, Nigeria show that this genre is by no means a monopoly of socialist economies. The balance sheet of rural capitalism in Zaire "is not just negative—it is catastrophic" (Young and Turner 1985:322). A thoroughly inadequate infrastructure, consistently low level of public investments, producer prices and fiscal pressures designed to discourage food production, inefficient and corrupt marketing parastatals—these are only some of the most obvious factors that explain the disastrous performance of Zairian agriculture. At the root of the agrarian crisis in Zaire lies a clientelistic distributive system in which access to land is largely the privilege of the state bourgeoisie. In such a system the extraction of a marketable surplus from the peasant sectors is the prime reward expected by land owners. Just as traditional land rights may be conveniently disregarded for the sake of profit, so may the basic needs of rural workers be neglected. The logic of the profit motive is a cruel one indeed for the plantation worker whose daily wage approximates $0.20, and whose only escape route is to go back to a subsistence-type economy (McGaffey 1982:103). When carried to the point of extortion, profit maximization becomes counterproductive for both patrons and clients. As one observer noted: "The productivity of capital in Zaire has always been low because large numbers of men are able to avoid the pressure to offer their labor in exchange for wages; it is often both possible and more productive to go fishing or to grow one's own food" (McGaffey 1982:103). Zaire's growing food deficits bear testimony to this law of diminishing returns.

Although the Nigerian case is more complex, the trend towards a Zairian pattern is unmistakable. The shift from "nurture" capitalism to "pirate" capitalism, to use Sayre Schatz's felicitous phrasing (Schatz 1984:55), underscores the preeminent role of the state as a source of personal enrichment. In Nigeria, as in Zaire, land figures prominently in the array of prebends available from the state, but it is incorporated into a radically different policy framework. Beginning in the 1970s, there has been a concerted effort on the part of Nigerian authorities to increase food production through generous state subsidies, integrated development schemes, state food farms, and large-scale irrigation projects. A critical component of this policy was the Integrated Rural Development Projects (IRDP), which were aimed at raising agricultural productivity through technological inputs, improved infrastructure, credit, marketing, and extension facilities. The trend toward large-scale capitalist farming was further accelerated by President Shagari's Green Revolution. All this, however, did not prevent massive food shortages and, as food imports began to compete with domestic food crops, many farmers responded to market pressures by switching to commercial crops, thereby aggravating the conditions that initially spurred the imports. What was missing from these grandiose schemes was a recognition of the potential contribution that small farmers could make to food self-sufficiency. Monumental profits were reaped by bureaucrats and speculators of various stripes through importing farm technology and food commodities (as the Dikko affair plainly demonstrated), or in short, through "pirate" capitalism; at the very same time, very little was done to apply the remedies of "nurture" capitalism to the small and poor farmers. As one knowledgeable observer noted:

> Poor farmers are forced to sell grain immediately after harvest at low prices to meet taxes, debt repayments and ceremonial expenditure on manufactured items. Later in the season they work as wage labor for middle and rich farmers in order to obtain food at high prices, thereby neglecting their own farms. The market therefore does not allocate resources. It articulates a whole system of inequality which involves control over commodities, money, labor power and means of production (Forrest 1981:247).

What has been referred to as "the emergence of the inert economy" (Schatz 1984:56) in the Nigerian context is not just a reflection of "pirate" capitalism; much of the inertia currently affecting Nigerian agriculture is also traceable to the persistence of rural inequality as a byproduct of this kind of capitalism.

This necessarily brief excursus into the ideological background of agricultural policy choices requires a few additional comments. (1) Whether inspired by socialist or free market principles, agricultural production in Africa is directly affected by the types of social organization available to smallholders, a point excellently argued by Michael Bratton in his recent discussion of self-managed farmers' associations in Zimbabwe (Bratton 1985). His conclusions apply to other states as well. Majangano (reciprocal labor exchange) in Zimbabwe, umuganda (self-help) in Rwanda, and ton (youth association) in Mali designate certain forms of social organization that are significant in mobilizing human and material resources, even though largely unrelated to socialist or capitalist options. (2) Ideological preferences are also irrelevant in terms of the perverse effects of market manipulation by urban-based elites. As Bates has shown, the distortions that such manipulation entails inevitably work against the interests of agricultural producers and to the benefit of the urban sector. (3) Ideology is again reduced to a rather indeterminate status when viewed against the background of the external constraints under which African economies are laboring.

Before turning to a more detailed analysis of these external impediments, let us briefly consider the more salient points made by Bates in his groundbreaking study, *Markets and States in Tropical Africa* (1981). Not only has he provided the most convincing set of arguments for an "internalist" explanation of Africa's agrarian crisis; his arguments also constitute the most devastating critique of the part played by African governments in bringing the crisis into existence.

If food policies in Africa are generally unresponsive to nutritional needs, it is because these policies are overwhelmingly geared to furthering the economic and political interests of the urban elites, most conspicuously the elite of the political class. By keeping producer prices for food crops well below the level of world market prices, African governments have consistently favored urban consumers while discriminating against peasant producers.[4] Furthermore, by setting official exchange rates at artificially high levels, governments have succeeded in both cutting down the cost of imported commodities (including food imports for urban consumers and agricultural technology for rich farmers) and reducing the effective prices paid to producers of export crops and food crops. By subsidizing agricultural inputs—fertilizer, seeds, tractors, and so on—they tend to promote the interests of "coteries of privileged, modern farmers" (Bates 1981:49) at the expense of small-scale agricultural producers. The cumulative effect of these policies and practices has been to create almost limitless opportunities for profit and corruption among the political class (mainly through the control of marketing boards and other parastatals) and to drastically reduce incentives for increased food production.

Bates' tightly argued critique also helps us understand the factors that lie behind (1) the rapidly expanding scope of parallel economies and (2) the informal deals that, at this level, bring together politicians and peasants as they jointly seek to evade official price controls and marketing regulations.

> Whereas at the level of official policy the interests of the peasants and the bureaucrat are in conflict, at the level of unofficial practice they are often consonant, given the structure of the incentives to which the official policy gives rise. To put it bluntly, the policies offer joint gains through corruption. The bureaucrat can offer protection against the very policies he is mandated to impose: for a portion of the gains, he can help the peasant evade market controls. And the peasant, rather then attacking government policy directly, can often do better by seeking to become an individual exception to it; he can do this by offering bribes (Bates 1981:42).

From this dismal rendering of African food policies one can hardly avoid the conclusion that rural poverty is fundamentally related to the powerlessness of the peasant sectors. Not only do the rural poor lack minimal control over their immediate environment and economic circumstances, they also lack all opportunities for taking part in the elaboration of the policies that affect their livelihood most directly. This situation is true not only of the domestic policies fashioned by African governments but also of the decisions affecting world commodity prices and market structures. That power relationships have a significant bearing on problems of poverty and hunger is undeniable; what remains uncertain is whether such relationships may be decisively altered at the domestic or international level.

• THE INCIDENCE OF EXTERNAL CONSTRAINTS •

The question of the relationship of external constraints to food production invites consideration of at least two major schools of thought, one associated with dependency theory and the other with the principle of comparative advantage. Although they each provide logically coherent explanations of rural poverty, they both leave out critically important features of the international environment. The fatality of external capitalist controls is just as open to doubt as the Ricardian blessings of specialization of production in free market conditions.

Dependency theory was the dominant theme in the 1960s and 1970s, but is now pronounced "dead in the water" even by radical analysts (Rogowski 1985). Whether there is any basis for such claims is beyond the scope of the present discussion; suffice it to note that only marginal analytic returns have been gained from various attempts at testing its applicability to the African scene. Reduced to its simplest expression, dependency theory argues that Third World poverty is dialectically linked to the expansion of capitalism into the periphery. Only through the extraction of an economic surplus from the periphery, that is, through the wholesale exploitation of Third World resources, could capitalism gather momentum while creating the conditions of peripheral misery and underdevelopment. Despite countless variations on this theme, its shortcomings are all too evident. (1) Patterns of dependency cover a wide spectrum of relationships and cannot be reduced to a simple dualism between core and periphery. (2) Some of the so-called dependent countries have in fact shown a surprising ability to reverse or at least decisively alter their relationship of dependency vis-á-vis core countries. (3) The terms of exchange between core and periphery are by no means eternally fixed but are susceptible to mutually beneficial adjustments. These are only some of the more problematic issues raised by dependency theory. Although there can be little question that rural poverty is *historically* linked to the processes of capital accumulation inaugurated under the auspices of the colonial state, today's market structures and prices call attention to an entirely different set of parameters.

From the standpoint of comparative advantage theory, rural poverty is only the most tragic symptom of the inability of African states to make effective use of their resources. Specifically, the roots of hunger and poverty are traceable to the failure of African governments to place sufficient emphasis on export crops, which they can produce at a comparatively low cost. Their comparative advantage lies in the full utilization of their productive potential as producers of tea, cocoa, coffee, cotton, peanuts, and so forth within the context of a free market economy. Rather than switch to food crops, a more rational course would be to use the foreign exchange derived from the sale of cash crops to import food from the West; thus, the opportunity costs of achieving nutritional self-sufficiency are avoided. The assumption, in brief, is that "the income generated by the sale of export crops . . . would make it possible to purchase far greater amounts of wheat and corn than could have been produced domestically with the same inputs" (Lofchie and Commins 1984:9).

The problems with this line of reasoning are that it: (1) overlooks the considerable elasticity of consumer demand for tropical exports; (2) assumes a situation of competitive bidding among foreign buyers, when in fact a near monopsony obtains; and (3) underestimates the extreme competitiveness among producers of tropical crops, in stark contrast with the near absence of competition among corporate buyers. There are indeed basic limitations to the applicability of competitive advantage to Africa, as excellently demonstrated by Michael Lofchie and Stephen Commins. If producers of tropical commodities are unable "to gain price leverage in the international market place," it is critically related to such factors as the "ready availability of synthetic or substitute products for such commodities," the dominant position occupied by "a handful of powerful multinational trading corporations . . . (such as) General Foods, Nestlé, Lipton and Brooke Bond," and the emergence of export crop production as "an enormously competitive field" (Lofchie and Commins 1984:11–12). What Lofchie and Commins refer to as "market failure" is largely responsible for the sharp deterioration of Africa's terms of trade, a process that shows no sign of coming to an end, Lome III notwithstanding.

Yet another facet of the current food crisis is Africa's mounting debt burden, perhaps the most dramatic illustration of the propensity to spend more on imports than is being earned from exports. To cite one example, although Mozambique spends an estimated $568 million annually in hard currency to cover the cost of imported fuel, spare parts, and other commodities, its total earnings from exports barely reach $110 million (May 1985). The growing indebtedness of African states imposes upon them debt-servicing obligations that tend to further restrict the pool of financial resources needed to improve agricultural production. Furthermore, the austerity measures, including the elimination of food subsidies, forced upon African states by the International Monetary Fund (IMF) as a condition for the extension of new loans entail political repercussions that few governments are able to face. The elimination of government subsidies that hold down the price of bread and other commodities inevitably tends to trigger explosions of popular discontent, as happened in Khartoum in 1985, in Tunis in 1984, and in Cairo in 1977. In each case urban rioting (sometimes referred to as IMF riots) came about as a result of major increases in the price of bread (33 percent overnight in Khartoum, 100 percent in Tunis, and 50 percent in Cairo). Whether to comply with IMF guidelines at the cost of political instability or to reject such guidelines and go into receivership is the basic dilemma currently facing a number of African states.

Equally serious is the dilemma confronting donor states as they must choose between treating the symptoms of rural poverty or attacking its root. Food aid may indeed perpetuate the very conditions that make for poverty and hunger, surely one of the most ironic facts about the massive relief operations organized under the auspices of private and international organizations. In the short run, of course, hundreds of thousands of human lives have been saved by the joint efforts and dedication of relief workers and donor agencies, and this may be seen as ample justification for this monumental outpouring of cash and commiseration. On the other hand, the drawbacks are equally clear. As Kevin Danaher pointed out, "food aid can undermine local food production by flooding local markets and depressing food prices; it can also create dependencies on foreign aid or be used by recipient governments to manipulate the poor" (Danaher 1985:3). Furthermore, if the case of Zaire is any index, food aid may not even reach those who need it most, but end up being sold on the open market for the benefit of strategically placed businessmen and politicians.

Reflecting on "why much of the money spent on agricultural development in Africa has simply not paid off," Clifford May (1985:74) suggested that

> a large part of the explanation may be that aid organizations must work with governments that helped create the problems in the first place, and the granting of any aid, relief or development, to regimes fighting civil wars frees resources that can be used to intensify and prolong those wars. Because war is a cause of famine, aid can in that way indirectly contribute to the spread of hunger. To deny aid on that basis, however, punishes the innocent far more than the guilty.

The alternative to working with African governments while ignoring their share of responsibility in creating famine conditions is to withhold development aid unless and until appropriate economic reforms are implemented. This course is the thrust of the 1981 World Bank Study, *Accelerated Development in Sub-Saharan Africa,* better known as the Berg Report, and is also a major feature of Ronald Reagan's Economic Policy Initiative for Africa (EPI), intended to provide $500 million in aid over a five-year period to those countries that are willing to initiate fundamental changes in their agricultural policies. Whether such pressures and inducements may effectively promote local enterprise and break the hold of parastatal agencies on the production and marketing of agricultural commodities remains unclear.

Clearly, the alternatives facing African governments are not reducible to single options such as acceptance of external dependency versus going it alone, free enterprise versus state-controlled economies, and concentration on food crops versus specialization in the production of cash crops. Behind these alternatives lie more fundamental choices. At what cost and through which strategies may the weight of external constraints be mitigated? Which mix of private enterprise and state controls is best suited to improve the productivity of the rural sectors? What proportion of cash-crop earnings must be given up for the sake of long-term savings in the area of food production?

That there are no simple answers to these questions does not make them any less pertinent as an academic concern; that these questions transcend the boundaries of any single discipline is equally clear. If nothing else, these questions should prompt us to seek out the answers at the level of interdisciplinary collaboration. In Africa as elsewhere, agriculture is far too important to be left to the production scientists. Only through a genuine and sustained collaborative effort among social and production scientists may one begin to address the multiple causes of poverty and hunger in Africa and help mitigate the devastating effects of this massive affliction.

• NOTES •

1. Twenty-six African countries earn more than half their foreign exchange from a single mineral or export crop; 37 countries depend on one or two items for as much as 80 percent of their overseas earnings. By the late 1970s, for example, 75 percent of Senegal's export earnings came from peanuts, and four-fifths of Chad's were generated by the sale of raw cotton.

2. The contradictory implications of the economy of affection are symptomatic of the imprecision surrounding its meaning. On the one hand, the economy of affection is viewed as having a dampening effect on "the revolutionary potential of peasants and workers". On the other hand, it is described as "the most important factor that facilitated the liberation or the struggle for independence in African countries." According to Hyden:

> Without access to the economy of affection as a hinterland, if you want to use that analogy, many of those brave fighters that actually challenged colonial rule would have found it very difficult to pursue their struggle. And, may I add here, it was probably the lack of appreciation of this economy among the colonial powers that actually made them in the long run lose the battle (Hyden 1985:55).

Why the economy of affection should both stimulate and restrain the "liberation efforts" of African peasantries remains unclear.

3. For a sample of divergent conceptualizations, see the 1985 special issue of the *Canadian Journal of African Studies* entirely devoted to "Mode of Production: The Challenge of Africa" (XIX:1).

4. The case of Tanzania is not atypical. According to a 1982 World Bank report, the government paid coffee farmers less than half of the fair market value for their production; rice farmers received less than one third of market value for their produce.

• SUGGESTED FURTHER READINGS •

Barker, Jonathan, ed. 1984. *The Politics of Agriculture in Tropical Africa*. Beverly Hills, California: Sage Publications.

Bates, Robert H. 1981. *Markets and States in Tropical Africa: The Political Basis of Agricultural Policies*. Berkeley: University of California Press.

Eicher, Carl, and John Staatz, eds. 1984. *Agricultural Development in the Third World*. Baltimore: Johns Hopkins University Press.

Gran, Guy. 1983. *Development by People*. New York: Praeger Publishers.

Heyer, Judith, Pepe Roberts, and Gavin Williams, eds. 1981. *Rural Development in Tropical Africa*. New York: St. Martin's Press.

Hopkins, Raymond, and Donald Puchala. 1978. *The Global Political Economy of Food*. Madison: University of Wisconsin Press.

Hopkins, Raymond, Donald Puchala, and Ross Talbot, eds. 1979. *Food, Politics and Agricultural Development*. Boulder, Colorado: Westview Press.

Lappe, Francis Moore, Joseph Collins, and David Kinley. 1980. *Aid as Obstacle*. San Francisco, California: Institute for Food and Development Policy.

Moyana, Henry. 1980. *The Political Economy of Land in Zimbabwe*. Harare, Zimbabwe: Mambo Press.

Young, Crawford, Neil Sherman, and Tim Rose. 1981. *Cooperatives and Development*. Madison: University of Wisconsin Press.

·4·

Agricultural Development Ideas in Historical Perspective

JOHN M. STAATZ
CARL K. EICHER

Although economists have been concerned with growth and development since at least the time of the mercantilists, development economics has existed as a separate branch of economics just since about 1950. The history of the field can roughly be divided into two periods: (1) the economic growth and modernization era of the 1950s and 1960s, when development was defined largely in terms of growth in average per capita output; and (2) the growth-with-equity period since around 1970, when the concern of most development economists broadened to include income distribution, employment, nutrition, and a host of other variables. The prevailing view of agriculture's role in development changed profoundly during these two periods.[1]

This chapter presents an outline of the changing view of agriculture in economic development since 1950. The chapter begins with a brief discussion of the evolution of agricultural development theory and practice during the growth and modernization era of the fifties and sixties. The relatively passive role assigned to agriculture in the economic growth models of the 1950s, the increasing recognition of the interdependence between agricultural and industrial growth during the 1960s, the lessons learned from the agricultural development experience of the 1950s and 1960s, and the contribution of radical and dependency scholars to an improved understanding of the process of agricultural and rural development are examined. The next section is a discussion of the increased emphasis given to agricultural and rural development during the growth-with-equity period that began around 1970. During this period there was a sharp increase in microeconomic research on agricultural production and marketing, intersectoral linkages, rural-factor markets, migration, and rural small-scale industry; and there was a policy

This chapter is based on an earlier article (with the same title) by the authors that appeared in *Agricultural Development in The Third World,* edited by Carl K. Eicher and John M. Staatz (Baltimore: John Hopkins University Press, 1984), pp. 3–30. Used with permission of the publisher.

shift to integrated rural development and basic-needs programs.

· THE ROLE OF AGRICULTURE IN DEVELOPMENT
ECONOMICS, 1950–1969 ·

Western Development Economists' Perspectives on Agriculture

Most Western development economists of the 1950s did not view agriculture as an important contributor to economic growth.[2] Development was often equated with the structural transformation of the economy, that is, with the decline in agriculture's relative share of the national product and of the labor force. The role of development economics, as seen by these economists, was to facilitate that transformation by discovering ways to transfer resources, especially labor, from traditional agriculture to industry—the presumed engine of growth. Agriculture itself was often treated as a "black box from which people, and food to feed them, and perhaps capital could be released" (Little 1982:105).

Development economics throughout the 1950s and 1960s was strongly influenced by W. Arthur Lewis's 1954 article, "Economic Development with Unlimited Supplies of Labour." Seldom has a single article been so instrumental in shaping the work of an entire subdiscipline of economics. In the article, Lewis presented a general equilibrium model of expansion in an economy with two sectors: a modern capitalist exchange sector and an indigenous noncapitalist sector, which was dominated by subsistence farming.[3] The distinguishing characteristics of the capitalist sector were its use of reproducible capital, its hiring of labor, and its sale of output for profit. "Capitalist" enterprises could be owned privately or by the state. The subsistence sector was pictured as the "self-employment sector," which did not hire labor or use reproducible capital. Lewis's model focused on how the transfer of labor from the subsistence sector (where the marginal productivity of a laborer approached zero as a limiting case) to the capitalist sector facilitated capitalist expansion through reinvestment of profits. The labor supply facing the capitalist sector was described as "unlimited" for the following reason: "When the capitalist sector offers additional employment opportunities at the existing wage rate, the numbers willing to work at the existing wage rate will be greater than the demand: the supply curve of labor is infinitely elastic at the ruling wage" (Meier 1976:158). In Lewis's model, expansion in the capitalist sector continued until earnings in the two sectors were equated, at which point a dual-sector model was no longer relevant; growth proceeded as in a one-sector neoclassical model. Lewis's analysis was later extended by Gustav Ranis (1963, 1964), Ranis and John Fei (1961), and Dale Jorgenson (1961).

Lewis pointed out that the capitalist sector did not need to be industry (it could be mining or plantations) and that the noncapitalist sector could include handicrafts. Most analysts, however, equated the capitalist sector with industry and the noncapitalist sector with traditional agriculture; they argued that "surplus" labor and other resources should be transferred from agriculture to industry in order to promote growth.[4] Many development economists concluded that since economic growth facilitated the structural transformation of the economy in the *long run,* the rapid transfer of resources (especially "surplus" labor) from agriculture to industry was an appropriate *short run* economic development strategy.[5] But Bruce Johnston observed that "This preoccupation with 'surplus labor' often seems to have encouraged neglect of the agricultural sector as well as a tendency to assume too readily that a surplus can and should be extracted from agriculture, while neglecting the difficult requirements that must be met if agriculture is to play a positive role in facilitating overall economic growth" (Johnston 1970:378).

The propensity of development economists to give relatively little attention to agriculture's potential "positive role in facilitating overall economic growth" was based in part on the empirical observation that agriculture's share of the economy inevitably declines during the course of development for at least two reasons. First, the income elasticity of demand for unprocessed food is less than unity and declines with higher incomes; hence, the demand for raw agricultural products grows more slowly than consumption in general. Second, increasing labor productivity in agriculture means that the same farm output can be produced with fewer workers, implying a transfer of labor to other sectors of the economy. Because agriculture's share of the economy was assumed to be declining, many economists downplayed the need to invest in the agricultural sector in the short run.

The relative neglect of agriculture in the 1950s was reinforced by two other developments. In 1949 Raul Prebisch and Hans Singer independently formulated the thesis that there is a secular tendency for the terms of trade to turn against countries that export primary products and import manufactures. From this they concluded that the scope for growth through agricultural and other primary product exports was very limited. Prebisch and his colleagues at the Economic Commission for Latin America (ECLA) of the United Nations therefore advocated that priority be given to import substitution of manufactured goods rather than to production of agricultural exports.[6] The "secular-decline hypothesis" became an article of faith for some development economists and planners; thus the tendency to downplay agriculture's potential role in development was reinforced.

The second important event affecting development economists' view of agriculture was the publication of Albert Hirschman's influential book, *The Strategy of Economic Development* (1958). In this book, Hirschman introduced the concept of linkages as a tool for investigating how, during the course of development, investment in one type of economic activity induced subsequent investment in other income-generating activities. Hirschman defined the linkage effects of a given product line as the "investment-generating forces that are set in motion, through input-output relations, when productive facilities that supply inputs to that line or utilize its output are inadequate or nonexistent. Backward linkages lead to new investment in input-supplying facilities and forward linkages to investment in output-using facilities" (Hirschman 1977:72). Hirschman argued that government investment should be concentrated in activities where the linkage effects were greatest, since this would maximize indigenous investment in related or "linked" industries. Hirschman asserted that "agriculture certainly stands convicted on the count of its lack of direct stimulus to the setting up of new activities through linkage effects—the superiority of manufacturing in this respect is crushing" (Hirschman 1958:109–10). Therefore, Hirschman argued, investment in industry would generally lead to more rapid and more broadly based economic growth than would investment in agriculture. Hirschman's analysis thus reinforced ECLA's policy recommendation that priority be given to import substitution of manufactures.

Ironically, Lewis's two-sector growth model, which led many development economists to focus heavily on the role of industry in economic development, led others, in the early 1960s, to stress the interdependence between agricultural and industrial growth. In an article comparing a Lewis-type "classical" model with a neoclassical growth model, Jorgenson (1961) argued that growth in nonfarm employment depended on the rate of growth of the agricultural surplus. Jorgenson's analysis and similar analyses by Ranis (1963, 1964), Ranis and Fei (1961), and Stephen Enke (1962a, 1962b) showed that food shortages could choke off growth in the nonfarm sector by making its labor supply less than infinitely elastic. These authors therefore concluded that in order to avoid falling into a low-level equilibrium trap, in the early stages of development a country probably needed to make some net investment in agriculture to accelerate the growth of its agricultural surplus.

Many agricultural economists found it "shocking . . . that general economists such as Jorgenson and Enke . . . felt it necessary to argue the case for *some* investment in agriculture" (Johnston 1970:378). In a seminal article entitled "The Role of Agriculture in Economic Development" (1961), Johnston and John W. Mellor drew on insights from the Lewis model to stress the importance of agriculture as a motive force in economic growth. They argued that, far from playing a passive role in development, agriculture could make five important contributions to the structural transformation of Third World economies: It could provide labor, capital, foreign exchange, and food to a growing industrial sector and could supply a market for domestically produced industrial goods. They argued further that the nature of the interrelationships between agriculture and industry at various stages of development had important implications for the types of agricultural and industrialization strategies that would be most likely to succeed.

Johnston and Mellor's article and William H. Nicholls's influential article, "The Place of Agriculture in Economic Development" (1964), were instrumental in encouraging economists to view agriculture as a potential positive force in development, and they helped to stimulate debate on the interdependence of agricultural and industrial growth. This in turn led to a growing interest in the empirical measurement of intersectoral resource transfers during the course of development.

The work of neoclassical agricultural economists during the 1960s stressed not only the interdependence of agriculture and industry and the potentially important role that agriculture could play in economic development but also the importance of understanding the process of agricultural growth per se if that potential was to be exploited.[7] The need for a better understanding of the process of agricultural growth was further emphasized by some of the agricultural development experiences of the 1950s and early 1960s.

The Influence of the Agricultural Development Programs of the 1950s and 1960s on Western Development Thought

Debates among Western economists about the role of agriculture in development did not take place in a vacuum; they were strongly influenced by the rural development experiences of Third World nations. Indeed, an important characteristic of the literature on agricultural development since the 1950s has been its movement from a priori theorizing toward empirical research.

Despite the emphasis that development economists placed on industrialization during the 1950s, governments of many low-income countries and donor agencies undertook a number of activities aimed at increasing agricultural output and rural incomes. The experience gained in these efforts was important in developing a better understanding of intersectoral relationships and the constraints on agricultural growth.

During the 1950s the approach of European and North American agricultural economists to development was colored by the historical experiences of their own countries and by their training in the then current theories of development economics. For example, most Western agricultural economists working on problems of Third World agriculture during this period believed that the problem of rural surplus labor could be resolved by transferring "excess" rural workers to urban industry. It was also widely assumed that Western agricultural advisers could directly transfer agricultural technology and models of agricultural extension from high-income countries to the Third World, that community development programs could help rural people overcome the shackles of traditional farming and inequitable land-tenure systems, and that food aid could serve humanitarian needs and provide jobs for rural people.

Agricultural development efforts of the 1950s placed heavy emphasis on the direct transfer of agricultural technology from high-income countries to the Third World and on the promotion of the U.S. model of agricultural extension. These efforts were based on what Hayami and Ruttan (1971) called the "diffusion model" of agricultural development. The diffusion model assumed that Third World farmers could substantially increase their agricultural productivity by allocating existing resources more efficiently and by adopting agricultural practices and technologies from the industrial countries.

Like the diffusion model, the community development effort of the 1950s and early 1960s assumed that small farmers were often poor decisionmakers who required outside assistance in planning local development projects (Stevens 1977b:5). Community development grew out of the cold-war atmosphere of the 1950s, when Western foreign assistance programs were searching for a non-revolutionary approach to rural change. Community development advocates assumed that villagers, meeting with community development specialists, would express their "felt needs" and unite to design and implement self-help programs aimed at promoting rural development. The community development effort also implicitly assumed that rural development could be achieved through the direct transfer of Western agricultural technologies and social institutions, such as local democracy, to the rural areas of the Third World.[8]

The failure of many agricultural extension programs to achieve rapid increases in agricultural output and the inability of community development projects to solve the basic food problem in many countries (particularly India in the mid-1950s) led to a reevaluation of the diffusion model of agricultural development. Two elements were critical in this reappraisal. First, it became apparent that in many countries there were important structural barriers to rural development, such as highly concentrated political power and asset ownership. The research by economists such as Doreen Warriner (1955), Wolf Ladejinsky (see Walinsky 1977), Thomas F. Carroll (1961), Philip M. Raup (1967), and Solon Barraclough (1973) on land tenure and land reform in Asia, North Africa, and Latin America documented how institutional barriers inhibited the expansion of agricultural output. These authors argued that, in some countries, basic institutional reforms were prerequisites to effective agricultural extension and community development. The second element leading to a reevaluation of the diffusion model was research by scholars such as W. O. Jones (1960), Raj Krishna (1967), and Jere R. Behrman (1968) that documented the responsiveness of Third World farmers and consumers to economic incentives and helped to demolish the myth of the "tradition-bound peasant." The findings of these studies suggested that if farmers were not responsive to agricultural extension efforts, perhaps it was because extension workers had few profitable innovations to extend. This viewpoint was advanced most forcefully in T. W. Schultz's highly influential book, *Transforming Traditional Agriculture* (1964).

Schultz's book was iconoclastic. Schultz argued that Third World farmers and herders, far from being irrational and fatalistic, were calculating economic agents who carefully weighed the marginal costs and benefits associated with different agricultural techniques. Through a long process of experimentation, these farmers had learned how to allocate efficiently the factors of production available to them, given existing technology. This implied that "no appreciable increase in agricultural production is to be had by reallocating the factors at the disposal of farmers who are bound by traditional agriculture. . . . An outside expert, however skilled he may be in farm management, will not discover any major inefficiency in the allocation of factors" (Schultz 1964:39).

Schultz's argument that traditional agriculture was characterized by allocative efficiency, despite low levels of per capita output, became known as the "efficient-but-poor hypothesis." Citing evidence from Guatemala (Tax 1953) and India (summarized in Hopper 1965) to support this hypothesis, Schultz argued that major increases in per capita agricultural output in the Third World would come about only if farmers were provided new, more productive factors of production, that is, new agricultural technologies and the new skills needed to exploit them. The cause of rural poverty, in other words, was the lack of profitable technical packages for Third World farmers and the lack of investment in human capital needed to cope with rapidly changing agricultural technologies. Schultz later attributed the low levels of investment in agricultural research and rural education in most Third World countries to national policies that undervalued agriculture (Schultz 1978:1981).

Transforming Traditional Agriculture called for a major shift from agricultural extension toward investment in agricultural research and human capital. The book, which appeared five years after the establishment of the International Rice Research Institute (IRRI) in the Philippines and one year after the establishment of the International Center for Maize and Wheat Improvement (CIMMYT) in Mexico, reinforced the increasing emphasis being given to agricultural research by the Rockefeller and Ford foundations and other donors in the 1960s. As a result of IRRI's and CIMMYT's success in developing high-yielding dwarf varieties of rice and wheat, which were rapidly adopted in many areas of the Third World during the 1960s, the Green Revolution, or high-payoff input model, replaced the diffusion/community development model as the dominant agricultural development model for field practitioners (Hayami and Ruttan 1971).

The appearance of the high-yielding grain varieties had important effects on the theory as well as on the practice of agricultural development. Several authors, such as Kazushi Ohkawa (1964), Mellor (1966), and Ohkawa and Johnston (1969), noted that the new grain-fertilizer technologies were highly divisible and scale neutral, allowing them to be incorporated into existing systems of small-scale agriculture. Therefore, these authors argued, intensification of agricultural production based on high-yielding cereal varieties offered the opportunity to provide productive employment for the rapidly growing rural labor force, and it also produced the wage goods needed for an expanding industrial labor force. The high-yielding varieties, it was argued, made it possible to achieve both employment and output objectives.[9]

The early enthusiasm for the Green Revolution was met by a barrage of criticism by Francine Frankel (1971), Keith Griffin (1974), and others. These authors argued that the new varieties often benefited mainly landlords and larger farmers in ecologically favored areas, but they frequently impoverished small farmers and tenants, particularly those in upland areas, by inducing lower grain prices and evictions from the land as landlords found it profitable to farm the land themselves using mechanization.

Although some authors, such as Lester Brown (1970), did tend to oversell the accomplishments of the Green Revolution, in Asia the impact of the new varieties was substantial. They have had a smaller effect in Latin America, however, where a high percentage of small farmers live in poor natural resource zones (Pineiro et al. 1979), and they have had little impact in Sub-Saharan Africa. Overall, high-yielding varieties accounted for about half the area planted to wheat and rice in the Third World in the early 1980s (Dalrymple 1985).

Grant Scobie and Rafael Posada (1984) and Yijiiro Hayami (1984) have evaluated some of the income distribution effects of the new varieties. These authors find that *within* villages there has been little difference between small farmers' and large farmers' rates of adoption of the modern varieties. Farmers in upland areas, however, may have been hurt relative to farmers in irrigated areas because the new varieties are more suited to irrigated conditions. Low-income consumers, who spend a high proportion of their income on foodgrains, have been major beneficiaries of the larger harvests and lower prices made possible by the Green Revolution. One of the important lessons of the 1950s and 1960s is that, with rising population pressure on land throughout the Third World, technological change must be included as a central component in both the theory and practice of agricultural and rural development.

Radical Political Economy and Dependency Perspectives on Agriculture

Western development economics was challenged in the 1960s and 1970s by the emergence and rapid growth of radical political economy and dependency models of development and underdevelopment. The radical political economy models have their roots in the writings of Lenin on imperialism and Karl Kautsky on agriculture, and in the post-World War II writings of Paul Baran and other Marxist economists. Baran, in an important article entitled "On the Political Economy of Backwardness" (1952), argued that in most low-income countries it would be impossible to bring about broad-based capitalist development without violent changes in social and political institutions. Although Baran was clearly ahead of his time in identifying institutional and structural barriers to development and the need to put effective demand at the center of development programs, he tended, as did many of the Western development economists he was criticizing, to see small-scale agriculture as incapable of making major contributions to economic growth. For example, Baran accepted the view that the marginal product of labor often approached zero in agriculture, and therefore "there is no way of employing it [labor] usefully in agriculture." Farmers "could only be provided with opportunities for productive work by transfer to industry." Baran, like many economists of the time, believed that "very few improvements that would be necessary in order to increase productivity can be carried out within the narrow confines of small-peasant holdings" and that, therefore, farm consolidation was necessary.

Marxist analysis of agricultural and rural development was further advanced in the 1950s and 1960s by several Latin American scholars, who often blended Marxian analyses with dependency theory.[10] The dependency interpretation of underdevelopment was first proposed in the 1950s by the Economic Commission for Latin America, under the leadership of Raul Prebisch. The basic hypothesis of this perspective is that underdevelopment is not a stage of development but the result of the expansion of the world capitalist system. Underdevelopment, in other words, is not simply the lack of development; it is a condition of impoverishment brought about by the integration of Third World economies into the world capitalist system. Although a number of different views of dependency have been put forward by scholars such as Osvaldo Sunkel (1972), Celso Furtado (1970), André Gunder Frank (1966), J. Galtung (1971), and others, the following definition of dependency by T. Dos Santos has been widely cited: "By dependency we mean a situation in which the economy of certain countries is conditioned by the development and expansion of another economy to which the former is subjected" (Dos Santos 1970:231).[11]

Dependency theorists implicitly argued that trade was often a zero-sum game—that low-income countries ("the periphery") were pauperized through both a process of unequal exchange with the industrialized world ("the center") and repatriation of profits from foreign-owned businesses. Capitalist growth in the periphery was not self-sustaining; it was stunted by policies favoring import substitution of luxury goods and export of agro-industrial products, often produced on large estates. These policies limited the internal market for consumer goods (including food and other agricultural products) and led to impoverishment of the mass of small farmers. Meaningful reform was blocked by an alliance of the landed elite, local bourgeoisie, and multinational firms, all of which benefited from the dependency relationship.

In the 1960s, dependency theory was imported into Africa from Latin America. Since the mid-1960s Samir Amin has provided leadership in developing a Marxist version of dependency theory. In *Accumulation on a World Scale* (1974b) and *Unequal Development* (1976) Amin presented an analytical framework of underdevelopment in Africa based on surplus extraction and the domination of the world capitalist system. Amin has provided valuable insights into the development process, but his prescriptions for African agriculture have vacillated over time. During the 1960s Amin favored animal traction, promoted industrial crops, and argued that traditional social values were a serious constraint on development at the village level. He also argued that the transition to privately owned small farms was a precondition for socialism (Amin 1965:210–11, 231). By the early 1970s Amin had reversed himself and recommended the collectivization of agricultural production, and he abandoned his support for animal traction and industrial crops (Amin 1971:231; 1973:56).

These criticisms notwithstanding, the radical scholars made several important contributions to the understanding of agriculture and rural development. First, they helped demolish the myth of "a typical underdeveloped country" by stressing that each country's economic development had to be understood in the context of that country's historical experience. For example, they argued that Schultz's concept of "traditional agriculture"—a situation where farmers have settled into a low-level equilibrium after years of facing static technology and factor prices—abstracted from the historical process of integration of individual Third World economies into the world capitalist system, and therefore was not a very useful analytical concept. Second, in arguing that rural poverty in the Third World resulted from the functioning of a global capitalist economy, the radical writers focused attention on the relationships between villagers and the wider economic system. Unlike Schultz, who attributed rural poverty to the lack of productive agricultural technologies and human capital, radical scholars stressed the importance of the linkages and exchange arrangements that tied villages to the rest of the economy. Third, the radical economists directly attacked what Hirschman (1981a:3) has called the "mutual benefit claim" of development economics, the assertion that economic relations between high-income and low-income countries (and among groups within low-income countries) could be shaped in a way to yield benefits for all. In disputing this claim, the radical scholars stressed that economic development was more than just a technocratic matter of determining how best to raise per capita GNP. Development involved restructuring institutional and political relationships, and the radicals urged neoclassical economists to include these political considerations explicitly in their analyses. In Alain de Janvry's words, "Economic policy without political economy is a useless and utopian exercise" (de Janvry 1981:263).

Both the radical analyses and the Western dual-sector models of the 1960s suffered from some of the same shortcomings: abstract theorizing, inadequate attention to the need for technical change in agriculture, lack of attention to the biological and location-specific nature of agricultural production processes, and lack of a solid micro foundation based on empirical research at the farm and village level. Recognition of some of these shortcomings was an important element leading to a reevaluation of the goals and approaches of development economics and of the role of agriculture in reaching those goals in the period following 1970.

· THE GROWTH-WITH-EQUITY ERA SINCE 1970 ·

The Broadening of Development Goals

Around 1970, mainstream Western development economics began to give greater attention to employment and the distribution of real income, broadly defined. This shift in emphasis came about for at least three reasons. The first was ideological, a response to the radical critique of Western development economics, especially the critique of the "mutual benefit claim" discussed previously. The goal of economic growth for Third World countries was seriously questioned by this critique, and some development economists may have felt the need to redefine the goals of development more broadly in order to preserve the legitimacy of their subdiscipline.

Second, from the 1960s onwards it became apparent that rapid economic growth in some countries, such as Pakistan, Nigeria, and Iran, had deleterious, and in some cases disastrous, side effects. Hirschman argued that development economists were forced to reevaluate the goals of their profession because

> the series of political disasters that struck a number of Third World countries from
> the sixties on . . . were clearly *somehow* connected with the stresses and strains

accompanying development and "modernization." These development disasters, ranging from civil wars to the establishment of murderous authoritarian regimes, could not but give pause to a group of social scientists who, after all, had taken up the cultivation of development economics in the wake of World War II not as narrow specialists, but impelled by the vision of a better world. As liberals, most of them presumed that "all good things go together" and took it for granted that if only a good job could be done in raising the national income of the countries concerned, a number of beneficial effects would follow in the social, political, and cultural realms.

When it turned out instead that the promotion of economic growth entailed not infrequently a sequence of events involving serious retrogression in those other areas, including the wholesale loss of civil and human rights, the easy self-confidence that our subdiscipline exuded in its early stages was impaired (Hirschman 1981a:20–21).

The third reason for the reevaluation of development goals was the growing awareness among development economists that even in countries where rapid economic growth had not contributed to social turmoil, the benefits of economic growth often were not trickling down to the poor and that frequently the income gap between rich and poor was widening (see, for example, Fishlow 1972; Nugent and Yotopoulos 1979; and Streeten 1979). Even where the incomes of the poor were rising, often they were rising so slowly that the poor would not be able to afford decent diets or housing for at least another generation.

Rather than simply waiting for increases in average per capita incomes to "solve" the problems of poverty and malnutrition; economists, political leaders in the Third World, and the leaders of major donor agencies argued in the early 1970s that greater explicit attention needed to be paid to employment, income distribution, and "basic needs," such as nutrition and housing. For example, when Robert McNamara was president of the World Bank, he called on it to redirect its activities toward helping people in the bottom 40 percent of the income distribution scale in low-income countries (McNamara 1973).

These growth-with-equity concerns stimulated a number of important theoretical and policy debates during the 1970s. The first debate concerned the interactions between income distribution and rates of economic growth. A number of economists during the 1970s included income distribution explicitly in their frameworks of analysis, and several examined the interdependence between income growth, income distribution, and other development goals, such as literacy and health.[12] These analyses focused on changes not only in the *size* distribution of income during the course of development (for example, Chenery et al. 1974; Adelman and Morris 1973) but in the *functional* distribution. For example, attention was given to the impact of economic growth on small farmers (Stevens 1977a; Fei et al. 1979) and on women (Boserup 1970; Tinker and Bramsen 1976; Spencer 1976).

A second debate centered on employment generation and the possible existence of employment-output trade-offs in industry and agriculture. Although Folke Dovring (1959) had shown that the absolute number of people engaged in agriculture in developing countries would probably continue to grow for several decades, most economists during the 1960s still assumed that urban industry would absorb most of the new entrants to the labor force. By 1970, however, it had become apparent that urban industry in most countries could not expand quickly enough in the short run to provide employment for the expanding rural labor force. Hence, the concern of development planners shifted to finding ways to hold people in the countryside (Eicher et al. 1970).

The concern about creating rural jobs raised a number of questions in both agriculture and industry about the relative output and employment-generation capacities of large and small enterprises. In agriculture, debate centered on how much emphasis should be given to improving small farms as opposed to creating larger and more capital- intensive farms, ranches, and plantations. Empirical evidence from the late 1960s and early 1970s revealed that the economies of size in tropical agriculture were more limited than previously believed and that the improvement of small farms often resulted in greater output *and* employment per hectare than did large-scale farming. In industry, the small-versus-large debate led to a number of empirical studies of rural small-scale enterprises (see Chuta and Liedholm 1984). In both agriculture and industry the concern with possible employment-output trade-offs also stimulated research on the choice of appropriate production techniques.

During the 1970s economists and planners also began to give explicit consideration to the impact of development programs on nutrition. Empirical studies revealed that increases in average per capita income did not always lead to improved nutrition and that at times malnutrition actually increased with growing incomes (Berg 1973; Reutlinger and Selowsky 1976). Therefore, many analysts argued that nutrition projects targeted to the poor and malnourished were needed to supplement other development activities (Pinstrup-Anderson 1981).

Implications for Agriculture

The change in orientation of development economics in the early 1970s implied a much greater role for agriculture in development programs. Because the majority of the poor in most Third World countries live in rural areas and because food prices are a major determinant of the real income of both the rural and urban poor, the low productivity of Third World agriculture was seen as a major cause of poverty. Furthermore, because urban industry had generally provided few jobs for the rapidly growing labor force, development planners increasingly concentrated on ways to create productive employment in rural areas, if only as a holding action until the rate of population growth declined and urban industry could create more jobs. (Nonetheless, investment policies in many countries continued to favor urban areas [see Lipton 1977].) The need to create productive rural employment was underlined by a growing awareness of the increasing landlessness in many parts of the Third World, particularly South Asia (Singh n.d.), Latin America (de Janvry

1981), and a few countries in Africa (Ghai and Radwan 1983).

It soon became apparent that if agriculture was to play a more important role in development programs, policymakers needed a more detailed understanding of rural economies than that provided by the simple two-sector models of the 1950s and early 1960s. In the late 1960s and early 1970s there was a rapid expansion of micro-level research on agricultural production and marketing, farmer decision-making, the performance or rural-factor markets, and rural nonfarm employment.[13] This micro-level research documented the complexity of many Third World farming and marketing systems and complemented the macro-level work begun in the 1950s on modeling agricultural growth and intersectoral relationships.

Research Findings of The 1970s

Modeling Agricultural Growth

As policymakers looked to agriculture to provide more employment and wage goods for the rapidly expanding labor force, attempts to model the process of agricultural growth assumed increased importance. Hayami and Vernon Ruttan's induced-innovation model of agricultural development was a major contribution of the 1970s. Hayami and Ruttan (1971) argued that there are multiple technological paths to agricultural growth, each embodying a different mix of factors of production, and that changes in relative-factor prices can guide researchers to select the most "efficient" path for a country. This argument implied that countries with different-factor endowments would have different efficient growth paths and that the wholesale importation of agricultural technology from industrialized countries to the Third World could lead to highly inefficient patterns of growth. Hayami and Ruttan argued that relative-factor prices not only affected technological development but often played an important role in guiding the design of social institutions.[14]

Other major efforts to model the process of agricultural growth included detailed agricultural-sector analyses (such as in Thorbecke and Stoutjesdijk 1971, and Mantesch et al. 1971); the work of Mellor and of Johnston and Peter Kilby discussed below; and the attempt by some radical scholars, notably de Janvry (1981), to move from a purely global, abstract explanation of rural poverty to a neo-Marxist analysis on a micro level.

Intersectoral Relationships

The 1970s also witnessed a great expansion in the theoretical and empirical research begun by economists in the 1960s on the interdependence between agricultural and nonagricultural growth. Particularly noteworthy was the work of Mellor and of Johnston and Kilby (1975).[15] Mellor argued that it was possible to design employment-oriented strategies of development based on the potential growth linkages inherent in the new high-yielding grain varieties.[16] Mellor's analysis drew heavily on empirical evidence from India. Unlike many authors who mainly stressed how the new varieties could increase total food supplies, Mellor emphasized that the new varieties could also raise the incomes of foodgrain producers, thereby generating increased effective demand for a wide variety of labor-intensive products. Indeed, Mellor saw most of the potential growth in employment being outside the foodgrain sector itself, in sectors producing labor-intensive goods such as dairy products, fruit, other consumer products, and agricultural inputs. This expanded employment was made possible by the simultaneous increase in the effective demand for these products and in the supply of inexpensive wage goods in the form of foodgrains. Much of Mellor's analysis focused on the types of agricultural and industrial policies needed to exploit these growth linkages of the new grain varieties.

Johnston and Kilby analyzed "the reciprocal interactions between agricultural development and the expansion of manufacturing and other nonfarm sectors" (Johnston and Kilby 1975:xv). In particular, they focused on the factors affecting the rates of labor transfer between sectors and the level and composition of intersectoral commodity flows. Drawing on empirical evidence from England, the United States, Japan, Taiwan, Mexico, and the Soviet Union, Johnston and Kilby argued that the size distribution of farms was a critical determinant of the demand for industrial products in a developing economy. They showed that broad-based agricultural growth was more effective than estate production in stimulating the demand for industrial products and hence in speeding the structural transformation of the economy. Johnston and Kilby's analysis strongly supported the view that concentrating agricultural development efforts on the mass of small farmers in low-income countries, rather than promoting a bimodal structure of small and large farms, would lead to faster growth rates of both aggregate economic output and employment.

Factor Markets and Employment Generation

Concern for creating jobs stimulated research during the 1970s on rural labor markets and employment. Krishna (1973) addressed the basic methodological problem of defining underemployment and unemployment in rural economies. Noting that most unemployment studies use definitions appropriate to industrial economies, Krishna identified four different criteria commonly used to classify people as underemployed or unemployed: (1) a time criterion, according to which a person is underemployed if he or she is gainfully occupied for less time than some full-employment standard; (2) an income criterion, by which an individual is underemployed or unemployed if he or she earns less than some desired minimum; (3) a willingness criterion, which defines a person as underemployed or unemployed if he or she is willing to work longer hours at the prevailing wage; and (4) a productivity criterion, which defines a worker as unemployed if the worker's marginal product is zero. Krishna showed that different policy measures were appropriate for dealing with each type of underemployment.

During the 1970s several economists, particularly those associated with the

International Labour Office (ILO), spoke of dethroning GNP as the target and indicator of development and replacing growth strategies with employment-oriented approaches (see, for example, Seers 1970). During the first half of the 1970s the ILO dispatched missions to Colombia, Sri Lanka, Kenya, the Philippines, and Sudan to draw up programs to expand employment (ILO 1970, 1971, 1972, 1974, 1976b). The ILO missions "studied just about everything—population, education, income distribution, appropriate technology, multinationals" (Little 1982:214), but they frequently lacked the detailed information needed to evaluate where and to what degree employment-output trade-offs existed in these countries. The impact of the ILO studies was further limited as research during the 1970s demonstrated that, because 60–80 percent of the poor in most Third World countries were employed in some fashion, the critical policy issue was not one of creating jobs per se but one of increasing the productivity of workers already employed in small-scale agriculture and nonfarm enterprises. The ILO studies were, nonetheless, important in stimulating research on labor markets and on the impact of factor-price distortions on output and employment.

A large number of studies during the 1970s that evaluated the performance of labor markets in low-income countries generally found that at peak periods of the agricultural cycle there was little unemployment in rural areas, although at other periods of the year there were labor surpluses. The studies also documented that earlier researchers had frequently overestimated the size of these surpluses because they had failed to take account of the considerable time devoted to rural nonfarm enterprises and to walking to and from fields. Studies also confirmed that labor markets in most countries were generally competitive, with wage rates, particularly in rural areas, following seasonal patterns of labor demand (see Berry and Sabot 1978).

The labor-market research also documented that when labor was misallocated, in many situations the misallocation was due not only to imperfections in labor markets, but to poorly functioning markets for other factors of production as well. Overvalued exchange rates and subsidized credit, for example, often encouraged excessive substitution of capital for labor in low-wage economies. Concern about the impact of such factor-price distortions on output and employment stimulated research on the choice of technique in agricultural production and processing (see Byerlee et al. 1983) and on the functioning of rural financial markets in low-income countries (Adams and Graham 1984).

In the late 1960s and early 1970s the concern for employment generation led to questions about the productivity and labor-absorption capacity of large farms and ranches versus those of small farms. A large number of scholars (for example, Dorner and Kanel 1971; Barraclough 1973; Berry 1975; and Berry and Cline 1979) documented the strong economic case for land reform in many Third World countries because of the higher employment and land productivity potential of small family farms. The higher land productivity was largely due to greater use of labor (mainly family labor) per unit of land. Although there was widespread agreement among these scholars that land reform was an attractive policy instrument for raising farm output, increasing rural employment, and improving the equality of income distribution, political support for land reform waned during the 1970s (de Janvry 1984).

Rural-to-Urban Migration

Rural-to-urban migration was a major area of research during the 1960s and 1970s because the rate of rural-to-urban migration in most Third World countries far outstripped the rates of growth of urban employment. This led to rising levels of open urban unemployment. The concern of policymakers therefore shifted quickly from trying to transfer surplus labor from agriculture to industry to trying to reduce "excessive" rates of urbanization.

Research by economists on migration in the Third World was sparked by Michael Todaro's attempt in the late 1960s to explain the apparently paradoxical phenomenon of accelerating rural-to-urban migration in the context of continuously rising urban unemployment in Kenya. Todaro (1969) proposed a model (later extended by John Harris and Todaro 1970) in which a potential migrant's decision to migrate is motivated primarily by the difference between his or her expected (rather than actual) urban income and the prevailing rural wage. The Harris-Todaro model implied that attempts to reduce urban unemployment by creating more urban jobs could paradoxically result in more urban unemployment rather than less. By leading potential migrants to believe that their chances of getting an urban job had increased, urban employment programs induced greater rural-to-urban migration. Harris and Todaro therefore argued that urban unemployment could best be addressed by reducing the incentives to migrate to the cities, for example, by raising rural incomes via a broad range of agricultural and rural development programs.[17]

The second approach to studying migration was spearheaded by several radical political economists who focused on the social, as opposed to the private, benefits and costs of migration. Samir Amin, for example, argued that although rural-to-urban migration might be privately profitable for the migrant, it imposed important social costs on the sending area, including the loss of future village leadership and the instability of rural families. Amin argued that these costs exceeded possible gains to the area from wage remittances to the home villages.

Although the net welfare impact of migration is obviously an important question, many of the studies by radical scholars lacked empirical data to support their conclusions. In a balanced and constructive assessment of both neoclassical and radical political economy studies of migration in southern Africa, Knight and Lenta (1980) concluded that there was not a clear picture of the net welfare impact of migration in the countries supplying labor to the mines in South Africa.

Product Market Performance

Rapid income growth and urbanization put increasing pressures on markets for agricultural products, particularly food, during the 1960s and 1970s. In response, economists undertook a number of studies to evaluate the performance of agricultural product markets and suggest improvements.[18] These studies generally found little support for allegations of widespread collusion and extraction of monopoly profits by private merchants in Third World countries. They did, however, document how insufficient infrastructure and the lack of reliable public information systems and other public goods often reduced market efficiency and lowered farmers' incentives to specialize for market production. The studies were often critical of state monopolies in the domestic food trade, citing the frequent high costs of state marketing agencies. The studies identified important roles for the state in providing public goods (better information systems, standardized weights and measures, and so on) to facilitate private trading, price stabilization, and regulation of international trade. More recently, there has been discussion of ways the state can ensure adequate food supplies to the poor without disrupting normal market channels.

Farming Systems Research and Farmer Decisionmaking

During the late 1960s and the 1970s economists increasingly investigated the factors that influenced farmers' decisions concerning whether to adopt new crop varieties and farming practices. This work eventually led to the development of farming systems research. Farming systems research attempts to incorporate farmers' constraints and objectives into agricultural research by involving farmers in problem identification, on-farm agronomic trials, and extension (CIMMYT Economics Staff 1984).

Interest in farming systems research and the new household economics also led to efforts to model the farm household as both a production and a consumption unit (see Singh et al. n.d.). Inspired by A. V. Chayanov's (1966) work on the behavior of Russian peasants in the early 1900s, the farm-household models stressed the need to understand how government policies could simultaneously affect both the production and the consumption decisions of small farmers. For example, these models showed that marketed surplus of a crop might, in some circumstances, actually decline as the crop's price was increased (even if production of the crop rose) because the price increase would raise farm family income, and some of this increased income would be spent on the good whose price had risen.

Summary: Research in the 1970s

The results of microeconomic research during the 1970s contributed to an accumulation of knowledge about the behavior of farmers; constraints on the expansion of farm and nonfarm production, income, and employment; the linkages between agricultural research and extension institutions; and the complexity and location-specific nature of the agricultural development process. One of the major accomplishments of the 1970s was a large increase in knowledge about agricultural development in Sub-Saharan Africa, an area often ignored by development economists during the 1950s and early 1960s (see Eicher and Baker 1982). But the increased orientation to micro-level research may have resulted in relatively less attention being paid to macroeconomic research on food policy and the role that agriculture can play in the structural transformation of Third World economies. A major challenge, therefore, is to incorporate the micro-research findings into models that examine agriculture's role in a general equilibrium (or disequilibrium) context.

Development Programs of the 1970s: Integrated Rural Development and Basic Needs

Reacting to some of the disappointments of the Green Revolution and the agricultural growth-oriented programs of the 1960s, donors and Third World governments turned increasingly their attention to integrated rural development and basic-needs projects in the 1970s. Integrated rural development attempts to combine in one project elements to increase agricultural production and to improve health, education, sanitation, and a variety of other social services. Like the community development projects of the 1950s, integrated rural development projects of the 1970s sometimes expanded social services much faster than they expanded the economic base to support them, and they often proved to be extraordinarily complex and difficult to implement and administer. Moreover, the inability of integrated rural development projects to increase rapidly agricultural production often stemmed from the lack of appropriate technical packages. Uma Lele (1975) reviewed seventeen integrated rural development projects in Africa and found that most of the projects were based upon inadequate knowledge of local technical possibilities, small-farmer constraints, and local institutions. The projects also tended to have very high administrative costs, making them difficult to replicate over broader areas. By 1980 many donors, such as the World Bank and the U.S. Agency for International Development, had retreated from integrated rural development projects or had redesigned these projects to give greater emphasis to agricultural production.[19] The rise and decline of integrated rural development (1973–1980) was in some ways very similar to the fate of community development between 1950 and 1957 (Holdcroft 1984).

In the mid-1970s the basic-needs approach was popularized by the International Labour Office (ILO 1976a) and subsequently spearheaded by a group of economists within the World Bank under the leadership of Paul Streeten. The basic-needs approach holds that development projects should give priority to increasing the welfare of the poor directly through projects to improve nutrition, education, housing, and so on, rather than focus mainly on increasing aggregate growth rates.[20] The basic-needs advocates supported their case by citing impressive gains in life span, literacy, and nutrition in Cuba, Sri Lanka, and the People's Republic of China—countries that had emphasized basic needs. But the constraints on the basic-needs approach were highlighted by Sri Lanka's inability during the mid-1970s to continue to finance the centerpiece of its program, universal free rice rations, which forced the government to shift to a more growth-oriented strategy. Likewise, the rising cost of food subsidies in China raises questions about China's ability to sustain its policy of cheap food for urban consumers (Lardy 1984).

Although investments in health, nutrition, education, and housing can contribute importantly to the welfare of the poor and to the rate of economic growth, the experience with the basic-needs approach suggests that low-income countries also need to emphasize building the economic base to finance these investments. By the early 1980s many economists were once again giving greater emphasis to economic growth and to the sequence of different types of development activities, such as investments in irrigation and health facilities. This shift in emphasis did not imply a rejection of the growth-with-equity philosophy of the 1970s. Rather, it reflected an increasing recognition of the impossibility of achieving a decent living standard for the bulk of the rapidly growing populations in poor countries simply by redistributing existing assets. This recognition led the World Bank to shift to a more growth-oriented strategy in the early 1980s and the basic-needs approach faded into the background.[21]

The research results and development experiences of the 1970s suggest that in order to attain more rapid, more broad-based agricultural growth and rural development, the following components will have to be emphasized in the coming decades: strengthening of institutions in low-income countries for agricultural research, administration, policy analysis, and training; renewed emphasis on analyzing agricultural development issues in broader macroeconomic frameworks; reevaluation of the roles of international trade, food aid, and agricultural specialization in an increasingly interdependent world food economy; and movement towards more interdisciplinary approaches to problemsolving. All these require expansion of the human-capital base of Third World countries. One of the clearest lessons of the 1960s and 1970s is that agricultural and rural development require strong local institutions and well-trained individuals. International research centers and expatriate advisers are at best complements to, not substitutes for, domestic research systems and policy analysts. Because problems in the food system are typically multifaceted, there is also a need to move toward more interdisciplinary approaches to problemsolving. Food policy research and farming systems research (see Fresco and Poats in this book) are examples of areas where such interdisciplinary approaches are proving useful.

· NOTES ·

Larry Lev, Carl Liedholm, Michael Morris, and Robert Stevens offered insightful comments on an earlier draft of this paper. Bruce Johnston (1970) extensively reviewed the literature of the 1950s and 1960s on the role of agriculture in development.

1. Development economics began to emerge as a subdiscipline of economics in the post-World War II period with the work of Nurkse, Mandelbaum, Rosenstein-Rodan,

Singer, Prebisch, and others. The first major text on economic development was W. Arthur Lewis's influential *The Theory of Economic Growth* (1955). Lewis's emphasis on economic growth set the tone for work in development economics during the "growth era" of the 1950s and 1960s. In the introduction Lewis wrote, "The subject matter of this book is growth of output per head of population . . . and not distribution" (p. 9). Lewis did, however, include an appendix entitled "Is Economic Growth Desirable?" For reviews of the history of development economics, see Hirschman (1981a), Streeten (1979), Reynolds (1977, chap. 2), and Little (1982).

2. This section draws heavily on Johnston's excellent review of the literature through 1970 on the role of agriculture in economic development.

3. For an excellent summary of the Lewis model, see Meier (1976:157–63); see also Lewis (1972). For an analysis of the impact of Lewis's model on development economics, see Gersowitz et al. (1982).

4. Lewis's statement that the marginal productivity of laborers in the noncapitalist sector approached zero as a limiting case stimulated a large number of efforts to measure the extent of surplus labor in agriculture. For a review of these efforts, see Kao, Anschel, and Eicher (1964). For a critique of the concept of surplus labor in agriculture, see Schultz (1964, chap. 4).

5. William H. Nicholls (1964) was one of the first critics of the rapid transfer of surplus labor as a short-run strategy.

6. For a summary of this thesis, see Prebisch (1959). For critical reviews, see Kravis (1970) and Little (1982, chap. 4). In recent years Prebisch has modified his views about import substitution (see Prebisch 1981).

7. The 1960s literature on agricultural development is captured in the volumes edited by Eicher and Witt (1964), Southworth and Johnston (1967), and Wharton (1969).

8. The community development approach emphasized the provision of social services, which presaged the basic-needs approach to development in the late 1970s, described later in this chapter. By emphasizing social services, community development differed from other Western development efforts of the 1950s and 1960s, which focused mainly on increasing average per capita incomes.

9. These arguments were most fully developed by Mellor and by Johnston and Kilby in the 1970s. See the discussion of these authors' work in the second section of this chapter.

10. French scholars also made important contributions to the Marxist analysis of agricultural development during the 1960s and 1970s (see Petit 1982).

11. For critiques of the dependency school of thought in Latin America, see Cardoso and Faletto (1979), and de Janvry (1981).

12. A standard reference is the influential book *Redistribution With Growth* by Chenery et al. (1974). See also Seers (1970), and Adelman (1975).

13. See, for example, the volumes edited by Stevens (1977a); and Jones (1972).

14. For attempts to test the induced-innovation hypothesis empirically, see Binswanger and Ruttan (1978).

15. See also the volume edited by Reynolds (1975).

16. Mellor's views are articulated in *The New Economics of Growth: A Strategy for India and the Developing World* (1976). See also Mellor and Lele (1973).

17. The major extensions of the Harris-Todaro model and the empirical tests of it are summarized in Todaro (1980).

18. Many of these studies are reviewed by Lele (1977) and Riley and Staatz (1981). For a critique of some of these studies see Harriss (1979).

19. For excellent reviews of integrated rural development, see Ruttan (1975), de Janvry (1981), and Johnston and Clark (1982).

20. The basic-needs approach is not simply a call for increased social welfare spending, however; it is also based on recognition of the importance of investment in human cap-

ital in economic growth and of the synergism of nutrition, health, and family-planning decisions. For an excellent discussion of basic-needs projects and their relationships to rural development, see Johnston and Clark (1982, chap. 4).

21. The World Bank's experience with basic needs is summarized by Streeten (1981).

• SUGGESTED FURTHER READINGS •

Amin, Samir. 1974. *Accumulation on a World Scale: A Critique of the Theory of Underdevelopment*. New York: Monthly Review Press.

Dalrymple, Dana G. 1985. The Development and Adoption of High Yielding Varieties of Wheat and Rice in Developing Countries. *American Journal of Agricultural Economics* 67:5:1067-1073.

Eicher, Carl K., and Doyle C. Baker. 1982. *Research on Agricultural Development in Sub-Saharan Africa: A Critical Survey*. MSU International Development Paper No. 1. East Lansing: Department of Agricultural Economics, Michigan State University.

Eicher, Carl K., and John M. Staatz, eds. 1984. *Agricultural Development in the Third World*. Baltimore: Johns Hopkins University Press.

Hayami, Yujiro, and Vernon W. Ruttan. 1971. *Agricultural Development: An International Perspective*. Baltimore: Johns Hopkins Press.

Johnston, Bruce F. 1970. Agriculture and Structural Transformation in Developing Countries: A Survey of Research. *Journal of Economic Literature* 3:2:369–404.

Johnston, Bruce F., and Peter Kilby. 1975. *Agriculture and Structural Transformation: Economic Strategies in Late-Developing Countries*. New York: Oxford University Press.

Lele, Uma. 1975. *The Design of Rural Development: Lessons from Africa*. Baltimore: Johns Hopkins University Press for the World Bank.

Lewis, W. Arthur. 1954. Economic Development with Unlimited Supplies of Labour. *Manchester School of Economic and Social Studies* 22:2:139–91.

Mellor, John W. 1975. *The New Economics of Growth: A Strategy for India and the Developing World*. Ithaca, New York: Cornell University Press.

Schultz, Theodore W. 1964. *Transforming Traditional Agriculture*. New Haven: Yale University Press.

·5·

Social Science Perspectives on Food in Africa

SARA BERRY

Recent assessments of the performance and prospects of African economies portray a deepening crisis, centered on the problem of food supplies. Since the early 1970s a rapidly rising number of Africans have had an increasingly difficult time getting enough to eat. By all accounts, domestic food supplies are falling further and further behind domestic needs. Both governments and consumers face serious problems in procuring the kinds and quantities of food they want at prices they can afford to pay. Chronic hunger and malnutrition are widespread and escalate quickly into famine in times of drought or national financial crisis. Easing shortages with food from foreign sources has also become more difficult in the last decade. World prices of grains have risen; unstable petroleum prices have put heavy strains on many African countries' balances of payments and worsened their terms of trade. Agricultural exports have not increased sufficiently to cover rising import bills. Food aid to Africa has grown at unprecedented rates in the last decade, but it is adequate neither to meet short-term needs nor generate a long-run solution to the crisis.

Social scientists attribute African economic stagnation and food deficits to everything from global economic and political conditions to backward African farming practices. Although most social scientists agree that the food crisis is the result of many causes, they disagree about the relative importance of these causes and their interactions. Explanations range from: (1) Africa is the unfortunate victim of a world economy geared to serve the interests of wealthy industrial countries; to (2) Africa's economic problems are the result of poor policy choices made by Afri-

This chapter is based on an earlier article by the author entitled "The Food Crisis and Agrarian Change in Africa: A Review Essay," *African Studies Review* 27:2 (1984):59–112, which was originally prepared for the Joint African Studies Committee of the Social Science Research Council and the American Council of Learned Societies. Used with permission of the publisher.

can governments, or the inability of these governments to implement sound policies effectively, or both; and (3) the technology needed to increase the productivity of African farming systems has not yet been developed. The social science literature cannot be reduced to a single, consistent explanatory argument—many studies have produced multiple interpretations.

This chapter does not attempt to synthesize the social science literature on food in Africa, but to review some of the important lines of interpretation and debate. The discussion is organized as follows: (1) the quality of available evidence about agricultural performance in Africa; (2) African agriculture and the world economy; (3) the form and effects of African governments' policies towards agriculture; (4) environmental constraints on expanding food production and subsequent implications for technological development; (5) the idea of peasant rationality and its implications for understanding agrarian change and policy; (6) relations between African systems of kinship, domestic organization, and agricultural practices; and (7) the effects of rural commercialization on economic and social differentiation and structural change. In conclusion, a few comments are offered about directions for further research.

• SEARCHING FOR THE EVIDENCE—WHAT DO WE KNOW ABOUT AGRICULTURAL PERFORMANCE? •

International agencies from the World Bank to the Organization of African Unity (OAU) have interpreted Africa's food crisis as a crisis of production, arising partly from historical factors and partly from excessive efforts by African governments to regulate and control economic activity within their countries (OAU 1981; World Bank 1981). Since 1960, the international agencies argue, population growth, urbanization, and rising incomes, especially in urban areas, have caused demand for marketed foodstuffs to outrun domestic productive capacity. This is especially true for commodities such as wheat and rice, which make up a major part of urban residents' diets but are not commonly grown in Africa. Consequently, food imports have increased rapidly at a time when the cost of other essential imports—notably petroleum products—has risen sharply also. The resulting pressure on African countries' balances of payments has been further exacerbated by the lagging output of crops, according to the World Bank (1981). In turn, lagging production stems from African governments' neglect of agriculture or their adoption of inappropriate policies toward trade, foreign exchange, and domestic prices.

To support the argument that Africa faces a crisis in agricultural production, official and scholarly publications regularly cite aggregate production figures for Africa as a whole. The reliability of national data on agricultural output is open to serious question. Agricultural censuses and sample surveys, no matter how well organized and administered, are subject to numerous sources of error and uncertainty, stemming from problems such as farmers' unwillingness to disclose information to potential tax assessors and selecting a representative sample of producers in countries where there is no reliable census from which to prepare a sampling frame. In recent years, moreover, the reliability of official marketing data as an indicator of production has been reduced by the very factor to which the World Bank attributes much of the crisis—increased governmental regulation of economic transactions. Price controls, taxes, and state agricultural marketing schemes have driven many transactions out of official marketing channels. Official control of export marketing has, for example, caused large-scale smuggling in countries such as Ghana and Niger (Jeffries 1982; Collins 1976) and, as in Tanzania, undermined governments' own programs of stabilization and rural development (Lele and Candler 1981; Hyden 1980).

If the output exists but is hidden, where does it go? Does it go into illegal or "parallel" markets or into higher standards of consumption for self-sufficient rural households? Has output in fact declined? Local evidence suggests that all of these things have happened, but there is no reliable statistical basis for estimating their relative importance within particular localities, let alone on national or regional levels. It is likely that official statistics for output have diverged further and further from actual output in recent years, but neither the magnitude of the divergence nor, in many cases, even the direction of the divergence is known.

To sum up, our ignorance of aggregate trends in agricultural output has increased. In most cases the data are simply not good enough to warrant firm conclusions about national—let alone continental—trends in agricultural output. Nonetheless, such data are regularly cited both to show that agricultural production in Africa is declining and to support arguments that this decline is primarily due to global and/or national economic and political trends.

• AFRICAN AGRICULTURE AND THE WORLD ECONOMY •

Much discussion of the impact of international economic forces and agencies on African agriculture has revolved around a rather sterile debate over whether Africa suffers from too much or too little integration into the world economy. Both arguments have a substantial legacy of scholarly support. The first view—that African agriculture suffers from excessive international influence—has gone through several versions. Early critics of the colonial legacy decried African economies' dependence on agricultural exports on the grounds that agricultural commodities face unstable world prices and deteriorating terms of trade, both of which make African economic development more difficult (Robson and Lury 1969). This argument encouraged newly independent African governments to adopt crash programs to diversify output through industrialization, programs that often absorbed more revenue and foreign exchange than they generated. Later arguments shifted the emphasis of discussion from the disadvantages of agricultural production per se to the belief that capital accumulation on a world scale tended to siphon off surplus from peripheral areas of the world economy, keeping African labor cheap and relatively unproductive, in and outside agriculture (Amin 1976; Leys 1974).

Recently, rising food prices and imports have once again focused attention on agricultural production and the disadvantages faced by African farmers in international markets. Some scholars have argued that if Africans cannot hope to compete effectively against developed countries' tariffs on tropical imports or against the market power of international merchants of grain, improved seed, and fertilizer, Africans should seek to protect themselves by becoming self-sufficient in foodstuffs (Franke and Chasin 1980; OAU 1981; Food and Agriculture Organization 1978b). Unfortunately, this self-sufficiency is difficult to achieve because there are poor marketing systems and/or because it is profitable for African traders and officials to deal in imported and donated food supplies (Harriss 1979). Ironically, a goal of self-sufficiency in food may also play directly into the hands of foreign suppliers of improved agricultural inputs and techniques, thus increasing other imports rather than total self-sufficiency. However, withdrawal from the world market is no panacea, either in practice or as an intellectual solution to Africa's agrarian problems.

Arguments supporting an open door policy rather than a self-sufficiency policy also need to be scrutinized. The World Bank and other international agencies base their arguments for free trade on calculations that indicate that Africa's comparative advantage lies in traditional export crops (World Bank 1981; Pearson et al. 1981). What do such calculations mean? World markets are not perfectly competitive, and Africa's most competitive exports, at world market prices, are not necessarily those that represent the best returns to African resources. In addition, even if African governments were to dismantle their own tariffs and foreign exchange controls, they would continue to face these same barriers to trade in the industrialized countries they sell to.

Another dimension to the self-sufficiency versus open door debate is that foreign governments and donor agencies already intervene directly in African domestic food production. Foreign agencies and even private firms sponsor an increasing number of rural development plans and projects in Africa which, in turn, provide a market for foreign advice and inputs. Competition among donors has even become an impediment to their own as well as to host governments' efforts to reach agricultural producers (Franke and Chasin 1980; Pinckney et al. 1982). In the wake of the long drought of the mid-1970s, for example, donor activity in some Sahelian countries grew so intense that local officials were fully occupied in administering foreign aid, and the same thing is happening in the Horn of Africa in the 1980s.

The very agencies that exhort African governments to relinquish controls over foreign transactions also hold these governments responsible for managing their balances of payments and maintaining their creditworthiness in international financial circles. By opening their doors to U.S. farm surpluses and international agribusiness, African governments increase their vulnerability to fluctuations in world supply and to the market power of multinational firms, and, consequently, African citizens demand state protection against the risks and losses of international trade. It is inherently contradictory to argue that African governments should intervene less in their citizens' activities in order to increase their participation in the international economy. In today's global economy, integration into world markets requires that governments take responsibility for managing foreign transactions, which in turn requires effective management of the domestic economy.

· THE ROLE OF THE STATE ·

Neither the form nor the consequences of African governments' policies can be deduced from the logic of their circumstances—whether described in terms of dependence, underdevelopment and class structure, or in terms of market forces and technological imperatives. Although African bureaucrats sometimes behave like "an executive committee of the [national or international] bourgeoisie," extracting surpluses from African farmers without making any effort to increase their productive capacity (Leys 1978; Wolpe 1972), this phenomenon alone is not sufficient to explain the behavior of postcolonial regimes. Exploiting peasants is not unambiguously advantageous for the accumulating classes, as writers from Nicholai I. Bukharin and Evgenia Preobrazhensky (1922) to Alain de Janvry (1981) have pointed out, nor do bureaucrats and capitalists always work together in Africa or anywhere else.

On the other hand, neoclassical economists repeatedly exhort African governments to confine their economic activities to functions which the market cannot or will not perform such as providing public goods and controlling the level of aggregate demand, but these economists never discuss the conditions under which such a strategy might be feasible. Failure to address this issue sometimes leads to outright contradiction. For example, in a development scheme in Mali the government failed to procure adequate supplies of millet and sorghum because the official price did not cover farmers' costs of production. Then a private firm was called in and managed "to persuade farmers to deliver some 10,000 tons of cereals annually" *at the official price* (World Bank 1981:54). Far from demonstrating the World Bank's thesis that price incentives are the most effective way to raise agricultural output, this example suggests that private enterprise has a comparative advantage in its exercise of extraeconomic coercion!

More generally, the literature on the food crisis fails to explain why African governments have rather consistently failed to adopt the right policies even if the right policies were identified. The argument that politicians and bureaucrats are not farmers and, hence, neither understand farmers' problems nor act in their interests, is hardly convincing. Many African politicians and officials are farmers' sons or daughters, and some own and even manage agricultural enterprises of their own (Heyer et al. 1981). On a theoretical level, it is insufficient to attribute government policy to the attitudes of individual bureaucrats. In one of the few attempts to explain governmental policy choices, Robert H. Bates suggested that state policies that discourage agricultural production reflect rational efforts by politicians and bureaucrats to raise government revenues or consolidate state power (Bates 1981). African countries with relatively good records of agricultural performance have been those in which agricultural producers have acquired political power and used it to design and enact policies favorable to agriculture, as occurred in Ivory Coast and Kenya. Bates concluded that the key to agricultural progress elsewhere in Africa is for farmers to gain power and use it to shift relative prices, government taxes, and subsidies to their favor.

Like neoclassical economists, Bates apparently assumed that, once an agricultural faction gained a foothold in the government, the resulting improvement in agricultural incentives would be readily accessible to most producers, and the leaders of the farmers' party would not try to use their power to appropriate all or most of the resulting gains. The history of European settlers' political strategies and their resulting impact on agricultural policies in Kenya, Rhodesia, and South Africa suggests, however, that agricultural price supports and subsidies do not automatically trickle down to the mass of small farmers (Palmer and Parsons 1977; Wilson 1971; Heyer et al. 1976). Even the avowedly promarket regimes of Kenya, Malawi, and the Ivory Coast favor estate agriculture, promote parastatals, and enact legislation to facilitate large land purchases (Kydd and Christiansen 1982; World Bank 1978; Heyer et al. 1976). Bates reminded us, appropriately, that politicians and bureaucrats are as rational or self-interested as are farmers; however, he did not show that it is any easier to construct a theory of the state than to build theories of market performance from the presumption of individual rationality (Bates 1981).

That most postcolonial regimes in Africa took office under pressure (from below, above, and within) to take responsibility for developing their economies means they are obliged to adopt an interventionist stance towards economic activities and institutions. Their mandate is a contradictory one. Because agriculture is the principal source of foreign exchange, domestic incomes, and employment for most African economies, governments need to raise agricultural production to finance higher levels of imports and widen the domestic market. Also, agriculture provides the principal tax base from which to draw government revenues and is the major source of savings for nonagricultural investment. Extracting surpluses from farmers reduces agricultural output and income, and vice versa. Thus, the formulation and implementation of rural development strategies is a subject of debate and political contention within the governing class.

In addition, both the form and effects of state policies toward agriculture are shaped by relationships among farmers, traders, and consumers, and between these groups and state agencies and personnel. Although few farmers' parties have emerged in postcolonial Africa, farmers play an active role in shaping state actions—both through organized political action and by encouraging their descendants to seek wealth and influence outside of agriculture. Studies of farmers' behavior and local rural conditions hold an important place in the social science literature on food in Africa.

· ENVIRONMENTAL CONSTRAINTS AND TECHNOLOGICAL DEVELOPMENT ·

Concern over lagging agricultural production in Africa has stimulated considerable research on cultivation techniques and ways to improve them. Agronomists have made progress in identifying environmental constraints to agricultural output and productivity. African soils are fragile, subject to intense heat and extremes of moisture or dryness, and tend to deteriorate quickly under conditions of increasingly regular or intensive exploitation. Agricultural yields are often low, and raising them requires enormous inputs of labor, except in areas where it is possible to practice long-fallow systems of cultivation (Kamarck 1976; Kowal and Kassam 1978; Ruthenberg 1980). Even if enough labor were available, possibilities for increased output are constrained in semiarid areas by the brevity of the rainy season and in humid areas by soil erosion and leaching, which increase with more intense cultivation. Population densities in many parts of Africa are low compared with other tropical regions; it used to be argued that Africans were not impelled by population pressure to devise ecologically appropriate methods of intensifying agricultural production (Ruthenberg 1980; United States Department of Agriculture 1981).

Recent research fosters a growing appreciation of the appropriateness of indigenous methods of cultivation (see references in Berry 1984; Eicher and Baker 1982). Agronomists recognize that, due to the physical fragility of tropical soils, deep plowing often contributes to leaching and erosion; however, traditional cultivation methods such as heaping, ridging, intercropping, and minimum tillage prevent deterioration of the soil structure (Lal and Greenland 1979). Farm-management researchers collect detailed data on input-output coefficients, costs of production, and technical requirements of alternative crop regimes and methods of cultivation, then use this data to measure the profitability of alternative sets of farming practices (Heyer 1971; Upton 1973; Collinson 1982; Norman 1972). These studies contribute to a growing consensus that labor, rather than land, is often the crucial constraint to African agricultural production.

The discovery that African farmers are often more concerned with saving labor than with conserving cultivated land strengthened economists' faith in the economic rationality of African farmers. Farmers' indifference to new crops with labor requirements that conflict with those of established ones, or to new techniques that only increase yield at the cost of considerably increased labor inputs, now appears to be consistent with local-factor endowments and is, hence, economically efficient (Tourte and Moomaw 1977; Richards 1983a; Cleave 1974). This leads to a new appreciation of some traditional farming practices that agronomists had previously denigrated because of their low yields. For instance, mixed cropping, long fallowing, and cultivation of crops such as cassava may maximize returns to labor, especially in seasons of peak demand, and are worthy of greater attention by extension agents and agricultural researchers. Further research demonstrates that various practices such as mixed cropping, combining upland and valley plots, and cultivating drought-resistant but low-yielding crops such as finger millet, bulrush millet, sorghum, and cassava tend to reduce variations in total farm output and thus contribute to farmers' security (Richards 1983b). On the basis of these findings, agronomists modify or redesign research strategies, and international agricultural research institutes hire some economists who place new emphasis on developing crop varieties or cultivation methods that will not destroy tropical soil structures or threaten the security or savings in labor time provided by traditional practices (Terry et al. 1981; Plucknett et al. in this volume).

Although scholarly understanding of African agricultural practices has clearly advanced in recent years, problems remain. Adaptation of Green Revolution technology to specific African microenvironments remains spotty, although there have been some notable successes. High-yielding varieties of maize are widely grown in Kenya, Zambia, and Zimbabwe; high-yielding varieties of hybrid oil palms, in Nigeria and Sierra Leone (Eicher and Baker 1982). However, many researchers continue to have an overly simplistic concentration on single-factor explanations: They have simply substituted labor for land as *the* scarce factor in African agriculture, and, consequently, have focused research entirely on relieving this constraint. Thus it has been argued that mechanization is both inevitable and desirable as a strategy for expanding productive capacity, especially for expanding the capacity to grow domestically foodstuffs that are currently imported (Gaury 1977; Hart 1982). In keeping with this argument, several governments, particularly in West Africa, have launched or underwritten large-scale schemes for mechanized rice production. Not only do such projects often absorb more foreign exchange or government revenue than they generate (Pearson et al. 1981), they may prove environmentally damaging. The technique used to cultivate rice on large commercial farms in northern Ghana has been described as "mechanized shifting cultivation." It tends to destroy the physical structure of the soil, exhaust soil nutrients, disrupt local food supplies, and foster social tension and conflict rather than alleviate food shortages or reduce imports (Shepherd 1981).

Other studies conclude that African farmers' practices are often closely calibrated to local environmental conditions; these studies emphasize the importance of economic and social constraints to farmers' incomes and productivity. David Norman and others point out that inefficiency in agricultural production often reflects poverty rather than ignorance or mismanagement (Norman 1972). Moreover, technical change is not always an unmixed blessing. For example, agronomists have long argued that closer integration of crop and livestock production will yield important technical complementarities, such as manuring and animal traction, for African farmers. However, these technical benefits from mixed farming might be realized only at great cost—for example, if cattle are kept near arable fields during the cropping season, their foraging may threaten crops and generate conflict between farmers and herd owners (Delgado 1978; Norman et al. 1981). Technical progress is sometimes a mixed blessing and may founder on its own inherent contradictions.

· RATIONAL PEASANTS AND IMPERFECT STRUCTURES ·

By the end of World War II, Europeans were becoming increasingly aware that colonial rule was not only cumbersome and costly, but also unnecessary to the advancement of European economic interests in Africa. During the colonial period, if not before, Africans were drawn irreversibly into world markets. Once the immediate task of postwar reconstruction had been undertaken, the colonizers could afford to relinquish formal political control, secure in the knowledge that Africans would find it in their own interest to continue to do business with their erstwhile rulers. Growing acceptance of the desirability and feasibility of decolonization parallelled social scientists' new belief in the economic rationality of individual Africans and in the power of this rationality to explain economic trends. The publication of W. O. Jones's (1960) essay, "Economic Man in Africa," on the eve of independence reflected the tenor of the times.

Economic rationality can mean different things in different contexts. In formal decisionmaking models, it is usually defined as the ability or willingness to make choices in accordance with a consistent ordering of preferences among alternative outcomes. Since in reality the future is uncertain, outcomes are never actually known in advance, and it is therefore impossible to prove conclusively that behavior is perfectly rational. In practice, when people say that African farmers are rational, they mean that farmers act not in accordance with instinct or custom but on the basis of reasoned assessments of their circumstances. Appreciation of this point contributes to advances in understanding African ecologies and the indigenous methods of cultivation previously described, and certainly represents an advance over the notion, often expressed by colonial officials, that African farmers act without thinking.

It is not always easy to predict what rational farmers will do under changing circumstances because they can apply multiple rationales to a situation. For example, in the following scenario profit maximization and risk aversion, often held to reflect mutually exclusive preferences or attitudes, are complementary ones: If the price of a crop fluctuates seasonally so that farmers who need to exchange some of their crops for cash may be forced to sell cheap at harvest time and buy dear for home consumption later in the year, then the response of farmers to store their crops for their own consumption increases these farmers' real income and reduces their vulnerability to risk. In general, the presumption that individuals are rational does not enable us to predict their behavior. Furthermore, efforts to explain agricultural performance in terms of the rationality of peasants (or planners) frequently prove inconsistent or tautological. One recent attempt to take account of the impact of international price fluctuations on economic policy points out that international prices of peanuts and rice are more unstable than that of millet. Therefore, the authors argue, if Senegalese planners dislike instability, their comparative advantage lies in producing more millet, less rice, and fewer peanuts. If they enjoy gambling, presumably they should specialize completely in peanuts! The argument is perfectly circular (Jabara and Thompson 1980).

Even if one assigns unambiguous motives to particular economic acts, it does not follow that the analysis of individual behavior is sufficient to explain social processes. History results from the interactions of individuals—the behavior of some affect the circumstances of others. For example, economists often argue that higher prices for agricultural commodities will lead to faster growth of agricultural output and incomes. Their case rests primarily on studies of farmers' responses to changes in price that focus on a single crop (no other variables are considered). These studies may be useful for purposes of exposition, but are inadequate for thinking about agricultural performance and policy. In practice, there are many variables, and their consequences must be accounted for in order to predict the effects of price changes. If the price of maize rises while other prices remain unchanged, farmers may produce more maize by shifting land and labor from other crops, leaving total output unchanged (Helleiner 1975). In some cases, increases in official prices induce farmers to sell to government buyers crops that they would otherwise have consumed, stored, or sold locally—thus creating acute shortages in local markets or contributing to malnutrition and hunger in rural families (Chauveau et al. 1981; Harriss 1979).

Factors other than crop prices may also affect output or sales of an agricultural commodity. Changes in weather, access to markets or traders' margins, to say nothing of the effects of expectations, may all obscure or offset the effects of price increases. Statistical estimates often show relatively weak correlations between price and output. Because a weak relationship may, in principle, be attributed to the effects of unspecified or unobservable variables, it cannot be said to refute the strength of price incentives. Hence, whether studies conclude a strong or weak correlation, these findings are regularly interpreted as supportive of the strength of price incentives. Like the argument that total agricultural output is declining in Africa, faith in the universality of positive supply response continues partly because it cannot be put to a conclusive test.

Studies of price trends in unorganized markets have also produced conflicting evidence. In reviewing marketing studies by W. O. Jones and others, Barbara Harriss noted that their evidence on the structure and performance of West African markets often conflicts with their conclusion that such markets are reasonably competitive (Harriss 1979:210). Historical and ethnographic literature has suggested that markets worked well in the past not because they were highly competitive, but because commercial intelligence, brokerage functions, and credit were controlled by well-organized kinship or community-based networks (Baier 1980; A. Cohen 1969). At present, economists are well aware that much agricultural marketing in Africa takes place outside official channels. However, there is little understanding of how unofficial markets work. Harriss concluded: "There is no research to show whether present stagnation is a result of a high response to low official prices . . . or a low response to high parallel market prices, or a high response to parallel market prices that are lower than official prices" (Harriss 1979:375). Generally, empirical grounds for believing that higher crop prices promote agricultural development do not seem to warrant the enthusiasm with which the case is often put.

Finally, it is not very useful to base policy conclusions solely on analyses of individual farmers' responses to changing economic incentives. Economists' criticisms of African governments for reducing incentives to agricultural producers often are implicitly comparing the existing situation to one in which state intervention is nonexistent. Economic theory and facts of African political economy suggest that this comparison is unrealistic. No market system functions in a political vacuum; no environment for perfect competition ever survived for long, if at all. A competitive environment is a hazardous one: Competition not only drives down prices and profits but impels people to try to protect themselves from its vicissitudes. Competition breeds market controls as well as lower costs, and even competitive markets seldom remain competitive indefinitely. The choice facing African governments is often not one of selecting between controlled prices and competitive prices, but one of choosing to regulate prices themselves or letting other factors take control.

• DOMESTIC ORGANIZATION AND FARMING PRACTICES •

Understanding the context of resource allocation in African farming systems requires examining the actual organization of agricultural production. African farmers are involved in a great variety of domestic organizations and kin-based farming units. These defy easy categorization, but clearly are not the self-contained nuclear household that constitutes the principal unit of production and consumption in most paradigms of peasant agriculture (see Cohen and McMillan in this volume). To analyze agricultural performance in Africa, it is necessary to take account of forms of domestic organization and their influence on farming practices.

In a recent review of Africanist literature on household and lineage, Jane Guyer questioned the value of typologies of domestic organization in Africa: "The concept of the lineage and typologies of lineage systems disguise far too much of the variability in ways things get done: children brought up, livings made, authority achieved and assigned, land distributed, bridewealth paid, residence determined and all the myriad other activities which can be organized along genealogical lines" (Guyer 1981:89). Similarly, we gain little understanding of processes of agrarian change from typologies that try to establish unique correlations between forms of domestic organization, ecological conditions, cultural systems, and/or stages of economic development. The prevalence of kinship as an idiom of social organization in Africa has led to various attempts to specify kin-based paradigms of agricultural production. For example, matriliny has been associated with horticulture (Lancaster 1976) and underdevelopment (Goody 1962); hunting and gathering, with bands, segmentary lineage systems, or male supremacy (Meillassoux 1981); low-density farming, with family labor (Lancaster 1979); precapitalist economies, with a kinship mode of production (Terray 1974); and so forth. Such typologies rarely withstand comparative analysis nor do they help to explain change.

Nonetheless, because kinship is a common principle of social organization in African communities, it is of potential significance for the organization of production and investment. If relations of descent, affinity, or coresidence constitute a basis for making claims on property, commodities, labor, or protection of other people, then kinship relations and residential patterns are likely to influence the ways in which productive resources are acquired and used (Hill 1963; S. Berry 1975).

The structure of a household may be as important as its landholdings or size for determining the amount or composition of its output. Husbands and wives often farm separately; exert different degrees of control over the labor, output, and consumption of other household members; and participate differentially in extra-household relations (Guyer 1981). Commercialization or technical change may affect men and women differently, leading to changes in the division of labor within domestic units or to changes in participation in extra-household transactions or to both. In such cases, the impact of commercialization on agricultural performance will not be captured by analyses that treat the household as a monolithic decision-making unit.

In recognition of this problem, some Francophone ethnographers avoid using the term "household" altogether, preferring to speak of units of production, consumption, accumulation, and so forth, in order to distinguish both the functions and the constitutions of each. Such distinctions may be analytically helpful as well as empirically precise. J. M. Gastellu showed that the spread of cash cropping in Senegal has not led to marked differentiation among the Serer people, partly because production and accumulation are carried out by overlapping but not identical groups of kin (Gastellu 1977). Uterine brothers farm together under the direction of the eldest, and they, together with their wives and children, constitute a unit of joint-income management for purposes of consumption. Once consumption needs of the group have been met, individuals remit surplus income to groups of their own matrikin for joint investment in livestock. Wives and husbands belong to the same unit of consumption but to different units of accumulation. Thus, elder men who control the process of agricultural production are prevented from monopolizing the resulting surplus and using it to amass property on their own account.

In some extended families, accumulation is not only permitted but encouraged. Serakule kinsmen in Gambia pool their savings to purchase heavy agricultural equipment from the state, and they have recently begun to grow rice on large, mechanized, and irrigated farms worked by labor mobilized within corporate kin groups of up to one hundred or more persons (Watts 1983: personal communication). In contrast, efforts by well-placed officials to launch large-scale mechanized rice cultivation in northern Ghana—using state subsidized machinery and inputs, hired labor, and questionable manipulations of local land-tenure practices—have proved ecologically destructive, socially disruptive, and often commercially unviable (Shepherd 1981; Johnny et al. 1981). African agricultural performance is not shaped by the pervasiveness of kinship, as a principle of African social organization, but by the way in which specifically constituted forms of domestic organization interact with changing economic, technical, and political opportunities and pressures.

The importance of understanding domestic relations in the context of farmers' linkages to the wider political economy is not simply a matter of historical accuracy. Maintaining ties with kin groups or communities of origin is important throughout contemporary Africa—not only for people legally barred from settling in urban, industrial centers, as in South Africa, or for those paid so little they are forced to cling to declining rural economies and anachronistic structures in order to subsist, but also for those with surplus income who wish to invest it in valuable assets and/or power and prestige. To the extent that Africans' access to property, labor, patronage, or the resources of the state depend on membership in a descent group or community of birth, it is understandable that Africans of all socioeconomic levels invest in maintaining or enhancing their own standings in such groups (see Cohen in this volume).

In some areas, the development of commercial farming is directly associated with a rising incidence of polygyny and level of bridewealth payments (Cheater 1981). The Ghanaian officials and mechanized rice farmers mentioned previously were not strangers to the local community when they defrauded other local farmers of their ancient land rights. These officials were often local sons who used their memberships in local lineages to gain virtually unlimited access to local land. This is not an isolated example (Berry 1985). Elites as well as peasants often spend time and money cultivating home-based ties, in part because property rights, credit, and political mobilization are mediated through these ties. Commercialization, technical change, and the emergence of independent national governments affect relations among rural families, the division of labor within farming households, and patterns of productive activities; in fact they affect the entire structure of rural society.

· DIFFERENTIATION AND SOCIAL CHANGE ·

In contrast to studies that identify patterns of agricultural performance based on the behavior of individual farmers, a substantial literature on agrarian change in Africa explains both farmers' behavior and agricultural performance in terms of the structure or dynamics, or both, of rural economy and society. Discussion centers on the degree to which agricultural commercialization, technical change, or the agricultural policies of colonial and postcolonial regimes affects patterns of inequality or the form and intensity of social cleavages and conflict.

Some studies suggest that the impact of commercialization and centralized governments on African rural economies has been relatively superficial. Hyden argued that "African peasants are less integrated in the cash economy than peasants elsewhere" (1980:10), and that peasant households, though not entirely self-sufficient, manage resources independently of one another and enjoy considerable autonomy with respect to outside institutions such as the market and the state. "African rulers have been unable to make the peasants effectively dependent on their policy measures" (Hyden 1980:33); indeed, bureaucratic interference often drives farmers to take refuge in parallel markets or virtual self-sufficiency. Hyden's views are shared by a number of people concerned with Africa's food deficits who argue, contrary to the World Bank's interpretation, that food crop production in Africa is relatively unresponsive to market forces. The U.S. Department of Agriculture (USDA) states baldly that, for most African farmers, "the reason for growing export crops is to sell them, while the reason for growing food crops is to eat them" (USDA 1981:25). This position is challenged by researchers who point out that the need for cash to pay taxes, purchase medical and educational services, and acquire many household necessities forces even very poor families to sell a good part of their agricultural output and to buy part of the staple food they consume (Cowen 1983).

Most social scientists agree that the expansion of capitalist enterprise and national governments has affected profoundly the structure of rural society and its relation to wider economic and political systems, but disagree over the nature of these effects. Scholars argue that commercialization and government intervention: (1) transformed large areas of rural Africa into labor reserves; (2) turned African cultivators into peasants, who control their own means of production but depend on externally controlled markets and agencies for the returns to their productive efforts; or (3) created class divisions in rural Africa similar to those in other capitalist societies. A brief review of each of these arguments follows.

The labor reserve argument is based on the historical fact that both private firms and colonial regimes needed a steady supply of cheap labor. To provide it, colonial administrations frequently demanded that Africans pay taxes in cash, and simultaneously restricted Africans' access to land or other sources of independent income to compel them to seek wage employment. Farmers in West African societies that were already involved in commercial relations with Europeans through the slave trade were often able to supply European merchants with cheap agricultural commodities. Export crop growers hired migrant workers from poorer or more remote areas to work on their farms. Thus, many rural areas became labor reserves for capitalist-dominated sectors (Arrighi 1970; Amin 1974a).

The extent to which labor migration impoverished rural communities is a subject of long-standing debate. Argument revolves around several interrelated questions: (1) Was production lost or maintained because withdrawal of migrant workers' labor power from the community was compensated by the self-exploitation of their relatives who stayed at home? (Berg 1965; Amin 1974a); (2) Did migrants' remittances to their communities represent a net inflow of purchasing power to their home areas or were remittances more than offset by reverse flows of foodstuffs, school fees, and so forth? (Essang and Mabawonku 1974; Parkin 1979; Amin 1974a); and (3) What was happening to the structure of rural economies?

Some have suggested that because African peasants were not dispossessed, migrant workers' families continued to feed themselves and sometimes the migrants as well, enabling capitalist firms to pay lower wages and increase their profits (Wolpe 1972; Meillassoux 1981). In this way, colonial capitalism tended to fossilize rather than destroy traditional economies, creating a semiproletarianized working class whose continued ties to the land promoted self-exploitation and dependence rather than peasant autonomy. The homelands of South Africa are sometimes cited as an extreme example. Although South African whites have clearly profited handsomely from cheap black labor, the homelands' dependence on remittances of workers to cover basic consumption requirements may act as a drain on the national economy's investable surplus rather than as a source of additional national wealth (Simkins 1981; Knight and Lenta 1980). By the 1970s, the impoverishment of the homelands was so acute that migrant workers' subsistence needs were far from being met, in spite of workers' rights to land there.

Although the effects of the labor reserve system have been overwhelmingly negative in South Africa, other labor-exporting areas have not fared as badly. In parts of postcolonial Kenya, workers' remittances help to finance purchases of rural land and increase peasant production for the market (Collier and Lal 1980; Stichter 1982). In parts of Kenya and Uganda, migrants straddle the boundary between rural and urban sectors with considerable success, sometimes establishing two households so that individuals may circulate between urban and rural areas, practicing forms of gainful employment in both (Parkin 1979; Richards et al. 1973). Circulatory migration and occupational diversification are also common in western and southern Africa (Mayer 1980; Colvin 1981; Amin 1974a), and migrants often invest part of their earnings in livestock or other rural assets (Delgado 1978; Norman et al. 1981). Migrant labor contributes to rural differentiation as well (Mayer 1980; Collier and Lal 1980). Such evidence casts doubt on the significance of rural-urban boundaries as primary divisions of economic specialization or socioeconomic differentiation. In short, the argument that commercialization, or capitalist penetration, or both, transformed rural communities into labor reserves is only part of the story.

Cheap labor was not the only resource sought by Europeans from their African colonies. In some areas, increased agricultural production for the market was condoned or encouraged, by both colonial and postcolonial regimes, in order to provide export earnings or cheap foodstuffs in the local economy. Aided by rising world market prices for agricultural commodities, the early 1950s saw a resurgence of peasant production for the market, both in older areas of cash-crop production and in areas where peasantization was discouraged before the war. At various times, the growth of commercial opportunities created conditions for the emergence of a class of local accumulators in African agriculture and a corresponding demand for hired labor (Hill 1963; Lawson 1972; Kitching 1980). The degree to which these tendencies resulted in the division of rural society into capitalist farmers and landless workers depended, in part, on the role played by the state in abetting or undermining the emergence of an African bourgeoisie.

Although colonial regimes acted at times to protect the profits of European capitalists in trade, mining, industry, and agriculture, they were not invariably hostile to African accumulators. For colonial regimes whose tax base depended, at least in part, on the prosperity of African farmers and traders, the rise of an indigenous bourgeoisie was not an unmitigated disaster however much it might have been opposed by European farmers and traders faced with African competitors. And although prosperous Africans confronted their colonial rulers with a political threat—wealthy Africans might have the means to challenge the power of the colonial state—these Africans could often be induced to collaborate instead. By the late colonial period, administrators were increasingly conscious of the role a class of prosperous peasants, or "progressive farmers," might play in containing or defusing rural discontent, producing agricultural commodities for both domestic and foreign markets, and generating revenue for the state. Colonial policy toward African agriculture is better understood as a relentless struggle to cope with the contradictory implications of peasant accumulation and impoverishment than as a simple extension of the cheap labor policies of European settlers and industrialists (Lonsdale and Berman 1979; Berman and Lonsdale 1980).

Postcolonial governments vacillate between extracting surpluses from farmers and subsidizing them. Marketing boards are both convenient and costly as instruments for mobilizing agricultural surplus. Overly aggressive pricing policies often lead farmers to cut back production of export or other officially marketed crops, seek refuge in parallel markets, or engage in political protest; thus, purchases often decline (Beer and Williams 1975; Beckman 1978; Lamb 1974). African governments frequently attempt to exploit local accumulators and to coopt them by nationalizing lucrative enterprises or by using official prerogatives to gain preferential access to land, capital, or market opportunities. Postcolonial governments of varying ideological persuasions demonstrate a common penchant for state farms, parastatal enterprises, and joint government-private ventures in large-scale farming. Governments often provide generous loans, subsidies, infrastructure, and technical assistance to a small number of large private farms (Heyer et al. 1981; Asante in this volume). Such policies reflect officials' pursuits of private gain and states' desires to nationalize key productive activities in order to manage more effectively the process of economic development. Such intervention often serves to promote rural differentiation, but not necessarily in the form of an emerging rural bourgeoisie and proletariat.

Today, as in the colonial period, rich farmers are often clients or members of the state and they receive access to credit, inputs, extension services, and market opportunities on much more favorable terms than do the majority of farmers. This is not the whole story, however. Prosperous farmers may invest outside of agriculture, seek to commute their wealth into direct political power, or do both. In the process, they may be absorbed into the national elite or come into conflict with other elite factions over access to power and the management of the economy. Conflict between white farmers and industrialists over access to black labor was a significant aspect of South African politics in the 1930s (Morris 1976), and the Convention People's Party in Ghana went to considerable lengths and expense to neutralize the power of indigenous capitalists, both inside and outside of the cocoa-growing sector (Beckman 1978). Elsewhere, rural profits have been invested in trade, education, and even manufacturing, creating a class of indigenous ac-cumulators that cuts across rural-urban boundaries and often across the public and private sectors as well (Berry 1985; Kitching 1980). In some cases, relations be-tween the government and a particular rural elite have changed over time, as with the Mourides in Senegal whose ability to deliver the votes of their rural followers earned them substantial profits as well as power in the 1950s, but whose power waned as Senghor's party consolidated its control of the state (Cruise O'Brien 1970). In short, "coping with the contradictions" and "crises of accumulation" are problems not only for colonial states, but for postcolonial regimes as well (Lonsdale and Berman 1979; Berman and Lonsdale 1980).

• CONCLUSION •

Social science perspectives on food in Africa are varied, to say the least. This diver-sity can be productive. Although this review of the literature does not indicate a consensus, it does suggest directions for further study. It is increasingly evident that food deficits and agricultural performance in Africa spring from many causes including international economic and political processes, national politics, pat-terns of government expenditure, legal and judicial systems, local institutions and social relations, technical possibilities, and methods of cultivation. The multitude of causes suggests to policymakers that it is probably not very useful to assess in isolation the impact of any specific interventions—price controls, input subsidies, dissemination of improved techniques, land reform, etc.—without considering that any intervention affects many variables, and, in turn, many variables also in-fluence the impact. It is necessary to try to understand how national, international, and local processes interact to shape conditions and patterns of agricultural pro-duction and distribution in Africa. It is also important to confront the diversity of African farming systems and rural economies and to develop explanatory frameworks that help to account for this diversity rather than to try to reduce Afri-can agricultural processes to a series of universally applicable propositions about human behavior or social structures. To capture the realities of African agricultural practices and policy options, such frameworks should consider conditions of ac-cess to productive resources and economic opportunities, as well as how resources are allocated among alternative uses. These frameworks should also seek to analyze, not castigate, the ways in which the acquisition and exercise of power—at all levels of social interaction—influence economic performance, and vice versa.

• SUGGESTED FURTHER READINGS •

Bates, R. 1981. *Markets and States in Tropical Africa*. Berkeley: University of California Press.

Collinson, M. P. 1982. *Farming Systems Research in East Africa*. East Lansing: Michigan State University, Department of Agricultural Economics.

Eicher, C., and D. Baker. 1982. *Research on Agricultural Development in Sub-Saharan Africa*. East Lansing: Michigan State University, Department of Agricultural Economics.

Guyer, J. 1981. Household and Community in African Studies. *African Studies Review* 24:2/3:87–138.

Heyer, J., P. Roberts, and G. Williams, eds. 1981. *Rural Development in Tropical Africa*. New York: St. Martin's Press.

Mayer, P., ed. 1980. *Black Villagers in an Industrial Society: Anthropological Perspectives on Labour Migration in Southern Africa*. Cape Town: Oxford University Press.

Richards, P. 1983. Farming Systems and Agrarian Change in West Africa. *Progress in Human Geography* 7:1:1–39.

·6·

The African Environment

CHARLES GUTHRIE

An overview of Africa's physical and human features places contemporary food issues in a broader perspective. This chapter has six interrelated sections. In the first section the focus is on Africa's size and regions. A discussion of climate and vegetation patterns follows in section two, and in section three the characteristics of the major agricultural systems are described. Population, the subject of the next section, has been divided for discussion into distribution, density, growth rate, age and sex structure, and urbanization. Section five contains highlights of some of the important structural characteristics of African economies: poverty, the central role of national government policies, and the development of economic islands and extractive industries. The final section presents the cultural diversity of the continent in terms of political geography, ethnicity, language, and religion.

· SIZE AND REGIONS ·

Africa is the second largest continent in the world and has a total land area that is large enough to encompass sizable portions of the rest of the world's land mass (see Figure 6.1). For example, all of Europe from Portugal to Moscow would fit into Africa north of the equator. Africa is more than three times larger than the United States; the Sahara Desert alone equals the size of the forty-eight contiguous states of the United States. Distances in Africa are staggering reminders of its size: it is almost 7,200 kilometers from Capetown in the south to Cairo in the north and approximately the same distance from the tip of the Horn in the east to Dakar, Senegal, in the west. The Nile is reputed to be the longest river in the world; the Zaire River is more than 4,600 kilometers long and drains a river basin of 3.6 million square kilometers, one of the world's largest.

There are conventional ways to divide Africa geographically. A common one establishes six regions: (1) North—five countries bordering the Mediterranean

FIGURE 6.1.   The Size of Africa

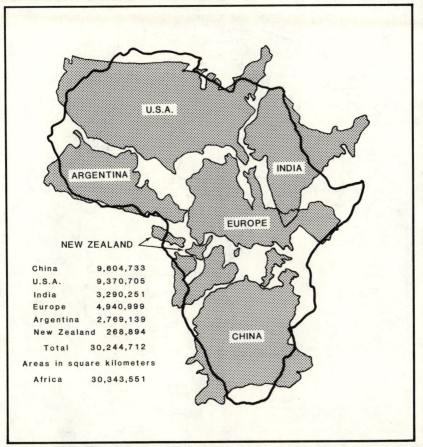

China	9,604,733
U.S.A.	9,370,705
India	3,290,251
Europe	4,940,999
Argentina	2,769,139
New Zealand	268,894
Total	30,244,712

Areas in square kilometers

Africa	30,343,551

Source: Revised from World Eagle. 1983. *Africa Today: An Atlas of Reproducible Pages*. Wellesley, Massachusetts: World Eagle. Pg. 14.

plus the disputed Western Sahara; (2) West—seventeen countries including all of the Sahel or southern fringe of the Sahara; (3) Northeast—the Sudan and the three countries of the Horn of Africa; (4) East—six countries, three of which were formally united for ten years in the East African Community; (5) Central—seven countries; and (6) Southern—fourteen countries (see figure 6.2). These totals include seven island countries. This chapter and volume focus on Sub-Saharan Africa, sometimes called Black Africa, which is all of Africa except the northern region. Although the entire continent has been linked by major historical themes, the culture, history, and Arabic language of North Africa tie that region more closely to the Islamic Middle East and the Mediterranean than to the rest of the African continent.

FIGURE 6.2. African Countries and Political Regions

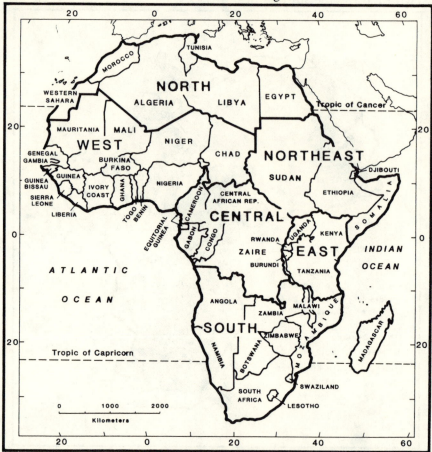

• CLIMATE AND VEGETATION •

Africa, unlike any other continent, is divided almost evenly by the equator, a fact that helps determine climatic, rainfall, and vegetation zones. Tropical Africa is most commonly defined as that area between the Tropic of Cancer and the Tropic of Capricorn, although some writers include all of Sub-Saharan Africa except the Republic of South Africa in the tropical region. Since most of Africa falls within the tropics, it does not experience the wide fluctuations in temperature typical of North America and Europe. Temperatures in most of tropical Africa range from warm to hot. Because temperatures are consistently warm, vegetable matter decomposes too rapidly to allow the buildup of extensive topsoil (See Popenoe in this volume). Continuously warm temperatures, that is, no hard freezes, also mean that there is no seasonal relief from bacteria or disease-bearing insects, which take a heavy toll of human life and domestic livestock.

Designating Sub-Saharan Africa as a single, tropical zone does not mean that climate and vegetation are uniform. There are differences in altitude, prevailing wind conditions, and distance from the ocean throughout Sub-Saharan Africa that have created practically every kind of climate and vegetation. Africa's deserts occupy 40 percent of the continent. Dense rain forests along the equator account for only 7 or 8 percent of the land mass, contrary to popular Western myths that equate Africa with jungle. The most extensive vegetation is actually savanna, which extends between forest and desert areas and ranges from woodlands to grasslands. A series of undulating plateaus throughout the continent averages about nine hundred meters above sea level, which makes these areas much cooler than their latitude suggests. The plateaus are occasionally broken by mountainous areas, which also alter climatic and vegetation patterns.

The patterns of natural vegetation are based on the availability of water, principally water as rainfall. A distinctive characteristic of the climate in Sub-Saharan Africa is the rainy and dry seasons. Rainfall patterns are closely associated with the annual movement of air masses that converge from north and south upon a broad, irregular equatorial zone, the Intertropical Convergence Zone (ITCZ). The position of the ITCZ shifts between the Tropic of Cancer and the Tropic of Capricorn with the annual movement of the sun (see Figure 6.3). The heaviest rainfall tends to center on this moving convergence zone that brings summer rainfall (around July) to regions north of the equator and winter rainfall (around January) to the south. Although other factors also affect rainfall, this movement of the ITCZ accounts for an annual average rainfall pattern distributed symmetrically around the equator and largely determines when rainy and dry seasons will occur. Most of Sub-Saharan Africa has one rainy season per year, but the area straddling the equator has two (see Figure 6.5).

One result of the rainfall patterns is the symmetrical arrangement of vegetation zones on both sides of the equator (see Figure 6.4). General outlines are clear, although they do not show important subregional and local variations that are caused by elevation, soil types, and human activity. In any discussion of natural vegetation, it is essential to remember that there are few areas of Africa that have not been severely modified through tree cutting, burning, cultivation, and herding. Rain forest lies along the equator where hot, wet conditions (more than 1500 millimeters of annual rainfall) give rise to dense growth that stretches in an unbroken line along the West African coast from Sierra Leone to Cameroon and extends inland to eastern Zaire. Poor soils, diseases, and the absence of a sufficient drying period in these areas discourage the cultivation of cereal grains. Forms of shifting cultivation, crop rotations, and intercropping have evolved as effective adaptations to these environmental conditions.

North and south from this equatorial wet zone the forest thins as it makes a gradual transition to savanna. There is wide variation in savanna vegetation, but as one travels farther north or south, trees become less frequent and shrubs and grasses increase. Human use of the savanna area has been heavy through the centuries, from hunting, pastoralism, and various forms of shifting and intensive cultivation.

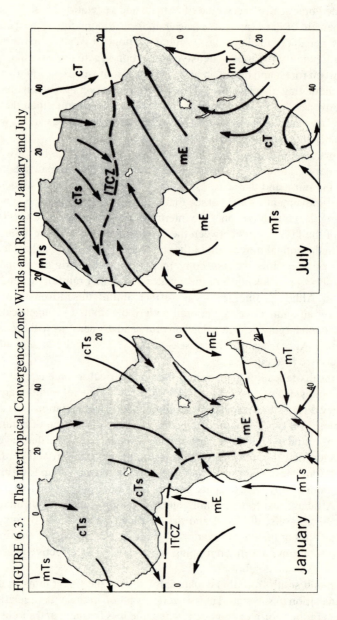

FIGURE 6.3. The Intertropical Convergence Zone: Winds and Rains in January and July

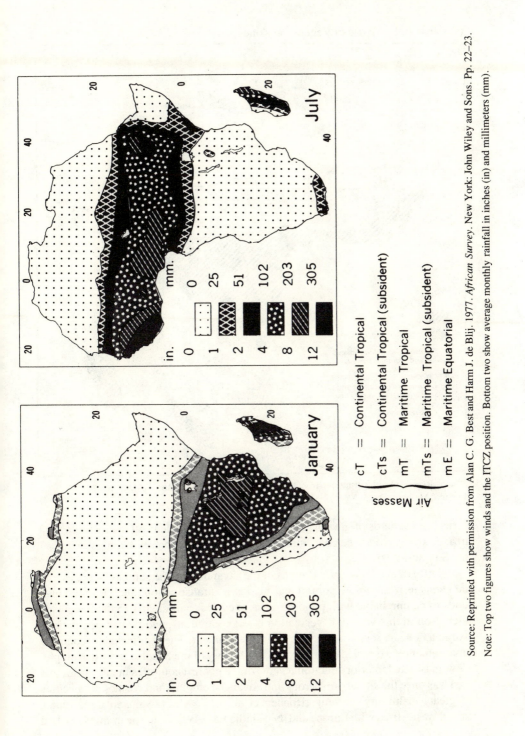

Source: Reprinted with permission from Alan C. G. Best and Harm J. de Blij. 1977. *African Survey*. New York: John Wiley and Sons. Pp. 22–23.

Note: Top two figures show winds and the ITCZ position. Bottom two show average monthly rainfall in inches (in) and millimeters (mm).

FIGURE 6.4.   African Vegetation Zones

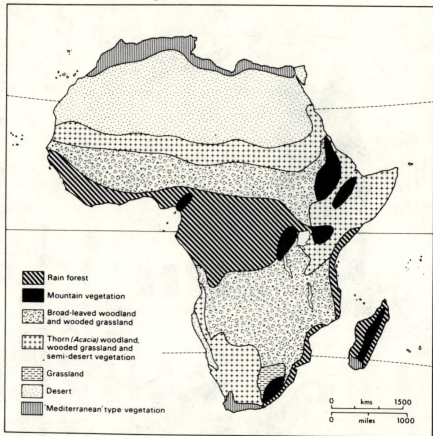

Source: Reprinted with permission from Ieuan Ll. Griffiths. 1984. *An Atlas of African Affairs.*
London: Methuen. P. 15.

Africa's great herds of grazing game animals were once plentiful in this ecological
area; now they tend to be concentrated in large parks and preserves, mostly in East
and Southern Africa.

Northern and southern extremes of the savanna become semiarid steppes that
are characterized by low rainfall and high evapotranspiration rates. Rainfall also
tends to be unreliable with periodic drought cycles, particularly in the Sahel (see
Nicholson in this volume). Vegetation is not continuous, and human populations
live in a delicate relationship with their environment. The political and economic
environment have varied dramatically. The history of the Sahel is a vivid example.
Now an isolated interior containing some of the poorest countries in the world, this
area was once the site of prosperous and advanced empires and cosmopolitan cities
of great wealth and learning (Boahen et al. 1971). Trans-Saharan trade routes
linked West Africa with Europe and the Middle East. When European ships reached

West Africa in the fifteenth century, new trade routes developed that bypassed the Sahel, and its trade centers declined.

The steppes gradually change to desert. Forty percent of Africa is considered desert; not all of the desert lands are uninhabitable. A number of areas, even in the driest desert, have springs around which oases have developed, and these are farmed intensively. Other areas occasionally have rain, making possible the growth of some grass for grazing.

Africa has a rainfall problem. Shortage of rain is a continual problem for areas such as the Sahel and the Kalahari in the southwest; the more significant problem for most of Sub-Saharan Africa is the annual distribution rather than the quantity of rainfall. The movement of the ITCZ results in many areas receiving all or most of their rainfall within a four-to-six-month period, barely sufficient time for crops to mature. The remainder of the year may be completely dry or have scanty rainfall that cannot be of any practical use for growing crops. These areas are marginal ones for food production: the dynamic balance between the human population and an adequate food supply is easily upset by slight climatic changes, population increases, or degradation of natural resources.

This problem can be illustrated by comparing rainfall distribution in Chicago, Illinois, and Kano, Nigeria (see Figure 6.5). Both areas receive about the same amount of rainfall annually, but Chicago's rainfall is distributed throughout the year, making possible an ample growing season for a variety of crops. By contrast, Kano's rainfall is concentrated in a five-month period, from May through September—a length of time insufficient for many crops and marginal for others. The Chicago area is considered to be a breadbasket; the area of Kano is practically desert. Harare, Zimbabwe, and Nairobi, Kenya, represent other contrasts in rainfall distribution in tropical Africa. Nairobi is near the equator and has two rainy seasons defined as the long and short rains. More southern Harare has a single rainy season like Kano, but with greater total rainfall and a more even distribution than in Kano. The most common pattern for Sub-Saharan Africa is the distinct single rainy season and single dry season; however, there is a wide belt along the equator with two rainy reasons (see figure 6.5).

• PATTERNS OF AGRICULTURE •

Most of Sub-Saharan Africa's food production still takes place on small farms with people using hand tools such as the hoe. Large-scale mechanized farming in Africa is seldom oriented toward domestic food production. The approximate distribution of traditional crop and livestock production systems is shown in Figure 6.6. In the semiarid regions, nomadic or settled pastoralists are dominant (see McGee in this volume).

Africans have perfected a variety of complex cultivation methods that maintain soil fertility over the long term and are efficient in their use of human labor; these methods are shifting cultivation, rotational fallow, and intercropping (Allan

FIGURE 6.5.   Annual Rainfall Distribution Patterns

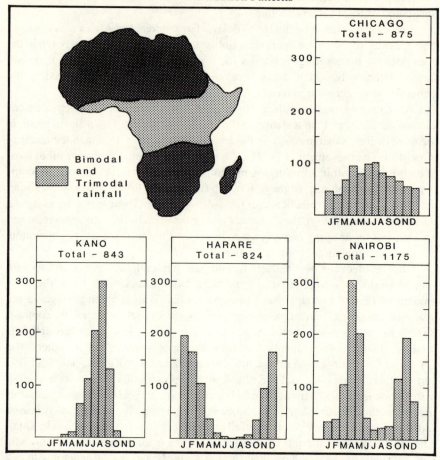

Sources: Rainfall data for four locations were supplied by Sharon Nicholson. The Nairobi data were from Merango (Fort Hall). Modal patterns of annual rainfall were derived from a map in Marcel Leroux. 1983. *The Climate of Tropical Africa: Atlas*. Paris: Editions CHAMPIONS.

Note: There are two or even three (bimodal or trimodal) rainy seasons per year along the equator, whereas most of Africa has only one (unimodal) rainy season per year.

1965; Miracle 1967; Okigbo and Greenland 1976). Shifting cultivation requires that an area be cleared of trees and shrubs that are then burned to produce ash. The ash is scattered on the plot for fertilizer, and seeds are planted in conjunction with the rainy season. A field prepared in this manner each year will usually support only two or three annual crops before farmers must move elsewhere and repeat the process. There are many variations of this basic method, all of which require extensive woodland (land and plant cover) and assume a low population density. Although some strongly criticize this system as wasteful, it is now acknowledged as extremely well designed for Africa's low fertility soils and low population densities (Boserup 1965). Other African systems of cultivation rotate crops to allow for periods of fallow.

A discussion of the distribution of dominant agricultural systems masks the complexity within each zone of a wide variety of carefully evolved human responses to diverse climatic, soil, and vegetation conditions. These diverse methods have served African societies for centuries, and these methods depend upon extensive woodland. Growing concentrations of population have forced farmers and herders to abandon the safeguards that were vital to the success and stability of their customary practices. Farmers do not leave plots to fallow long enough to restore soil fertility, those who practice shifting cultivation return to previously used fields before the tree or brush cover has been renewed, and herders overgraze. The result in much of Africa is soil exhaustion, deforestation, and soil

FIGURE 6.6. Traditional Agricultural Systems in Africa

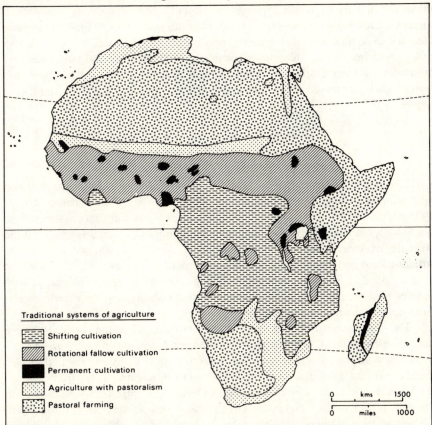

Source: Reprinted with permission from Ieuan Ll. Griffiths. 1984. *An Atlas of African Affairs*. London: Methuen. Pg. 119.

erosion (Brown and Wolf 1985).

In the early 1960s, most African countries were self-sufficient in basic food staples. The paramount fact of Africa's economic performance in the two decades since independence has been its uninterrupted decline in per capita food production (see Figure 6.7). It is not entirely correct to blame the overtaxed traditional systems of food production for this decline. In many instances the systems have managed to increase food production by incorporating some innovative technologies and by cultivating more land using customary technologies (United States Department of Agriculture [USDA] 1981). Unfortunately, there are limits to the availability of new lands to cultivate, and new lands are often of lower quality, which is why they were not previously used. The primary problem has not been agricultural but the dramatic increase in population that has sent per capita production statistics plummeting. A related trend, increasing migration from the rural areas to the cities and towns, weakens the agricultural sector because it is often the more ambitious and skilled people who leave for the better opportunities in the urban areas. This migration expands the urban non-food-producing population, thereby increasing demands on the rural sector to produce more food. It has been clear for some time that these demands may be met only by a technological shift in many areas from land-extensive cultivation to land-intensive and labor-intensive cultivation. Intensive cultivation requires the kinds of inputs that can maintain land fertility under increased use. Thus far the shift has not taken place to a significant degree.

• DEMOGRAPHIC PATTERNS •

Africa's total population in 1985 is approximately 550 million people, of which approximately 450 million live in Sub-Saharan Africa. Thus Sub-Saharan Africa's 1985 population is almost double that of the United States and almost a tenth of the world's population (United Nations 1985). More important than this number is the character of Africa's population: its distribution, density, growth rate, age and sex structure, and patterns of migration and settlement. All of these factors influence food availability, economic development, degradation of natural resources, opportunities for education and employment, political stability, and the manifold pressures upon African countries to change.

The African continent as a whole is not yet overpopulated and has more arable land to cultivate (USDA 1981), but this continental generalization has to be qualified. There are vast desert or desertlike areas that are virtually uninhabited such as the Sahara to the north, the Namib and Kalahari to the southwest, and the northeastern Horn. Environmental or climatic factors have discouraged dense settlement in other areas such as the Sahel or parts of Central Africa. At the other extreme, there are certain areas in which population density is high and well beyond the ability of the land to support it through agriculture alone. These areas include southern West Africa, especially the coastal area of Nigeria, the East African lakes region, and

FIGURE 6.7. Comparative Indices of Food Production per Capita, 1950 to 1984

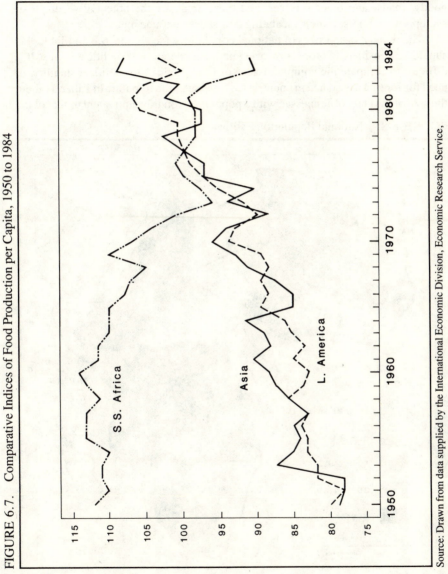

Source: Drawn from data supplied by the International Economic Division, Economic Research Service, U.S. Department of Agriculture.

Note: 1977 is the base year; 1977 production is scored 100.

parts of the Ethiopian highlands and South Africa. These few areas of dense population account for more than half of Africa's total population. High density pockets
are often non-food-producing areas that have grown and developed rapidly at the
expense of less populous areas. These high density areas make the greatest demands upon national governments for food deliveries, employment, consumer
goods, roads, and other services; and these areas are the potential seedbeds of
sociopolitical unrest if their escalating demands cannot be met.

The widely varied sizes of national populations (see Figure 6.8 and Table 1.1)
should be considered before comparing national economic or political issues. It is
difficult to compare the complex issues of food production, political stability, or
need for foreign assistance in countries as diverse as the Republic of Liberia (about
the size of the state of Tennessee with a population roughly equivalent to that of the

FIGURE 6.8. National Population Estimates

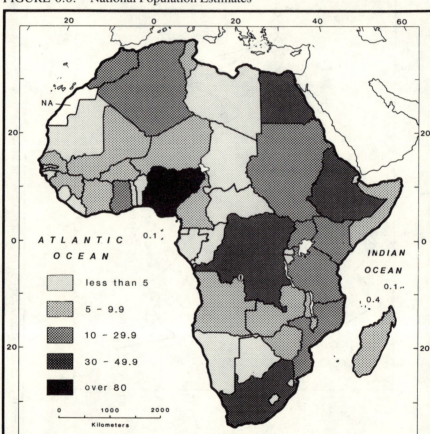

Source: Food and Agriculture Organization. 1985. *1984 FAO Production Yearbook*. Rome:
Food and Agriculture Organization.

Note: Population is expressed in millions of people.

FIGURE 6.9. Comparative Population Growth Rates, 1950 to 2000

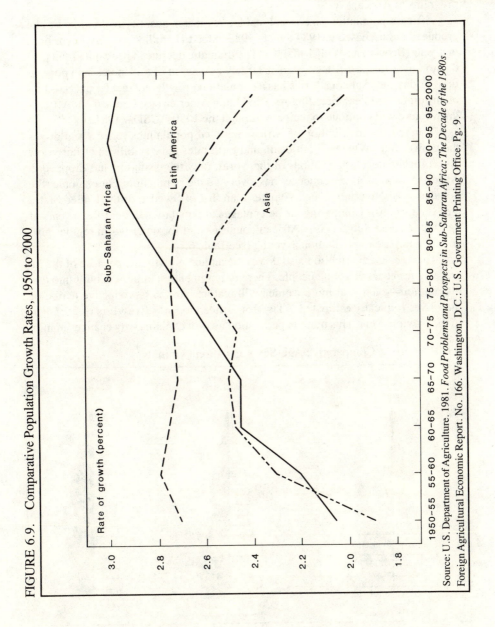

Source: U.S. Department of Agriculture. 1981. *Food Problems and Prospects in Sub-Saharan Africa: The Decade of the 1980s.* Foreign Agricultural Economic Report. No. 166. Washington, D.C.: U.S. Government Printing Office. Pg. 9.

city of Atlanta) and Nigeria (with a population of at least 84 million people). Such a consideration of population puts into perspective the U.S. assistance to Liberia, more than $76 million in 1983. This assistance was one of the largest U.S. bilateral programs in Africa.

Africa's population size is not stable. A greater quantity of food had to be produced or purchased in 1984 than in 1983 to feed 16 million more Africans born that year (Brown and Wolf 1985:30). The dramatic decline in per capita food production over the past fifteen years is largely a function of this increase in population. Today Sub-Saharan Africa has a population growth rate that far exceeds that of any other continent including Asia and Latin America (see Figure 6.9). Africa's growth rate will continue to increase through the 1980s (USDA 1981:9).

The age-sex distribution of African national populations reflects and drives the growth rate. Whereas both death and birth rates have stabilized at fairly low levels for the developed nations of the world, only the death rate has dropped in Africa. Africa, as a consequence, has a very young population. For example, the population of Nigeria is much younger than that of Sweden or the United States (see Figure 6.10). Comparing the percentages of population under fifteen years of age for selected Sub-Saharan African countries and for other world regions also shows that Africa's population is young (see Table 6.1).

The age-sex distribution also drives the annual growth rate because of the increasing numbers of young people. There is a momentum of growth built into this distribution—each year more women will mature into the reproductive period of their lives (typically estimated to last from fifteen to forty-five years of age) than in the previous year. This trend in population growth explains why changes in indi-

FIGURE 6.10. Comparative Age-Sex Population Pyramids

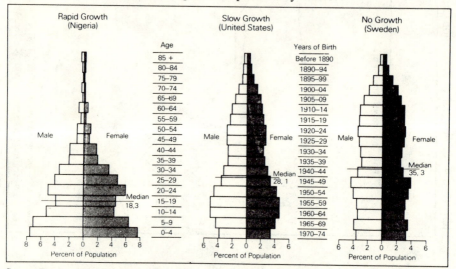

Source: Reprinted with permission from John M. Pritchard. 1979. *Africa: A Study Geography for Advanced Students*. Revised metric edition. London: Longman. Pg. 64.

TABLE 6.1. Percentage of Population Under Fifteen Years of Age in Selected
            Countries, 1984

Sub-Saharan Africa		Other World Regions	
Country	Percent	Country	Percent
Nigeria	48	Mexico	44
Kenya	50	Brazil	37
Ghana	47	China	34
Zimbabwe	48	Soviet Union	25
Zaire	45	USA	22
Ethiopia	43	West Germany	18

Source: Adapted from Lester R. Brown and Edward C. Wolf. 1985. Reversing
Africa's Decline. Worldwatch Paper 65. Washington, D.C.: Worldwatch
Institute.

vidual behavior are not reflected immediately in population growth rates. Africa's population growth rate is not now expected to peak until at least 1990, when it will exceed 3 percent annually (UN 1985; USDA 1981). Three percent is the highest growth rate of any world region. Even without consideration of changes in tastes and standards, the age distribution alone is enough to increase the demand on natural and social resources. Swelling numbers of young demand food, education, medical services, housing, and so on. As they reach maturity, these people demand land to farm and other employment opportunities.

Another demographic trend is increased urbanization, with wide variation among countries. Although Sub-Saharan Africa remains the least urbanized region of the world, its urban growth rate is currently one of the highest and averages between 5 and 6 percent annually (UN 1985; World Bank 1985). This trend is accentuated by drought and famine, which drive people to seek refuge near the towns and cities. Whereas only 15 percent of all Africans lived in urban areas in 1950, 59 percent will live there by 2025. Urbanites consume food, but rarely produce it.

· ECONOMIC PATTERNS ·

The backdrop to any discussion of Africa's economic environment must be the admission that this is a poor continent. Africa's standard of living is low by any indices: gross national product, gross domestic product, per capita income, literacy, per capita food production, and so on. The United Nations Conference on Trade recently published a study naming the world's thirty-six poorest countries: twenty-six of these are in Sub-Saharan Africa (see Figure 6.11). These twenty-six poorest

African countries are located predominantly, although not exclusively, in the Sahel and the Horn, areas of marginal rainfall and inadequate food production that have been brought vividly to the attention of the world through the well-publicized famines and droughts of the early 1970s and mid-1980s.

Seven decades of European colonial domination oriented Sub-Saharan African agricultural systems toward exports to Europe at the expense of domestic food production (see Davis in this volume). Investments were made to develop the colonial infrastructure to meet the needs of European settler populations and European colonial states. A few Africans were able to benefit from their own initiatives within the colonial systems, but colonial regimes did not usually invest in the development of smallholder agriculture, except to encourage the growing of selected crops for export. At the same time, especially in East and Southern Africa, colonial systems forced and encouraged African men to leave their villages, temporarily or permanently, to work for European settlers on farms, in mines, and in the growing towns. Individual and family interest began to shift away from farming toward the urban-based and European-dominated export economy. One effect of this shift was a deterioration in rural living conditions, either absolutely or relative to improving urban conditions. These rural areas remain unattractive to many young Africans; the areas are viewed as uninteresting and lacking in opportunities.

Political independence failed to alter Africa's economic dependence upon exporting raw materials or to halt rural-urban migration. Independent African leaders were slow to face the gargantuan task of reorienting their national economies and strengthening food production for internal consumption. Perhaps these leaders listened too much to what was then the prevailing wisdom of development economists (see Staatz and Eicher in this volume).

The dangers of this failure are illustrated by Zambia. At independence Zambia's highly developed copper industry accounted for more than 90 percent of exports and 60 percent of government revenues (Griffiths 1984:130). At that time, 1964, world demand and prices for copper were high. By the 1970s the international market had collapsed, and with it went Zambia's revenue. There are many other instances of economic dependence upon one or two key minerals or cash crops; a prominent example is Nigeria and oil. Most African leaders are now painfully aware of their economic predicament, and national planning is beginning to reflect a new emphasis on rural and agricultural development. The extent to which these plans are implemented remains to be seen (see Asante in this volume).

Migration away from the rural areas takes resources away from agriculture; the people who leave represent labor, skills, and talent that could be used to expand food production. This process occurred in the United States and Europe as these countries modernized their agriculture; yet these countries concurrently experienced a dramatic increase in industrial employment, and their expanding economies facilitated the development of mechanized agriculture in which fewer producers were supported by machinery. Industries supplied machinery and other inputs, and the urban employed population supplied an effective demand for food, fibers, and products derived from crops and livestock. Capital-intensive agricul-

FIGURE 6.11.   African Countries Now Classified Among World's Least
Developed

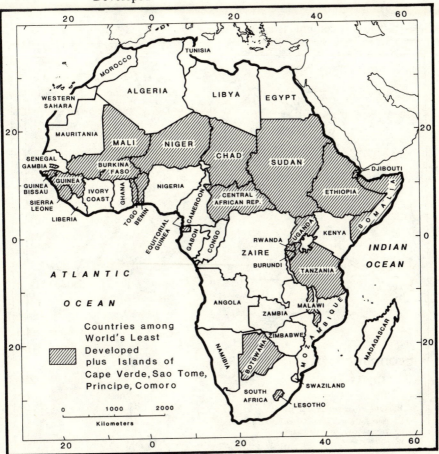

Source: United Nations. 1984. *The Least Developed Countries 1984 Report*. New York: United
Nations.

ture replaced labor-intensive agriculture. African countries are developing in a
very different world economy. Developed industrial countries already dominate
the world's limited markets. African national economies, unable to expand, have
been further weakened by the oil price shock of the early 1970s, continuing high
oil prices, and a continuing world economic recession. Agriculture must continue
to employ large amounts of labor because national industry cannot.

The urban and industrial areas to which people are migrating are economic
islands (see Figure 6.12). These tend to be isolated zones of development that are
distinct in many respects from the less populated and more neglected rural sur-
roundings. These islands are: (1) major centers of commerce, industry (sometimes
mining), and educational and economic opportunity; (2) hubs of national and inter-

national transportation and communication networks; and (3) the primary zones for national and international investment. Surrounding areas are often cut off from

FIGURE 6.12.   Economic Islands in Africa

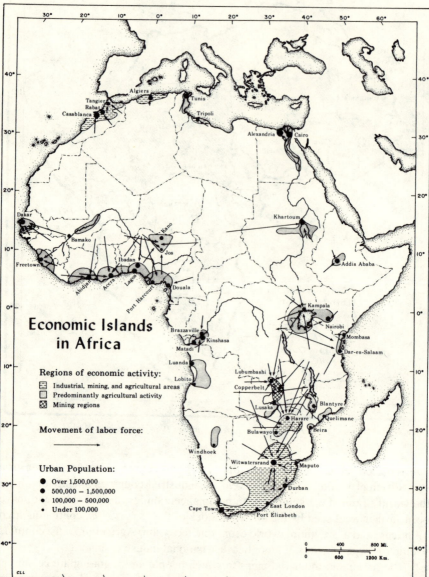

Economic Islands
in Africa

Regions of economic activity:
- Industrial, mining, and agricultural areas
- Predominantly agricultural activity
- Mining regions

Movement of labor force:

Urban Population:
- Over 1,500,000
- 500,000 – 1,500,000
- 100,000 – 500,000
- Under 100,000

Source: Reprinted with permission from Michael L. McNulty. 1986. The Contemporary Map of Africa. In *Africa*, Phyllis M. Martin and Patrick O'Meara, eds. 2nd Edition. Bloomington: Indiana University.

the benefits enjoyed by the islands, and such unbalanced development is self-reinforcing.

Africa is often described as rich in minerals, and references are made to its great untapped wealth. This is true but misleading. The African continent does possess a good share of the world's mineral resources, but there are important qualifiers, namely, the following: (1) These resources are not evenly distributed among nations. (2) Mineral rich nations often have no other marketable resource and are dependent on the highly unreliable demands and prices of the world market, as noted previously for Zambia. (3) Many large extractive industries are controlled by multinational corporations. Decisions regarding reinvestments are made in the best interests of the corporation, which are not necessarily those of the country. (4) Successful mining industries sometimes require more from the domestic economy than they offer in return. (5) Finally, the lion's share of Sub-Saharan Africa's mineral wealth is in the Republic of South Africa, where the system of apartheid prevents the black majority of the population from receiving an equitable share of the wealth produced.

· SOURCES AND PATTERNS OF IDENTITY ·

There are many sources of African identity and no single homogeneous Africa or African identity. This chapter has made many general statements about Sub-Saharan Africa. Unfortunately, generalizing in this way may obscure for some people the existence of heterogeneity. Ethnicity, language, colonial history, and religion are all important sources of diversity and identity.

Approximately eight hundred to one thousand named ethnic groups exist in Africa. It may be difficult to grasp the significance of this preponderance of ethnic groups for the whole continent. Consider then that one country, Nigeria, contains approximately two hundred groups. Nigeria has the largest population of any Sub-Saharan African country, but several other countries each contain at least seventy-five different ethnic groups. Figure 6.13 illustrates the multiplicity and general locations of these African ethnic groups, but the map is not meant to imply that there are fixed boundaries. Ethnic identities change over time, people migrate, and marriage and settlement patterns often result in the intermingling of peoples with different ethnic backgrounds. Nonetheless, each ethnic group has its unique cultural traditions that generate a sense of belonging and identity (see Cohen in this volume). A shared language is another primary feature of an ethnic group. The linguistic diversity of Africa is striking. Of the approximately three thousand different languages (not dialects) in the world, one third are found in Africa.

In the late nineteenth century, the major West European imperial powers established claims to parts of Africa, fixed boundaries, and then administered these territories as colonies (see Davis in this volume). Existing ethnic territories were lumped together, and ethnic groups were often divided by new colonial boundaries (see Figure 6.14). Two of the most significant legacies of that era are (1) the artifi-

FIGURE 6.13.   General Ethnic Territories in Africa

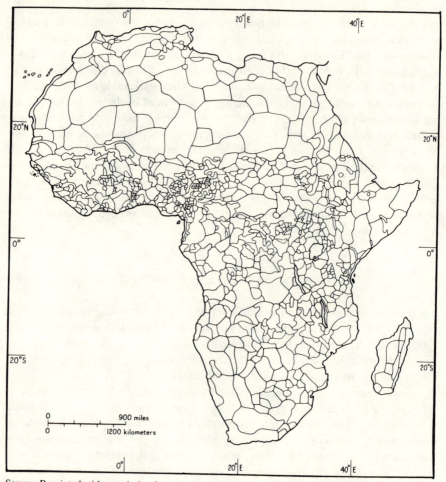

Source: Reprinted with permission from Alan C. G. Best and Harm J. de Blij. 1977. *African Survey*. New York: John Wiley and Sons. Pg. 102.

ciality of Africa's current national boundaries and (2) the continuing division of Africa into Anglophone, Francophone, and Lusophone (Portuguese-speaking) countries.

For three quarters of a century Europeans forced a unity upon their colonies to serve European ends. African ethnic and linguistic diversity was obscured, and territorial boundaries were redefined by administrative and economic unities imposed within each European sphere. The struggles for decolonization and national independence confirmed the arbitrary borders imposed by the colonial powers and incorporated into each independent African state many conflicting ethnic, linguistic, and colonial identities. The world community gave its approval to newly formed African nation states as each took its seat in the United Nations and began to act as an independent political unit. Unfortunately, it soon became apparent, as the euphoria and momentum of independence waned, that some of the basic requirements for statehood were missing in many African countries. There was no broadly accepted ruling group or theory of government, and a unifying sense of nationality or national consciousness was lacking. Under growing political and economic pressures, one African nation after another rejected as unworkable the political models that they had inherited from their former colonial rulers, and internal power struggles began to emphasize the lack of elite and popular identification with the state. It is increasingly questionable whether the present pattern of fifty-

FIGURE 6.14.   European Colonial Territories in Africa

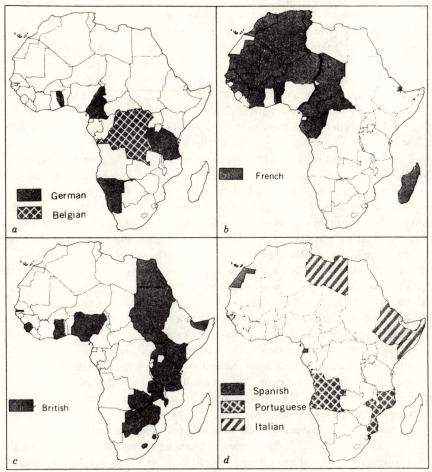

Source: Reprinted with permission from Alan C. G. Best and Harm J. de Blij. 1977. *African Survey*. New York: John Wiley and Sons. Pg. 89.

three independent African states (plus Western Sahara) will continue (Calvocorresi 1985:5).

Numerous African languages were spoken within each colony, but to participate in the colonial economy Africans were forced to learn and adopt the language of their oppressors. The consequences of this situation are apparent today throughout Sub-Saharan Africa, as the dominant language of government and trade in most countries is the former colonial language: English, French, or Portuguese. One exception to this is Swahili, the official state language of Tanzania and Kenya. Most children growing up in Sub-Saharan Africa today learn three or four languages: (1) that of their own ethnic group, (2) that of at least one neighboring ethnic group with which they interact, (3) possibly a regional trade language such as Hausa in Nigeria or Swahili in East Africa, and (4) the official (usually European) language used in their state.

Religion is another source of diversity. There are three major religious systems in contemporary Africa: Islam, Christianity, and indigenous African religions. Islam and Christianity may be considered indigenous only in the sense that they have been practiced in various parts of the continent for several centuries. Christianity's considerable influence in North Africa in the early Christian era was swept away by Muslim Arab conquests from the east that began in the seventh and eighth centuries. Only Ethiopia maintained Christianity as the state religion into recent times. Africa north of the Sahara evolved rapidly into dominant Arab cultures with cities that were major world centers of Islamic civilization. This dominance of Arabic language and culture and the strong ties with the Middle East are the reasons North Africa is usually separated from our discussions of Sub-Saharan Africa.

Islam has continued to spread south of the Sahara, blending easily with the highly tolerant indigenous religions until it now dominates two thirds of Africa north of the equator, as well as coastal areas of East Africa (see Figure 6.15). European missionaries introduced Christianity into Sub-Saharan Africa before and during the colonial era. An important reason for the influence of Christianity today is its link with education. Christian missionary schools were often the only schools open to Africans during the colonial period, and many current political leaders received their education in these schools. Although it has grown steadily, Christianity is a majority religion in fewer than ten countries, and no African country except Ethiopia can claim Christianity as North African states claim Islam. Islam and Christianity have been occasional sources of tension and conflict in contemporary Sub-Saharan Africa, primarily in an indirect way through the strengthening of regional or ethnic loyalties. Yet many African families tolerate more than one religion among kin without conflict, and political leaders are usually accepted without concern for their religious persuasion.

A number of key aspects of Sub-Saharan Africa's natural and human environment have been presented in this chapter to facilitate the understanding of African food issues. Two broad themes have emerged that characterize contemporary Africa: rapid change and diversity. These themes and African and world responses to the challenges of feeding and developing Africa are addressed in more detail in other chapters in this volume.

FIGURE 6.15. Distribution of Islam in Africa

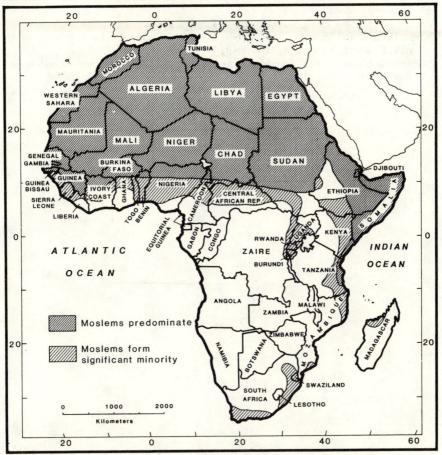

Source: Revised from World Eagle. 1983. *Africa Today: An Atlas of Reproducible Pages*.
Wellesley, Massachusetts: World Eagle. Pg. 47.

· SUGGESTED FURTHER READINGS ·

Best, Alan C. G. and Harm de Blij. 1977. *African Survey*. New York: John Wiley and
    Sons.
Calvocoressi, Peter. 1985. *Independent Africa and the World*. New York: Longman.
Griffiths, Ieuan. 1984. *An Atlas of African Affairs*. London: Methuen.
Hance, William A. 1975. *The Geography of Modern Africa*. 2nd edition. New York: Col-
    umbia University Press.
Maquet, Jaques. 1972. *Africanity: The Cultural Unity of Black Africa*. New York: Oxford
    University Press.

Martin, Phyllis, and Patrick O'Meara, eds. 1986. *Africa*. 2nd. ed. Bloomington: Indiana University Press.

Mazrui, Ali A. 1980. *The African Condition*. London: Heinemann.

Oliver, Roland, and Michael Crowder, eds. 1981. *The Cambridge Encyclopaedia of Africa*. Cambridge: Cambridge University Press.

Prothero, R. Mansell. 1972. *People and Land in Africa South of the Sahara*. London: Oxford University Press.

·7·

Climate, Drought, and Famine in Africa

SHARON E. NICHOLSON

In the early 1970s a seemingly unprecedented drought struck the West African Sahel, the semiarid southern margin of the Sahara. Famine claimed over one hundred thousand lives in 1973 alone; cattle herds were ruined; and millions of people fled into refugee camps and urban centers (Glantz 1976). This disaster provoked much controversy concerning its cause and whether or not it denoted a longer-term trend toward more desertlike conditions. Climatologists offered a variety of hypotheses—including changes in tropical winds, sea-surface temperatures, and global temperatures—to account for the observed variations in rainfall. Another hypothesis by J. G. Charney (1975) proposed that degradation of vegetation in this semiarid region, perhaps caused by human activities, increases the capacity of dry ground to reflect solar radiation, a factor that might lead to long-term, possibly permanent rainfall reduction. The concept of desertification also became prominent, furthering the hypothesis that human intervention, perhaps more than climate, is turning these marginal lands into deserts. Following a short improvement in rainfalls in the mid-1970s, the intensification of drought conditions in West Africa and renewed occurrences throughout East and Southern Africa have once again focused attention on questions of the cause and effect of drought.

Resolving the controversy concerning the roles of human activities and climate and assessing various related theories depend, in part, on increasing our understanding of long-term climatic variation in Africa. We need to know whether long-term climatic trends are affecting regions of Africa, whether such droughts have chronically plagued the continent, and whether the impact of the recent drought was in proportion to the actual rainfall decrease that the region experienced. Similarly, knowledge of the nature of climate in Africa and its variation in past centuries will help to assess the proper way to cope with, or develop and manage, the fragile environments that predominate throughout the African continent.

The study of long-term climatic fluctuations is hindered by a scarcity of useful meteorological data. Meteorological station records that extend back a century or more are rare outside of Algeria and South Africa. Freetown, Dakar, St. Louis, Banjul, Mombasa, Alexandria, and Accra are among the few places that have such records. Colonial administrations set up a number of meteorological stations in the 1890s; however, observations from these stations were generally discontinued after a couple of decades. Most countries initially established reasonable station networks in the 1940s or 1950s, but even today little or no data are available for large areas of the continent. This situation contrasts sharply with Europe and, to a lesser extent, the United States, where dense observing networks have been in operation for at least one hundred years and where numerous stations were established as early as the seventeenth and eighteenth centuries. The basic lack of data in Africa creates a severe problem in regions of greatest climatic interest, semiarid drought-prone regions such as the Sahel or the Kalahari where large temporal and spatial variability of rainfall demands a dense observing network to obtain representative pictures of climatic conditions.

To look at African climatic variation over a period of centuries or millenia, researchers rely on a variety of less precise types of data. These derive from several disciplines (see Table 7.1). Geology and palynology (pollen studies) present climate related information on lake-level variations, vegetation, dunes, changes in stream regimes, and other environmental features. These indicators, although most useful for studying variation over millennia, occasionally provide information pertinent to the more recent historical past. For this latter period the best sources of information on Africa's climates prove to be historical records and geographical descriptions of drought, famine, floods, agriculture and harvest quality, landscape, climate, and weather. Among the great variety of possible sources are archives, local chronicles, works of Arab geographers, travelers' and settlers' journals, ships' logs, maps, early geographical journals, colonial reports, and newspapers (Nicholson 1979).

Although these sources contain a potential wealth of information, the imprecise nature of these sources may render their interpretation somewhat difficult. For example, local chronicles such as the "Tarikh es-Soudan" record the earlier fallible witness of memory or oral tradition: Information was selected by the chronicler, and dates were usually estimated. Weather and climate reports in journals, diaries, or historical treatises frequently contain secondhand information, information that often obscures the location and date of origin and occasionally substitutes theory for observation. Some writers may have generalized the climate of all of Western Africa from observations in Dakar and Accra that covered one or two possibly unrepresentative years or from observations that exaggerated harshness or favorableness of an environment. Much information is relative or subjective: an observing standard was lacking. "Forests" mentioned in native accounts of Timbuktu possibly were sparse, isolated stands of trees that exist today and bear little resemblance to our own concept of a forest (a European visitor, accustomed to more humid environments, may term the same region a veritable desert). A reference to drought might also be ambiguous: a drought is not defined solely by rainfall being less than a certain threshold amount, but also by such factors as the population to

TABLE 7.1. Types of Data Useful for Historical Climatic Reconstructions

I. Landscape Descriptions

1. Forests and vegetation: are they as today?
2. Conditions of lakes and rivers:
    (a) Height of the annual flood, month of maximum flow of the river
    (b) villages directly along lakeshores
    (c) size of the lake (e.g. as indicated on map)
    (d) navigability of rivers
    (e) desiccation of present-day lakes or appearance of lakes no longer
        existing
    (f) floods
    (g) seasonality of flow; condition in wet and dry seasons
3. Wells, oases, bogs in presently dry areas
4. Flow of wadis
5. Measured height of lake surfaces (frequently given in travel journals,
    but optimally some instrumental calibration or standard should accompany
    this)

II. Drought, Famine and Other Agricultural Information

1. References to famine or drought, preferably accompanied by the following:
    (a) where occurred and when occurred: as precisely as possible
    (b) who reported it; whether the information is second hand
    (c) severity of the famine or drought; local or widespread?
    (d) cause of the famine
2. Agricultural prosperity:
    (a) condition of harvest
    (b) what-produced this condition
    (c) months of harvests, in both bad years and good years
    (d) what crops grown
3. Wet cultivation in regions presently too arid

III. Climate and Meteorology

1. Measurements of temperature, rainfall, etc.
2. Weather diaries
3. Descriptions of climate and the rainy season: when do the rains occur,
    what winds prevail?
4. References to occurrence of rain, tornado, storm
5. Seasonality and frequency of tornadoes, storms
6. Snowfalls: is this clearly snow or may the reporter be mistakenly
    reporting frost, etc?
7. Freezing temperatures, frost, hail
8. Duration of snow cover on mountains (or absence)
9. References to dry or wet years, severe or mild winters, other unusual
    seasons

be fed and their habitual standard of living and ability to accommodate rainfall shortages. All of these factors, which need to be considered in interpreting droughts, may have been different centuries ago. Despite these difficulties, when such information is cautiously interpreted, complemented with indicators that are more precise (for example, lake levels), and corroborated by several sources and types of indicators, a rather reliable climatic history of the last few centuries may be derived. This knowledge, combined with more sophisticated understanding of

FIGURE 7.1. Fluctuations of Lake Levels and Climate in Africa During the Last 4000 Years

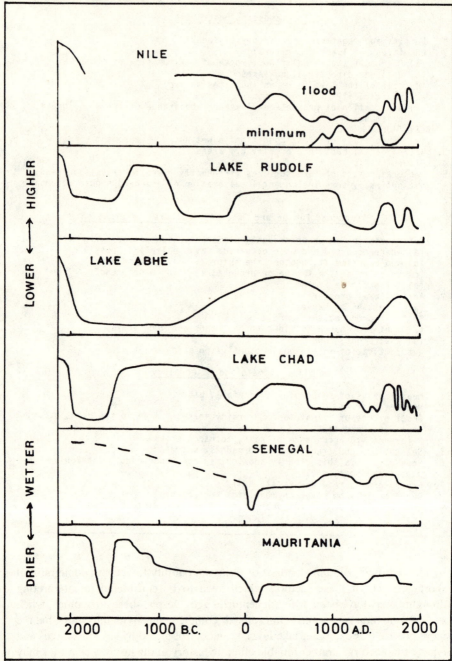

Source: Sharon E. Nicholson. 1976. A Climatic Chronology for Africa: Synthesis of Geological, Historical and Meteorological Information and Data. Ph.D. Thesis. Department of Meterology. University of Wisconsin, Madison.

current climatic conditions, provides tentative answers to pressing questions concerning climate, human population, environment, and development in Africa.

• THE COURSE OF AFRICAN CLIMATE DURING HISTORIC TIME •

Climatic and environmental conditions that prevailed over Africa long ago were quite unlike those we know today. Toward the end of the last ice age, from about twelve thousand to twenty thousand years ago, forests all but disappeared as the desert expanded to cover most of the continent (Nicholson and Flohn 1980). As recently as five thousand years ago, the desert had vanished—lowland marshes formed in the northwestern Sahara, while Neolithic man herded cattle in the central Sahara surrounded by fauna grazing on what was apparently a savanna landscape. Lakes dotted what are now arid regions of Mauritania; fish hooks uncovered in archaeological sites there attest to human occupation and a livelihood that is no longer possible. Rift valley lakes were several hundred feet deeper than at present, and they expanded to form a huge hydrologic system. Lake Chad, almost entirely desiccated in 1985, was then over a hundred meters deep and expanded to ten times its normal twentieth century size. Onset of more arid conditions over most of Africa occurred about three thousand years ago (see Figure 7.1). Conditions generally resembling those of the current century have prevailed during the past two millenia, but during the past two millenia extensive periods of significantly more humid or more arid climate than the present have also occurred.

One such period of humid conditions in northern Africa occurred from the ninth through fourteenth centuries, the time of the middle ages in Europe (Nicholson 1979). Globally, this was a climatic period significantly unlike the present. Warmer conditions generally prevailed in middle and high latitudes of the northern hemisphere, and wetter conditions persisted in many tropical and subtropical regions. Evidence for this period in Africa is sparse and difficult to interpret, but some conclusions may be drawn. From Mauritania eastward to Ethiopia, cultural activities and landscape and hydrologic indicators suggest that relatively humid conditions prevailed in regions that are now semiarid or arid. Several towns in Mauritania are said to have flourished on caravan trade that took place along routes directly across the El Djouf desert, routes now unsuitable due to a lack of water along them. The Gangara people, occupying the sandy plains of central Mauritania from the eighth to the fifteenth centuries, practiced wet cultivation in areas that are now desert. Portuguese exploring Mauritania around 1500 described a relatively long season of storminess and rich mountain wadis, artesian wells that tapped a water table as much as eight meters higher than at present, and running water that gullied dunes in western Mauritania.

Bogs and river terraces in parts of Morocco and Algeria suggest similar wetter conditions existed there. Lake Chad remained several meters higher from about the tenth through thirteenth centuries, a time when the desert massif of Tibesti was heavily populated (see Figure 7.2). The flow of the Nile and lake levels throughout

FIGURE 7.2.   Variations in the Level of Lake Chad During the Last 1000 Years

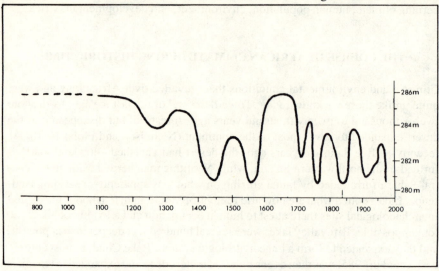

Source: Reprinted with permission from V. Maley, 1981. *Études palynologiques dans le Basin du Tchad et Paléoclimatologie de l'Afrique nord-Tropicale de 30.000 ans à l'époque actuelle.* Traveaux et documents de l'ORSTOM, no. 129, 58. Paris: ORSTROM.

East Africa and the Rift Valley provide further evidence of this wetter episode. In the twelfth century, El Idrisi found elephants and giraffes in the Sudan desert near Dongola, an area where the mean annual rainfall is now twenty millimeters. Around the fourteenth or fifteenth century these more humid conditions declined in most areas. A relatively dry episode persisted for one or two centuries, but the precise timing of this episode and the areas most affected by it cannot be firmly established.

For the last few centuries, evidence of climatic conditions is available for many more regions of the continent (Nicholson 1978, 1980, 1981). In the semiarid subtropics of northern hemisphere Africa, including Ethiopia and at least parts of East Africa, the Chad Basin, and the western Sahel, wetter conditions than at present prevailed throughout most of the sixteenth through nineteenth centuries, although some extended periods of severe drought did occur. Equatorial latitudes were probably relatively dry during these centuries. Little information is available for Southern Africa until late in the eighteenth century, but from that time trends were similar to those in the Sahel—namely, wetter conditions through the end of the nineteenth century interrupted by an extended dry period of several decades early in that century. A major change occurred throughout most of Africa around the 1890s, as well as in tropical regions globally: increasingly arid conditions commenced in most areas.

A variety of indicators, including chronologies of famine and drought, lake and river levels, and geographical descriptions, suggest more humid conditions

FIGURE 7.3.   Chronology of Famine and Drought in Chad, Senegambia, the Niger Bend, and Northern Algeria, 1500 to 1900

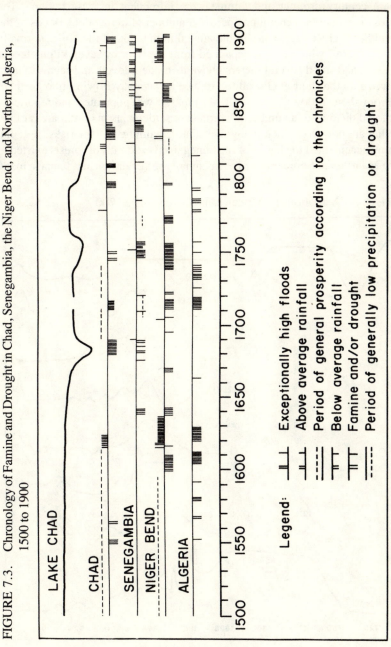

Legend:

Exceptionally high floods
Above average rainfall
Period of general prosperity according to the chronicles
Below average rainfall
Famine and/or drought
Period of generally low precipitation or drought

LAKE CHAD
CHAD
SENEGAMBIA
NIGER BEND
ALGERIA

1500 1550 1600 1650 1700 1750 1800 1850 1900

Source: Sharon E. Nicholson. 1980. Saharan Climates in Historic Times. In *The Sahara and the Nile*, M. A. J. Williams and H. Faure, eds. Pp. 173–200. Rotterdam: A. A. Balkema.

once existed in the West African Sahel (see Figure 7.3). According to chronicles of Timbuktu, Senegambia, and Bornu (near Lake Chad), except in the mid-eighteenth century drought and famine were infrequent in these regions. The chronicles also mention general prosperity. A number of tremendous floods of the Niger and Senegal Rivers occurred; the annual inundation of the Niger normally reached Timbuktu, which is now separated from the river by seven kilometers of sand. Lake Chad stood several meters above its modern levels and seems to have overflowed into the Bahr el Ghazal to produce a waterway flowing into northern Chad. From about 1500 to 1700, the Tibesti massif was populated and reportedly wooded, and there were a number of permanent settlements in border areas of the Sahara that are now dry. Thick mangrove stands, palm trees, tamarisks, redgum, and thorny acacia lined the banks of the Senegal River; stands of forests existed in southern Mauritania. Sources describe savanna-type vegetation and fauna in many

FIGURE 7.4.   Variations in African Lake Levels Since 1700

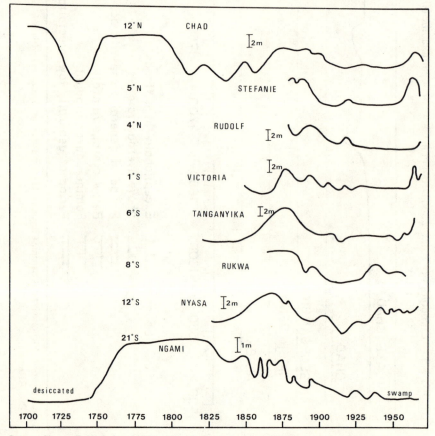

Source: Sharon E. Nicholson. 1978. Climatic Variations in the Sahel and Other African Regions During the Past Five Centuries. *Journal of Arid Environments* 1:3–24.

regions along the southern fringe of the Sahara from Mauritania and Mali across to the Sudan and numerous wells in western portions of the now totally barren desert. Previous Nile floods indicated higher rainfall in the Ethiopian highlands; previous low summer Nile flows implied relatively dry conditions in the equatorial regions of East Africa. Climate descriptions of the Guinea coast of West Africa provide further evidence of low-latitude dryness.

Landscape descriptions and faunal evidence suggest that, before 1800, many semiarid regions of Southern Africa—including the Kalahari, the Karroo, and the dry northwestern Cape—were considerably more humid than in later times (see Figure 7.4). Lake Ngami, now a swamp, was deep enough to produce powerful waves that washed hippos and fish to shore. Rushy grasses, swamps, springs, and periodical rivers thrived in now-barren Karroo. Antelopes, buffalo, and other fauna reminiscent of East Africa roamed plains that are now dry. Although it is impossible to determine how long such conditions prevailed, it was at least for several decades.

Within the centuries of relatively humid conditions in the semiarid subtropics, several major drought episodes occurred. In the Sahel, one such episode lasted for about seven years in the 1680s; another lasted for nearly two decades in the 1740s and 1750s. A third drought episode culminating in the 1820s and 1830s may be traced throughout much of the continent and seems to signal a general trend toward increasing aridity beginning after 1800 (see Figure 7.5). Some drought-affected areas included Senegal, Mali, Mauritania, Burkina Faso, Chad, northern Nigeria, Eastern Africa, the Ethiopian highlands, Zambia, Zimbabwe, Namibia, Botswana, Angola, and drier regions of South Africa. Southern African lakes, swamps, wells, and rivers dried up; well-watered plains turned to barren karroo; farmers and tribesmen alike complained of continually decreasing rainfall; and extreme drought occurred in many years. The flow of the Nile was very weak, and Lake Chad in effect dried up.

Plenty of evidence suggests that this general desiccation was followed within decades by conditions considerably wetter than those occurring during the current century and that the subsequent change to semiarid conditions occurred around 1900 (see Figure 7.5). During these relatively humid decades in the 1800s, lake levels from Chad in the north to Ngami in the south increased dramatically (see Figure 7.4). Numerous lakes stood several meters above modern levels; they maintained for several decades levels achieved at most briefly, and generally not at all, during the twentieth century. Lake Chad again overflowed into the outlet called the Bahr el Ghazal, and the Senegal and Niger rivers rose to flood deep depressions along their banks. Niger floods were continually good in the 1870s and 1880s. In the Niger Bend region wheat production thrived to such an extent that wheat was exported to surrounding areas. Harvest quality was continually good in southern Algeria, the Niger Bend, Namibia, and drier regions of South Africa and Botswana. Numerous quantitative measurements of rainfall and river flow further confirmed these wetter conditions. Two striking examples are Freetown in Sierra Leone, where rainfall from 1880 to 1895 averaged 35 percent above the mean for

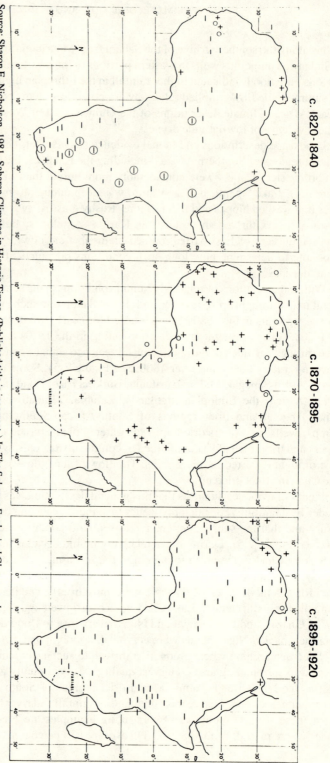

FIGURE 7.5   Schematic of Continental Rainfall Anomalies c. 1820 to 1840, 1870 to 1895, 1895 to 1920

c. 1820-1840

c. 1870-1895

c. 1895-1920

Source: Sharon E. Nicholson. 1981. Saharan Climates in Historic Times. (Published title is incorrect.) In *The Sahara: Ecological Change and Early Economic History*, J. A. Allan, ed. London: Menas Press. Pp. 35–59.

Note: + is above normal rainfall
        0 is normal rainfall
        − is below normal rainfall
        circled symbols denote regional indicators such as lakes and rivers.

1910 to 1940, and the Nile discharge, which was also 35 percent greater during the earlier period (see Figure 7.6). Wells dotted the western Sahara, and stands of forest existed in now barren regions of Mauritania and Mali.

Another major decline in rainfall occurred in the mid-1890s and culminated in severe drought in the 1910s for numerous regions across the continent (see Figure 7.6). Rainfall decreased, lake levels fell, and river flow decreased dramatically. A series of bad harvests plagued areas from Algeria and West Africa southward to the Kalahari and South Africa. The Sahel suffered many years of extreme drought. The situation in southern Africa was critical enough to prompt establishment of a commission to examine progressive desiccation and a serious proposal to flood the Kalahari in an attempt to bring back the "good" rains.

In summary, relatively humid conditions probably prevailed in the semiarid subtropical regions of Africa in earlier centuries. These conditions lasted from about the sixteenth through nineteenth centuries along the southern borders of the Sahara and in at least parts of the eighteenth and the nineteenth centuries in south-

FIGURE 7.6.   Trends of African Climatic Indicators (Lakes, Rivers, Rainfall and Harvests), 1880 to 1920

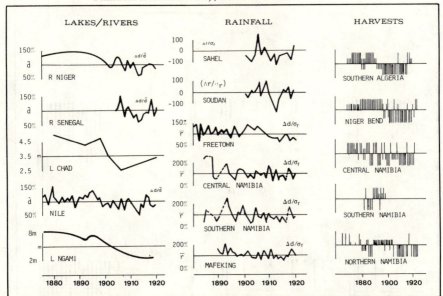

Source: Sharon E. Nicholson. 1981. The Historical Climatology of Africa. In *Climate and History: Studies in Past Climates and Their Impact on Man*. J. M. L. Wigley et al., eds. Pp. 249–270. Cambridge: Cambridge University Press.

Notes: Lake levels show the annual averages in meters. River discharge (d) and rainfall (r) are expressed as percentages, which represent standardized departures from normal (Δ d or Δ r) as a percentage of long term means (d̄ or r̄) or the standard deviation (σ d or σ r). Harvest quality is good when above the axes, poor when below.

ern Africa. Within this time at least three major drought episodes occurred in the Sahel; the last (in the 1820s and 1830s) may be traced throughout much of Africa. A dramatic return of wetter conditions—unlike any seen during the last nine decades—occurred late in the nineteenth century and persisted for two to three decades.

FIGURE 7.7. Rainfall Fluctuations in Three Regions of West Africa, 1900 to 1984

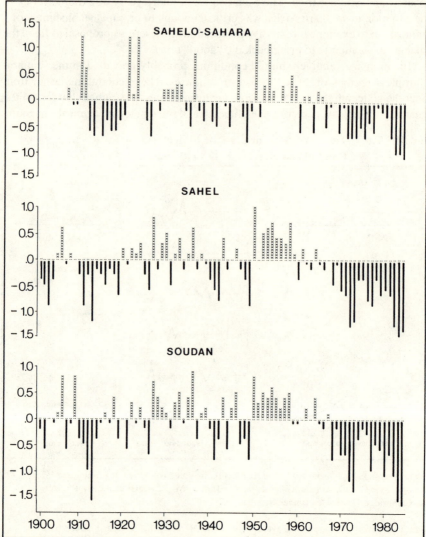

These three adjacent zones derive from vegetation classifications and extend east to west from the Atlantic through the country of Sudan. Sahelo-Sahara is the northernmost zone, with annual mean rainfall between 50 and 100 mm. The Sahel zone receives 100 to 400 mm, and the southernmost Soudan zone receives 400 to 1200 mm.

FIGURE 7.8. Rainfall Fluctuations in Three Regions of East and Southern Africa, 1900 to 1970

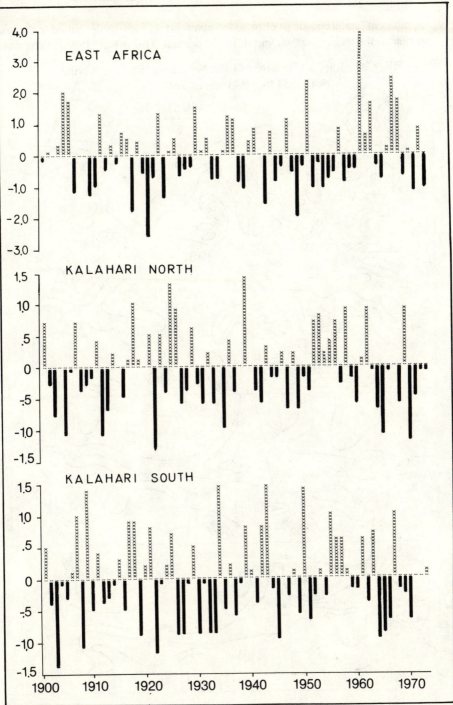

• AFRICAN CLIMATES IN RECENT TIMES •

An inherent characteristic of climate in subhumid regions, as described in the last chapter, is the large temporal variability of rainfall. This is well illustrated by fluc-

FIGURE 7.9.   Rainfall Departures from Normal in West and Northeast Africa, 1981 to 1984 (percentage)

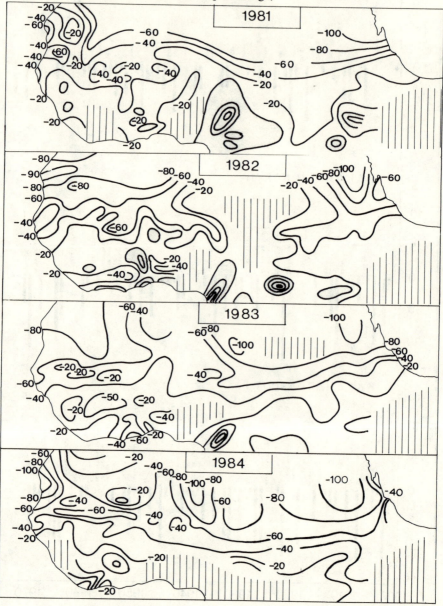

TABLE 7.2. Rainfall at Nine Stations in 1950, 1972 and 1983 and Mean Rainfall for 1950-1959 and 1970-1984 (millimeters)

Station	1950	1972	1983	Mean Rainfall 1950-1959	1970-1984
Bilma	40	21	0	20	9
Atbara	166	55	15	92	54
Nouakchott	183	103	66	172	51
Khartoum[a]	178	135	86(15)	178	116
Agadez	262	74	94	210	97
Tombouctoo	230	106	74	241	147
Nema	345	245	43	381	210
Dakar	797	130	159	609	308
Banjul	1489	583	358	1409	791

[a]At Khartoum, only 15 millimeters fell during the July-September rainy season.

tuations that have occurred during the course of the twentieth century. In Sahelian regions of West Africa (see Figure 7.7) three drought episodes have occurred: in the 1910s, the 1940s, and during the 1970s and 1980s (Nicholson 1983, 1985). The first and last have been particularly severe and longlasting. High rainfall was the rule throughout the 1950s. Similar fluctuations have occurred in Southern and East Africa, but drought episodes tend to be less severe and of shorter duration there (see Figure 7.8). In the Sahel, the longest spell of continually below normal rainfall lasted eighteen years. In the Kalahari, by contrast, the longest "dry spell" lasted five years, and most dry spells last just two or three years.

Countries most severely affected during the 1980s include Senegal, Mali, Mauritania, Burkina Faso, Ghana, the Ivory Coast, Togo, Benin, Niger, Nigeria, the Sudan, Ethiopia, Chad, Morocco, Mozambique, Angola, Zambia, Zimbabwe, Botswana, South Africa, Namibia, and probably others as well. Rainfall deficits were extreme in most of northern hemisphere Africa during the four years from 1981 to 1984 (see Figure 7.9), and the extent of the drought stricken area was relatively constant, but in Southern Africa the magnitude, extent, and even location of drought conditions varied greatly. The magnitude of rainfall fluctuations in West Africa is illustrated using several stations as examples (see Table 7.2). In most cases, means of rainfall recorded at stations across the Sahel from 1950 to 1959 are nearly double those recorded from 1970 to 1984, even at Banjul where rainfall is reasonably high. Individual annual totals varied by factors of three to five between 1950 and 1983. Although rainfall differences from one year to the next may be nearly as large in other areas of Africa, these conditions do not persist for such lengthy periods; thus the impact on human populations is likely to be much less than in West Africa.

The recent occurrences of drought throughout most of Africa, especially its lengthy persistence in the Sahel, have again brought to light numerous important issues concerning its cause and continuation. In particular, three provocative and critical questions are being posed. First, what is the cause of drought in Africa, and are human activities such as those involved in desertification a contributing factor? Second, how long are the droughts likely to persist, especially in West Africa, and do they signal a long-term climatic change in Africa? Finally, are we able to predict the occurrence of drought? A synthesis of historical information with modern drought studies provides tentative answers to these questions.

• CAUSES OF AFRICAN DROUGHT •

What seems to be an unprecedented drought in West Africa and its persistence over nearly two decades leads to speculation that human activities may be the cause. Increased population pressures and a breakdown of traditional livelihoods, life-styles, and economic systems lead to processes of desertification: extension of cultivation into too arid lands, poor agricultural practices, overgrazing, and removal of natural vegetation by fire or cutting. These processes dramatically alter the land-scape in ways that, according to some meteorologists, might reduce rainfall. Charney (1975), who originated this theory, was primarily concerned with the increased reflectivity of exposed soil surfaces along the desert fringe. Other studies focus on other physical changes such as higher temperature, increased atmospheric dust, and lower evapotranspiration (the process by which water is returned to the atmosphere through a combination of evaporation from soil and transpiration from plants) (Hare 1983; Kandel 1984). Although all these changes might result from human-induced desertification, all are also a product of drought-induced changes in the land surface.

If recent droughts are a result of the human pressures on the landscape that have dramatically increased in recent decades, events of this magnitude and extent should be unique to the twentieth century. However, the long-term record for Africa shows clearly that this is not the case. Through centuries, fluctuations between wetter and drier conditions have occurred, and past analogies to the present situation do exist. The best example for comparison is perhaps the episode early in the nineteenth century when drought ravaged most of Africa. The severity of the drought, as indicated by Lake Chad, actually rivalled that of the current drought. For the earlier episode, actual drought conditions persisted in the Sahel for about two decades, as long as the current drought, and predominantly dry conditions persisted during most of the first half of the nineteenth century. The dramatic decline from eighteenth century humid conditions that preceded the drought is quite comparable to the recent decline from the nearly pan-African wet episode of the 1950s.

Thus, neither the length or severity of recent droughts nor the rainfall pattern preceding them is unique for African droughts. Therefore, the characteristics of recent African droughts do not advance the argument that human pressures are responsible for the current drought episode.

Although the meteorological causes of drought in Africa are not well understood, the consensus is, nevertheless, that they are a result of major changes in general atmospheric circulation. Cited as reasons for this belief are global climatic associations with droughts and the extreme spatial patterns and extent of the African droughts. Some of the droughts, such as the one in 1972, coincided with unusual conditions throughout the tropics globally and, hence, cannot be attributed to local causes. Meteorological variables such as sea surface temperature or winds in the upper atmosphere also relate to drought. Furthermore, occurrences of drought and wetter conditions in West Africa are generally coupled with similar changes in rainfall in the semiarid regions of Southern Africa; in some years nearly the entire continent may be affected (see figure 7.10). This suggests further that local factors are unlikely causal factors of drought. Moreover, drought or wetter conditions in the semiarid regions of both northern and Southern Africa occurred simultaneously in both recent and past episodes, pointing to a meteorological origin of recent droughts.

Nevertheless, it is conceivable that human-induced changes may potentially influence climate. Numerous mathematical models and a few statistical studies suggest that changes in land surface, especially changes in vegetative cover and soil moisture, can influence rainfall patterns in certain regions. Regions most likely to be influenced in this way are semiarid ones where local thunderstorm activity, as opposed to frontal-type rainfall, is the dominant source of precipitation—this description applies to much of West Africa. Again, it is important to emphasize that these changes in land surface occur quite dramatically as a consequence of drought, so drought that is triggered by large-scale atmospheric circulation changes might be self-sustaining through its effects on the land surface. Many prominent scientists believe this to be the case for the Sahel. Through such factors as overgrazing, overcultivation, and removal of vegetation, people may help to strengthen this feedback loop, but the fundamental cause of African drought is meteorological.

• PROGNOSIS FOR THE FUTURE •

It is important to know for agriculture, planning, and development whether recent African droughts signal a long-term change of climate and, in general, if we have any capability of forecasting conditions in Africa. These questions are most critical in West Africa, where rainfall has continually diminished since the 1950s. There is no simple answer to either question, but some tentative conclusions may be drawn by considering documented fluctuations of past and present centuries.

Basically, we do not know if a long-term climate change is in process. Past

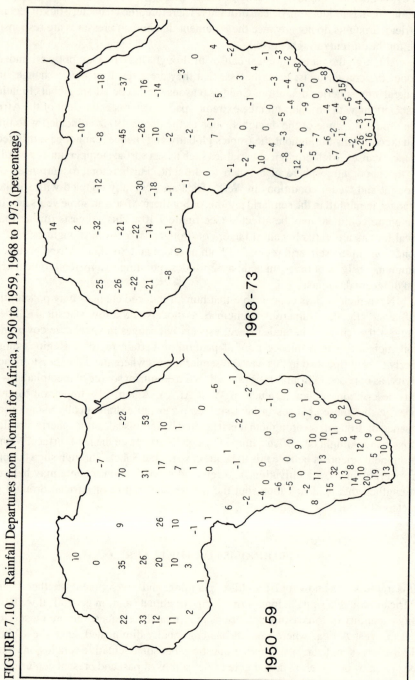

FIGURE 7.10.   Rainfall Departures from Normal for Africa, 1950 to 1959, 1968 to 1973 (percentage)

centuries have seen numerous long and continual declines in rainfall throughout semiarid regions of Africa; most notable are those occurring between about 1800 and the 1830s and again between the 1890s and the 1910s. Both drought periods were part of a sequence of nearly global climatic fluctuations, and both gave way to wet episodes within decades. Hence, the current trend provides no evidence of a long-term change in climate, but neither does it disprove this possibility.

Among the manifold approaches to meteorological forecasting are the use of mathematical models based on physical laws and associations and the use of various types of statistical methods (Nicholson 1982). One example of the latter is the use of "persistence," i.e., using past conditions to estimate future ones on the basis of a quantifiable memory in the system, or "this month is more likely than not to resemble last month." Persistence is routinely incorporated in seasonal forecasts within the United States, but its applications in Africa are probably limited. Another statistical method is to project future conditions from apparent trends or cycles in the data. Few consider this a sound approach simply because, for most physical systems, statistical characteristics are variable in time; they describe the past but, as they can change, they cannot prescribe the future. Trends, in particular, cannot be extrapolated forward in time because climatic fluctuations occur abruptly. However, past events suggest that the extreme drought in the Sahel in 1984 is unlikely to give way to really wet conditions within the next year or two; previous drought recovery has generally been more gradual.

Many authors have tried to forecast future rainfall conditions on the basis of apparent cycles. Again the approach is unreliable, as several examples will illustrate. As with trends, a regular recurrence of an event might suggest that a cycle is present during some time interval, but that cycle can abruptly disappear. Moreover, exact periodicities are rare. A cycle of about fifteen years can mean droughts at intervals of twelve to eighteen years, hardly a basis for predicting a given event. Most established regularities in meteorological time series are also small in magnitude, i.e., although detectable, they are probably too small to prescribe much of the variability of the factor (rainfall, for instance) that is being examined. A common notion derived from the chance occurrence of Sahelian drought in the 1910s, 1940s, and 1970s is that a cycle of about thirty years exists in the region. This view neglects the previous eighty-year absence of major drought in the region and should have been dramatically dispelled by the current episode. Drought has now persisted nearly twenty years, and the 1980s (a time of intensive and widespread drought) follow the wet episode of the 1950s by about thirty years. Our best hope for obtaining any long-range forecasting capability is further development of physical-mathematical models based on improved physical understanding of the dynamics of climate in Africa.

• IMPLICATIONS FOR POLICY AND PLANNING •

A number of policy implications stem from this analysis of past droughts and the meteorological basis of climatic change.

Climate as a Variable

In dealing with the African environment, climate must be treated as a variable, not as a constant. Climatic fluctuations are abrupt and extreme; both wet and dry episodes can persist for periods of one to several decades, thereby creating a false sense of normal conditions. In West Africa, rainfall in one decade may be nearly double that of the next. Drought is an inherent characteristic of the environment and recurs at inconstant intervals. Since the change from wetter conditions to persistent drought cannot be forecast, the true carrying capacity of land should be based on that of the driest years.

Difficulty of Prediction

Rainfall in most regions cannot yet be predicted or planned for on an annual or seasonal basis. Long-range forecasts of drought or even drying trends cannot be substantiated. Thus, the best approach to planning is a flexible one that minimizes the consequences of dry years and quickly adapts to take optimal advantage of wetter years.

Forecasting requires a deep understanding of both the physical processes affecting rainfall and of the interrelationship between Africa and the global climatic system. Meteorologists have made much progress in long-range forecasting in past decades: we may have seasonal or annual forecasts in the not-too-distant future. For at least the next decade or two, however, rainfall conditions in the Sahel can be expected to change without warning. In other regions of the continent, especially East and Southern Africa, the relationship between rainfall and global weather is well enough understood that it may soon be possible to provide forecasts for a season or even a year in advance; however, long-term fluctuations will remain unpredictable.

Adaptation to Climatic and Environmental Constraints

From a climatic viewpoint, the best approach to development in Africa is one in which lifestyles and support systems adapt to—and, when possible, make use of—the region's climate and fragile environment. Troublesome climatic characteristics include low and highly variable rainfall, prevalence of dry years, extreme magnitude of variability, rapidity with which new persistent conditions may be established, great geographic extent of the most extreme periods of abnormal rainfall, and the spottiness of rainfall in more normal years. The lifestyle of nomadic and seminomadic pastoralists is attuned to these conditions. In dry years, groups move to the few pastures that do receive rainfall; alternative support strategies are used during droughts. Further modern development might also proceed in a way compatible with the environment. As Vermeer (1981) showed for Mauritania, some areas are more prone to drought conditions, suffering more frequently or more intensely than other areas with the same mean climatic characteristics. In order to mitigate the impact of future droughts, planners could identify drought-prone areas, then lessen pressure on these lands. Furthermore, lessening the concentration of land use at individual sites (for example, wells or cities) and spreading it over the entire region could take advantage of spotty rainfall and also minimize human impact on the land surface.

Interrelationship Between Human Activities and Climate

The possibility that human activities in the Sahel can affect its climate cannot be ruled out. There is much evidence that landscape changes that occur as a result of drought can influence the system and reinforce drought. These landscape changes affect vegetation cover, reflectivity of ground surface due to removal of vegetation and the quality of soil, and the storage of moisture in the ground. The effects of varying conditions of rainfall are the controlling influence on the landscape but some changes can occur through human activity even in the absence of drought.

When agriculture and pastoralism are extended into marginal areas during wet years, the environmental damage that occurs in these marginal areas during subsequent drought is accelerated and intensified. Conservative land-use strategies, protection of the vegetation, and soil conservation reduce the potential impact land use by humans might have on climate through feedback processes. They also minimize the impact of drought by promoting higher retention (reduced evaporative loss) of the meager rains that do fall during drought years. If environmental degradation is of a magnitude large enough to have an impact on climate, the effect is likely to be a prolongation and intensification of major droughts.

Need for Climatic Monitoring

A complete understanding of African climate and conclusive knowledge of the possible impact of mankind and environment on the region's climate require continuous monitoring of the system. Climatic networks must be reestablished and information transmitted to appropriate data banks. Land use and environmental changes must be monitored on local and regional scales. Population surveys may provide useful information in this context. Analysis of the monitoring results will help to better our understanding of people-environment-climate interactions. The data thereby gained also will help us to assess the appropriateness of strategies for coping with the environment and for minimizing its degradation in the face of extensive use.

• SUGGESTED FURTHER READINGS •

Hare, F. K. 1983. *Climate and Desertification: A Revised Analysis*. WCP-44. Geneva: World Meteorological Organization and United Nations Environment Program.

Jackson, I. L. 1977. *Climate, Water and Agriculture in the Tropics*. London: Longman.

Kandel, R. S. 1984. *Mechanisms Governing the Climate of the Sahel: A Survey of Recent Modeling and Observational Studies*. Club du Sahel D(84) 252, CILSS. Paris: Organization for Economic Cooperation in Development.

Nicholson, S. E. 1979. The Methodology of Historical Climate Reconstruction and its Application to Africa. *Journal of African History* 20:31–49.

1982. *The Sahel: A Climatic Perspective*. Club du Sahel D(82) 187, CILSS. Paris: Organization for Economic Cooperation in Development.

1983. Sub-Saharan Rainfall in the Years 1976–1980: Evidence of Continued Droughts. *Monthly Weather Review* 3:1646–1654.

Ojo, O. 1977. *The Climates of West Africa*. London: Heinemann.

Wigley, T. M. L., M. J. Ingram, and G. Farmer. 1981. *Climate and History*. Cambridge: Cambridge University Press.

·8·

Subsistence Strategies and Systems of Land Use in Africa

DANIEL McGEE

African societies engage in a wide variety of activities to meet their material needs. Activities involved in the allocation of food resources are termed subsistence strategies. A large body of literature in anthropology analyzes different subsistence strategies, and several authors have reviewed their variety and distribution in Africa (Gibbs 1965; Murdock 1959; Ottenberg and Ottenberg 1960; Vaughan 1977). There are four broad categories of subsistence strategies: hunting and gathering, fishing, pastoralism, and cultivation. A survey of 277 societies in Sub-Saharan Africa based on Murdock's "Ethnographic Atlas"[1] showed that approximately 86 percent depend primarily upon agriculture; 6 percent, upon animal husbandry; and animal husbandry and agriculture are codominant for another 3 percent. Of the remaining African societies, 2 percent rely primarily on fishing; 1 percent, on fishing and agriculture equally; and slightly more than 2 percent, on hunting and gathering (Vaughan 1977:21). These figures refer only to the dominant subsistence strategies and do not reflect the importance of minor activities. For example, it is important to note that agriculturalists in tsetse-free regions of western, eastern, and southern Africa obtain approximately 25 percent of their subsistence from animal husbandry (Vaughan 1977:21). Other studies indicate the nutritional importance of gathering activities to agriculturalists (Colson 1979; Scudder 1971). This chapter focuses on the ecological bases and social and political characteristics associated with the four broad categories of subsistence strategies.

· HUNTING AND GATHERING ·

According to archaeological evidence, hunting and gathering was the only subsistence strategy in Africa until around 5000 B.C. (Murdock 1959). It was at this time that a gradual shift away from hunting and gathering to agriculture and animal husbandry began in the areas of higher population densities, although this did not have a significant impact on much of Sub-Saharan Africa until later. Few societies rely primarily on hunting and gathering today. Hunter-gatherer population densities are comparatively low; land requirements range from twenty-one to twenty-six square kilometers per person (Allan 1965). The growth in populations in the last few centuries and the associated land shortages led many societies to engage in agriculture and animal husbandry, thereby forcing the last remaining hunter-gatherers onto marginal lands. Such environments include the tropical rainforest inhabited by the Mbuti pygmies, where rainfall is excessive, and the Kalahari Desert occupied by the !Kung, where rainfall is inadequate for cultivation or pastoralism. A number of East African societies, including the Dorobo, Waboni, and Sandawe, were still engaged in hunting and gathering until the middle of this century but have since adopted agriculture and animal husbandry (Murdock 1959:59–60).

Hunter-gatherers are characterized by small bands, usually under one hundred members. Band size is limited primarily by the availability of resources. Other limiting factors include the added work and cooperation involved in keeping large groups supplied (Lee 1979:367) and the imperative for mobility. Although land tenure is not divided at the individual level, bands are associated with specific territories, often bounded by natural landmarks. Because of the need to exploit a wide variety of resources seasonally in a large geographical area, most hunter-gatherers remain mobile. Mobility and low population densities are necessary to exist in ecological equilibrium. These are associated with low fertility rates, which are maintained through a variety of prenatal practices along with prolonged lactation, postpartum sex taboos, and infanticide (Howell 1979).

There is a loose sexual division of labor among hunter-gatherers: women are responsible for gathering, cooking and building huts; men, for hunting and the production of the implements used in that pursuit. Mbuti women do participate in hunting alongside the men by making noise to frighten the prey into the men's nets (Turnbull 1961). Although work in hunter-gatherer societies is divided by sex, the labor of neither sex is devalued. Egalitarianism is the rule, and cooperation by everyone is emphasized in all activities. Hunter-gatherers lack centralized political authority; decisionmaking is flexible and operates largely by consensus.

There is little specialization in African hunter-gatherer diets, which is consistent with the flexibility needed to exploit a wide range of available food sources when necessary. Therefore a wealth of knowledge about the regional flora and fauna is required. Although only a small percentage of Africans now rely primarily on hunting and gathering as a dominant subsistence strategy, hunting and gathering remains important. Those engaging in animal husbandry, agriculture, and fishing still depend on foraging to obtain relishes and supplementary foods such as honey and wild fruits, as well as raw materials for clothing, shelter, and fuel (Allan 1965; see Fox in this volume). Hunting and gathering is also important as an emergency activity when crops fail. The agricultural Gwembe Tonga, for example, make use of an even larger number of plant species than do the hunter-gatherer !Kung if bad years are taken into account (Scudder 1971).

· FISHING ·

Fishing is often classified as a hunting and gathering subsistence strategy, since it is a foraging activity. It is more useful, however, to consider fishing as a separate subsistence strategy because, as a primary mode of production, it is usually associated with much higher population densities and more complex social organizations than hunting and gathering (see Goldsmith in this volume). Fishing communities tend to maintain sedentary or semisedentary (for those who also cultivate) patterns of residence. In the semisedentary case, communities adjust to seasonal changes in rainfall by shifting between fishing and cultivation. The Unga of the Bangweulu swamps, for example, make seasonal migrations between swamps where they fish and higher cultivation lands (Brelsford 1946). Residence in the cultivation areas is controlled by a rigid system of land tenure and social organization administered by chiefs.

Fish may provide a plentiful and stable source of food if the resources available are properly managed. In the seasons when fish are plentiful, surpluses may be dried and stored for the dry seasons. When the water level drops, the banks left dry are used for temporary cultivation. Increasing production in fishing economies must be done with great care because overfishing or disrupting the reproductive cycle of the fish can be disastrous. Thus, respecting critical population densities (population densities approaching the carrying capacity) is essential since efforts to increase production beyond this point may result in significant declines in production.

· PASTORALISM ·

Pastoralism is not simply a stage in cultural evolution between foraging and farming, as was previously believed (Allan 1965:287). Pastoralism is a highly specialized subsistence strategy associated with specific environmental conditions and social patterns. The degree to which animal husbandry is combined with cultivation can be plotted on a continuum, with nomadic pastoralism at one extreme and mixed farming at the other. In this way pastoral peoples may be designated by the relative number of cattle they own. One definition marks pastoralists as having a cattle-to-people ratio of one-to-one or higher (Schneider 1981:63). Pastoralists are the predominant occupants of Africa's arid and semiarid zones, including the Sahel and savannah regions of East Africa. The ecological conditions in much of these areas are unsuitable for cultivation or sedentarization (Bremaud and Pagot 1968; Horowitz 1979). Both the regular movements of transhumant pastoralists and the irregular movements of nomadic pastoralists are dictated by the need to find water and pasturage, which fluctuate in geographical availability both seasonally and annually (Bremaud and Pagot 1968:318). Pastoralists engage in a number of activities to improve the availability of water and pasturage, including digging wells and burning off dry grass. Burnings not only enhance the growth of green grass but reduce scrub and help keep away tsetse and trypanosomiasis (Horowitz 1979:31).

Migrations have social and political dimensions as well. The allocation and control of water supplies such as public wells continue to be controversial political issues. Associational ties, including relations among different pastoral groups and between pastoralists and cultivators, are also important in the movements of pastoralists. The specialization and interdependence of cultivators and pastoralists is reinforced by ethnicity, as exemplified by the interactions of Fulani herders and Manga farmers in Niger: "Pastoralism and farming, according to local points of view, are not merely ecological commitments but also cultural ones" (Horowitz 1973:106).

Livestock is the central focus of pastoral life. African pastoralists rely on hearty breeds like Zebu cattle, which are more drought resistant and less susceptible to temperature changes than European varieties (Bremaud and Pagot 1968; see Simpson in this volume). Camels, sheep, and goats are also raised. For added insurance against disease and drought, most Sahelian pastoralists maintain a variety of livestock instead of concentrating on only one species. One problematic feature of African pastoral systems is overstocking. A number of factors contribute to this practice. African pastoralism, like hunting and gathering, is a labor efficient subsistence strategy. Large numbers of valuable (although smaller) cattle can be herded by a few people in a land extensive pastoral system; however, the inputs of water facilities, shelter, fodder, etc. needed to raise larger, fatter cattle would be much more costly and would require a larger labor force. Also contributing to overstocking is the belief that overstocking preserves the health of the herds by eliminating persistent vegetation-harboring ticks, flies, and worms that carry parasitic diseases (Hornby, as cited in Allan 1965:292). Finally, cattle are repositories of wealth in pastoral societies, and the well-being of individuals is measured in terms of numbers of cattle (Goldschmidt 1975). So cattle herd sizes are often maximized at the expense of cattle size.

Population densities maintained by pastoralists are higher than those of hunter-gatherers and lower than those associated with fishing or cultivation, ranging from about 0.8 people per square kilometer for the Massai to about 2.3 people per square kilometer for the Mukogodo (Allan 1965:291). Land requirements vary as determined by the number of livestock needed per family and the stock carrying capacity of the grazing or browsing land. Mixed systems of pastoralism and cultivation sustain a somewhat larger population density. Pastoral societies have a marked sexual division of labor, and men usually have a higher social status than women. Women are responsible for milking and for the distribution and selling of milk—their status is determined by the number of cows they milk (Stenning 1959). Men's duties include herding and taking care of the livestock; in fact pastoralism is associated with patrilineal descent (see Cohen in this volume). In many African societies, patrilineages are related to each other in ascending levels to form a segmentary lineage system (Evans-Pritchard 1940). Although bonded by kinship networks, pastoral societies do not have centralization of political authority, especially regarding the movement and welfare of animals.

• CULTIVATION •

Cultivators occupy a diversity of ecological zones, and the crops grown, methods of cultivation, and population densities vary among these zones. African farmers grow a wide variety of crops. Staple crops include cereals such as maize, millet, sorghum, rice, and wheat; roots and tubers such as cassava, yams, cocoyams, sweetpotato, and potato; and rhizomes such as bananas and plantains (see Hiebsch and O'Hair in this volume). The main function of staples is to provide carbohydrates. Traditionally nutritional sufficiency is achieved by supplementing staple consumption with complementary, nonstaple food plants that are valuable sources of proteins, minerals, and vitamins. These plants, sometimes called "relishes," include cultivated and foraged plants. Relishes actively cultivated include legumes such as cowpeas, peanuts, and pidgeonpeas; cucurbits; and okra. The germination and maturation of many wild varieties of relishes, including leafy greens, fruits, roots, and mushrooms, are fostered by patterns of land clearance and plot weeding (Fleuret and Fleuret 1980).

A number of factors influence crop selection. The amount of annual rainfall and its seasonal distribution are crucial limiting factors. Farmers in areas with poor rainfall must concentrate on drought-resistant crops such as millet, sorghum, and cassava. When the amount of rainfall changes markedly between seasons, African farmers lacking irrigation and other technological innovations to insure against drought experience profound changes in yields. The high labor inputs needed to grow certain crops such as yams are also important considerations. Soil types and qualities may affect crop selection, and soil degradation has forced farmers in some areas to grow different crops. For example, many Igbo farmers in Nigeria have adopted cassava in place of yams, as a consequence of soil degradation (Okere 1983). Since cassava is a poor source of protein, the resulting dietary change can be nutritionally problematic unless it is incorporated with additional protein supplements.

The land requirements of African cultivation systems generally vary in an inverse relationship to the intensity of the labor inputs necessary to maintain them. Intensive systems of permanent cultivation require large amounts of labor inputs and sometimes incorporate technological improvements such as irrigation, traction animals, and manure. The Kikuyu and Nyakyusa hoe cultivators of Kenya and Tanzania, respectively; the Diola in Senegal; and the Sukuma people along Lake Victoria are intensive cultivators. Extensive systems of cultivation, also referred to as "swidden" or "slash and burn" or "shifting" cultivation, require much less labor than do intensive systems and rely on natural processes to maintain the fertility of the soil. "Shifting agriculture is a well-adjusted and ecologically harmonious and stable system that can produce sustained yields without depleting the natural resource base. It does this by minimally interfering with the natural vegetation cover with mixed cropping systems, and thus closely modeling the nutrient cycle of a mature or nearly mature vegetation climax" (Hunter and Ntiri 1978:193). Extensive systems require large areas of land but are also very reliable, usually providing adequate but scanty yields even in the worst years. In this way they present less risk than intensive systems, which provide better yields only with adequate rainfall and good soils or with costly inputs.

William Allan referred to the level of production characterizing African systems as "the normal surplus of subsistence" and emphasized that African subsistence farmers do indeed produce surpluses in good years, but over the long run they only produce enough to maintain themselves (Allan 1965:38–48). Population densities for extensive cultivation may vary between 3 and 12 people per square kilometer, although for more intensive systems the population density can be as high as 40 to 150 people per square kilometer (Allan 1965:123, 173, 195). It should be emphasized that systems of cultivation can vary in intensity between extremes of extensive cultivation and intensive cultivation. The degree to which a system is considered extensive or intensive depends on the frequency of the rotation cycles. The R factor, which indicates the percentage of area cultivated at one time in relation to the total cultivable area used in a system, is a good method for classifying systems according to their level of intensity (Ruthenberg 1980:15–16).

Social organization among cultivators is as varied as the systems of production. Political power tends to be more consolidated in groups with intensive farming systems, and it serves to facilitate the allocation of land, labor, and other limited resources needed to maintain these larger sedentary populations. Kinship among cultivators is also related to the organization of production. Matrilineal descent predominates among hoe cultivators in Central and Southern Africa (see Cohen in this volume). The Lele of Central Africa, studied by Mary Douglas, are an example of a matrilineal society relying on shifting cultivation (Onwuejeogwu 1975:69). Patrilineal descent in African agricultural societies is associated with cultivation combined with animal husbandry; the relations between patrilineages are reinforced by the institution of bridewealth payments in the form of cattle. The Nyakyusa and Gikuyu in East Africa practice polygyny, a common feature of patrilineal systems. The role of women in African agricultural societies is very important and has unfortunately often been overlooked in past studies. Women provide a majority of the labor in many areas, especially in polygynous societies where women constitute most of the work force (see Spring in this volume).

• DYNAMISM AND COMPLEXITY •

Groups relying primarily on one subsistence strategy do not exist in a vacuum but interact with other groups employing different subsistence strategies in ways that often enhance mutual appropriation of resources. For example, the Fulani pastoralists in Burkina Faso take care of cattle for the Mossi and supply them with manure for cultivation (Hammond 1966). The Mossi, in return, allow the Fulani to keep some of the cattle's offspring and supply the Fulani with grain. Most systems of land usage are complex, employing more than a single subsistence strategy. For example, hoe cultivators usually engage in a significant amount of hunting and gathering; bushmeat is a valuable protein source and plants collected in the bush provide necessary minerals and vitamins. Elizabeth Colson (1979:23) stressed that this kind of adaptive diversity "provides not a maximal return under optimal conditions, but a reasonable return under a wide variation in environmental factors."

Systems of land usage are not static but rather represent transformations in strategies, organization, and intensity to provide for the changing needs of populations. This adaptive aspect of systems of land usage was used by Ester Boserup (1965) to explain agricultural growth as a response to increases in population density. Boserup has been optimistic about the ability of developing nations to meet their growing needs through agricultural innovation. Such optimism must be coupled with the caution that many innovations are deleterious over the long run. In order to predict whether or not technological inputs will ultimately have a positive impact, indigenous socioeconomic systems must be studied as they have evolved and as they interact in their ecological contexts.

• NOTES •

1. George P. Murdock, in "Ethnographic Atlas: A Summary," *Ethnology* VI (April 1967), classified 239 of the 862 societies in the atlas as being in Sub-Saharan Africa. In the study cited, Vaughan included Ethiopia, the Horn of Africa, and certain Muslim societies located south of the Sahara that Murdock did not classify as "Sub-Saharan Africa" (Vaughan 1977:23).

• SUGGESTED FURTHER READINGS •

Allan, William. 1965. *The African Husbandman*. Westport, Connecticut: Greenwood Press.
Evans-Pritchard, E. E. 1940. *The Nuer*. Oxford: Oxford University Press.
Hammond, Peter B. 1966. *Yatenga*. New York: The Free Press.
Horowitz, Michael M. 1979. *The Sociology of Pastoralism and African Livestock Projects*. A.I.D. Program Evaluation Paper No. 6. Washington, D.C.: United States Agency for International Development.
Lee, Richard. 1979. *The !Kung San*. Cambridge: Cambridge University Press.
Ruthenberg, Hans. 1976. *Farming Systems in the Tropics*. Oxford: Clarendon Press.
Turnbull, Colin. 1961. *The Forest People*. New York: Simon & Schuster.

·9·

Traditional Social Formations

RONALD COHEN

The first version of this article was written more than fifteen years ago for a three-volume set of readings, course materials, and bibliography that introduced Americans to *The African Experience* (Paden and Soja 1970). Much has changed in Africa, in America, and in anthropology since then, and the present essay addresses a multidisciplinary audience concerned about the problems of food in Africa. For people interested in African development it is important to obtain some understanding of traditional sociopolitical structures, i.e., those ways of feeling, believing, and behaving that have evolved in African societies. Accordingly, this chapter focuses on descriptive categories that distinguish Sub-Saharan African social formations from those in Western societies. African societies in the 1980s are complex and include many untraditional features, including some borrowed from Western societies, but traditional categories continue to be useful in understanding continuity and change in contemporary Africa.

For Africa, the term "traditional" refers to that quality of African social life for which contact with the Western world was not a significant part of the lives of the majority of the population. The concept of tradition thus refers to social life in which the direction of change and development in society is primarily determined by indigenous events and patterns of behavior. The concept of tradition may also refer to a condition in which neither leaders nor the masses are dedicated to the goal of changing the nature of their society. Such rapid and planned change is a primary focus of national ideology in modern Africa and is promoted actively by the state. In summary, traditionalism reflects a genuinely indigenous quality in each society and culture whose social and cultural institutions are rooted in its own adaptations to its own patterns of growth. This does not suggest that either mode, the traditional or the modern, is necessarily more valuable. Each has its own value in its own context. The Africans themselves and the conditions of their lives ultimately determine the mix of traditional and modern elements included in the development of their societies.

· THE INDIVIDUAL IN TRADITIONAL AFRICAN SOCIETY ·

Like all individuals, an individual African operates within a social system. The prevailing common feature in the African social tradition is the primary value that is placed on social relations regardless of the particular form of organization of the society itself. This strong bias in traditional cultural values and personal attitudes to life implies a greater overlap of "we" and "me" than occurs in contemporary Western societies.

Experience teaches Africans that group membership is necessary for marriage, for political membership in a community, and for obtaining a livelihood. Corporate kin responsibility is widespread throughout Africa, and the social security of kin membership has often been noted. Examples of kin responsibility are found in the treatment of those accused of crimes or moral offenses against neighbors. In patrilineal northern Nigeria an accused man must appear in court with his brothers, father, and perhaps his father's brothers and father's father. If the man is fined by the court, then all people related to him through the male line, both men and women, are responsible for payment. In matrilineal northwestern Zambia, accused men are accompanied to court by their brothers, sisters, mothers, and mothers' brothers and sisters. The appearance of family shows support, in fact all those related to an accused man through the female line are responsible with him to pay any fine.

Social advance in rank usually involves obtaining and maintaining an increasing number of social relationships. Also, an increase in the number of social relationships traditionally follows greater income or wealth. Although increased wealth may be spent on new consumer goods in modern Africa, in traditional Africa greater income or wealth requires a concurrent increase in the number of dependents, which results in more prestige and feelings of achievement for the individual concerned.

Within the sphere of traditional values, prescriptions clearly focus on interpersonal relations (Read 1959; Cohen 1967). Nigerian parents admonish their children constantly about norms (rules for behavior) to be learned concerning interaction with people. These are not abstract standards such as "honesty is the best policy." The Kanuri of Borno, Nigeria, say to their children "you must treat so-and-so in such-and-such a way" or "remember to take your shoes off when you pass in front of the chief's house" or "your religious teacher surpasses your father [in fatherly qualities]." Literally dozens of specific prescriptions about interpersonal behavior are drilled into children at a very early age.

The cultural contrast between traditional African values and those of Europe and the United States is dramatized by African writers and novelists. In William Conton's novel *The African,* the hero rages against "the European's exaggerated individualism, his constant exalting of the single human being, at the polls, in the classroom, and in the sight of God" (Fisher 1961). To suggest that Western life is antithetical to African life in terms of social relationships is misleading. However, the tradition in Western cultures that leads us to admire individuals who sacrifice social relationships for ideals when necessary is in sharp contrast to African cultures in which the value of social relations is considered to be the most important guide for individuals.

In contemporary Western societies the solitary hero is admired as one who acts in accordance with ideal standards of values rather than submitting to social pressures. On our television screens the cowboy combats evil in society and then rides off alone into the sunset. The viewer feels that the moral purity and Samson-like strength of the hero are revitalized in his solitary communion. Popular entertainment thus dramatizes an ideal of individualism which, in the life of the more average person, is eroded and corrupted by social and economic necessities of daily existence. Africans, conversely, feel that only through social life may the highest ideals of morality be realized. Among the Kanuri of Nigeria, for instance, the man who lives alone is called *ngudi* ("unfortunate"). He is not to be trusted because his lack of social ties indicates that he may not be bound by the moral precepts of his own society.

Traditional identities still represent strong personal loyalties. Therefore, in spite of the many decisions affecting a person's life in modern Africa that are made by bureaucracies, very strong social forces operate to maintain and even strengthen older identities. Traditional links with people in bureaucracies are used to obtain access to scarce resources such as scholarships, trade licenses, jobs, or government contracts. Opposing this tradition today are government attempts to create equal rights for all citizens, the impersonality of modern urban life, and the contractual nature of modern employment.

Kinship in Traditional Africa

Every individual born into an African society is a member of a local residence group and kinship system. In some cases these are the only organizations in the society, but in other cases these are the smallest scale social units that become embedded in larger organizations. In all cases, kinship involves three categories of interpersonal relations: genealogy, descent, and marriage.

Genealogy and Descent

Genealogy refers to relationships between an individual ("ego" in kinship terminology) and those persons related through a network of biologically traceable links. Relationships formed by genealogical links are less important to the social system than relationships formed by descent or marriage. Descent is an aspect of kinship that refers to the way in which loyalties, obligations, rights, and duties are passed on to succeeding generations. From the point of view of ego, descent refers to patterns of rights and obligations of new members born into a family with respect to other members of the family. Descent has a variable capacity to create groups that may act corporately. Descent groups are behaving corporately when they hold property in common and act as political units, marriage units, and even economic units.

The degree of corporateness is generally high for unilineal descent groups but low or absent for bilateral, or cognatic (the more commonly used term), descent groups. In bilateral descent groups, ego reckons descent through both biological parents and all four grandparents; in unilineal descent groups, ego reckons through only one parent, rendering corporate activity easier than in bilateral descent groups.

In Africa there are three types of unilineal descent: patrilineal, or agnatic, which reckons through males only; matrilineal, or uterine, which reckons through females only; and duolineal, sometimes called double unilineal or bilineal. Duolineal descent describes a situation in which ego is a member of two unilineal descent groups. The difference between bilateral and duolineal is that in bilateral groups ego is related by descent to four grandparents, but in duolineal groups ego is related by descent to only two grandparents, the mother's mother and the father's father.

One study estimated that the dominant descent principle is unilineal for 85 percent of African societies and cognatic for 15 percent of them.[1] Three quarters of the unilineal descent groups are patrilineal. Most of the remaining one quarter are traditionally matrilineal, and a small number of groups, almost all in West Africa, have duolineal systems. Why these regularities of patrilineal and matrilineal descent exist on a continent as large and as diverse as Africa is an important question, but one for which there is yet no clear answer. Unilineal descent groups are widely used for organizing corporate activities and social life. The adaptability of these groups is enormous, serving multiple functions across a wide spectrum of activities, and the means for their continuity are simple and universal—marriage and birth.

Matrilineal descent is associated with hoe agriculture, and there is a so-called matrilineal belt running from the Atlantic Ocean to the Indian Ocean across south-central Africa. Any tendencies to move away from a reliance on hoe cultivation seem to provoke tendencies to move away from matrilineal descent. The correlation between nomadic pastoralism and patrilineal descent is one of the oldest and best established in anthropology (Hobhouse et al. 1915:150–154). In the usual sexual division of labor, men care for herds of animals, and herds are easily and efficiently maintained as a corporate holding among a group of persons related through the male line (agnates) who live off the herd. Animals may be exchanged in connection with marriage alliances or sold to defray the direct costs of a marriage celebration, thereby making possible the recruitment of wives who continue the group through childbearing.

Division of descent groups into "nesting" or segmentary units seems to be a function of population mobility, within a geographic context. The less an African group has remained in settled stable villages using the locality itself (residence groups) as a basis for social organization, the greater the tendency for individuals in the group to unite on the basis of actual descent (lineages) or putative descent (clans). In a mobile population such as the northern Somali, several million people may be linked into one overall patrilineal descent system.

In agricultural terms, the social relations defined by an individual's descent group determine the individual's rights to use and to inherit farmlands and livestock as well as access to special resources such as bottom lands, other specially fertile lands, fishing and hunting rights, irrigation, wells, and tools. Although in both patrilineal and matrilineal systems women may inherit as well as men, in a patrilineal system inheritance tends to pass from a man to his sons, and in a matrilineal system inheritance tends to pass from a man to his sister's sons.

Marriage

The third category of kinship (after genealogy and descent) is relationship by marriage. Although there is a bewildering number of different marriage forms in Africa, some patterns predominate. Marriage inception almost always entails some form of material consideration or value provided by the groom and his group of kin, friends, and supporters to the bride and her group. George Peter Murdock (1959) estimated that compensation is provided in almost 90 percent of African societies: 80 percent is in the form of bridewealth payments and 10 percent is in bride-service arrangements. Bride-service means that the groom works for the bride's family for a period of time. For only one percent of the societies sampled is marriage inception accompanied by a payment (dowry) from the bride's group. A woman is traditionally considered to be of value to the prospective groom and his group, and to obtain such value some compensation must be made to the group surrendering the woman. Her value lies partly in her fecundity as a childbearer and partly in her contributions to the work force of the group she joins through marriage.

Marriage inception patterns in Africa differ for primary and secondary marriages. Primary marriages are first marriages for one or both partners; secondary marriages are subsequent unions. Generally in Africa women marry at an earlier age than men do; sometimes women marry before puberty. The later the individual's age at primary marriage, the less stringent are the rules of premarital chastity. Secondary marriages are less formal and less expensive than primary ones. Parties (men and women) to secondary marriages have more freedom to arrange the union independently than do parties to primary marriages. (The degree of increased freedom allowed depends also on age and social status.)

Both single spouse marriages (monogamy) and plural marriages (polygamy) are found in Africa. Polygamy may be subdivided into polygyny, in which a man has more than one wife, and polyandry, in which a woman has more than one husband. Polygyny is rather common traditionally in Africa, but polyandry is rare. Although common, polygynous societies in Africa do not practice the custom uniformly: in some of these societies only a minority of people actually live in polygynous families, but in others well over half of all marriages are polygynous at any given time.

Family Life

Family life in Africa may be classified into two types: (1) families that include only one married generation with their children (nuclear families)—these comprise 56 percent of our sample of African societies; (2) variant forms of extended, often polygynous families in which marriage units from two or more adjacent generations, linked by descent ties, live together as a family—these comprise 44 percent of our sample.

Family cohesion is related to the corporate quality of descent groups, which is expressed in kinship terms that sometimes confuse Westerners. Western bilateral kinship traditionally gives ego only one mother and one father, biologically and socially, and only the other children of that mother and father are addressed or referred to as brothers and sisters. African kinship terms often merge people of the same descent group and generation, for example the mother and her sisters may be referred to using the same "mother" term, and the father and his brothers by the same "father" term. In a patrilineal society all of the children of the "fathers" may be termed "brothers" and "sisters" to each other; the same is true for the children of the "mothers" in a matrilineal society. The sibling relationship is used to refer to people who Westerners would just as ambiguously refer to as cousins because they share no biological parents. Thus, there are varying degrees of proximity among persons who use sibling terms. Proximity may be expressed through the use of genealogical linkages, for example, people sharing the same father and mother, or the same father but different mothers, or fathers having the same father. In widely ramifying descent systems, sibling terms may be used for people sharing the same clan. At the level of the nuclear family, the distinction between full and half siblings is important at the death of a parent: full siblings still share a parent, but half siblings may have lost the parent who united them. The tendency for half siblings to break up at this point and go their own ways is a function of this genealogical difference between them.

Marital unions are more or less stable depending upon descent type, rural-urban residence, socioeconomic status of the husband, fertility of the wife, and the degree to which the wife is absorbed into her husband's group. Rural marriages are more stable than urban ones; marriages with low status husbands, more stable than those with high status husbands; fertile marriages, more stable than infertile ones; and marriages in which wives are highly absorbed into husbands' groups, more stable than those in which wives are not highly absorbed. Patrilineal descent is associated with a more stable family life than is matrilineal descent; bilateral descent is associated with both high and low stability. In general, traditional African marriages are less stable than Western marriages, even though there are celebrated cases such as the Nuer of Sudan and the Zulu of South Africa among whom divorce is rare or nonexistent.[2]

The great majority of marriages are patrilocal, or virilocal, which means that the wife moves to live with her husband, who may be living with a group of his agnates. In patrilocal societies with high divorce rates, many children lose household contact with their mothers. At divorce, the mother leaves the husband's house generally taking only unweaned children, who may have to be returned to their father's house when weaned. Children whose parents divorce in these societies must adjust to living with their mother's former co-wives or with subsequent wives of their father who become senior females in the household.

The relationship of co-wives is a difficult and tenuous one at best. Given widespread polygyny, the probability that a traditional marriage may involve co-wives is fairly high. Relations with the shared husband are defined by rules that protect what might be called a right of equal treatment, or as nearly equal as possible. The inequality of the man to woman ratio in such a marriage creates scarcity (access to the husband) and competition among wives. Such tensions are carefully controlled by rules. Among the Kanuri of Nigeria, a man must take nightly turns with each wife in his sleeping hut or room, whether he has sexual relations with her or not. To avoid such a responsibility is tantamount to open conflict.

A very widespread variant of the equal treatment rule is the situation of the senior wife, the first women married by the husband. She has special privileges and is regarded as the senior female authority in the household of her husband. Usually such authority continues down the marriage order; thus marriage order itself is the basis of a status hierarchy among the women. Varying degrees of sexual attractiveness, domestic skills, fertility, the importance of a particular wife's own descent group, and other qualities of the wives tend to influence the ordering and create jealousies and tension among co-wives.

The Household

The most impressive change in our understanding of African societies is the shift in emphasis by researchers away from descent groups and toward the domestic group or household (Guyer 1981). Although it is difficult or even impossible to know how African societies work without considering kinship arrangements, the central element today in the analysis of consumption, production, interpersonal relations, and personal success and failure is the household. Most farm-level studies use this working definition of household: the social grouping that eats together and works together most of the time. Households produce, buy, and sell food, and household members usually plan and decide as a unit how food will be distributed, stored, and sold (see McMillan in this volume).

Because of the changes associated with individual life cycles, households are structurally dynamic. Meyer Fortes (1958) noted three phases in the household group cycle. First, an expansionist phase occurs from the inception of marriages through the births of children, this phase being limited by the duration of the wife's fertility. Second, a fissioning phase occurs as children mature and move or marry out. Finally, a replacement phase occurs as the second generation assumes the roles of the parental generation.

High divorce rates mean that marriages are unstable, but households continue whether they lose or gain members. Households expand and contract due to births, marriages, deaths, and the gain or loss of servile members; they are much more enduring than marriages. As a result of unstable married life, the subsidiary unit, or the household, emerges from the broader descent group to serve as the primary unit of property ownership, the center of production and consumption relationships, and the smallest organized unit of the community.

The traditional ideal in Africa is a large, usually patrilocal extended family household with as much polygyny as economically possible. Starting with a husband and wife, the unit grows by adding wives and children, having the sons bring in their wives, and adding the children of the sons and their wives, etc., until often four generations live together in a large compound. Complex roles of conduct govern relations in such large units; life may be smooth and rewarding for those living in such arrangements that are well managed and cooperative. Traditionally, it is not uncommon for the unit to break up after the death of the compound household head. Some members then start their separate households, quite near each other if housing, farmlands, and good relations allow. In most areas, a wife moves to the husband's household at the time of marriage; so households lose daughters, as they grow up and move away, but gain unrelated women as new wives. At the death of a husband, especially in strongly patrilineal groups, the wife or wives often remain as members of the household, becoming wives to other males of their deceased husband's lineage, thus keeping intact the marital ties between lineages. This practice whereby brothers inherit wives of dead brothers is known as the levirate.

Power, success, labor, and status stem traditionally from large successful households. It is not surprising, therefore, that kinship is not the only means of adding members. African households often increase their size by adding foster children, apprentices, servants, debt servitude workers, and runaway in-laws who seek refuge among those whom their sisters married. Previously, slavery was another means of expanding households (Miers and Kopytoff 1977). In West Africa, it is not uncommon to find successful men heading households of forty or fifty people.

Households as agricultural production units are systems of jointly cultivated, dispersed farm plots under the direction and ownership of the household head. Adult men and women in a household may also cultivate a few farm plots on their own in addition to those directed by the household head. Land acquisition and ownership is a complex and changing mixture of communal and individual rights that requires a full chapter on its own (see McMillan in this volume). Most men, and often women as well, also work at occupations other than farming. This off-farm work is important to households because growing seasons are not year-round. Household members may do the same off-farm work or have different jobs. Thus, households are complex economic units with a flexible capacity for autonomous economic activity by each adult member. The degree to which the unit acts cohesively is a function of the relative ages of its members, how well they get along together, the managerial skills of the household head, and the autonomy strivings of the junior members.

Surveys of households in many parts of West Africa indicate that household heads may have different goals than other members (Ancey 1975). Heads want to run self-sufficient production and consumption units. They want annual and inter-annual security in economic and political matters and the corresponding prestige, leisure time, and social cohesiveness of the household. They want to be able to meet their social obligations, and they consider land access and ownership and political/administrative obligations to be important and linked. On the other hand, other household members may see off-farm income and marketed cash cropping and autonomy as their most important goals.

Two important and controversial trends are emerging to change traditional patterns. One is that the large extended family compound still exists in Africa, but there is a measurable trend away from it and towards nuclear or polygynous families. Recent researchers have found that up to 50 percent of rural households are nucleated, i.e., made up of two-generation families restricted to parents and children (Norman et al. 1981), although older data showed that about 33 percent of all households were nucleated (Smith 1955). There are grounds for hypothesizing that with increased mechanization, paid labor, and commercialization the tendency to nucleate households will accelerate (Cohen 1984).

The second trend is toward increasing reliance on paid labor. The number of people living as servile, nonkin members of households has been declining slowly since slavery ended at the beginning of this century. Other forms of servility are costly because the people must be clothed, fed, and housed. The use of paid labor, on farms especially, has been growing for both rich and poor households throughout Africa, and this trend makes it less necessary to keep a large household as a labor force (see Lennihan 1983). Labor is an important resource for more productive agriculture, and hired labor used at the right time in planting and land preparation may produce up to one-third more crop (Cohen 1984; Bernal 1985). Rural schooling for children decreases their farm work contribution, thereby increasing the need for hired labor.

In sum, African households have traditionally been the center of production and consumption and are the principal units of property rights and the basis for farming. They vary in size depending on individual and marital cycles and the power and success of the manager of the compound group. Changes today are toward smaller households and the use of paid labor instead of kin and dependent servile members for labor purposes.

Wider Scale Social Organization

Community patterning refers to the forms of organizations in which localized groups of people, in households and kin groups, interact with one another. Such units may be based on specific, fixed geographic areas or on larger, sometimes shifting systems of alliances founded on marriage or descent or both. Among the settled villages of West Africa, marriage and descent lines might not correspond;

geographic boundaries between these villages are well known, although they may change over time due to ecological, political, or economic conditions of the specific locality. On the other hand, community boundaries among the Tonga of Zambia can be defined as (1) neighborhoods, localized areas in which people have rights to use land, and (2) vicinages, wider groupings that include several neighborhoods and are defined as areas in which intermarriage between groups takes place (Colson 1970). All people outside of the vicinage are considered aliens, and among aliens the non-Tonga speakers are foreigners. Because vicinage is defined by affinal ties, it is a shifting set of alliances rather than a fixed one. Community boundaries in such cases cannot be said to be fixed. They are stable at any one time, but vary with the interaction (marriage) patterns of community members.

Another criterion for characterizing community organization in Africa is the mobility-stability continuum. Murdock (1959) developed a series of eight categories along a continuum. At one end of the scale are fully migratory or nomadic bands. Next are seminomadic communities whose members wander in small bands for at least half the year but occupy a fixed settlement at other times. Third are communities that shift as a whole from one fixed settlement to another, as in cases of floodplain living, or cases in which a majority is nomadic during part of the year while a remnant group stays behind to occupy the settlement. Fourth are communities with compact, but impermanent settlements that shift every few years, usually because of soil depletion. Fifth, increased locational stability is found in communities made up of dispersed neighborhoods, family homesteads, or households. Sixth are communities composed of separate small families in which several separated units are perceived locally as a single community. Seventh, more stable communities are those made of compact and relatively permanent settlements, not much different in structure and functions from one another. Finally, the most stable are complex communities in which a local village, town, or even city is surrounded by satellite outgrowths, hamlets, and households.

These categories do not account for the sometimes temporary, sometimes permanent, relocation of people fleeing drought or war, as in the Sahel and Horn of Africa in the 1970s and 1980s; nor do they account for the forced relocation in new territory of formerly stable groups subjected to the expansionist pressures of neighboring peoples. Thus there is another form of mobility characterizing such groups as the Tiv of Nigeria and the Nuer of Sudan. African governments have also engaged in planned resettlement to achieve a variety of humanitarian, development, and political goals. Planned resettlement projects include the forced relocation of refugees from wars and civil disorders and of other peoples who have lost their homes due to the damming of rivers, infestation with tsetse, drought, and famine (Hansen and Oliver-Smith 1982).

• POLITICAL ORGANIZATION IN TRADITIONAL AFRICA •

The ways in which African communities are organized politically reflect ecological, historical, and political factors in the society at large. A traditionally separate political sector does not always exist, and there is widespread lack of differentiation among functions in a majority of traditional African societies. Constituted authority not only serves strictly political functions, but is often responsible for a wide variety of economic, social, and religious activities. Although many of these community responsibilities have been diminished, even severely curtailed with the incorporation of local groups into modern nation-states, the traditional authorities continue to be important in most areas whether they are officially recognized or not.

Traditional polities, or independent political units before incorporation into colonial states, may be divided into two types: centralized and noncentralized (locally autonomous). Although there are varieties of political systems that seem to hover between these two basic types, the distinction is nonetheless useful and applies to a large majority of traditional African authority systems.

Noncentralized Societies

The least complex level of polity is hunting and gathering bands that may include twenty to fifty people each. Heads of constituent household units confer on decisions and resolve conflicts within the band (see McGee in this volume). Unresolved conflicts may lead to band fission, although such an outcome is generally considered to be injurious to all concerned because the resource base must then be divided. There may or may not be a headman; if there is, his power is limited.

Noncentralized agriculturally based polities have more problems than hunting bands over continuity of membership, rights to property, and prerogatives of office. As groups settle down into more or less permanent villages, however, the locality itself, rather than descent groups, tends to serve as the organizing basis for community relations. The more sedentary of locally autonomous societies commonly subdivide (fission) and use village subgroups as jural communities or polities. Once formed, these subgroups tend to become autonomous with regard to one another, although links among such units continue and vary with descent, trade, marriage, and political alliances for defense, and aggressive attacks on others.

Descent groups, in differing ways, form the core around which communities develop, as indicated over and over again in the anthropological literature on Africa. For example, when patrilineal descent and patrilocal residence practices come together, as they often do in Africa, then a core settlement of agnates starts to grow. Each adult man may head his own household, while linked as well to his agnates in surrounding houses. The senior male of the core heads the organization and represents it, either to other settlements or to neighboring wards of a village or town. In-marrying women provide and represent affinal links to other lineage groups nearby, as do out-marrying women of the descent group. Later arrivals include noncore members who agree to recognize the leadership of the headman.

Older, respected members of each lineage or of a large successful household often form a group of "elders" who meet and talk over village affairs. Major decisions, dispute settlements, and even marriage choices may come under their authority.

Crosscutting such lineage links, especially in eastern and southern Africa, are age-set organizations. These organizations generally unite all members of a community within specified age brackets. Such age groupings may provide specific services to the community. For example, those in older age groups act as leaders, authorities, and decisionmakers, and in the past, young men invariably assumed military roles, which in some cases involved enforced bachelorhood. A somewhat different crosscutting function is served by the widespread use of initiation rites and secret society memberships. Such initiations among locally autonomous sedentary peoples of Africa unite young boys within a community and often within several neighboring communities. Boys are removed from their families, tutored in sacred lore of the adult male societies, then reborn into their communities as beginning adults. The secret societies of initiated men enforce community norms, punish immoral or criminal behavior, and reinforce traditions of male dominance by fusing it with the power of supernatural entities who support community rules and authority—all dramatic means of social control.

Centralized State Systems

Chieftaincies and centralized states were found in many areas of precolonial Africa. The political structure, organization, and functions of these societies were dramatically changed by colonialism and later by integration into modern nation-states. Although they are no longer independent political units—all are now incorporated into or fragmented by the present nation-states—they represent an important category of traditional political organization and merit discussion.

Community patterning of precolonial states and chieftaincies was similar in most cases to that discussed for localized autonomous societies, with some important differences. Recruitment to office was through traditional lineage or clan organizations, and the jural community was enlarged in scale beyond that of the local settlement or clan group. Disputes were settled at various levels in an authoritative hierarchy: from local household heads to village heads to the chiefly offices beyond the village. Chiefs very often fulfilled functions in addition to that of conflict resolution; they were generally religious leaders, and as military commanders they united their peoples against outsiders.

These traditional African states varied in the degree to which they were able to maintain centralized control over their constituent parts (Vansina 1962:324–325). Generally these states were multiethnic polities that maintained some form of central bureaucratic organization surrounding a monarchy with dynastic qualities. Problems existed ubiquitously in relations between the central government and its constituent local settlements, in relations between the kingdom and surrounding peoples, and in the methods used to recruit personnel into the political system. The last problem was the major determinant of centralized power, which varied with the hereditary rights to office of subordinates in the state. When these rights were not clearly hereditary, or when slaves or eunuchs were used in positions of authority, the state was more centralized in the monarchy. When rights to power positions were more stringently hereditary, authority was more decentralized, and the monarch and kingdom were weaker.

Centralized political authority solved problems of organization that arose when local groups coordinated control of their external relations with surrounding groups. Some of these problems were isolated. First, difficulties resulted from the increasing cultural heterogeneity within a polity as it absorbed groups from outside. Associated with this issue were problems of social stratification among the various groups within the society. Second, there were problems when a group moved into a new territory and subordinated the local population. In this case the leaders could have established a dynasty. Third, there were problems when groups surrounding a centralized state were stimulated to emulate it for reasons of power, prestige, and defense. Fourth, there were problems when locally autonomous groups attached themselves to nearby ritual leaders in order to share in the blessings of supernatural powers. Fifth, new states could have been formed when vassal or tributary states became independent, or when integral parts of older states broke away under the leadership of dissident factions, royal usurpers, or rebellious nobles.

The Concepts of Tribe and Ethnic Group

A final aspect of traditional African society is of great importance and is extremely difficult to capture in any definitive sense. This is the concept of a whole society. Dubbed "tribe" in the past, this concept has given birth to contemporary ideas of tribalism and detribalization—usually urbanization and the loss of identity in the modern situation. Yet, as noted in this chapter, traditional African political patterns do not necessarily correspond to cultural or ethnic groupings. In addition, in Africa and elsewhere, political and cultural or ethnic identities have been forming, reforming, and disappearing for literally thousands of years.

Race and language are not clearly bounded within Africa's so-called ethnic entities. Vast numbers of Africans, perhaps most Africans, are multilingual, so language differences are not necessarily barriers between groups. Descent groups; language groups; religious groups; residential units such as towns, cities, local regions, and subregions; and even occupation, especially with respect to pariah activities such as blacksmithing, serve to give identity and a quality similar to ethnicity to segments of populations that subdivide so-called tribes and may even cut across several widely recognized ethnic groups.

Then what is an African tribe? The simple answer often used by former colonial officials, journalists, and political parties in contemporary Africa is that tribe refers to named groups possessing a common identity and a recognized cultural distinctiveness that form politically significant divisions in a nation. It often goes unnoticed that so-called tribes may have great internal variations, even named subgroups. Moreover, people define their own groups, even though the identity and composition of groups change through time (Fried 1968) due to complex reasons (Cohen and Middleton 1970).

An important point, seldom mentioned by the nonspecialist, is that a tribe is never an immutable entity. On the contrary, it is exactly the opposite. To be understood at all, the tribe must be seen as an adaptive identity that changes in relation to internal and external forces. Once this point is clear, it becomes nonsense to speak of reverting to tribalism or ancient tribal rivalries. Partly to emphasize the changing nature of tribe, and partly to allow more comparatively useful and acceptable units, social scientists in Africa and beyond are increasingly using the term "ethnic group" to refer to recognized culturally distinct groups that are significant units within modern nation-states. Processes of ethnic change and development and the relation of these ethnic groups to the nation-state are important foci for research in Africa today, as they are elsewhere in both the more-developed and less-developed countries of the world.

· CONCLUSION ·

To name something does not necessarily mean to know it. In Africa there are clusters and categories of peoples who have some traditional similarities with one another. Whether these clusters represent any real units in the past or in the present is a matter for research rather than speculation. Social formations are not fixed. They evolve out of fundamental human needs and environments that are shared by groups of people. All peoples want a good life for themselves, their families, and communities. The potentialities of local environments and the traditional cultures used to survive in them have influenced not only the development and differentiation of African peoples, but also their capacity to adapt to a changing world. Traditional Africa is not an exotic jigsaw puzzle of tribal groupings. Rather, it represents an important range of living options in our common human attempt to solve the universal problems of human existence.

· NOTES ·

This chapter is a shorter, revised version of an essay by the author entitled "Traditional Society in Africa," in *The African Experience: Volume 1: Essays,* ed. John N. Paden and Edward W. Soja (Evanston: Northwestern University Press, 1970), pp. 37–60. Used by permission of the publisher.

1. The quantitative data for the generalizations in this paper were obtained through the facilities of the African Data Bank, Council for Intersocietal Studies, Northwestern University. Sampling ranged in size from fifty-five to ninety-two and represented all areas of the continent. The author wishes to express gratitude to the program for permission to use

these materials and to Dr. Joseph Kaufert for helping with this segment of the work.

2. This statement implies comparison with countries such as the United States, where divorce rates in the 1960s reached 25 percent, i.e., 25 percent of all marriages ended in divorce. I define a high divorce society as one in which there is a greater than 50 percent chance that any union entered into will end in divorce, i.e., there is a greater chance for divorce than for nondivorce termination.

• SUGGESTED FURTHER READINGS •

Cohen, Ronald, and John Middleton, eds. 1970. *From Tribe to Nation in Africa*. San Francisco: Chandler.

Gibbs, James L., Jr., ed. 1965. *Peoples of Africa*. New York: Holt, Rinehart & Winston.

Guyer, Jane. 1981. Household and Community in African Studies. *African Studies Review* 24:87–138.

Hart, Keith. 1982. *The Political Economy of West African Agriculture*. Cambridge: Cambridge University Press.

Hyden, G. 1980. *Beyond Ujamaa in Tanzania*. Berkeley: University of California Press.

Norman, David, et al. 1982. *Farming Systems in the Nigerian Savanna*. Boulder, Colorado: Westview Press.

Murdock, George Peter. 1959. *Africa: Its Peoples and Their Culture History*. New York: McGraw Hill Book Co.

Onwuejeogwu, M. Angulu. 1975. *The Social Anthropology of Africa*. London: Heinemann.

·10·

Agriculture, Food, and the Colonial Period

R. HUNT DAVIS, JR.

The colonial period, dating from the 1880s to the 1960s, had a decisive impact on the course of African history. During this time, Britain and France governed most of the continent, joined by Belgium, Portugal, and Spain as rulers over smaller pieces of territory. Germany and Italy also possessed colonies in Africa, but Germany lost its colonies after World War I, and Italy forfeited its possessions as a result of World War II. South Africa, in effect an independent country after 1910, also exercised colonial control over South West Africa (Namibia). Only Liberia retained its sovereignty throughout the colonial era, and this was largely due to its position as part of the "informal" empire of the United States.

Colonialism meant more than just foreign rulers. In addition to the loss of political control, Africans also lost much of the economic control over their lives. Furthermore, colonial rule came at a time when the world itself was beginning a great change, as the interlocked forces of the industrial and social revolutions and the new imperialism of the late nineteenth century produced basic structural transformations. Coinciding with the colonial period was the birth of a new period of world history—contemporary history—which was separated by a real gulf from the preceding period of "modern" history. Geoffrey Barraclough (1967:9) noted, "We live today in a world different, in almost all its basic preconditions, from the world in which Bismarck lived and died." European colonial rule over Africa and much of Asia was one of the many forces that were to shape the outlines of contemporary history. For Africans, therefore, the colonial period came at a critical juncture—not only was there alien rule, but it was also a time of basic structural, social, economic, and political change for Africa and for the world as a whole.

Decisive though the colonial period was, assessing its impact on agriculture and other aspects of African life remains a matter of debate among historians (Davis 1973). Central to this debate is the question of whether the colonial or the precolonial period was the more crucial in shaping independent Africa. One interpretation stresses the centrality of the colonial period for understanding the most

151

recent era. Variations of this approach can either stress the positive aspects of colonialism—its contribution to the integration of Africa into the modern world through such developments as the introduction of Western education and medicine; the building of roads, railways, and ports; and the establishment of modern forms of government—or its negative aspects—the alienation of African land, the exploitation of African labor, the general disruption of the fabric of African life, and so forth. Whether the emphasis is on the positive or the negative aspects, however, the conclusion remains the same: the colonial period represented a decisive break with Africa's past.

A counterargument to the first interpretation is that the colonial period must be viewed in the context of African history as a whole. The colonial period has an obvious importance for the present, but no more so than any of the other periods in African history. The colonial period introduced new factors, but the ecology, economic factors unrelated to Europe, quality of leadership, and political problems and opportunities that affected the precolonial past were and continue to be significant. Indeed, some scholars such as Crowder (1968) argued that colonial rule had little impact on the lives of ordinary Africans. Historians who hold this perspective thus assert that "African development has run in an unbroken line from its most distant origins until the present" (Davidson 1969:3).

The third interpretation, which became prominent in the 1970s, is that of the dependency school. Basically, it consists of those disillusioned with independent Africa's seeming inability to develop itself. Taking their cue from the dependency theorists of Latin America, historians of this persuasion have written in terms of the "development of underdevelopment," producing works such as Walter Rodney's *How Europe Underdeveloped Africa* (1972). The colonial period thus can be seen as the final and most important stage in making Africa an economic appendage of the West.

As noted above, the three divergent interpretations all revolve around one central question: Which aspects of the African past best explain the African present? This question is also the principal concern of this chapter. How far must we go into Africa's past to understand the roots of current food problems? Clearly, developments during the colonial period made a significant contribution. In one of the classic statements of the current food crisis, Carl Eicher noted that

> the crisis stems from a seamless web of political, technical and structural constraints which are a product of colonial surplus extraction strategies, misguided development plans and priorities of African states since independence, and faulty advice from many expatriate planning advisers. These complex, deep-rooted constraints can only be understood in historical perspective (Eicher 1982:157).

Yet there were also agricultural and other developments prior to the colonial period that led in part to colonial strategies for the production and extraction of surpluses; events since independence have a contributory role as well. Therefore, although a discussion of agriculture and food during the colonial period forms the heart of this chapter, it is also necessary to consider briefly developments both before and following that era.

· EARLY AGRICULTURE IN AFRICA ·

Agriculture in Africa resulted from a process that was evolutionary in nature, spanning a lengthy period of time for each of the domesticated crops or complex of crops rather than stemming from a series of specific events. Local circumstances determined the pace at which different populations changed from food gathering to food production. In general, compelling reasons growing out of stresses on existing food systems were necessary to cause people to adopt stock keeping or cultivation or both. The diversity of crops, techniques, and traditions also suggest that farming emerged at various times in divergent areas of the continent, rather than from a single center of diffusion or a nuclear area for the development of plant domestication. Thus, from its inception food production in Africa involved the initiative of farmers in terms of adopting innovations when these changes became manifestly advantageous.

When did Africans first begin to farm? This question is asked frequently, as Thurstan Shaw conceded by noting: "In the present state of our knowledge any consideration of the beginning and development of agriculture in Africa must largely be a survey of our ignorance and a reasoned essay in speculation" (Shaw 1976:107). The archeological evidence indicates that wheat and barley entered Egypt from Asia not later than the sixth millennium B.C. It is likely, though, that the sites of earlier cultivators lie beneath the silt of the Nile delta. Archeological evidence also suggests that millets and wheat were grown in the central Sahara perhaps as early as 6100 B.C. and millets were grown in Mauretania at Dhar Tichitt by the middle of the second millennium B.C. In southeastern Africa, domesticated millets appeared before the end of the first millennium A.D. The archeological evidence, however, cannot answer the question of whether domesticated millets were in use in Sub-Saharan Africa for five hundred or five thousand years before that date (Shaw 1976).

Regardless of when food production took hold in various parts of Africa, it is clear that farming was well established throughout the bulk of the continent by the time the American crops—manioc (cassava), the sweet potato, corn (maize), and peanuts (groundnuts)—entered the scene after 1492. These crops spread rapidly, and frequently displaced earlier staples. Maize, for instance, became the most widely cultivated food plant in Africa long before the colonial period. African farmers demonstrated a receptiveness to new crops when the farmers recognized the advantages of the new crops over existing crops—namely that maize provided higher yields than existing cereals and that manioc could be harvested throughout the year and was resistant to drought and locusts (Hogendorn 1975:284–285).

Food production led to trade in agricultural commodities, part of the wider range of trading activities that were associated with a settled agricultural way of life. Generally, due in part to the high bulk/low value ratio of food and the absence of suitable transport, trade in agricultural products took place in local and regional markets in exchange for both local goods and those that came via the long distance trade routes. In West Africa in particular, the trade in agricultural commodities developed to a significant degree as part of the overall growth of advanced commercial networks. Sufficient cotton was raised in Nigeria, for example, to supply a textile industry in Kano that on the eve of the colonial period was said to serve two-thirds of the population of the western Sudan. Kola nuts from the Ashanti region of present-day Ghana constituted a highly valued agricultural commodity that was widely traded throughout West Africa, especially after the Islamic revolution of the late eighteenth and early nineteenth centuries (Hogendorn 1975:287). The slave trade also helped promote the production of foodstuffs for sale since it was necessary to feed both the slave cargos and the ship crews during the trans-Atlantic voyage.

• THE PRECOLONIAL CENTURY •

A principal feature of African agriculture in the colonial period was the large-scale production of cash crops for external markets. The roots of cash-crop agriculture, however, lie largely in the precolonial century. African farmers, as noted previously, had long been involved in selling some of their crops in local and regional markets. In limited instances, such as with kola nuts or the sale of foodstuffs to provision slave ships, cash crops had even emerged. Major portions of the continent had also been commercially linked with Europe through the slave trade (which had been based upon previous well-developed commercial systems, particularly those in West Africa). Industrialization in Europe, the emergence of the "humanitarian factor," and the abolition of slave trade—all developments that became important during the decades bordering on 1800—had combined to produce the era of "legitimate commerce" that was to last until the onset of colonial rule. Herein lay the first extensive production of cash crops for external markets. Commercially oriented agriculture also emerged in South Africa in association with the expansion of European colonial rule[1] and in East Africa where Arab-owned plantations had begun producing for external markets.

Industrialization in Europe had created a demand for raw materials from the tropics, especially for oil from palms and peanuts. At the same time, industrialization had helped create a political and economic climate conducive to ending the slave trade, which in turn had led to a sharp growth of slave labor within Africa that could be turned to agricultural enterprises. The palm plantations of the king of Dahomey constituted one example. Another was in Senegambia where "enterprising traders took their domestics and slaves down with them to the vicinity of the sea and had them grow ground-nuts," thus establishing the basis for the later migrant farmers of the region (Freund 1984:63). The new European demand had produced a sharp expansion in trade. For palm oil alone, British imports from West Africa grew from one thousand tons in 1810 to ten thousand tons in 1830; twenty thousand tons in 1842; thirty thousand tons in 1853; and forty thousand tons in 1855. Thereafter they averaged fifty thousand tons per year from 1860 to 1890. Peanut exports were negligible in the 1840s, but were to average twenty-nine thousand tons a year by the late 1880s (Hopkins 1973:128). This dramatic growth led one economic historian to conclude: "While the ratio of 'planted' to 'gathered' palm oil in total exports cannot be calculated, the fact of its existence, when coupled with ground-nut production, justifies the claim that for the first time in West Africa's economic history the international economy had an influence on the choice of crops and techniques employed in agriculture" (Munro 1976:48).

Along with the production of cash crops, two other features from the colonial economy affecting the relationship of agriculture to overall economic development had strong roots in the precolonial century. The first of these was the purchase of imported manufactured goods with the proceeds from exports. Manufactured goods had long been imported in small quantities along the trans-Saharan trade routes, and European slave traders had purchased their human cargos with textiles, frequently produced in Bengal, and other manufactured goods. The era of legitimate commerce saw a sharp upsurge in imports. "For instance, the quantity of cotton goods (measured by the yard) exported from the United Kingdom to West Africa increased thirty times in the short period between 1816–1820 and 1846–1850" (Hopkins 1973:128). The familiar colonial and postcolonial pattern of agricultural production for external markets, which provided income to purchase imported goods, thus was firmly established prior to the colonial era. Furthermore, this exchange not only failed to promote the development of domestic manufacturing but frequently undermined it through a flood of imports, as occurred in the Kano textile industry.

The second feature was the gradual intrusion of European merchants into the continent, who in turn forced aside their African counterparts. During the slave trade era, Europeans in most instances purchased slaves from African traders at the coast. Initially, Africans served almost exclusively as the middlemen in the sale of cash crops to European merchants. These transactions again took place at the coast. Starting in about the mid-1800s, however, British merchants pushed up the Niger with steamships, and French merchants penetrated the Senegal interior. In the process they usurped the middleman role from Africans, setting the stage for their full domination of large-scale commercial enterprise during the colonial era.

Although West Africa was the principal region for growing cash crops for exchange with European manufactured products, there were also important developments in the commercialization of agriculture elsewhere. In South Africa today, few Africans are able to earn a living from the land, and productive farming is almost exclusively the preserve of South African whites. However, prior to the massive loss of ownership and access to the land, and the rapid population growth of the twentieth century that intensified pressure on the little land that remained in their hands, African agriculturalists in South Africa responded to market opportunities. They adopted new tools and crops and became engaged in the money economy. Indeed, a distinct peasant class topped by a strata of small farmers flourished in the latter part of the nineteenth century (Bundy 1979). White farmers were also important, but they were not nearly as dominant in agricultural production as they later became. Elsewhere, commercially oriented plantations gradually emerged along the East African coast and islands during the mid-1800s as the Arab aristocracy began to use slave labor to produce export crops such as cloves, copra, and sesame seed. In contrast to the growing cash-crop economy of West Africa, however, the Arab plantations in East Africa did not provide a basis for agricultural expansion—essentially they were dead ends (Munro 1976:55; Freund 1984:70).

• THE COLONIAL PERIOD •

The colonial period grew out of developments that preceded it, particularly those of the precolonial century, but it also marked a dramatic break with the past. African dependency on the West was not a foregone conclusion in 1880, but by 1960 it was firmly in place. The changing conditions that produced the greatly altered relationships inherent in colonialism lay largely in Europe. Two major forces—the rise of the new nation states in Europe, primarily Germany and Italy, and the second industrial revolution that led to the geographical spread of industrialization that increasingly utilized science in the production process—combined to produce the "new" imperialism of the late nineteenth century. One result was the colonial conquest of Africa. As indicated earlier, there was a gradual expansion of European enclaves during the precolonial century, but most of Africa remained under indigenous rule in 1880. However, by the eve of World War I England and France had pushed into the interior from their various enclaves, vying with each other in their efforts to gain territory; Portugal had expanded its holdings in southern Africa in an effort to keep from being completely squeezed out; Germany and Italy had entered the fray; and a single individual, King Leopold of Belgium, ruled the single largest colony, the Congo Free State (also known as the Belgian Congo, now Zaire), as his personal possession—in fact, Europe ruled the entire continent except for Liberia and Ethiopia.

Europeans conquered Africa to benefit themselves primarily in two ways: to obtain commodities that they needed and to secure markets for their manufactured goods. Colonialism was essentially exploitative, although attempts were made to justify it in terms of "the white man's burden" or a "civilizing mission." Its purpose was to benefit the colonizers and not the colonized, and the purpose was the same whatever the nationality of the colonizer. Policies for securing maximum benefits from the colonies varied significantly, depending on the resource base of individual colonies as much as, if not more than, on the identity of the colonial power. Therefore, the following discussion approaches developments affecting agriculture and food in the colonial period more in terms of the resources available to the colonial rulers than in terms of the overall African policies of the various colonial powers. In other words, differences within the British empire in Africa were as great or greater than those between the British and French empires in Africa.

The initial colonial conquest involved the extensive use of force in both political and economic terms. Europeans used their military might to wrest political power from the hands of Africans. Forced taxation, forced cultivation, and forced labor constituted principal features of the economic systems of the early colonial era. Nowhere was force as intensively applied as in King Leopold's Congo. In order to generate the necessary capital for the colony's infrastructure, Leopold turned over large areas to concession companies. The companies resorted to mass terror to enforce the collection of wild rubber (demand for tires and other rubber products made rubber a highly profitable commodity). Although useful in the short run for establishing both economic and political control, in the long run the raw use of force proved incapable of developing the potential of the colonies to benefit the metropolitan countries. Exceptions such as compulsory cultivation in Angola and Mozambique notwithstanding, by the end of World War I the era of force had given way to other forms of exploitation (Freund 1984:114–118).

Mining was the most successful means colonial rulers had for extracting wealth from their colonies. Where mineral resources were available, they served as the core of the colonial economic system. The first great mineral discoveries were in South Africa; the discovery of diamonds there in 1867 was followed by discovery of the gold reefs of the Transvaal in 1886. Ultimately, the "revolution of diamonds and gold" in South Africa and the industrialization that followed were to destroy African cash-crop agriculture in that country. "European-owned mining and agricultural enterprises would compete with African agrarian societies for the resources [i.e., labor] necessary to production for the international economy" (Munro 1976:82). Copper became the mainstay of the Congolese economy by 1920 and of the Northern Rhodesian economy beginning in the 1930s. Tin mining flourished in northern Nigeria, and mining was also important in Southern Rhodesia. Most colonial territories, however, lacked significant mineral deposits or they lay untapped until after World War II. For instance, iron mining only became important in West Africa in the 1950s when production boomed from 70,000 to 2,180,000 metric tons between 1947 and 1957 (Munro 1976:179).

Early colonial authorities considered white settlers to be excellent agents for developing colonial territories, and there were many precedents of white settlers' involvement in development including those of South Africa and Algeria within the African continent. However, although small numbers of white settlers existed in many colonies, they never constituted the core of the economy except in Kenya, Southern Rhodesia, and (somewhat later) Angola and Mozambique.[2] Aside from South Africa, Kenya was the premier settler colony. Its commercial base depended mostly on white-owned farms. The success of these farms depended largely upon the protection they received from the colonial state. For example, African smallholders were prohibited from growing the profitable arabica coffee, and maize production was not promoted in Nyasaland (Malawi) in an effort to protect the markets for Kenya's white farmers. A few major European-owned plantations also emerged such as the Firestone rubber plantation in Liberia, Unilever palm oil plantations in the Belgian Congo, sisal plantations in Tanganyika, and sugar estates in Mozambique. These enterprises, though individually important, lacked major economic significance for the continent as a whole. After World War II, the export boom of the African economies enabled white settlement to increase rapidly. At the same time, however, Africa was moving rapidly toward independence. White settlers sought to entrench themselves politically, especially in Rhodesia with the 1965 Unilateral Declaration of Independence, but they failed in the attempt, except in South Africa where they had long held political sway.

Faced with a need to develop the economic potential of their colonies, lacking mineral resources in most of them, having learned that white settlers were not generally a satisfactory means for economic development, and having had commercial experience with trade in African-produced cash crops, colonial authorities in most territories soon settled on smallholder production of export crops. This smallholder production of export crops became the major means for supplying raw materials that would benefit the colonial powers and generate revenue to run the colonies and pay for imported goods. The focus on African-produced cash crops in turn had major implications not only for agriculture but for the overall development of the colonies. The remainder of this chapter focuses largely on the principal cash crops and how export agriculture affected the overall colonial economies. In turn the independent African states inherited these economies.

From the beginning of the colonial period the authorities specifically encouraged African smallholders to produce cash crops. After World War I, during the heyday of the colonial era, the colonial governments launched large-scale development projects to further the production of these crops. Some projects, such as the Gezira cotton scheme in the Sudan that began in the 1920s, enjoyed a considerable degree of success. Others, such as the mechanized peanut scheme in Tanganyika in the late 1940s, were disasters. For the most part, however, governments used direct taxation and various forms of promotion, such as the distribution of seeds, as ways to increase the production of export crops. The incentive of earning cash income to purchase consumer goods also stimulated cash-crop production. The result was to link Africans in an unprecedented way to the international economy.

The principal peasant cash crops of the colonial era were cotton, cocoa, peanuts, and palm products (kernels and oil). Coffee became important in the 1930s, though much of it was grown on white-owned farms or on plantations. The production of other important cash crops such as sisal, tobacco, and tea was largely under control of whites. Although African farmers grew export commodities throughout the continent, the greatest region of activity was in West Africa (see Table 10.1). Prior to World War II, cash crops were the mainstay of all but a few of the colonial economies; after the war, cash crops increasingly shared the spotlight with expanding mineral production. Those colonies with the most favorable weather tended to grow the crops, while neighboring areas served as reservoirs of labor. For example, the production of cocoa and palm products in West Africa took place in the southern forest zones, while the interior savanna regions provided migrant laborers to do the work of raising and transporting the crops.

Growing realization of the importance of cash crops led the colonial authorities to pay attention to their production. Where white settlers were important to the colony, Africans were excluded from growing export crops. Africans in Kenya were prohibited from growing coffee for this reason (Eicher 1982:20–21).

In some colonies the authorities also continued to utilize force to compel Africans to grow cash crops, as occurred with cotton and rice production in Mozambique (Vail and White 1978). For the most part, however, Africans were not under direct compulsion to raise export crops nor did they find themselves excluded from such activities. More typically, colonial governments combined basic economic incentives, such as direct taxation and the need for cash to purchase imported goods, with active promotion of specific crops. Often, however, government efforts at encouraging cash crops failed to produce significant results. On other occasions, African farmers took the initiative and established major export crops without government backing. The histories of cotton and cocoa illustrate these two contrasting outcomes.

From the start of the colonial era cotton was the cash crop that received the greatest attention. Indeed, the first major large-scale colonial development project, the Gezira scheme in the Sudan, produced cotton. The emphasis on cotton stemmed from the widespread nature of the textile industry in Europe. Not only was there a high demand for cotton products in Europe, but cotton goods also found a ready market in the colonies. Even an underdeveloped country such as Portugal was able to have a textile industry and find both the raw materials and the market for the finished product in its colonies. Thus cotton well exemplifies the heart of the colonial relationship: the colonies produced raw materials and imported manufactured goods, often made from the raw materials they exported. Not only did colonial governments discourage the growth of industries that could process cash crops locally, but the increasing availability of cheaper imports undercut existing industries such as the textile industry in Kano. A further result was that cities in Africa did not, for the most part, develop significant industrial labor forces, which in turn would have stimulated African agricultural production for internal markets.

The success of cotton as a smallholder crop was uneven. In Uganda, cotton production zoomed upward starting about 1905 and reaching substantial proportions by 1928 (see Table 10.1). Although the chiefs, who retained considerable authority, played an important role in the spread of cotton, small farmers also actively adopted the crop for the income it produced. The Gezira scheme was another success. In most areas, however, efforts at promoting cotton production yielded poor results: in Nyasaland (Malawi) inadequate information on the part of agricultural officials, wrong-headed efforts at enforcing certain planting times, diseases, pests, and other factors severely hindered the crop. During the first decade of the century, authorities promoted cotton growing to settlers. When settler production failed, the authorities sought to induce African farmers to grow cotton. The outcome, however, was largely a failure. In some areas, efforts at promoting cotton production failed due to the lack of sufficient economic incentives. British authorities attempted to push cotton in southern Nigeria, but plant diseases and pests hampered the effort as well as competition from cocoa, which provided a much more attractive alternative cash crop. In northern Nigeria, low fixed purchase prices provided little incentive to farmers. In the end, the peanut boom that began with the arrival of the

TABLE 10.1. Principal Export Cash Crops From Africa During the Colonial Period (1,000 tons)

Crop / Country/Region	Year								
	1895	1905	1920	1928	1934	1938	1941	1950	1955-58
Coffee									
Angola					16.4			33.9	72.8
Belgian Congo					17.0			33.4	58.9
Ivory Coast					1.3	10.1	28.0	57.7[a]	115.4[a]
Kenya		1.1	3.5	7.9		17.7			
Tanganyika						13.7			
Uganda		0.2	0.2	6.0	14.8	12.6		57.2[b]	120.0[b]
Cotton									
Belgian Congo (fibre)			0.02	9.6		42.0		51.0	42.0
French Equatorial Africa			4.2	0.8	5.0	9.0			
French West Africa					3.9	8.3			
Nigeria		1.9			4.6			12.8	30.5
Uganda		0.2		6.0		80.0		71.1[b]	93.4[b]
Sudan				36.0		62.7		66.5	86.7
Cocoa									
Cameroon			2.5		21.0	31.0			
Gold Coast	0.01	5.0	125.0	225.0	230.0	263.0	271.2	228.3	
Ivory Coast			2.5	16.0	26.0	55.0		61.8[a]	66.0[a]
Nigeria		3.9		45.0	63.0	96.0		101.6	109.1
Togo					8.6				
Bananas									
Cameroon				0.1	4.0	17.0			
Guinea (French)						22.0	53.0		
Peanuts									
Gambia		58.0	41.0	75.0		50.0			
Nigeria				109.0	189.0	250.0		321.9	422.1
Senegal		220.0		410.0	520.0	601.0[a,d]		200.3[a]	306.5[a]

Palm Kernels							
Belgian Congo					85.0		
Cameroon					36.0	84.6[a]	87.3[a]
Dahomey					52.0		
French Equatorial Africa					13.0		
Ivory Coast					36.0		
Nigeria	121.0	174.0	255.0	275.0	334.0	416.8	440.3
Sierra Leone					78.0		
Togo					13.0		
Palm Oil							
Belgian Congo					66.0	132.0	140.2
Cameroon					8.9	11.8[a]	15.2[a]
Dahomey					16.6		
Nigeria	54.0	78.0	125.0	139.0	122.0	175.8	179.2
Sisal							
Kenya	5.0	15.0	18.0		31.0		
Tanganyika	21.0		73.0		107.0	163.3[b]	226.5[b]
Tobacco							
Southern Rhodesia	1.6		9.6		9.2	43.4[c]	64.8[c]

Sources: For 1895-1941, Bill Freund, 1984, The Making of Contemporary Africa (Bloomington: Indiana University Press), pp. 141-42; for 1950 and 1955-58, Peter Duignan and L.H. Gann, 1975, Economic Achievements of the Colonizers: An Assessment, in Colonialism in Africa, 1870-1960, Volume IV, The Economies of Colonialism, edited by Peter Duignan and L.H. Gann (Cambridge: Cambridge University Press), pp. 628-83.

[a]French West Africa
[b]British East Africa
[c]Rhodesias and Nyasaland
[d]Duignan and Gann also provide figures for 1938, which are in general agreement with those of Freund except for peanut production for French West Africa. Their figures are 169.4 in contrast to the figure of 601.0 which Freund provides.

railway in Kano in 1912 doomed cotton-growing efforts. Similar results occurred in French West Africa (Hogendorn 1975:312–316; Munro 1976:128–129; McCracken 1982:102–105).

The history of cocoa as a cash crop differs considerably from that of cotton. First of all, African initiative was responsible for the introduction and growth of the cocoa industry. The Gold Coast (Ghana) was the site of the largest and most sustained development (Hill 1963). African farmers initially turned to the crop to replace palm oil, which was in decline, and production soared during the first two decades of the twentieth century (see Table 10.1). Major capital investment was required on the part of the producers. Prior to World War I, tens of millions of cocoa trees, which took six to seven years to mature, were planted annually by hired laborers paid cash wages on land that often had to be purchased. This investment pointed to the second feature of cocoa—it was tremendously profitable. The 50,600 tons exported from Ghana in 1913 were worth £2,489,000. In fact, the crop was so valuable that for the first twenty years of its development in the Gold Coast human portage was utilized to convey cocoa from its interior production area to the coastal ports. It is little wonder, then, that cocoa was able to gain the upper hand against competing economic alternatives such as palm oil, cotton, and rubber among African farmers in southern Nigeria (Hogendorn 1975:320–324). Only with the depression in the 1930s did cocoa production begin to level off. The depression also provided government officials with an opportunity to intervene in the marketing process through establishing marketing boards, which shifted much of the profit from the farmer to the government for its own uses.

Government encouragement of cash crops for export contrasted sharply with a near total neglect of food crop production. Except for supporting white commercial farmers, i.e., those in Kenya producing corn or in Northern Rhodesia (Zambia) producing foodstuffs for the workers on the Copperbelt, a hallmark of colonial agricultural policy was the almost total neglect of food crops. The focus of colonial agricultural policy, as indicated by its research efforts, was squarely on cash crops. The implicit assumption was that Africans would continue to grow sufficient food for themselves, as they always had. In some instances, as with cocoa, it was possible in terms of available land and labor for staple production to continue. Also, cocoa production tended to stimulate foodstuff production in neighboring areas since migrant workers needed to be fed and had a cash income to purchase food. At the opposite end of the scale was cotton. It interfered with the cultivation of foodstuffs because of the intensive labor demands of the crop, and because it generated very little income for the producers. As a result, cotton-producing areas often had severe food shortages (Freund 1984:131; Berry 1975:169–170). The direct impact of cash cropping on food production in both place and time thus varied considerably. For the most part, however, the key factor was the colonial governments' neglect of staple crops and the technology associated with them, leaving Africa with systems for the production and distribution of food that were increasingly inadequate to the task at hand.

Colonial economic development had other consequences for food production besides the emphasis on export crops and the neglect of food crops. One consequence was the diversion of labor from growing crops for food. Mining, particularly in the southern part of the continent, needed large numbers of African workers. In South Africa, for instance, the agricultural decline of the rural African areas was a direct result of demands by mine owners and white commercial farmers for African labor, demands they were able to satisfy through their monopoly of the political system. Some scholars view the whole of southern Africa as a vast labor reserve for the white-controlled South African economy. Elsewhere on the continent the most significant demand for labor was associated with cash-crop production. In West Africa the major export-producing regions, generally located near the coast, lacked sufficient labor. They thus created a labor demand that had to be met by migrant workers who generally came from the savanna and Sahelian regions of the interior. By the 1920s, sixty thousand to seventy thousand migrant laborers were working annually in the peanut-producing areas of Senegambia. As many as two hundred thousand workers entered the Gold Coast to work on cocoa farms in the 1950s (Hopkins 1973:223–224). In this manner, regions "became informally divided into 'rich' export producing zones and 'underdeveloped' reservoirs of migrant labor" (Freund 1984:135). This process had severe negative consequences for the agricultural sector in the labor-producing zones.

Colonial authorities fostered the development of an infrastructure that can best be described as "lopsided." Those components of the infrastructure necessary to facilitate the export of raw materials and the importation of manufactured goods were built and maintained; those components necessary for the internal development of the individual colonies were ignored. The railway maps of Africa during the colonial period provide vivid illustrations of the distorted infrastructures and the economies they served.[3] With the exception of railways in South Africa, nearly all of the railways ran from port cities on the coast to the interior: their purpose was clearly to support and promote an export economy. There was virtually no railway construction to enhance and encourage development within the colonies. The early realization that the growth of cash-crop production depended upon railway transportation provided a major stimulus for their construction. Even where other motives were involved for building specific railways, as for the St. Louis-Dakar line in Senegal or the Uganda railway, once in place they greatly facilitated cash crops such as peanuts on the Cayor Plain in Senegal or cotton in Uganda. In addition to promoting the spread of cash-crop production, railways also increased the flow of imported consumer goods into the interior and thus undercut local manufacturing (Hogendorn 1975:294–297). Similarly, the principal cities of the colonial period were usually port cities designed to handle the exports and imports vital to the colonial economy. Generally they also were the principal administrative centers. Consequently, their fundamental orientation was outward in nature, and they depended for their existence principally on external economic relationships.

African cash-crop agriculture came into existence to meet the needs of markets outside the continent. In other words, cash crops were for export and not for domestic consumption. Internal markets did, of course, exist for agricultural products. African farmers responded to the economic opportunity these markets presented in the same way that they responded to the markets for cash crops. Yet the overall trend during the colonial period was a diminution in the internal markets for African-produced foodstuffs. In some instances—as in South Africa, Southern Rhodesia, and Kenya—white farmers used their political clout to dominate markets to insure the sale of foodstuffs they produced through the utilization of lowly paid African labor. In other cases, imperial policy created markets in Africa for food produced elsewhere in a colonial empire: in French West Africa a major market was created for rice French planters grew in Indo-China.

Economic policies that favored imported goods over locally manufactured products also hindered the growth of markets for African foodstuffs by hampering the growth of an urban African wage labor force. Furthermore, the infrastructure of the colonies, geared as it was toward exports, did little to promote internal agricultural markets. Food-producing areas, unless along the line of rail, lacked adequate transport. Other farm-to-market links were also neglected. Finally, the infrastructure of support services for agriculture was totally oriented toward export crops, white commercial farmers, and land settlement schemes. For instance, the post–World War II expansion of biological research in Nigerian and other West African research institutes "was heavily biased toward export crops with repercussions for the development of staple food crop technology in the future" (Forrest 1981:224).

A final factor for consideration is that of demographic changes and their relationship to the production, distribution, and consumption of food during the colonial era. By 1980 Africa faced a food crisis that resulted in part from population growth having outstripped food production. Rapid urban growth in recent decades has made increasing numbers of Africans rely upon purchasing food rather than growing their own. Yet the cities in which they live are inadequately linked to the food-producing areas. A contributing factor has been the urban bias of most African rulers. At the end of the colonial period, population growth had not yet exceeded Africa's food production capabilities and, until the 1950s, towns in tropical Africa tended to remain small. The roots of the gap between population growth and food production, and the basis of urban growth and bias, however, lie in the colonial period. In the first place, Africa's population expanded at an increasing pace during the colonial period, perhaps by as much as 1.3 percent per year between 1930 and 1950 and by another 30 percent over the decade 1950–1960. The emphasis on cash-crop agriculture and the neglect of food crops, however, left Africa ill prepared to increase or even to maintain per capita food output, especially once urban growth became a factor—that is when each rural producer had to feed more and more people. Since the colonial infrastructure did not effectively link the urban with the rural areas, African farmers could not ship sufficient quantities of the food they did produce to the cities. Finally, the ruling elite incorporated the urban bias that had its roots in the education and training these Africans received during the colonial period. Thus once the new rulers assumed political office, like the colonial authorities before them, they neglected food production.

· THE COLONIAL LEGACY ·

At independence, Africa's agricultural structure and food production capabilities were substantially different from what they had been prior to the colonial era. Africa's new leaders were not in a position to depart radically from the agricultural strategies of their colonial predecessors, even if they were so inclined. Cash cropping, which had developed along the fringes of the continent during the precolonial century, constituted the principal economic entry into the world economy for the majority of newly independent African states. Intent upon building "modern" societies, which by the very definition of the time were oriented toward the urban sector, Africa's rulers continued to emphasize export crops in order to generate the foreign exchange earnings they considered necessary for (and were so advised by Western experts) modernizing their countries. Those aspects of the infrastructure needed for exports (mineral or agricultural) continued to receive attention, thus building further on the structural lopsidedness inherited from the colonial era. For example, the primary purpose of the major railway construction project of the independence era, the Tanzam Railway in Zambia and Tanzania, was to facilitate the export of Zambia's copper. And in Sudan the government undertook a major extension of the Gezira cotton scheme.

Africa's new rulers focused their attention on the cities, where ordinary people sought economic opportunity and an escape from the imagined drudgery and dullness of the rural areas. With independence, some of the resources that had previously flowed overseas were diverted to Africa's booming cities. To generate sufficient funds for urban development, African governments continued the marketing boards that their predecessors had established. To insure cheap food in urban areas, thereby insuring political stability, the governments extended the domain of marketing boards to include food crops. By necessity and by choice, however, urban areas imported much of the food they consumed from abroad. Thus earnings from agricultural and mineral exports went increasingly to import foodstuffs. Not only had Africa become dependent on external sources for manufactured goods, it was becoming increasingly dependent on many of those same sources for the food it consumed.

The economic growth of the postcolonial state in Africa rested, as had that of the colonial state, to a considerable degree on the farming population. If anything, however, African governments neglected farmers even more than had the colonial authorities. Burgeoning cities claimed so great a share of the return generated by exports of cash crops that producers of the cash crops received insufficient return for their commodities. This situation was exacerbated at times by low prices on the world market and eventually led to a decline in production. Although governments paid some attention to the export infrastructure, they placed far greater emphasis on the infrastructures of the urban areas, including the construction of public buildings that befitted the status of independent nations. In the meantime, planners and policymakers continued to ignore food production, seemingly acting under the assumption that African farmers would continue to produce food as they always had.

It was not until 1980 with the appearance of the Lagos Plan of Action that African governments began to orchestrate their efforts to overcome decades of neglect of the food-producing sectors of the economy and to reverse the per capita decline in food production that had emerged in the 1970s (see Asante in this volume). By this time, however, Africa found itself in the midst of a food crisis. Perhaps no single factor contributing to the crisis has been more dramatic than the population explosion. The number of Africans increased from 285 million to 551 million people between 1960 and 1985. Thus, in the way that the colonial period introduced factors built upon the precolonial heritage, new factors built upon the colonial heritage are being introduced.

What, then, has been the impact of the colonial period on the agricultural history of Africa? How much did it contribute to the food production gap and hunger that constitute the African food crisis of the 1980s? Clearly, the colonial period left a legacy of cash cropping, an export-oriented economy, structural lopsidedness, a reliance on imported manufactured goods, a neglect of food production, a bias toward urbanization and modernization, a diversion of labor away from food production, and the beginnings of an upsurge in population. Not all of these developments had their origins in the colonial period, as the discussion of the emergence of cash cropping and of the gradual growth of a dependence on imported manufactured goods in the precolonial century demonstrated. The first twenty-five years of African independence witnessed the emergence of cities on a large scale, a boom in population, environmental degradation of increasing severity, and political instability. None of these developments were very pronounced in the colonial era, even though they had their roots in that period, yet all have contributed significantly to the contemporary food crisis.

An understanding of why Africa is in the throes of a food crisis must begin with an examination of the impact of the colonial period on African agriculture and on the wider African economy. Between the 1880s and the 1960s, Africa changed from a continent of primarily self-sufficient agriculturalists unengaged with the world economy to a continent with far greater diversities of economic pursuits, whose remaining agriculturalists had, by and large, become inextricably linked to the world economy. As a result of this fundamental transformation, the colonial period established to a significant degree some of the basic parameters for the production, distribution, and consumption of food in Africa.

• NOTES •

1. Although most of the continent remained free of colonial control until after 1880, throughout the nineteenth century there was a steady expansion of colonial rule in present-day South Africa in association with a substantial European settler population. Elsewhere there was a limited colonial expansion that "consisted largely in the seizure of points here and there along the coast which appeared most appropriate for controlling long-distance commerce, often under the cover of suppressing the slave trade" (Freund 1984:73). These included the British in Sierra Leone (1787), at the mouth of the Gambia (1816), on Lagos

TABLE 10.2. Colonial European Settler Population in Africa

Country/Region	Period	
	Pre-World War II	Pre-Independence
North Africa	(1,311,081)	(1,770,000)
Southern Africa		
South Africa	2,003,512	3,088,492
South-West Africa	31,049	73,464
Other	6,068	11,018
Subtotal	(2,040,629)	(3,172,974)
Tropical Africa		
Southern Rhodesia	55,419	221,490
Angola	30,000	172,529
French West Africa	19,061	62,236
Belgian Congo	18,680	109,457
Kenya	17,997	55,759
Mozambique	10,000	65,798
Northern Rhodesia	9,913	74,540
Other	34,639	140,364
Subtotal	(195,709)	(902,173)
Total	3,547,419	5,845,147

Source: Floyd Dotson and Lillian O. Dotson. 1975. The Economic Role of Non-Indigenous Ethnic Minorities in Colonial Africa in Colonialism in Africa, Volume IV. The Economies of Colonialism, edited by Peter Duignan and L.H. Gann (Cambridge: Cambridge University Press) Pg. 612.

Island (1851), and increasingly along the Gold Coast after 1850; and the French founding of a territorially extensive colony in Senegal in the 1850s, and establishment of fingerholds on the Ivory Coast and in Gabon. Portuguese rule, especially in East Africa, actually constricted during the precolonial century.

2. European settler communities in Africa numbered approximately 3.6 million in the mid-1930s and 5.9 million prior to independence. The total population of the African continent in 1960 was approximately 285 million. The greatest settler concentrations were in the north and in the south (the figures for North Africa date from 1931 and 1954 respectively; those for the rest of the continent from 1935 to 1936 and various dates in the 1950s and early 1960s respectively) (see Table 10.2).

3. For an excellent set of maps that show the railways of Africa and their relationship to cash-crop and mineral production areas, see Kwamena-Poh et al. (1982:60–65, 70–71). Railway construction since independence has served largely to entrench the export function of Africa's railway system.

• SUGGESTED FURTHER READINGS •

Berry, Sara S. 1975. *Cocoa, Custom and Socio-Economic Change in Rural Western Nigeria*. Oxford: Clarendon Press.

————. 1984. The Food Crisis and Agrarian Change in Africa: A Review Essay. 1984. *African Studies Review* 27:2:59–112.

Bundy, Colin. 1979. *The Rise and Fall of the South African Peasantry*. Berkeley, California: University of California Press.

Freund, Bill. 1984. *The Making of Contemporary Africa: The Development of African Society Since 1800*. Bloomington: Indiana University Press.

Heyer, Judith, Pepe Roberts, and Gavin Williams, eds. 1981. *Rural Development in Tropical Africa*. London: Macmillan Publishing Co.

Hill, Polly. 1963. *The Migrant Cocoa Farmers of Southern Ghana*. Cambridge: Cambridge University Press.

Hogendorn, Jan S. 1975. Economic Initiative and African Cash Farming: Pre-colonial Origins and Early Colonial Developments. In *The Economics of Colonialism in Africa, 1870–1960*. Peter Duignan and L. H. Gann, eds. Pp. 283–328. Cambridge: Cambridge University Press.

Munro, J. Forbes. 1976. *Africa and the International Economy, 1800–1960: An Introduction to the Modern Economic History of Africa South of the Sahara*. Totowa, New Jersey: Rowman and Littlefield.

Palmer, Robin, and Neil Parsons. 1977. *The Roots of Rural Poverty in Central and Southern Africa*. Berkeley: University of California Press.

Yudelman, Montague. 1975. Imperialism and the Transfer of Agricultural Techniques. In *The Economics of Colonialism in Africa, 1870–1960*. Peter Duignan and L. H. Gann, eds. Pp. 329–359. Cambridge: Cambridge University Press.

·11·

African Soils:
Opportunities and Constraints

HUGH POPENOE

Many different causes have been proposed for the food problem in Africa, the only major continent where per capita agricultural production is declining. Seldom is mention made that Africa is less endowed with suitable growing conditions than other major world regions. No volcanic chain is running the length of the continent as in Latin America nor are large delta areas present as in Asia. Much of the continent is also affected by an erratic semiarid or arid climate. All of these climatic and geological features affect the quality, productivity, and management of soils.

This discussion of African soils proceeds from the following definition: soil is a three-dimensional, dynamic, and natural body occurring on the surface of the earth, which is a medium for plant growth and whose characteristics have resulted from the forces of climate and living organisms acting upon parent material, as modified by relief, over a period of time. This concept is often expressed in the following form:

$$s = (cl, p, r, o, t)$$

where: s = soil, cl = climate, p = parent material, r = relief, o = organisms (including humans), and t = time (Donahue et al. 1971).

Usually the best agricultural soils in the tropics are "new" soils, those of the large river deltas, in areas of recent volcanic activity, and on not too steep mountain slopes that are continually rejuvenated through the action of mild erosion. In Africa, these soils are concentrated in a very few narrow river basins and in some of the volcanic highlands in East Africa, Cameroon, Rwanda, and Burundi. Much of Africa is very old geologically, and the parent material is acidic or granitic. The topography is mostly flat or undulating, and the derived soils are old, highly weathered and, consequently, low in nutrients. Under a layer of natural vegetation, nutrients are constantly recycled by plants and active earth fauna. Earthworms in some areas are reported to recycle fifty tons of soil per hectare in a year (Nye 1955).

169

Many landscapes are also dotted with termite mounds, which serve to concentrate particles of clay and add some relief to monotonous plains. If this vegetation is removed, much recycling halts, and rains quickly wash nutrients out of the soils.

The distribution of different soil types in Africa is related to climatic patterns. Sandier soils with more nutrient reserves are found in drier regions, whereas soils higher in clay but lower in nutrients are common in wetter areas. Soil moisture is the main limiting factor in the arid and semiarid zones. In the subhumid and humid tropics, soil erosion, nitrogen, and phosphorus are the most significant limiting factors. Some of the most widely distributed soils in the different climatic zones will be discussed in terms of their management problems.

• SOIL AND MANAGEMENT PROBLEMS •

Humid Tropics

The most common soils in the wet equatorial belt are the Oxisols (also known as Latosols or Ferralsols) and Ultisols (alternatively called Red-Yellow Podzols or Acrisols). Both soils are generally acid and low in nutrients. Traditional exploitation has occurred mainly through shifting cultivation and, more recently, by production of plantation crops such as cacao, oil palm, and rubber. Shifting cultivation, although not highly productive, is an easy method of recycling nutrients and controlling weeds, pests, and diseases (Andreae 1980). However, as human population density increases, the forest fallow period decreases and the system begins to deteriorate. Useful alternative subsistence systems include various types of agroforestry, such as the cultivation of annual crops under perennial crops, that diminish the loss of nutrients occurring when annual crops such as cassava, corn (maize), or upland rice are planted as monocultures.

Subhumid Tropics

Alfisols (Red-Yellow Mediterranean or Planosols) dominate the subhumid tropics in Africa, particularly in the western part. Traditionally, these soils have been used for shifting cultivation since they are highly susceptible to erosion. The International Institute of Tropical Agriculture (IITA) in Ibadan, Nigeria, has devoted many resources to the development of more permanent types of agriculture. Although minimum tillage techniques looked promising at first, eventually they proved only to delay soil losses for a few years, and bench terraces have been of little value.

Current work on alley cropping appears quite promising and may be the eventual solution for the production of food crops (Kang et al. 1984). In this system lines of leguminous trees such as *Leucaena* or *Gliricidia* are planted three or four meters apart. At the onset of the rains the trees are pruned to provide mulch for the soil. Firewood or animal fodder may also be extracted. Such crops as corn, cowpeas, or soybeans are planted in the alleys between the trees. In the dry season, the trees are allowed to grow, thus shading and protecting the soil. Such a practice protects the soil against erosion and helps to recycle plant nutrients.

Hydromorphic Soils

These soils might include almost all soil orders but are characterized as soils that occur with a high water table (at least part of the year) or occasional flooding. A recent Netherlands survey team estimated that the wetland area of West Africa is about one-half million square kilometers. These soils are underutilized in many parts of Africa compared with other regions of the world—especially Asia, where these are the most productive soils and have the highest priority for development. Although they are productive, these soils require large investments in reclamation, drainage, human disease eradication, and water control. In spite of these problems, Africa may witness considerable expansion of production in these regions during the next decade.

Wetland rice is one of the most productive crops where water can be controlled. It is also one of the best examples of sustainable agriculture. In China this system has produced continuous crops for four thousand years on the same piece of land (King 1911)! Stability in the system is provided by the influx of nutrients in irrigation water, the control of weeds by flooding, and the high rates of biological nitrogen fixation found in many rice fields. Flooded soils usually have less acidity, less aluminum toxicity, and more available phosphorus than their upland counterparts. One problem encountered in West Africa by bringing these extensive areas into production is iron toxicity. However, this problem can be ameliorated through management practices and the use of crop varieties resistant to iron toxicity. Furthermore, iron toxicity tends to decrease with time if lands are continuously used. There is no doubt that the wetter areas of Africa have the greatest potential for increased food production; they also require the most research in order to overcome biological problems and soil constraints.

Semiarid Tropics

The main limiting factor in this region is the distribution and amount of rainfall. Below normal rainfall in the semiarid tropics results in crop failures, which is why much of the famine in Africa occurs in the semiarid region. A positive factor in the region is that soils are less highly weathered than in the more humid regions and are, therefore, usually less acidic and higher in plant nutrients. Soil crusting may occur, and in some areas salinity may be a problem. Consequently, management techniques are oriented toward the manipulation and conservation of soil moisture.

Several soil management methods have been devised to conserve and concentrate soil moisture. Soil imprinting may be done by hand or with animal-

and tractor-drawn equipment. In this system, pockets are dug or impressed in soil where crops are planted. Sometimes small channels may be constructed that slope down to the impressions. At the beginning of the rainy season, water accumulates in the impressions around the plant allowing a good root system to develop. The pockets also trap organic matter and fine soil particles and partially protect seedlings against wind. The International Crops Research Institute for the Semi-Arid Tropics (ICRISAT) has developed another method that uses tied ridges: small lateral dikes are constructed in furrows, thus preventing runoff and concentrating rainfall. By this method crop yields often double.

One of the main management strategies for the drier tropics is to use appropriate plants that require less rainfall. Since livestock raising is widespread in this zone, browse shrubs and trees have received some attention. With their deep root systems they more efficiently use soil moisture, prevent erosion, and may serve as an important source of browse in the dry season. (However, these need to be protected from grazing for two or three years after establishment.) One popular tree, the *Acacia albida*, bears leaves in the dry season and loses them in the rainy season. Thus other crops can grow beneath these trees during the rains. Since they bear foliage in the dry season, they are an important source of shade and fodder. The firewood crisis in this part of Africa has also promoted much interest in these fast growing trees (see Webley in this volume).

Other edible crops particularly adapted to drier climates are sorghum, millet, Bambarra groundnut, buffalo gourd, tepary bean, and the marama or tsai bean. Sixty-day varieties of corn and cowpeas have also been successfully grown in this region, and two industrial crops—jojoba and guayule—have been recently introduced into several places.

• IMPROVING SOIL FERTILITY •

The two plant nutrients most often lacking in African soils are nitrogen and phosphorus. Either can be replaced with chemical or organic fertilizers. Although the use of chemical fertilizers has increased substantially in recent years and is one of the most cost-effective inputs into agriculture, their manufacture requires large amounts of fossil fuels, which are scarce in most African countries. For a comparison of energy use in fertilizer between developed countries and developing countries (most of which are found in the tropics), see Table 11.1.

The developing countries use a larger percentage of their commercial energy in the agricultural sector, especially in fertilizers, than the industrial countries use. (The manufacturing of fertilizers consumes more energy than any other agricultural activity in developing countries.) Since developing countries must import most of this energy, it poses a drain on foreign currency reserves.

Approximately two thirds of the energy used for fertilizers is used in the production of nitrogen, which is most often made with natural gas. Nitrogen can also be produced in agricultural systems through biological processes. The largest pro-

TABLE 11.1. Share of Total Commercial Energy Used in the Fertilizer and
             Agricultural Sectors of Developed and Developing Countries

Region	Percent of Energy Used In		Percent of Agricultural Production Energy Used In Fertilizer Sector
	Fertilizer Sector	Agricultural Production	
Developed Countries	1.3	3.4	40
Developing Countries	2.7	4.0	68
World	1.5	3.5	45

Source: Mudahar, M.S. and Hignett, T.P. 1981. Energy and Fertilizer--Policy
Implications and Options for Developing Countries. International Fertilizer
Development Center IFDC-T-19.

ducers of nitrogen, leguminous plants (members of the bean and pea family), produce (fix) nitrogen through an association with organisms (*Rhizobium sp.*) in their
root zone. Many food plants such as cowpeas, soybeans, peanuts (groundnuts),
and pigeon peas fix large amounts of nitrogen in this way. Leguminous trees are
used in agroforestry and alley cropping systems because of their nitrogen contribution.

Soil fertility can also be improved through the addition of locally produced
organic materials. In areas where animal production is common, the use of animal
manures increases the nutrient content of soil and improves its structure and water
holding capacity. In one system commonly used in Africa, called "foraging for fertility," animals are allowed to graze or browse in surrounding grasslands during the
day; as nightfall approaches they are penned in small corrals; in the morning they
are released to graze again. The manure that accumulates is removed for use on
small garden plots. In this manner, animals scavenge nutrients from a large area
for people to use in the intensive production of food crops. Many households also
make compost: crop residues, weeds, animal wastes, kitchen refuse, ashes, and
even house sweepings are placed in piles to decompose. The decomposition process eliminates most weed seeds, insect pests, and diseases; thus it yields a fertilizer (or compost) suitable for gardens.

• SOIL EROSION AND CONSERVATION •

Many African soils are highly susceptible to erosion, particularly the Alfisols.
Rainfall is usually more intense under tropical conditions than in temperate climates and thus erosion risks are higher in the tropics. Erosion is greatest on steep
slopes and on bare soils, or soils with poor vegetative cover. The traditional practice of shifting cultivation minimizes erosion since the soil is protected most of the

time by a dense stand of vegetation.

Several methods of reducing soil erosion are commonly practiced. One of these methods, alley cropping, has already been discussed. Planting row crops on slopes so the rows follow contour lines reduces erosion. Several rows may also be alternated with strips of grass so that the velocity of water flowing downhill is reduced, which in turn reduces the water's erosive capacity. Terraces and minimum tillage techniques may also minimize soil losses. The most important systems for erosion control are those that keep the ground constantly covered with vegetation. Farmers in the more humid regions plant several crops such as cassava, corn, cowpeas, squash, and bananas interspersed throughout the same field. Since these crops have different periods of maturity, they are harvested at different times; thus, when one is harvested, the others continue to protect the soil.

• FIRE AS AN AGRICULTURAL TOOL •

Much maligned fire is important in many tropical agricultural systems. Fire can eliminate large amounts of unwanted vegetation; reduce insect pests, diseases, and weeds; and, in some cases, improve the soils. Temperate climate agriculture is favored by cold winters, which break life cycles of weeds and pests. In the humid tropics no such mechanism exists, but fire can perform some of the same functions.

Shifting agriculture, which produces about 60 percent of the food in Africa (Okigbo 1984), utilizes fire to improve soil fertility and break life cycles. In this system the vegetation is felled and subsequently burned; the remaining ash increases the nutrient content of the soil. The farmer extracts one or two crops from the clearing before weeds and pests threaten to overwhelm production. The farmer then moves to a new site and repeats the process. Although nitrogen is lost from the burned vegetation, none is lost from the soil as a direct consequence of fire. Some, however, is lost subsequently by leaching. Ash also improves soil acidity, or pH; this is especially useful where aluminum toxicity may be a problem. The use of fire is also important in many rangeland areas. Since grass is usually more resistant to burning than many broadleaved species, burning reduces competition between the two and the grass can dominate. Burning may also reduce livestock pests such as tsetse fly and ticks. Moreover, the new growth after burning is much more palatable and nutritious for livestock.

• SUSTAINABLE AGRICULTURE, FARM SIZE, AND LABOR •

Much has been written recently about agricultural systems that are ecologically balanced, require low levels of industrial inputs, and do not degrade with time. Wetland rice of Asia is a prime example since many fields have continuously provided annual crops for four thousand years. Obviously, most of the agriculture of Sub-Saharan Africa is much younger and has not withstood this test of time. Shifting cultivation is perhaps the nearest counterpart, but this system is much less intensive and degrades very rapidly if the ideal equilibrium between fallow and cropland is upset by the growth of human populations.

Many African countries are caught in the dilemma of whether to follow an agricultural strategy that seeks to maximize output through large infusions of industrial inputs or one that seeks to develop a more self-sustaining system that reduces reliance on expensive imports. Policies are partly dictated by the amount of nonagricultural resources available in each country, which in turn dictates how much can be imported or manufactured and also the amount of nonfarm employment available. Some countries such as Rwanda, Burundi, and Malawi are following a labor-intensive agricultural strategy by necessity, whereas others such as Nigeria are opting for more reliance on industrial inputs. The dilemma in Africa is exacerbated by the relatively high wages of nonfarm laborers in rapidly industrializing areas, as compared with the wages of farm laborers—nonfarm laborers' wages are four to six times higher than farm laborers' wages. (In Asia nonfarm laborers' wages are two or two and one-half times higher than farm laborers' wages.)

Recent studies in several tropical countries show that food production per area rises dramatically as farm size drops below three hectares (Harwood 1979). Small farms are usually more productive per area than large farms because the smaller system can be much more diversified—such small-farm techniques as kitchen gardens, intercropping, multiple cropping, two- or three-story agriculture, and the use of many different species are difficult, at best, in a large, mechanized system. Also, small farms usually make better use of organic residues and integrate animals into the system. Therefore, a country that wants to maximize agricultural production could develop a strategy to increase the number of small farms. Unfortunately, although small farms produce more per area than large farms, farmers on small farms receive less total income than farmers on large farms. Thus, the question is often asked: should a country maximize agricultural production or income per farmer? One of the most important dilemmas in tropical agricultural production for our times is this trade-off between yields per hectare and income per farmer.

In general, the most effective industrial input for increasing food production is fertilizer. Costs are returned in the same season that fertilizer is purchased, unlike costs for machinery. Fertilizer use is also scale neutral—yields are increased as much on large farms as on small ones. That developing countries use 68 percent of their energy devoted to agricultural production for fertilizer manufacturing (compared to 40 percent for developed countries) indicates that they are confident of the effectiveness of fertilizers. The most important strategy for a country attempting to increase production on small farms is probably to use chemical fertilizers—that is if foreign exchange reserves are available to purchase them.

Unlike fertilizer use, the use of farm machinery is not scale neutral. Farm machines are primarily used to displace labor; the reduced labor costs result in more income for the owner-operator, but reduced labor results in less employment. Therefore, farm machinery is most useful in countries that have an industrial capacity to absorb labor. A problem in many African countries is that farm labor may be scarce; however, in many countries unemployment is very high since urban areas are increasing at the fastest rate in the world largely because of the influx of people from rural areas. Unless labor can be effectively absorbed in the cities, much more needs to be done to make rural employment more rewarding. This is particularly important for the many African countries that have the problem of scarce farm labor. The quick solution of adding farm machinery is often only a temporary panacea. National agricultural strategies should address the labor issue as well as food production. Some countries in other continents have adopted the strategy of development of technologies that increase productivity per farmer while not risking displacing farmers.

· CONCLUSION ·

Some of the opportunities and constraints for increasing agricultural production on African soils have been addressed. The technology to improve food production on a plot of land exists. We can usually tell a farmer how much chemical fertilizer and machinery to use to obtain maximum yields. What we often cannot tell him is whether he should fertilize with chemicals or use machinery. The ultimate answers often depend on policy issues ranging from farm credit, marketing and prices, to the larger issues of farm size, labor absorption, and national strategies.

· SUGGESTED FURTHER READINGS ·

Ahn, Peter M. 1970. *West African Soils*. Vol. 1. Oxford: Oxford University Press.

Food and Agriculture Organization (FAO). 1974. *Shifting Cultivation and Soil Conservation in Africa*. Rome: Food and Agriculture Organization.

Greenland, D. J., and R. Lal, eds. 1977. *International Conference on Soil Conservation and Management in the Humid Tropics*. London: John Wiley & Sons.

International Rice Research Institute (IRRI). 1980. *Soil-Related Constraints to Food Production in the Tropics*. IRRI and New York State College of Agriculture and Life Sciences. Ithaca, New York: Cornell University.

Jones, M. J., and A. Wild. 1975. *Soils of the West African Savanna*. Farnham Royal, Slough, England: Commonwealth Agricultural Bureau.

Moss, R. P., ed. 1968. *The Soils Resources of Tropical Africa*. Cambridge: Cambridge University Press.

National Academy of Sciences (NAS). 1972. *Soils of the Humid Tropics*. Washington, D.C.: NAS Printing and Publishing Office.

Nye, P. H., and D. J. Greenland. 1965. *The Soil Under Shifting Cultivation*. Farnham Royal, Slough, England: Commonwealth Agricultural Bureau.

Sanchez, Pedro A. 1976. *Properties and Management of Soils in the Tropics*. New York: John Wiley & Sons.

·12·

Major Domesticated Food Crops

CLIFTON HIEBSCH
STEPHEN K. O'HAIR

Cereal grains and farinaceous crops are the principal components of Sub-Saharan African diets. These crops provide 65 percent of the nutritional energy requirements in all regions (see Table 12.1) and more than 50 percent in all countries—even those with highly nomadic people such as Somalia or those as cattle-oriented as Botswana. These starchy energy sources, except for cassava roots and plantain, also provide significant quantities of protein due to the large quantities consumed (see Table 12.3). Legume grains are produced and consumed in smaller quantities than these other crops in all regions (see Table 12.2), but are a valuable portion of the diet due to their high protein content (see Table 12.3).

The distribution of staple food crops depends on cultural preferences and adaptation of the crop species to ecological zones defined by rainfall, temperature, and soils. South of the Sahara Desert, zones of rainfall form parallel belts running west to east and then circling clockwise with northern Zaire as the hub. Zones continue southward through East Africa and backtrack westward to the Angolan coast (see Figure 12.1). Moving south from the Sahara and toward the center of the hub, rainfall and humidity generally increase. Cereal grains—millet, sorghum, and corn (maize)—are the major staples from the semiarid regions, where millet is dominant, to the drier forested areas (receiving less than 2000 millimeters of annual rainfall), where corn is dominant. Root crops, principally cassava, and bananas and plantains are the major staples in the wetter forested regions, but corn is also grown there. Rice production is increasing in higher rainfall areas and where irrigation is available, particularly on wet-natured soils. Wheat is adapted to cooler highland areas found in East Africa and southwest Angola. The Sahel, Northeast Africa, and southern Africa are drier regions where cereal crops are the most important staples (see Table 12.1). A wide range of rainfall is found south of the Sahel and in East Africa, where cereal and farinaceous crops are consumed in nearly equal quantities. Due to higher rainfall in Central Africa, farinaceous crops, particularly cassava, are the predominant food energy source. Rice and wheat are

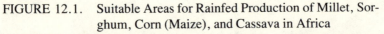

FIGURE 12.1.   Suitable Areas for Rainfed Production of Millet, Sor-
               ghum, Corn (Maize), and Cassava in Africa

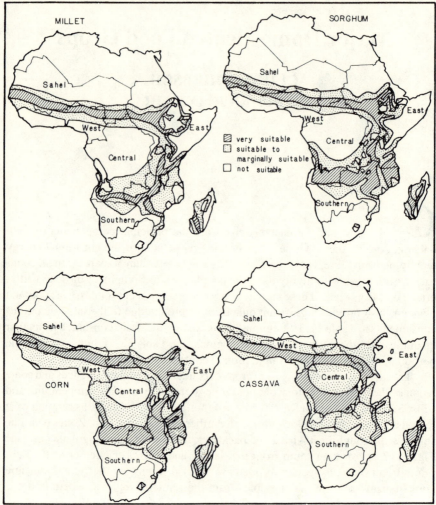

Source: Revised from U.S. Department of Agriculture. 1981. *Food Problems and Prospects in
Sub-Saharan Africa: The Decade of the 1980s.* Foreign Agricultural Economic Report No.
166. Washington, D.C.: U.S. Government Printing Office. Pp. 63–67. Originally from Food
and Agricultural Organization. 1978. *Report on the Agro-Ecological Zones Project.* Vol. 1.
Methodology and Results for Africa. Rome: Food and Agriculture Organization.

becoming major staples among many of the urban populations.
    Leguminous grain crops are produced and consumed in all rainfall belts, or
from semiarid to humid regions (see Table 12.2). The pulses of major importance
are: (1) cowpeas in the drier lowland tropics, particularly of West Africa; (2) lima

TABLE 12.1. Average Annual Production and Per Capita Production Index, 1981-1983, and Caloric Intake, 1972-1974, for Staple Food Crops in Sub-Saharan Africa

African Region[a]	Food Crop Production 1981-1983							Per Capita Index Base = 100 1969-1971 (Percent)	Caloric Intake Percentage 1972-1974		
	Cereals (1000 metric tons)				Roots & Starchy Fruits in Cereal Equivalents[b] (1000 metric tons)					Roots, tubers and	
	Sorghum and Millet	Corn	Rice Paddy	Wheat	Cassava	Other[c] Root Crops	Banana and Plantain		Cereal	Plantains	Total
West Sahel	4167	269	328	--	200	52	--	87	72	3	75
South of Sahel	7250	3547	3007	--	7302	9424	2171	87	41	36	77
Central	100	931	272	11	6616	191	686	89	19	56	75
Northeast	4497	3319	39	1132	50	198	25	85	60	7	67
East	1660	1984	214	87	3197	1108	1675	91	30	35	65
Southern	520	4718	2162	193	1848	232	117	81	59	16	75

Source: Adapted from two reports: (1) USDA (United States Department of Agriculture). 1981. Food Problems and Prospects in Sub-Saharan Africa: The Decade of the 1980's. Foreign Agricultural Economic Report No. 166. Economic Research Service. Washington, D.C.: USDA. Pg. 32. (2) USDA. 1984. Sub-Saharan Africa Outlook and Situation Report. Economic Research Service. Washington, D.C.: USDA. Pp. 31-33.

aWest Sahel and South of Sahel combine to form the West African region in Figure 6.2, except Cameroon is included in South of Sahel due to its proximity and food production similarity to this region.

bRoots, tubers and plantains reported at approximately equal water content as cereals (12 percent) to allow for more direct food production comparison. Average water content and multiplication factor used to convert from fresh wet to dry reported weight are cassava, 64 percent and 0.41, and other root crops and bananas and plantians, 70 percent and 0.34.

cOther root crops include yams, cocoyams, sweet potatoes and white potatoes.

beans in the humid lowland tropics; (3) common or kidney beans in cooler regions, particularly at higher elevations in East Africa; and (4) pigeon peas with a wide range of adaptation and good potential. Leguminous oilseed crops, high in both oil and protein, are peanuts (groundnuts), which are adapted to drier subhumid environments but grown in all regions, and soybeans, which have good potential in subhumid to humid areas but are not now commonly grown.

The declining per capita production of food in Sub-Saharan Africa is of major concern. Except for Ghana, Angola, and Mozambique, all major countries produced more food from 1981 to 1983 than from 1969 to 1971. Yet due to the fastest population growth rate of any continent—2.5 to 3.0 percent growth annually—per capita production of food for all regions was down by 9 percent or more in the same fourteen-year period (see Table 12.1). Per capita food production improved only in Ivory Coast and was within 2 percent of 1969 to 1971 levels in Liberia, Kenya, Rwanda, Burundi, and Malawi. The potential for a per capita increase in food production is great in most areas since the population density and average yields are relatively low. Yields in Sub-Saharan Africa of roots, tubers, and pulses average 70 percent of yields in Latin America and Asia; yields in Sub-Saharan Africa of cereals average 50 percent of cereal yields in Latin America and Asia (U.S. Department of Agriculture 1981).

At one time it was thought that traditional diets low in animal products were the cause of malnutrition, particularly protein deficiency. However, malnutrition generally does not occur unless the normal quantity and variety of food in the traditional diet are restricted by adverse conditions such as those that may occur seasonally or that are experienced by the poorest residents or by adverse changes in eating habits that can occur with urbanization and other forms of migration. The bulk of the diet provides energy from carbohydrates (starch and sugar), oil, and protein sources at recommended levels from 2200 to 3000 kilocalories per day for adolescents and adults. Carbohydrate-rich cereal grains and farinaceous crops (roots and starchy fruits) provide most of this energy, but it may also be supplied by legume grains (see Table 12.3), other plants, and animal products. Protein also is needed in large quantities—29 to 38 grams per day for adults. Protein quality (composition) as well is critical—the building units of human protein are amino acids, eight of which must be supplied at minimum levels by dietary protein (see Wagner in this volume).

The protein requirement can be satisfied by a particular diet if three criteria are met: the total energy supply is adequate, 5.0 to 5.3 percent of the total energy supply is from protein, and all eight essential amino acids are supplied in sufficient quantities. The ratio of energy supplied from protein to total energy supplied (the P/E ratio) is 0.9 percent for cassava, 1.6 percent for plantain, 4.6 percent for yam, 5.9 percent for potato, 4.7 percent for maize, 4.9 percent for rice, 5.3 percent for pearl millet, and 5.9 percent for wheat (Payne 1975, as cited in Aykroyd et al. 1982). These ratios have been adjusted to account for the most limiting amino acid in each food. In order to prevent protein deficiency, high protein supplements can be added to a staple or diet that has a P/E ratio beneath the requirement level.

TABLE 12.2. Average Annual Production, 1981-1983, and Estimate of Supplies for Consumption, 1975-1977, for Legume Grains in Sub-Saharan Africa

| | Production (1000 metric tons) | | | | Daily per Capita Supplies (g/head/day) | | | | |
| | Pulses | | Oilseeds | | | | | | |
African Region[a]	All	Dry Beans[b]	in Shell Peanuts	Soybeans	All	Dry Beans[b]	Cowpeas	Shelled Peanuts	Others
West Sahel	538	--	1044	--	52	15	9	15	13
South of Sahel	1148	151	575	75	29	2	14	9	4
Central	188	133	76	14	30	11	--	15	4
Northeast	1319	32	654	12	36	<1	--	4	31
East	1161	965	213	12	71	43	5	10	13
Southern	359	144	397	87	29	7	2	9	11
Total	4713	1425	2959	200	Mean[c] 38	10	6	9	13

Sources: Adapted from two reports: (1) FAO (Food and Agriculture Organization). 1984. 1983 FAO Production Yearbook 37:132-135. Rome: FAO. (2) W.R. Aykroyd, Joyce Doughty and Ann Walker. 1982 Legumes in Human Nutrition. FAO Food and Nutrition Paper No. 20. Rome. FAO. Pg. 104.

aWest Sahel and South of Sahel combine to form the West African region in Figure 6.2, except Cameroon is included in South of Sahel due to its proximity and food production similarity to this region.

bSpecies of beans in FAO production statistic not indicated. Species in daily per capita supplies mainly common beans (Phaseolus vulgaris) and lima beans (Phaseolus lunatus). Discrepancy for the Sahel may be due in part to the inclusion of secondary legumes such as tepary beans (Phaseolus acutifolius) in per capita supplies.

cWeighted by human population of the region.

TABLE 12.3. Average Nutritional Composition of Major Food Crops and Three Animal Products of Sub-Saharan Africa

Crop Product	Water (Percent)	Energy Kcal/100g	Protein[a] (Percent)	Carbohydrate (Percent)	Fat (Percent)
Cereals					
Corn, meal	12	360	9.5	73.0	4.0
Sorghum	11	340	10.0	73.0	3.0
Pearl Millet	10	330	13.0	65.0	5.0
Rice					
brown	12	360	7.5	76.0	2.0
white	12	360	6.7	81.0	0.4
Wheat					
whole grain	12	350	12.2	70.0	2.5
white flour	12		10.9	78.0	1.2
Roots, Tubers and Starchy Fruits (Fresh)					
Cassava	64	142	1.1	34.0	0.3
Yam	73	103	2.5	23.0	0.3
Taro	74	98	2.0	22.0	0.1
Cocoyam	64	137	2.2	32.0	0.2
Potato	78	82	1.8	19.0	0.1
Sweet Potato	71	115	1.5	27.0	0.3
Plantain	67	124	1.1	31.0	0.3
Banana	74	100	1.4	23.0	0.3

(Recalculated with Percentage of Water equal to Cereals, Grouped by Protein and Averaged)

Cassava & Plantain	12	340	2.8	83.0	0.7
Sweet Potato & Banana	12	345	4.6	80.0	0.8
Yam, Taro, Cocoyam, Potato	12	335	6.9	76.0	0.6
Legumes					
Cowpeas	12	340	23.0	61.0	1.6
Beans	12	340	20.0	63.0	1.2
Pigeon Peas	12	340	20.0	63.0	1.2
Peanuts	12	520	21.0	22.0	43.0
Soybeans	12	390	35.0	31.0	18.0
Animal Products					
Fish, lean fillet		73	17.0	0	0.5
Beef, lean		202	19.0	0	14.0
Egg, chicken		158	13.0	0.5	11.5

Sources: Adapted from three reports: (1) B.S. Platt. 1962. Tables of Representative Values of Foods Commonly Used in Tropical Countries. Medical Research Crops Special Report 301. (2) Stephen K. O'Hair. 1984. Farinaceous Crops. In Handbook of Tropical Food Crops. F.W. Martin, ed. Boca Raton, Florida: CRC Press. Pg. 109-137. (3) W.R. Aykroyd, Joyce Doughty and Ann Walker. 1982. Legumes in Human Nutrition. FAO Food and Nutrition Paper No. 20. Rome: FAO. Pg. 108.

aPrincipal deficient essential amino acids are: lysine among cereals; methionine among roots, tubers and starchy fruits; and methionine and cystine among legumes.

Many animal products and legume grains contain more than double the protein of the starchy staples. Including these animal products and legumes in the diet can significantly raise the total protein content. In addition, cereal grains and legume grains have complementary levels of amino acids in their protein content. Cereal grains are generally most deficient in the essential amino acid lysine, which prevents people from utilizing to the full the more than adequate levels of methionine and cystine. Legumes are high in lysine and low in methionine and cystine. When a cereal and a legume are consumed together, more of the cereal protein can be utilized due to the additional lysine from the legume. More of the legume protein can be utilized due to the increased levels of methionine and cystine from the cereal. A diet of a cereal and a legume in which the legume constitutes 5 percent of the total has a P/E ratio of over 6 percent. In more general terms, if a diet combines both cereals and legumes, then all essential amino acids can be supplied in the ratios needed, making a complete protein.

The proteins of legumes and starchy roots and fruits are not complementary but additive as the deficient amino acids in the two crop groups are the same. Therefore, if a diet of legumes, starchy roots, and fruits is to meet the protein requirement, then larger quantities of legume grains are needed, to compensate for deficient amino acids, in order to raise the protein percentage of the diet after adjustment for protein quality. Processing, such as milling cereals and peeling root crops, can reduce protein quantity and quality.

The most common way to prepare the staple starches is by grinding them into flour, then boiling the flour in water to make porridges of various consistencies, from thin gruels to those that are stiff enough to be shaped. Doughs, which may be first fermented, are made into various breads by boiling, steaming, baking, and frying. Beer is commonly made in most areas. Pulses are boiled alone or in combination with vegetables and spices, and are generally eaten with a cereal or farinaceous crop product. Peanuts are eaten raw, roasted, or as pulses.

· CEREAL GRAIN CROPS (CLIFTON HIEBSCH) ·

Cereal grains are of major importance in Sub-Saharan Africa, providing 45 percent of the total caloric intake. Cereal grains are easy to produce and have fair to good protein content and high carbohydrate supply (see Table 12.3). Seed of cereal crops can be stored for long periods, which makes cereals particularly valuable in regions with intermittent and unpredictable food supplies. This is true in areas of Africa with wet and dry seasons. Cereal grain crops are members of the grass family. Seed have a single unit, producing a seedling with a single seed leaf; seed of legumes such as bean have two seed leaves. The plant is erect with a cylindrical stem that is hollow between nodes, with exceptions of corn (maize) or sorghum. The seed head is formed at the top of the stem, except for corn that forms an ear about halfway up the stem at the base of a leaf. Leaves are attached directly to the stem and are long, slender and tapered with veins parallel to the length. Cereal grain crops are annuals or are managed as annuals, completing their life cycle in one year.

The three major cereal grain crops in Sub-Saharan Africa are corn, sorghum, and pearl millet. Rice and wheat production is small but increasing in certain areas. Rice, corn, sorghum, and pearl millet form a continuum according to their adaptation to available water. Rice performs best under flooded conditions—both naturally occurring flood plains and controlled irrigation—and under heavy rainfall where soils are kept continuously wet. Corn is produced in dryer forested regions or wetter savannahs, where annual rainfall is less than 2000 millimeters (mm) and soils are well drained. In wetter regions banana, cassava, and other root crops constitute the principal starch source. In drier regions, first sorghum and then pearl millet produce crops most reliably. The points of transition from corn to sorghum to pearl millet are gradual, with overlap of regions and even mixing in the same field. The switch from one cereal to another is dependent not only on total rainfall but on distribution within the year, reliability of rainfall within the rainy season, and moisture-holding capacity of the soil. Pearl millet, the most drought tolerant, progressively replaces sorghum as the primary crop as annual rainfall falls below 750 mm; it is the most common crop where annual rainfall is from 400 to 500 mm.: it is produced where as little as 250 mm of rain falls per year. Short season sorghums can be grown in regions with 400 mm of annual rainfall. The differences in tolerance to marginal water supply among crops correspond to a crop's water-use efficiency. Corn, sorghum, and millet—highly water use efficient crops—produce 2.0, 2.4, and 2.5 times, respectively, as much yield per unit of water used as rice produces per unit of water used (Shantz and Piemeisel 1927). Wheat requires cool temperatures and moderate rainfall and performs better at higher elevations.

Fertility management requirements of the five cereal crops are similar; lowland rice is the most unique among them. Management inputs must account for the resources of the farmer and country, as well as the limitations of the crop and environment, to create reasonable yield objectives and to determine practices that are not too costly or risky. Within these constraints, nitrogen is often the most limiting factor for cereal crops. The amount of nitrogen fertilizer needed for a cost-effective yield depends on the supply in the soil, the crop needs, and prices. It generally varies from 0 to 15 kilograms per hectare (kg/ha)—for soils with good nitrogen supply such as newly cleared forest land or for crops with low yields such as pearl millet when grown in drought-prone regions—to 150 kg/ha for high-yielding, well-watered corn. The need to supplement with other nutrients depends upon the supplying capacity of the soil and the needs of the crop and must be determined locally. Nitrogen, phosphorus, and potassium are the nutrients most commonly deficient in soil, but eight others—out of the total of thirteen essential plant nutrients obtained from the soil—occasionally may be the deficient factors that limit cereal crop growth in less usual situations. Each succeeding crop grown on the same plot of land increases the probability of nutrient inadequacy. Nutrients deficient in the soil can be supplied: (1) by growing a leguminous, green manure crop prior to the cereal to supply nitrogen; (2) by spreading ashes from burned vegetation or cook fires (ashes contain all nutrients but nitrogen and sulfur, which are vaporized in the fire); (3) by adding compost or animal manure that have not been leached by rains; and (4) by fertilizer.

The nutritive value of the cereal grains listed in Table 12.3 can vary greatly due to such factors as genetics and processing. For example, the protein content for most types of pearl millet ranges from 10 to 15 percent, but for some genetic types it is as high as 23 percent. Rice still in the hull or husk is known as paddy rice, and these fibrous husks are removed to produce brown rice. When brown rice is milled to produce white rice, the outer layer, or bran, which is 15 percent protein, is abraded away. This process reduces the weight (by 10 percent) and both the quantity and quality of the protein in the remaining material. Similarly, to mill bread wheat to produce white wheat flour, the protein-rich bran and embryo, or germ, is removed, resulting in weight loss of up to 28 percent, lower protein content, and reduction in the usable portion of the protein due to a disproportionate loss of the amino acid lysine. In some areas of Africa corn is pounded wet and 20 percent of the protein and much of the lysine are removed with the hull and germ. Sorghum and millet are generally utilized or ground whole and so have little nutrient loss. Breeding programs are under way to increase the protein and lysine level of several cereals, especially corn.

The development of semidwarf wheat, rice, sorghum, and millet has been a milestone in plant breeding; semidwarf varieties are better suited to the use of nitrogen fertilizers. Local varieties of these crops are relatively tall; when fertilized, they become even taller with heavier seed heads atop the stems, which then fall over (lodge), especially with moderate to high levels of nitrogen. Semidwarf varieties maintain short, stiff stems at higher nitrogen levels and are capable of seed yields up to four or five times that of local varieties. Shorter stature is also advantageous to corn, but to a lesser extent since the heavy seed head or ear is not at the top, so corn plants are less likely to lodge, regardless of height. Shorter plants are also advantageous because they tend to put more of the production into the grain and less into stalk. Many of the semidwarf varieties also have greater disease resistance; reduced sensitivity to day length, thereby providing increased adaptive range; and a shorter growing season. Local farmers in some regions, however, have rejected semidrawf varieties of sorghum and millet because the long stems of traditional varieties are used for building materials. This example illustrates how important it is to understand the many ways that local farmers utilize different plant parts.

Corn

Corn (or maize) is widely grown in most food crop producing areas of Africa. Under good soil and weather conditions, corn has the potential to produce high yields due to its abundance of leaves and high rate of photosynthesis. This cereal thrives on soils that are deep, well drained, have good water holding capacity, and are relatively fertile. Corn performs poorly on highly acid or waterlogged soils because root growth is restricted. Common varieties of corn mature in 100 to 120 days, with flowering occurring 55 to 65 days after planting. Favorable environmental conditions during flowering are critical for maximum yields. The tassel (male flower) at the top of the plant produces the pollen. For proper development of the ear (female flower), each grain in the ear must be fertilized individually by pollen landing on the silks that protrude from the end of the ear. Hot, dry conditions can kill the pollen, causing inadequate fertilization and improperly filled ears.

The time of planting in regions with wet and dry seasons is important because delayed planting may reduce yield. It is very important to control early season weeds; late season weeds are less of a problem since they are often suppressed by the corn canopy. Diseases attacking corn are more severe when humidity is high, which is why this crop is not grown extensively in high rainfall areas. Varietal resistance is the main defense against these diseases. Usually field insects are tolerated, but crop rotation, planting dates, and insecticides may be used to help control these pests in some situations.

In Africa, corn food products are varied but may be grouped according to processing methods: (1) ground or pounded and then boiled, (2) ground or pounded and then baked or fried, (3) boiled whole, (4) baked whole, and (5) fermented. The following are some examples of corn preparations in Africa. Corn bread, or *kenkey,* in Ghana is made by fermenting wet flour, wrapping it in corn husks, and then cooking it. A porridge made of flour mixed with hot water is called *akassa* in Ghana. In Swaziland a corn gruel called *inembe* is used as a supplement in the diet of nursing infants. Beer, or *utshwala,* is made from corn and sorghum.

Corn breeding, and the creation of hybrid and synthetic varieties, have been facilitated because male and female flowers are at different locations on the plant. Hybrids, crosses between inbred lines, have been widely accepted in commercial plantings because of higher yields under good management. Seed of hybrid corn is, however, expensive and must be purchased for each corn crop to maintain high yields. High yields from hybrid corn also depend on following other cultural practices such as heavy fertilization, high plant densities, weed control, and pest control. Synthetic varieties are created by allowing cross pollination of several superior races. Growers producing synthetic varieties may keep their own seed for several years. Subsistence farmers often produce open pollinated varieties because they perform as well in their production system and are less expensive.

Sorghum

Sorghum (or Guinea corn) apparently originated in Ethiopia and Sudan and has been extensively grown throughout Africa since early historical times. This cereal is capable of producing a crop in situations in which rainfall is too low to produce satisfactory corn yields. Sorghum is adapted to a wide range of soil types and textures, from sandy to clayey, but is not well adapted to acid soils common to rain forests, which have developed under conditions of heavy rainfall and leaching. This crop is generally grown in regions with distinct wet and dry seasons, often with limited rainfall even during the wet season. Soils in those regions may be moderately high in native nutrients since nutrient leaching is minimal with low rainfall. Water may be so scarce that there is little response to fertilizer. Sorghum is widely distributed in warm climates because it matures in ninety days to six or eight months.

Under poor management or dry conditions, yields are approximately 700 kg/ha. Yields increase two to three times under favorable conditions and proper management. Sorghum is susceptible to a number of root, leaf, and grain diseases. Insect damage may result in death of the stalk, damage to leaf tissue, and empty seed. Losses from these diseases and pests can be reduced by producing more resistant varieties, removing infected plants and crop residues, rotating crops, and applying chemicals.

Sorghum is harvested by cutting the heads from the stalks, then drying and storing the heads. The grain is threshed by beating the heads manually. In Sub-Saharan Africa sorghum grain is consumed primarily as a stiff porridge, although in Botswana sorghum is used to make beer. In the processing to make beer, more than 50 percent of the calories are lost. *Couscous* and *hura* are dishes made from sorghum that are found in the daily diet of northern Africans. Couscous is a popular dish consisting of finely ground sorghum flour rolled into balls, which is eaten with green leaves or other vegetables and seasoned with a spicy sauce of chili and peppers. Hura is based on a mixture of sorghum and millet. The cereals are cooked and served as a porridge.

Compared to some other major crops in the world, breeding and selection of high-yielding varieties of sorghum have been limited. Because of sorghum's drought tolerance, future research should prove valuable for the drier regions of Africa.

Pearl Millet

Pearl millet, also known as bulrush or cattail millet, is the staple crop for many semiarid regions of Africa, particularly in the Sahel. It tolerates drought conditions better than sorghum and also tolerates low fertility soils. Until recently the importance of pearl millet has been overlooked because it is traditionally grown on relatively unproductive land. But due to the expanse of semiarid land in Africa, millet's potential to contribute to the food supply is great. Because it is grown in the most drought-prone and unproductive locations, average yields in Africa are now only 600 kg/ha, lower than either sorghum (700 kg/ha) or corn (1300 kg/ha).

Millet production is affected by several plant and environmental characteristics. Because millet is often planted in seasons with short periods of rainfall, it is important to plant at the beginning of the rains. Planting at this time also helps reduce losses from some insects. Since millet seed size is small, it is planted shallowly and a fine seed bed must be prepared. Early plant growth of pearl millet is slow; thus, it is important during this time to protect the small millet from weeds, which compete with it for moisture. Several diseases and insects attack millet, but with normal yields, chemical control is rarely economical; removal of the infected plants is the most economical option. Most millet varieties are photoperiodic, i.e., the millet does not flower unless the period of daylight is less than twelve hours. To a great extent the reproductive cycle, including seed production, begins on a certain date instead of a certain number of days after planting. This is advantageous for forage production since more leafy animal feed can be produced during a long vegetative period prior to flowering. Pearl millet has been found to produce flowers and set seeds in temperatures from 25° C to 45° C. By contrast, corn pollen is killed by temperatures at the upper end of this range, and grain formation is prevented. At maturity, millet seeds are exposed and may be damaged by birds; therefore, early harvest is important, and mature fields demand labor to scare birds away.

Little breeding development has been done on millet. Research is being done on varieties that are not daylength sensitive to increase the range of adaptability of given varieties through successful growth in seasons and locations with different daylengths. The main objective in breeding, however, is to develop shorter varieties that will not lodge when fertilized with nitrogen and will have the potential for holding heavier seed heads. Most native varieties of pearl millet are tall, from 2 to 5 meters. Grain weight is a relatively small percentage of the total plant. Dwarf types from 0.5 to 3.0 meters have been developed through breeding. Breeding for disease resistance is also being conducted. Based upon experience with sorghum, it is possible that pearl millet yields will be increased in even drier regions by improved varieties and cultural practices.

Rice

African rice species have been cultivated in parts of West Africa for three thousand years. For the last two thousand years, Asian rice seed have been introduced repeatedly. A lack of the unique technology that is required to grow rice accounts for currently limited rice production in Africa, but since 1920 Africa's rice production has increased because of large irrigation resettlement schemes, availability of mechanization, and training of African farmers by Chinese specialists. Rice has potential for increased production in Africa due to its adaptability to a wide range of waterlogged soils. Other cereals perform poorly in these environments. Rice and rice culture are of three basic types: lowland, floating, and upland. Lowland, or paddy, rice is produced under nearly continuous, controlled flooding. Floating, or deep water, rice is produced under uncontrollable flood conditions. Upland rice requires wet soil and is produced on fields that are generally not flooded but which receive high rainfall. All three types are produced in Africa; lowland and upland rice have the greatest potential there.

Lowland rice is the most highly managed type and produces the greatest yields—yields of 4000 kg/ha are common and 7000 to 8000 kg/ha are obtainable. After the land is prepared, it is flooded and the soil is puddled (worked when wet to make an impenetrable layer) to reduce seepage. Paddy rice may be direct seeded or, to more efficiently utilize the land, transplanted from a nursery when three to four weeks old. Flooding creates an environment quite different from upland conditions and affects management tactics. To illustrate, flooding makes soil acidity more conducive to plant growth, increases the availability of phosphorus, increases nitrogen losses and also adds natural nitrogen through biological nitrogen fixation by blue green algae, and changes weed, disease, and insect populations. To prevent germination of the seed in the seedhead, fields are drained one to two weeks prior to maturity when possible, or varieties with postmaturation dormancy are used.

Floating rice is direct seeded or transplanted to coordinate with expected flooding of rivers. As the water level rises, floating rice elongates by as much as 0.3 meters a day, reaching over 6 meters in some cultivars. The seed head is held above the water level. As floodwater recedes, the leaves and stems fall into a mass while the seedhead is held vertically, allowing for maturation and harvest. Yields rarely exceed 1500 kg/ha, but no other food crop can grow under such flood conditions.

Upland rice can be produced in areas of high, uniformly distributed rainfall where the soil is continually moist for four to six months. It is direct seeded at the beginning of the rains. Upland rice is not tolerant of dry conditions, particularly during flowering. Erratic rainfall, poor weed control under nonflooded conditions, and diseases are some reasons why upland rice has lower yields than irrigated rice. Rice is harvested by cutting seedheads when the grain is slightly moist. The grain is dried slowly to prevent cracking. Rice is thrashed by people or animals walking on it, or by beating the sheaves against wooden blocks or ladders, or by mechanical thrashers.

Rice breeding and selection is conducted in many parts of the world with the center of activity at the International Rice Research Institute (IRRI) in the Philippines. As discussed in the introduction, greater yields from nitrogen fertilization have been realized through the development of varieties with shorter, stiffer stems that resist lodging. Other breeding objectives include developing varieties with higher protein, more resistance to diseases and insects, and tolerance to adverse soil conditions.

Wheat

Wheat has been produced in Sudan and the Sahel for several centuries on small irrigated plots during the dry season. Current wheat production in Africa is small, located primarily in the cooler highlands of Ethiopia, Kenya, and Sudan, but is slowly increasing as irrigation schemes increase. Bread wheat, which originated in the Near East, is the principal type produced. Durum wheat, used for macaroni and pasta, is grown to a lesser extent. Semidwarf bread wheat varieties developed at the International Center for Maize and Wheat Improvement (CIMMYT) in Mexico produce higher yields, particularly in fertile soils, have greater resistance to rusts, and possess better baking quality than taller traditional varieties. Because of lodging resistance and increased capacity to utilize nitrogen fertilizer, the semidwarf varieties often yield up to 5000 kg/ha in research plots—four to five times the yield of local varieties. Small farms commonly produce between 1000 and 2500 kg/ha of these semidwarf varieties.

Even though most wheat is currently produced in higher cooler regions, other parts of Sub-Saharan Africa can produce wheat satisfactorily if it is planted at the beginning of the cooler, dryer season, particularly where irrigation is available. Recent development of semidwarf varieties that mature in one hundred days takes advantage of these short, cool periods. Humid conditions during vegetative growth favor leaf diseases that cause yield losses. Wheat is planted at high seeding rates—120 to 150 kg/ha for semidwarf varieties, with little space between plants. Therefore, cultivation is difficult and weed control requires a weed-free seed bed, crop competition, and perhaps herbicides. If planted too late, grain fill occurs during warmer months and yield is decreased. Warmer, dryer conditions near maturity aid in proper drying of the crop.

Bread wheat is in demand in Africa, particularly in urban areas, because of its unique baking characteristics. Bread wheat is high in the protein gluten, which is capable of entrapping gas formed from leavening agents and stretching to form small bubbles that cause bakery products to rise. In areas where wheat has been grown traditionally, it is also used to make porridge and beer.

Development of semidwarf short-season bread wheats by CIMMYT has increased the potential for wheat production in Africa. Due to the requirement for cool to moderate temperatures and the rising demand, however, production will probably continue to fall behind consumption.

• FARINACEOUS CROPS (STEPHEN K. O'HAIR) •

Farinaceous crops are grown for their starchy, nonseed storage organs; they serve as a low cost source of readily digestible carbohydrates in many African diets. The leaves of several of these crops are regularly eaten as relish and are high in protein. Bananas and cassava are the most common farinaceous crops grown in Africa, followed by sweetpotato, yams, cocoyam, taro, and potato. All are vegetatively propagated, but each crop has special qualities and growing requirements. Planting usually begins at the onset of the rainy season, generally in mixed plantings with other vegetables and fruits. Industrially produced fertilizer is usually applied only to crops, such as bananas, intended for sale in the international market.

Diseases and pests are numerous, commonly transported with the planting material, and spread by man throughout wide production areas. Each crop has special problems, some of which are very regional. Control measures include destroying diseased plants, avoiding land with a history of disease, rotating crops, carefully selecting planting material based on parent-plant health, utilizing disease-free tissue-cultured plants, and planting resistant cultivars. Foliage diseases and pests are less of a problem in mixed plantings.

Yields vary considerably depending on cultivar, plant age at harvest, and local environmental conditions, which include soil fertility and pest and disease presence. Cultivar names vary from one region to the next, and no attempt is made here to present specific names. In general, the food preparation measures are similar to those of the potato. Although the processing of farinaceous crops into food items is not a major industry, there is potential for expanded local use of industrially produced products such as chips, bread, flour, and other dried products.

Many research and development needs are common and include: (1) reduce labor inputs in all aspects of production; (2) improve quality control in the production and handling of planting material; (3) develop appropriate soil management practices to maintain soil fertility and prevent soil erosion; (4) evaluate cropping systems; (5) germplasm collection, breeding, and selection (for pest and disease resistance; tolerance to drought, high soil acidity, and low soil fertility; and improved quality); (6) review current marketing and distribution systems and improve efficiency; (7) develop means to minimize production gluts and periods of unavailability; (8) develop and improve processing, postharvest storage, and utilization; and (9) train extension personnel in appropriate production innovations.

Cassava

Cassava, or manioc (French), is a very adaptable crop that is considered outstanding in its food producing ability and economy of production. It grows well in many soil types and excels over other crops in production on marginal lands unsuitable for most crops. However, it does not tolerate waterlogged conditions. Cassava originated in Brazil and was carried to Africa by traders. Over one-third of world cassava production is now in Africa; the largest producing country is Zaire, followed by Nigeria and Tanzania.

Cassava is planted by hand. Instead of using seeds, farmers plant sections of the plant stem as propagules. Unless rainfall is minimal, less than 750 millimeters, the crop does not respond to supplemental irrigation. In drought situations, cassava conserves moisture by shedding its leaves. Major factors leading to yield reduction are weed competition during the early stages of plant growth, diseases, and pests. When disease resistance is not present, yields can be reduced by as much as 50 percent if healthy, pathogen-free propagules are not utilized.

Individual plants are uprooted by hand as needed, or large roots can be individually harvested from the plant in a nondestructive manner. All plants are usually harvested from eight to eighteen months after planting. Plants can be left in the ground for several years (with the roots enlarging each year), but these become fibrous and woody and have a lower starch content. Average yields are nine metric tons per hectare (Mt/ha) per annum, but the highest experimental yields exceed sixty Mt/ha. Thus, the potential for higher yields is great. Harvested roots deteriorate to an inedible state within a few days after harvest, so they must be consumed quickly or special storage techniques must be employed including keeping the roots in a cool, humid location.

Without processing, the roots and leaves of some cultivars may be toxic due to the presence of cyanogenic glucosides (HCN). Toxicity from cassava may develop when considerable quantities with a high HCN content are consumed, particularly if the high HCN content is a result of poor processing or if the diet is poorly balanced nutritionally. Cultivars low and high in HCN are termed "sweet" and "bitter," respectively, due to a bitter taste that usually accompanies HCN. Juice extraction, cooking, fermentation, or combinations of these are processing treatments that aid in reducing HCN to safe levels.

Most cultivars have white fleshed roots with up to 30 percent starch, and in many parts of Africa the young, tender leaves and growing tips are collected and cooked as potherbs (similar to spinach). Cassava leaves are composed of up to 40 percent protein on a dry-weight basis, but the sulfur amino acids are low or missing, thus cassava diets need the addition of foods high in methionine to supply complete protein. Several different foods in West and Central Africa are made from cassava roots including: *chikwange*—a heavy boiled or steamed bread; *fufu*—a cooked paste; and *gari*—grated and fire dried root. Gari and well dried whole roots, known as *cossettes* in Zaire, can be stored for extended periods in dry locations. Dried roots can be pounded to flour and made into fufu.

Plantains and Bananas

Bananas and plantains are grown as food and cash crops in regions having a major wet season. The distinction between banana and plantain is largely a reflection of their end use where bananas are sweet dessert fruits and plantains are starchy, nonsweet cooking fruits. The greatest advantage for both over other starchy crops is that they are productive over a number of years; land preparation and planting occur only once every five or six years. Cultivars are dervied from *Musa acuminata* (A genome) or are hybrids of *M. acuminata* and *M. balbisiana* (B genome). The former prefer a long, wet season, but the latter tolerate a monsoon type of climate with a pronounced dry season, typical of that found in most of Sub-Saharan Africa. Countries with the greatest production in decreasing order of annual production include: Uganda, Nigeria, Rwanda, Zaire, Tanzania, Ghana, Cameroon, Ivory Coast, and Burundi. Plantains are the major crop in each.

Both crops are adapted for growth from sea level up to eighteen hundred meters and can be grown on a wide range of soils, if there is good drainage. The best soils are of volcanic or alluvial origin, well drained, and with a high humus content. Suckers are planted up to four meters apart. Cash-crop production includes the use of herbicides and, during rapid plant growth periods, fertilization or manuring. Diseases are the most serious problems, but due to the value of the exported product, fruit rots are the most well known. Insect pests can be controlled in severe situations with biological control; introducing predatory insects is successful in many locations. The time from planting to harvest ranges from nine to eighteen months with yields ranging up to 45 Mt/ha for the first year's crop, and up to 75 Mt/ha per annum in subsequent years. Typical bunch weights average 20 kg. Bunches are often wrapped in dried banana leaves to protect the fruit during local shipment. Otherwise, no special practices are used to store fruit that is to be consumed domestically.

Most bananas consumed locally are eaten as cooking bananas. Unpeeled green plantains are roasted over charcoal fires, and peeled green bananas and plantains are fried, boiled, or steamed. Peeled ripe bananas are fried or eaten uncooked as a dessert fruit. Alternatively, bananas and plantains are brewed and converted into alcoholic beverages. Nutritionally, bananas are similar to other starchy staples. Of the farinaceous crops, they are second highest in vitamin A content, after the yellow fleshed sweet potatoes. The dessert bananas tend to have more moisture and less carbohydrate than the plantains.

Breeding has primarily been limited to producing disease resistant dessert types. It is believed that several commercially grown cloned varieties resulted from chance mutations during natural vegetative propagation, which suggests that there is great potential for using genetic engineering and plant tissue culture to develop new clones.

Sweetpotato

Sweetpotatoes, also known as yams (in the United States) and *patates douces* (French), are completely different than the true yam (*Dioscorea* spp). They are perennial herbaceous twiners that are cultivated as annuals. Roots thicken to form tubers with white to red skins. The top producing countries (in decreasing order of production) include: Burundi, Rwanda, Uganda, Tanzania, Kenya, Zaire, and Nigeria. Sweetpotatoes are commonly grown from sea level up to one thousand meters and have good drought tolerance as well as high rainfall tolerance, providing there is adequate drainage and good soil aeration. They also tolerate low soil fertility, and their potential production range is great.

The shape and color of the leaves and roots are used to distinguish clones, but most cultivated varieties (cultivars) produce white-fleshed roots. Stem cuttings or sprouts taken from storage roots are hand planted into moist soil at densities up to 30,000 plants/ha in monoculture; mixed plantings are less dense. Weed control during the first month of growth allows the plants adequate time to develop a complete canopy, which limits additional weed competition. Sweetpotato weevil damage to the roots and stems is the major production problem.

Roots are harvested as needed four to six months after planting. Larger roots can be carefully removed ahead of smaller roots, allowing smaller roots additional time to enlarge. Yields average 6 Mt/ha in farmers' fields, but experimental yields are as high as 53 Mt/ha, showing the considerable potential for improving farm yields. Since sweetpotatoes are harvested as needed, postharvest storage is only for a few days. If longer storage is expected, care must be taken to minimize root damage during harvest and transport. In addition, the roots must be cured prior to storage by exposing them to high temperatures and humidity for three to four days.

Yellow fleshed cultivars contain higher amounts of vitamin A than white fleshed cultivars; therefore, when diets are low in vitamin A it is best to choose the former. Roots are usually boiled and consumed without additional preparation. Young leaves and tender shoots are used as potherbs in some regions and add to the protein and vitamin content of the meal. Little is known about variability in leaf protein content, a topic worth investigating. The amount of genetic variability for many qualities is great and, since sweetpotatoes can produce large amounts of carbohydrates in a relatively short time, they are a promising crop for the future.

Yams

Yams, or *igname* (French), are important tuber crops in many parts of Africa. They are herbaceous climbers producing enlarged, starch filled, stem tubers. Cultivated types include: the white (guinea) yam, the yellow (quinea) yam, the lesser or potato yam, and the water or greater yam. Other types are grown on a regional basis—some for their production of toxic substances. Production is primarily in Nigeria, Ivory Coast, Ghana, Dahomey, and Togo (together these countries grow over 96 percent of the world's supply of yams). Harvested yam tubers have a distinct dormancy period lasting several months. Thus, they are better suited than fresh cassava for long distance transport and export. Once dormancy requirements are completed, the tuber is reabsorbed by the plant during the production of new shoots. A new tuber is formed by the end of the season. This cycle can continue for several seasons, and each resulting tuber grows larger than the previous one. Tuber weight can vary from 0.5 to 10 kilograms.

Yams are more specific in soil requirements than other root crops, growing best in fertile well-drained soils. Mounds or beds are formed to improve drainage or concentrate top soil. Propagules, averaging 200 grams, are taken from the sprouting end of the tuber. Plant populations range up to 20,000 plants/ha in monoculture. Mulching is recommended to control weeds and conserve moisture if a prolonged dry period is expected. Weeds need to be controlled during the first two to three months after emergence; as the vines grow, they are manually trained onto poles. Tuber rots are probably the greatest production problem.

Harvesting is done by hand beginning six to ten months after shoot emergence. Nondestructive harvesting is occasionally practiced, the first harvest beginning as soon as four months after emergence. Yams can be stored and cured much the same as sweetpotatoes. Aside from other methods noted earlier, boiled yams also are pounded or mashed and eaten as fufu. Some species contain dios-corene and, prior to cooking, are sliced and soaked in salt water or running water for several hours or days to remove this toxic substance.

Cocoyam and Taro

The cocoyams and taro are among the most shade tolerant of terrestrial food plants. These edible aroids are often confused with each other and, in Africa, are both known as cocoyam. Both store starches in stem structures termed "corms," and both are perennial herbs with erect, heart-shaped leaves. Major production areas are in Nigeria, Ghana, and Ivory Coast, producing approximately 40, 28, and 4 percent of world production, respectively. Cultivars are distinguished by cormel (secondary corms) and leaf pigmentation. Taro cultivars are mostly white fleshed, and cocoyam flesh may be white, pink, or yellow. The cylindrical corms are produced at or below the soil surface. In cocoyam, few to many lateral, starch-filled, club-shaped cormels develop below the soil surface around the corm base. The stem of the taro leaf is attached to the lower surface, not the base.

The aroids grow best along rivers and streams and in regions such as coastal areas where rainfall is regular. Soil type is generally not a limiting factor. Taro has a better tolerance of saturated soils than does cocoyam, which must be grown on beds if flooding is likely. Some taro clones can be grown under continuously flooded conditions if the water is flowing. Others prefer little or no flooding. In general, cultural practices for these crops are similar to those used for other root crops. Corms or parts of corms are used as propagules. Diseases appear to cause the greatest problems; corm and root rots are the most important of these. Planting cocoyams in well-drained soil tends to reduce root rot problems.

Harvesting begins seven to fifteen months after planting. Cocoyam cormels are of marketable size when they are as large as the potatoes that are sold in U.S. markets. Harvesting begins with removing soil from the base of the cocoyam plant, then the larger cormels are removed and the soil replaced. This process can be repeated two to three times until the entire plant is harvested. Marketing in Africa is limited to selling fresh corms and cormels in local or nearby city markets. Cocoyam cormels have a long shelf life and are better suited than taro for long distance transport. Young, unopened leaves and, occasionally, fully expanded leaves of selected clones are eaten as cooked potherbs. The starchy taro corm or cocoyam cormels are prepared as potatoes are. For populations dependent on wetlands for energy foods, edible aroids may be a better choice than rice from the standpoint of human nutrition. Taro equals the potato in amino acid content, and taro leaves are nutritious. Cocoyam corms are not usually eaten by Africans, but are sometimes boiled and fed to swine.

Potato

The potato is a minor, yet potentially important staple food in Africa. Its production in Sub-Saharan Africa is limited to regions where night temperatures are cool at least four months of the year, and the best production occurs between the altitudes of 390 to 2,100 meters. Most production now is in (by order of decreasing volume) Kenya, Uganda, Burundi, Rwanda, and Tanzania.

Potatoes are propagated from whole tubers that have been stored from one crop to the next. Certified, disease-free propagules are recommended for planting. These propagules can be produced locally by trained personnel or may be imported from Europe. The latter are rather expensive and generally uneconomical. Water requirements are rather exacting, since potatoes do not tolerate moisture stress during tuber formation stages. A large number of diseases and pests are associated with potato production. Most clones were developed in Europe and are referred to by their European names in Africa.

Harvesting begins with uprooting the plant about one hundred days after planting. Tubers develop close to the soil surface, so harvesting is relatively easy. Yields range up to 10 Mt/ha, considerably less than the 20 to 42 Mt/ha recorded in temperate regions that employ high technology cultural practices. Potatoes can be stored for several months in well-ventilated shelters receiving diffuse light; inspection on a regular basis is necessary to remove spoiled tubers. Although potatoes are a source of vitamin C, most of this is lost in the cooking process. Leaves are especially high in toxic solanine and are inedible. The future for potato production in Sub-Saharan Africa is good in many cool, high altitude regions. Crops such as sweetpotato are better adapted to warmer conditions.

The potential for expanded farinaceous crop production in Africa and the need for additional research are great. Probably the greatest need is to improve crop utilization. Therefore, most research should be oriented toward minimizing the seasonal surplus and scarcity of fresh products, developing new processed products, and developing efficient marketing systems.

• LEGUME GRAIN CROPS (CLIFTON HIEBSCH) •

Legume grains are valuable to the peoples of Sub-Saharan Africa for three reasons: (1) They provide cheap, concentrated, high quality protein to supplement the high carbohydrate cereals and farinaceous crops (see Table 12.3). (2) Leguminous oilseeds, i.e. peanuts (groundnuts) and soybeans, can provide large quantities of quality cooking oils (see Table 12.3). (3) Unlike most crops, legumes are not dependent upon expensive nitrogen fertilizer for high yields. (For crops other than legumes, the lack of nitrogen naturally present in the soil is often the most limiting factor to production.) Protein, which is essential for human and animal nutrition, is 16 percent nitrogen, and the ultimate source of protein is plants. Air is 78 percent nitrogen, but this nitrogen is in a form not usable by plants. Specific nitrogen-fixing bacteria infect the roots of legumes, and nodules are formed. Utilizing energy from the legumes, these bacteria in the nodules convert atmospheric nitrogen present in the soil to a form usable by the legumes for making protein. When a legume is produced for the first time on a site, the bacteria specific to that legume, if not naturally occurring in the soil, needs to be introduced in order to prevent nitrogen deficiency.

The three principal legume grains produced in Sub-Saharan Africa are peanuts, cowpeas, and beans (common beans and lima beans), all of which are geographically widespread. Pigeon peas are grown principally in East Africa, but due to their wide range of adaptation they have good potential for production in other areas. Soybeans also have potential for more widespread production; currently their production is small but increasing. Cowpeas, beans, and pigeon peas are classified as pulses, and peanuts and soybeans are referred to as oilseeds. These legumes are adapted to the same regions as corn, sorghum, and millet are. Cowpeas, peanuts, beans, and pigeon peas are often intercropped with these cereals; soybeans also could be managed in this way. Cowpeas, peanuts, beans, and soybeans are generally understory components in intercrops, with climbing cowpeas and beans using the overstory crop for support. After the cereal is harvested, the slowly establishing pigeon peas develop and mature. Many other legumes—Bambarra groundnuts, Kersting's groundnut, locust beans, rice beans, jack beans, sword beans, African yam beans, velvet beans—have localized or unknown production and potential. All legumes produce seeds in pods with two lobes. Flowers contain both male and female parts, making commercial hybrid production currently unfeasible. Legume plants may be erect, prostrate, or climbing. Erect types of pigeon peas and soybeans, prostrate and erect types of peanuts, and all three types of cowpeas and beans are cultivated. Many crops, including cowpeas, pigeon peas, and soybeans, have cultivars with varying photoperiod or daylength sensitivity. The length of the nights influences the date of flower initiation and grain formation. This sensitivity causes a cultivar planted on different dates to initiate seeds and mature on nearly the same date. Away from the equator, daylength varies during the year, and this trait can be advantageously used to time crops to mature toward the end of the rains to maximize water use and then allow for proper grain drying. All five crops have determinate and indeterminate cultivars. Vegetative growth stops in determinate cultivars when flowers and pods are formed. After vegetative growth stops, the plants flower and produce seed in a relatively short period of time, and all grain matures about the same time. Indeterminate cultivars, however, flower and produce seed over a longer period, helping reduce the risk of crop failure due to droughts during pod initiation.

If evenly distributed over the growing season, 600 millimeters of rainfall can produce good crops of cowpeas, peanuts, pigeon peas, beans, and soybeans—the first three crops can be produced with even slightly less rainfall (see Table 12.4). Short-season cowpeas are capable of producing grain during short rainy seasons with only 250 to 300 millimeters of rain. Pigeon peas, lima beans, and soybeans can tolerate heavier rainfall by virtue of greater disease resistance, which is required in humid environments, and for soybeans by their capacity to withstand periods of water-saturated soils. Wet soils are particularly harmful to peanuts, causing rotten pods. Pigeon peas are adapted to the widest range of rainfall. All of these crops do best if grain maturation occurs at the end of the rains, which allows for proper drying. This is particularly true for peanuts, which must dry shortly after being dug.

Weeds, insects, diseases, and nematodes can severely reduce yields. Weeds can be controlled by hand or machine cultivation or by use of numerous herbicides. Weed control by these means is particularly important when legumes are small. Generally, once a full leaf canopy is formed, the shade it provides controls weeds by cutting their sunlight. Prostrate cowpeas cover soil rapidly, minimizing the requirement for weeding; thus these are an excellent choice for intercropping with crops that develop ground coverage more slowly. Pigeon pea establishes slowly and early in its life competes poorly against weeds. Late mechanical weeding of peanuts is not recommended, as it may destroy the pod forming underground. If properly timed and selected, insecticides may be very cost effective. Cowpeas appear to be the grain legume most vulnerable to insects in West Africa. Stem borers cause reduced nutrient and water supply, and pod feeders cause pod abortion and improper seed development; these insects may cause more economic loss than the more obvious foliage feeders cause. Seedling diseases may be controlled economically by applying small quantities of systemic fungicides to the seeds prior to planting. Foliar diseases can reduce yields significantly. Effective foliar fungicides probably are not economical or desirable in most African situations, but resistant varieties and cultural practices may be used to remedy these problems. Close monitoring of fields and rotations may be used to reduce damage from nematodes.

Cowpeas

Cowpeas (southern peas, blackeye peas) are some of the most important food legumes in Africa and are used in different localities as a vegetable, pulse, fodder, and green manure. Cowpeas are adapted to the hot semiarid and subhumid tropical areas with 250 to 1000 mm of rainfall per year. This environment is found along the southern fringe of the Sahara Desert and in the east from Ethiopia to South Africa. Nigeria, Burkina Faso, Uganda, Niger, Senegal, and Tanzania grow most of the world's supply of cowpeas. Intercropped local varieties commonly produce 120 to 150 kg/ha; with improved practices and sole cropping they can usually produce 750 kg/ha (improved varieties have produced as much as 1500 kg/ha).

Cowpeas are adapted to a wide range of well-drained soil; they produce well on fertile soils and tolerate less fertile, acid soils. Local varieties tend to be prostrate, low yielding, indeterminate, and susceptible to diseases and insects. Introduced varieties are generally erect, higher yielding, determinate, less daylength sensitive, and often more pest resistant. Unfortunately, many introduced varieties do not cook easily. Pods and seeds are held high on the plant on a long fruiting

TABLE 12.4. Legume Grain Crop Environmental Preference and Plant Characteristics

| Legume Grain | Environmental Preference | | Plant Characteristics | | |
	Rainfall[a]	Soil	Disease Resistance	Days to Seed Maturity	Plant Type
Cowpea	semiarid to subhumid	well drained sandy loams	poor	65-200	erect, climbing, or procumbent
Common bean	subhumid	sandy, peat to clayey	poor	60-100	dwarf bush to climbing
Lima bean	subhumid to very humid	well drained	excellent	100-270	bush to climbing
Peanut	semiarid to subhumid	friable, well drained sandy loams	fair	100-150	low bunchy herb
Pigeon pea	semiarid to humid	well drained sandy to clayey loams	good	90-300	erect, semiwoody shrub
Soybean	subhumid to humid	well drained to slightly waterlogged	fair/good	80-200	erect bush

Source: K.O. Rachie and L.M. Roberts. 1974. Grain Legumes of the Lowland Tropics. Advances in Agronomy 26:1-132.

[a]Semiarid is less than 600 millimeters (mm), subhumid is 600 to 1000 mm, humid is 1000 to 1500 mm and very humid is greater than 1500 mm annually.

stalk, which eases both hand and machine harvesting. Humid conditions increase severity of several seedling and foliar diseases. Estimates of loss from disease are as high as 75 percent for seedling diseases, 50 percent for anthracnose, 30 percent for leaf spot, and 50 percent for viruses (Rachie and Roberts 1974). Diseases may be controlled by removing all top growth at the end of the season, planting disease-free seed, and producing disease-resistant varieties.

Cowpeas are consumed in three basic forms. They are frequently cooked together with vegetables and spices to make a thick gruel. Deep fried cakes (*akara* balls) are made from a dough of dehulled (seedcoat removed) cowpea flour mixed with onion and seasonings. Steamed bean cakes (*moin-moin*) are prepared from a similarly seasoned dough that is wrapped in leaves and steamed.

The International Institute of Tropical Agriculture (IITA) at Ibadan, Nigeria is the center for testing and evaluating cowpea varieties. Development of varieties resistant to insects, nematodes, and diseases is being pursued. Cowpeas are self-pollinating, thus they breed true to type. Once a superior variety is developed, growers can produce their own seed. Cowpeas should remain one of the most important food legumes in Africa for the foreseeable future.

Beans

The statistics on production and consumption in Sub-Saharan Africa show that beans are consumed in larger quantities than any other pulse (see Table 12.2). The term "bean" refers to several related species of grain legumes—mainly the common bean (*Phaseolus vulgaris*) and lima bean (*Phaseolus lunatus*)—that are adapted to different environments, though often produced in the same areas. Determining which species of bean is produced in a certain area is difficult: world production statistics lump the species as dry beans, and surveys often refer to them as "beans" without further differentiation. Common beans (also known as dry, dwarf, field, French, haricot, navy, pinto, runner, salad, snap, and string beans) and lima beans (also known as butter, Madagascar, pole, and sieva beans) are believed to have spread to Africa from tropical Americas. Common and lima beans fill the same role in the diet, and both have similar average yields of 500 to 700 kg/ha and maximum yields near 2500 kg/ha.

Common beans are adapted to cooler climates and are particularly important at higher elevations in Burundi, Rwanda, and Uganda. Common beans are best adapted to moderate temperatures, well-distributed rainfall, and medium-textured well-drained soils. They are not tolerant of frosts, high temperatures, droughts, or high humidity and are highly susceptible to diseases and insect pests that are encouraged by warm, humid environments. Black seeded cultivars are better adapted to the lowland tropics, but their higher tannin content makes them less acceptable and digestible than other cultivars. In spite of the constraints, common beans are sometimes grown in lowland humid areas and harvested as vegetables, at the snap bean stage, and as pulses. Lima beans are more adapted to higher rainfall and are a major pulse in the humid rain forests, with extensive production in Madagascar. Lima beans are adapted to a wider range of environments. They tolerate high temperatures, poor soil, and drought, but have higher yields in the hot, humid tropics. Lima beans are less susceptible to diseases and insect pests than most grain legumes. Both species of beans require moderately dry weather toward the end of seed formation in order to produce good quality dry seeds.

Common and lima beans have two basic plant types: bush and trailing, or climbing. Bush types are erect with strongly developed central stems and branches and are generally determinate. Climbing types are generally indeterminate and are often included in mixed-cropping systems, where they use other crops for support. Maturity occurs in two to five months for common beans and three to nine months for lima beans; the bush types generally mature earlier. Seeds vary greatly in size, shape, and color. Oblong, round, or kidney-shaped seeds of common beans and flat or round lima beans may be white, buff, red, purple, brown, black, or mottled.

The nutritional value of dry beans is high (see Table 12.3). Beans are usually consumed as dry seed after boiling in salted water to which other vegetables, spices, and, occasionally, meat have been added. This dish is eaten with a cereal or farinaceous food, often prepared as a porridge. Beans are also consumed as green, immature pods and seeds, and the leaves are sometimes used as a potherb. Beans, however, have drawbacks: dried beans require a long cooking time, some cultivars may cause flatulence, and some cultivars of lima beans contain toxic levels of hydrocyanic acid and require special preparation.

Considerable research has been conducted on variety development and cultivation practices particular to Europe, North America, and Latin America. The International Center for Tropical Agriculture (CIAT) in Cali, Colombia is the world, particularly the tropical world, center for research. Little research has been done in Africa. Application of current scientific knowledge could increase average yields by two to three times. After peanuts, pigeon peas, and cowpeas, lima beans may be the most important grain legume to address in African research programs because of its wide range of adaptation, excellent disease and pest resistance, high yield potential, and excellent nutritional quality.

Peanuts

Peanuts or groundnuts originated in Bolivia and spread to both East and West Africa during the sixteenth century. Peanut production has become important in Nigeria, Senegal, Sudan, Zaire, Niger, Uganda, Burkina Faso, Cameroon, Malawi, Chad, and Mali. Although a nutritious food crop, peanuts are grown primarily as a cash crop, and between 75 and 90 percent of production is processed or exported. Comparison of yields in Africa (600 to 700 kg/ha) with those in Asia (1100 kg/ha) and the United States (2900 kg/ha) indicates that there is great potential to increase production. There are two basic types of peanuts. The Spanish Valencia type is erect with pods clustered around the base and produces uniformly mature seeds in

90 to 100 days. The Virginia type includes runner and upright varieties with pods and seeds maturing continuously from 120 to 150 days. Virginia varieties require better growing conditions and have higher yields than the Spanish Valencia varieties.

Peanuts thrive in lowland tropics with moderate rainfall, producing good yields on 500 to 600 mm of rainfall when well-distributed during the growing season. A well-developed taproot contributes to their reputation as a drought-resistant crop. Production in the humid tropics is poor due to increased diseases and pests. Due to their unique flowering and fruiting characteristics, peanuts perform best on well-drained sandy-loam savanna soils. Flowers are formed where the leaf connects to the branch. After self-pollination, the ovary stalk (peg) elongates and pushes the fertilized ovary into the soil—where the peanut develops. The correct soils allow easy penetration of the peg and growth of the peanut, minimize mold growth due to generally drier conditions, and ease digging up the pods. Peanuts are produced on clayey soils in Africa, but yields from these are lower.

Several production practices for peanuts are affected by their unique underground fruiting pattern. The crop may be planted on a ridge to improve drainage and increase ease of harvest. Due to the short stature of peanuts, they provide little competition for weeds, so good weed control is important for high yields. Cultivation or hoeing for weed control should be done before pegging to prevent damage to the developing pods. Peanuts have a unique nutritional requirement for relatively high calcium levels around the pods for proper development of the seed. Peanuts should not be left in the ground long after maturity, nor should the dug peanuts remain wet for a long period, otherwise the mold *Aspergillus flavus* could form and produce the chemical aflatoxin, which is quite poisonous and carcinogenic. Pods should be lifted from the ground together with the above-ground parts attached to them, then placed inverted in a wind row or small stack to minimize soil contact. Drying should continue in the field or on drying mats until the moisture content in the peanut drops to 10 percent.

Peanuts are commonly roasted, boiled, or eaten raw as a snack for consumption by producing households, but most of the production is exported or processed into oil and high protein cake, the solid left after oil is extracted. When processed on a small scale, cold, roasted peanuts are pressed to extract oil. Oil is commercially produced by cooking peanut pulp in a humid atmosphere, then extracting the oil by a hydraulic press. Commercial processing of unshelled roasted peanuts results in 27 percent oil, 41 percent cake, or meal, and 32 percent shell. The decorticated (without seedcoat) cake is approximately 47 percent protein.

This crop will continue to be important in African agriculture as a nutritious food and profitable cash crop. Production is relatively simple and requires little fertilizer or crop protection input. Diseases limit higher yields, and breeding programs are placing major emphasis on the development of disease-resistant varieties.

Pigeon Peas

Pigeon peas probably originated in Sub-Saharan Africa. Many are grown in home gardens, making estimates of total production difficult. Most field plantings are found in East Africa, particularly in Malawi, Tanzania, and Uganda. This legume is adapted to a wide range of environments and is being grown at low to medium elevations and in semiarid to humid regions; its resistance to fungal diseases allows it to grow well in the humid lowland tropics. Pigeon peas do best on deep, well-drained soils and are tolerant of saline or alkaline ones, but do poorly on acid and waterlogged soils. Yields of dry seeds from 300 to 3000 kg/ha are obtainable; yields of 500 to 1000 kg/ha are more common.

Pigeon peas are a woody, short-lived perennial with a productive life of five to six years, although the crop may be managed as an annual, producing the first seed crop 90 to 300 days after planting. Most varieties flower and produce seed in response to daylength, so the amount of time between planting and seed set can be manipulated with planting dates and variety selection. This legume is valuable as a component of intercrops, as a cover crop, and as bush fallow. Because early growth of pigeon peas is slow, it is seldom used as a sole crop; more commonly it is found intercropped with yam, corn, sorghum, or millet. Plant height ranges from 0.7 to 4.0 meters for erect and branching types, and both types may be used to support other climbing plants. During the first two to three months of growth, 500 to 600 millimeters of rainfall are required. Then, in soils with no restrictive layers, the pigeon peas produce a deep taproot that allows for drought tolerance during the remainder of the growing season. Pigeon pea competes less successfully than other legumes against weeds because of the pigeon pea's slow early growth; thus, weed control during the first four to six weeks is especially important. After full canopy forms, the plant competes well.

This legume is an excellent green pea vegetable and dry seed pulse. It requires a longer cooking time than other legumes require, due to its hard seedcoat, which varies depending on the variety of pigeon pea and weather conditions during and after seed maturation. Pigeon peas are palatable and more easily digested than some legumes, due to their lower quantities of metabolic inhibitors and flatus-producing sugars. The leaves are eaten as greens and used for forage, and the stems are used for fuel.

Breeding and selection of adapted pigeon pea varieties for Africa is in its infancy. Breeding objectives include high-yield capability, early maturation, determinate production of seed for more uniform maturation, increased drought resistance, clustering of flowers for harvest convenience, resistance to disease and insects, and better quality for seed and for cooking. Its value as a livestock feed in savannas during the dry season is currently being investigated.

Soybeans

Soybeans have been produced in China and parts of Asia for centuries, but did not spread throughout the world until the twentieth century. Production in Africa is limited now due to a lack of market availability and knowledge about domestic utilization and production practices. Soybeans have great potential, as they consistently produce more high quality protein and oil than any other crop. Yields of 1000 to 2000 kg/ha are obtainable when conditions are favorable. Most soybeans are produced in temperate areas and in the tropics at intermediate elevations, but soybeans can be produced in lowland tropics as well. This crop is adapted to soils ranging from sand to clay loams. They are less drought resistant than cowpeas, but can tolerate more waterlogging.

Africa's soybeans are produced primarily as a cash crop that is processed locally or exported. Oil, extracted for industrial uses and cooking, constitutes 18 percent of the bean. The remaining soybean meal is greater than 44 percent protein and can be ground into soybean flour; up to 10 percent soybean flour may be mixed with manufactured cereal products to significantly increase protein content without affecting taste. Soybeans consumed by humans should be boiled to eliminate a beany flavor and a protein digestive inhibitor.

A wide range of genetic material is available to assist in the selection and breeding of soybeans for Africa. Breeders are trying to develop varieties with less sensitivity to daylength and temperature; earlier maturity for short growing seasons; better palatability for direct human consumption; greater tolerance of high soil temperature; more resistance to diseases, insects, and nematodes; and improved seed quality.

• SUGGESTED FURTHER READINGS •

Aykroyd, W. R., Joyce Doughty, and Ann Walker. 1982. *Legumes in Human Nutrition*. FAO Food and Nutrition. Rome: Food and Agriculture Organization.

Dovlo, Florence E., Caroline E. Williams, and Laraba Zoaka. 1976. Cowpeas—Home Preparations and Use in West Africa. Ottawa: International Development Research Center.

Hahn, S. K. 1977. Sweet Potato. In *Ecophysiology of Tropical Crops*. P. de T. Alvin and T. T. Kozlowski, eds. Pp. 237–247. New York: Academic Press.

Harper, A. E. 1964. *Modern Banana Production*. London: Leonard Hill.

Litzenberger, Samuel C. 1974. *Guide for Field Crops in the Tropics and the Subtropics*. Washington, D.C.: Technical Assistance Bureau, United States Agency for International Development.

Martin, J. H., W. H. Leonard, and D. L. Stamp. 1976. *Principles of Field Crop Production*. New York: Macmillan Publishing Co.

Onwueme, I. C. 1978. Sweet Potato. In *The Tropical Tuber Crops*. Pp. 167–195. Chichester, England: John Wiley & Sons.

Rachie, K. O., and L. M. Roberts. 1974. Grain Legumes of the Lowland Tropics. *Advances in Agronomy* 26:1–132.

Simmonds, N. S. 1966. *Bananas*. London: Longman.

Smith, O. 1977. *Potatoes: Production, Storing, Processing*. Westport, Connecticut: AVI Publishing Company.

Stoskopf, Neal C. 1985. *Cereal Grain Crops*. Reston, Virginia: Reston Publishing Co.

Stover, R. H. 1972. *Banana, Plantation and Abaca Diseases*. Kew, Surrey, England: Commonwealth Mycological Institute.

Thirty Years of Cooperative Sweet Potato Research 1939–1969. 1970. *Southern Cooperative Services Bulletin* 159.

United States Department of Agriculture. 1981. *Food Problems and Prospects in Sub-Saharan Africa: The Decade of the 1980s*. Foreign Agricultural Economic Report No. 166. Washington, D.C.: Economic Research Service, United States Department of Agriculture.

Von Loesecke, H. W. 1950. *Bananas*. New York: Interscience Publications.

Wardlaw, C. W. 1961. *Banana Diseases*. London: Longman.

·13·

Livestock in the Economies
of Sub-Saharan Africa

JAMES R. SIMPSON
ROBERT E. McDOWELL

S ub-Saharan Africa is rich in animal biomass. There are many indigenous species of game, reptiles, birds, rodents, ants, termites, locusts, and others, which either support humans through food or are detrimental to crop production (R. E. McDowell 1984). Africa also has the usual domesticated species (livestock): camels, cattle, goats, poultry, swine, and equines, none of which are indigenous to Africa. As Africans shifted from gathering and hunting to agriculture, these introduced livestock became sources of food and providers of other goods and services such as manure for soil fertility and traction power for agriculture. Presently, the whole of Africa is highly dependent on its animal population. The purpose of this chapter is to provide an overview of the contributions of food animals, particularly those of livestock. Chapter 14 in this volume focuses on nondomesticated animals.

• ECONOMIC IMPORTANCE •

The estimated annual value of domestic livestock production in Sub-Saharan Africa is approximately $10 billion—about half of this is from meat, fiber, and skins and half is from nonfood products and services (International Livestock Center for Africa [ILCA] 1983). Additional contributions from meat, tourism, and trophies associated with game animals are valued at another $3.5 billion per year (McDowell et al. 1983). Seafood from rivers, lakes, and coastal waters add another $3 billion per year of food supplies. Total annual output from animals (livestock, game animals, and seafood), considering only their food value, equals or exceeds the $8.5 billion annual output from crops (Brumby et al. 1984). Output of products per livestock unit in Sub-Saharan Africa is low by developed-country standards. Nevertheless, these modest quantities of meat, milk, and eggs serve as an important source of high quality protein to complement African diets based on starch crops. There are tradeoffs, however: even though cattle are important for traction and manure and contribute to the protein supply, the animals also consume crop residues that could otherwise enrich the soil.

Milk is a precious commodity, especially for pastoralists and agropastoralists for whom it is a major source of food. Pastoralists must continually decide how to allocate available milk—either as family food or as a nutrient source for calves. The purchase of many foods—maize and other grains, tea, sugar, fats, and oils— by pastoralists and agropastoralists increases and decreases inversely to the availability of milk produced by their own animals. During the wet, rainy season, milk is available for both humans and calves. During the dry period when supplies of milk are reduced, the consumption of purchased foods and the cash outflow increase markedly. As the human population has increased in the arid and semiarid areas, emphasis has tended to shift from meat production to milk production. Hence, milk production has increased by 2 to 3 percent per year over the past decade, whereas meat production has increased only 1.3 percent per year in that time (ILCA 1985).

Income from livestock provides the main source of cash for both pastoralists and agropastoralists in virtually all of Sub-Saharan Africa. Livestock and livestock product sales enable low-resource farmers to earn cash to purchase inputs such as fertilizer and better seed to increase grain production, which suggests that expanded livestock output serves as a catalyst for growth. Exchanges of milk or small ruminants (sheep and goats) for grains between pastoralists and agropastoralists are important, particularly in arid and semiarid areas. The grazing of crop residues by pastoral herds leads to manure deposits that better support crop production (Brumby et al. 1984; Von Kaufmann 1982).

Livestock provide key factors of production in agriculture. Manure for fuel and fertilizer, and draft power for land preparation, are often more important than the edible products produced (see Table 13.1). In fact, meat production is frequently a minor product to both pastoralist and agropastoralist, although it is the product most African governments encourage. The contribution of nonfood items (fiber, skins or hides, and other inedible products) is noteworthy in many areas. It is also important to recognize that animals are multifaceted, very liquid savings mechanisms: livestock provide security of capital and a source of cash, especially in times of drought. Furthermore, they are a means for producers to build up equity capital and are one of the few good investments open to a wide segment of Africa's rural population. In good times livestock serve as a social convenience for bride price, weddings, etc.; in bad times animals are one of the few hedges available against financial and food disasters. Livestock contribute 20 to 30 percent of the gross domestic product in most countries of Sub-Saharan Africa. This percentage, although very large, underestimates the total value because difficult to measure contributions such as traction power and manure have not been included. Furthermore, livestock production may continue to grow because a sizeable proportion of Africa's urban dwellers are sufficiently affluent to effectively demand more and

TABLE 13.1. Classification of Contributions of Livestock to Human Welfare

Classification	Some Contributions
Food	milk, meat, eggs, prepared products
Fiber	wool, hair
Traction	agriculture, cartage, packing, herding, power, irrigation pumps, threshing grains, passenger conveyance
Waste	fertilizer, fuel, methane gas, construction, recycled as feed
Conservation	grazing, seed distribution
Pest Control	fallow between crops, plants in waterways
Cultural	exhibition, fighting, hunting, racing, status symbol, religious, barter, ceremonial
Inedible Products	horns, hooves, bones for processing into feed supplements and other products
Income	ready source of cash for daily needs and production inputs
Storage and Investments	capital, grains

Source: Adapted from R.E. McDowell. 1977. Ruminant Products: More than Meat and Milk. Morrilton, Arkansas: Winrock International Livestock Research and Training Center.

higher quality livestock products. It is critical to understand that Africans themselves desire greater per capita livestock products—it is not just a goal foreigners hold for Africans.

• DOMESTIC LIVESTOCK •

Cattle

Cattle first arrived in Africa from Western Asia about 5000 to 2300 B.C. (Payne 1970). Three types were introduced by nomadic peoples or by migration: the Hamitic "Longhorn" of Egypt, the "Shorthorn" of Egypt, and the Zebu. These types are not related to the Longhorn of the United States or the Shorthorn breed developed in England. The first admixtures of Zebu with Longhorn or Shorthorn or both probably took place as early as 2000 to 1500 B.C. at various centers in North and East Africa. Cattle that resulted from indigenous admixtures between humped and humpless cattle are generally classified as Sangas. A typology of more than fifty breeds in Sub-Saharan Africa is found in *The World's Beef Business* (Simpson and Farris 1982).

In the early 1980s there were about 174 million head of cattle in Africa, or 0.34 head per person. In contrast, the world average for this time was 0.26 head per person (see Table 13.2). Cattle are mainly concentrated in the east central part of Africa (see Figure 13.1). Examination of livestock inventories and meat production in Sub-Saharan Africa on a country by country basis reveals considerable differences among them. For example, cattle inventory varies from less than one-tenth of a head per person in Zaire to 3.6 head per person in Botswana. Another

FIGURE 13.1.   Distribution of Cattle in Africa

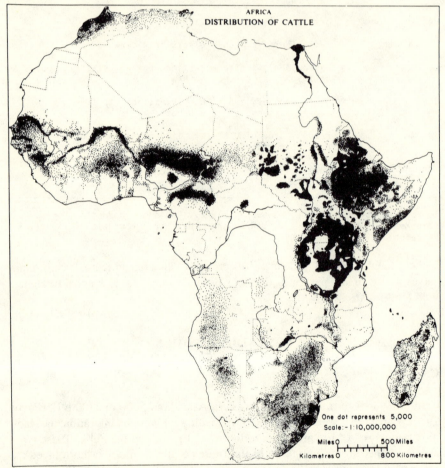

Source: Reprinted with permission from M. M. Rweyemamu. 1981. Surveillance and Control of Virus Diseases: Africa. In *Virus Diseases of Food Animals*. Vol. 1. *International Perspectives*, E. P. J. Gibbs, ed. London: Academic Press. Pp. 79–100. Originally from Interafrican Bureau for Animal Resources. 1976. Nairobi: Survey of Kenya.

measure, production of beef and veal per head of cattle (obtained by dividing total national production, including estimates of home slaughter, by total cattle inventory), further reveals that differences are very large, ranging from just 8.3 kilograms (kg) in Ethiopia to 25.7 kg in Rwanda. There are good reasons for these differences. About 40 percent of cattle are raised on rangelands, mainly by traditional pastoral groups, while virtually all of the remainder are kept in traditional (subsistence or small farmer) mixed crop-and-livestock systems. Crop residues play a critical role in cattle feeding and account for approximately half of cattle feedstuffs.

Sheep and Goats

About one-seventh of the world's sheep and goats are found in Africa. Distribution of inventory varies widely, from 0.04 head of livestock (both species) per person in Mozambique to 5.74 head per person in Burkina Faso (Simpson and Evangelou 1984). The average for Sub-Saharan Africa is 0.66 head per person. Yearly production of lamb, mutton, and goat meat varies widely, from 0.2 kg per person in Mozambique to 18.5 kg in Somalia. The yearly average for Sub-Saharan Africa, including both sheep and goats, is 2.4 kg per person (Jahnke 1982). The following inventories of goats indicate their relative importance in Africa: there are 0.31 head per person in Africa, only 0.10 head per person for the world, and 0.03 head per person in Europe (see Table 13.2). Sheep are a well-recognized commercial enterprise in developed countries as in Africa and number 0.37 head per person in Africa and 0.36 head per person in Europe. In Africa sheep are used for meat, and goats are for both milk and meat (Wilson 1984a).

Camels

Approximately 71 percent of the world's 17 million camels are found in the very arid regions (less than 400 millimeters of annual rainfall) of Sub-Saharan Africa. Camels are the oldest domestic species in Africa, having arrived via migration during the Pleistocene period about 3 million years ago (Wilson 1984b). They are most widely used for riding and transport, but certain ethnic groups such as the Somali and Afar in Ethiopia, Somalia, and Sudan maintain large herds almost solely for milk production. Camels prefer grass but shift to browse when grass quality is poor. They can consume plants from highly saline areas. Camels have a tolerance to plants that have a high salt content to conserve water; thus camels are well suited to arid and semiarid areas (Demment and Van Soest 1983).

TABLE 13.2. Cattle, Sheep and Goat Production in Africa and Selected Areas, 1983

Item	Units[a]	Africa	World	Europe	USA
Population, human	1,000,000	514.0	4,670.0	490.0	234.0
Cattle					
Annual Inventory	1,000,000 head	174.0	1,225.0	133.0	115.0
Per person	Head	0.34	0.26	0.27	0.49
Beef & Veal					
Total production	1,000 Mt	2,954.0	44,627.0	10,327.0	10,742.0
Production per person	kg	5.6	9.6	20.9	45.9
Production per head of cattle in inventory	kg	17.0	36.4	77.7	93.4
Sheep					
Annual Inventory	1,000,000 head	190.0	1,137.0	174.0	12.0
Per person	Head	0.37	0.24	0.36	0.05
Sheep meat					
Total production	1,000 Mt	775.0	6,139.0	1,150.0	170.0
production per person	kg	1.51	1.31	2.4	0.7
Production per head of sheep in inventory	kg	4.1	5.4	6.6	14.2
Goats					
Annual inventory	1,000,000 head	157.0	476.0	14.0	1.4
Per person	Head	0.31	0.10	0.03	0.01
Goat meat					
Total production	1,000 Mt	611.0	2.043	84.0	--
Production per person	kg	1.2	0.4	0.2	--
Production per head of goats in inventory	kg	3.9	4.3	6.0	--

Source: Adapted from FAO (Food and Agriculture Organization). 1984. Production Yearbook. Rome: FAO.

[a]Metric ton (Mt), kilogram (kg).

Swine and Poultry

There is only a relatively small amount of production and consumption of pork and poultry meat in any country of Sub-Saharan Africa. For example, just 2.8 kg of poultry meat are produced on a per person–per year basis. In contrast, production is about 15.2 kg per person per year in Europe and 30.9 kg per person per year in the United States. The production per person comparisons demonstrate the importance of these two commodities in diets of two major developed areas relative to their importance in diets of Sub-Saharan Africa.

Per capita consumption figures are useful, but it is more important to understand the reasons for differences in consumption levels. Concerning poultry, production systems in developed countries are based on confinement and a total concentrate ration. Inventory turnover in the United States is high, about seven to nine weeks, and so is the total production: 19.1 kg of meat are produced per bird in the annual inventory (the number at any one time in the year). In contrast, approximately 2.2 kg of meat are produced per bird in the annual inventory in Africa where there is very little confinement in poultry operations, despite the great benefits in reduced mortality, disease control, and feeding efficiency.

There are no blueprints to describe the roles of poultry or swine in optimizing resource utilization or to quantify their relation to food and development in Africa. However, Robert McDowell and Peter Hildebrand (1980) identified poultry in eight of the ten major agricultural systems in Africa and swine in five of these ten systems. Both species have traditionally been scavengers, converting byproducts and waste such as garbage, vegetable tops, sweet potato or yam vines, unmarketable roots, grasses, insects, and other consumable materials. Prices for poultry products in certain urban areas are such that grains, dried fish, and ground nuts, ordinarily used for human consumption, are being profitably used as feed for poultry. Nigeria has developed a number of commercial swine units. Other countries will no doubt follow this example.

Africa's production of pig meat may be analyzed in terms similar to that of poultry with the additional analysis of the role religion plays. In many areas, such as those with Moslems, consumption of pig meat is taboo. Furthermore, pig products may be dangerous due to trichinosis (disease from eating undercooked pork containing a parasitic worm) and to the ease with which other parasites can be transmitted to humans.

Techniques to enhance swine and poultry production are well known, thus there is great potential for reduced production costs and expanded output. However, these technologies cannot be employed until a multitude of economic and institutional constraints are overcome. Swine and poultry production must be intensive to realize efficiencies. Also, expanded demand will be mainly from the urban population. Consequently, even though these two species may potentially make a major contribution to meeting food needs in Africa, progress will be made only as each country experiences economic growth. An important benefit is that expansion of poultry and swine production would stimulate grain production in

TABLE 13.3. Swine and Poultry Production in Africa and Selected Areas, 1983

Item	Units[a]	Africa	World	Europe	USA
Population, human	1,000,000	514.0	4,670.0	490.0	234.0
Chickens in Annual Inventory	1,000,000	650.0	7,063.0	1,237.0	379.0
Chickens per person	Birds	1.26	1.51	2.52	1.62
Poultry Meat					
Total Production	1,000 Mt	1,449.0	28,624.0	7,424.0	7,234.0
Production per person	kg	2.8	6.1	15.2	30.9
Production per bird in Annual Inventory	kg	2.2	4.1	6.0	19.1
Pigs	1,000 head	11,045.0	773,599.0	173,555.0	53,935.0
Pigs per person	Head	0.02	0.17	0.35	0.23
Pigmeat					
Total Production	1,000 Mt	392.0	54,000.0	19,756.0	6,850.0
Production per person	kg	0.76	11.6	40.3	29.3
Production per pig in Annual Inventory	kg	35.5	69.8	113.8	127.1

Source: Adapted from FAO (Food and Agricultural Organization). 1984. Production Yearbook. Rome: FAO.

[a] Metric tons (Mt), kilograms (kg).

some areas, leading to even more economic activity—exactly what is needed for development.

• LIVESTOCK PRODUCTION SYSTEMS •

Agricultural production systems of Sub-Saharan Africa are numerous, highly complex, and vary widely depending on ecological zones and social patterns. For example, ten major smallholder crop-and-livestock systems and twelve subsystems have been identified in this region as compared with only four major systems in Latin America (McDowell and Hildebrand 1980). If the ten systems are redefined from a descriptive to a management viewpoint, three classifications can be identified: pastoral, transhumant, and sedentary.

Pastoral systems are associated with rangelands in arid and semiarid zones. These rangelands consist of natural or seminatural vegetation suitable for herds of wild or domestic ungulates (Pratt and Gwynne 1977). Although pure pastoralism is restricted to dry areas, there may be migrations into wetter areas and, in fact, there are several higher rainfall areas with a tradition of pastoral land use (Jahnke 1982). Pastoralists have no fixed home base, and their mobility is high. They utilize mixed species of ruminants, mainly camels and goats and sometimes cattle and sheep (Wilson 1984a, 1984b). Multispecies are preferred in order to reduce risks from loss by disease. The complementarity of species in feeding behavior and reproductive patterns—to ensure optimal use of rangeland resources and obtain maximum milk for food—is well recognized by pastoralists. As indicated in Table 13.4, the linkage between pastoralism and agriculture is weak. Some pure pastoralists may own or have access to plots or arable land for cropping, but their security rests principally in consumption of animal products and the barter of milk or small ruminants for grains.

The term "transhumant" denotes land-use systems in which livestock husbandry and cropping are practiced in association with each other. The relationship may be close, or the herding and cropping may be parallel activities without interaction. Quite often the two activities are not even carried out by the same management unit. Transhumants, in contrast to pastoralists, have a fixed base; however they are quite mobile depending upon rainfall distribution. The transhumant system prevails mainly in marginal areas with 300 to 600 millimeters of annual rainfall, i.e., those posing high risks for cropping. R. T. Wilson (1982) identifies two types of transhumance in Mali: dryland cropping and flood plain grazing with cropping. But H. E. Jahnke (1982) identifies at least four transhumant subsystems. Jahnke points out that transhumance is also practiced in Mali in subhumid areas with 600 to 1,000 millimeters of annual rainfall, where herd movements alleviate the threat of tsetse flies and the disease of trypanosomiasis. The characteristics of livestock production in Mali illustrate the complexity of livestock systems in Sub-Saharan Africa and the wide differences among systems, even in a single country, as a result of apparently small differences in a host of conditions.

TABLE 13.4. Major Characteristics of Livestock Production Systems in Mali

Item	Pastoral			Rainfed millet cropping	Agropastoral	
	Pure	Dryland cropping	Flood plain grazing and cropping		Irrigated rice cropping	Rainfed cash/subsistence cropping
Contribution of livestock (% gross revenue)	95	90	60	25	15	10
Rainfall (mm)	<400	300-600	200 (floodplain)	400-800	500 (irrigation)	700-1400
Importance of agriculture	nil to negligible	low	can be quite important	considerable	very important	paramount
Linkage with agriculture	very weak	some cultivation, manure exchanged for stubble grazing	cultivates or arranges to produce crops	cultivates own crops: work oxen important and consume crop residues		
Current carrying capacity:						
People	very low	low/medium	high/very high	medium	high	medium/high
Livestock	low	low/medium	medium/high	low/medium	medium/high	----------
TLU per capita[a]	0.8-1.6	0.4-1.6	1.2-1.6	0.4-1.6	0.4-1.2	0.4-0.8
Market production	40% barter mild/grain	50-60% sale milk/animals	45-50% sale animals/grain	10-50% sale animals	60% (sells rice)	60% (cash crops)
Mobility	high with no fixed base	high with fixed base	high wet season fixed base	low, short distances during cropping season, permanent base		

Source: Adapted from R.T. Wilson. 1982. Livestock Production in Central Mali. ILCA Bulletin No. 15. Addis Ababa: ILCA (International Livestock Centre for Africa).

[a]Total livestock units (TLU).

Transhumant herders generally practice cropping, but they obtain 60 to 90 percent of their food and income from livestock. These people use mixed herds of cattle, goats, and sheep. They place the highest value on milk for food or barter for grains. Manure is gathered during the dry season to ensure higher crop yields. Each household is usually geographically divided during the wet season—some members of the household tend livestock, which are grazing rangelands, and other members of the household cultivate crops. During the dry season, livestock are brought back to the household area to utilize crop residues as feedstuffs.

A third system, sedentary, denotes those people who have a permanent base. Subsets of this system denote those people (1) in mixed farming (crop-and-livestock systems) or agropastoralism, (2) in livestock ranching, and (3) who are landless or nearly so. Sedentary systems are found in all the major ecological zones: arid, semiarid, subhumid, humid, and highlands.

The main emphasis in the sedentary agropastoral subsystem is cropping; dependence on animals for income is variable, as illustrated for Mali in Table 13.4. Animal holdings are usually composed of multiple species. Livestock may be herded on fallow lands or rangelands away from the household during the cropping season and allowed to feed on crop residues during the dry season. Services rendered by animals are at least as important as the food they provide. Animal traction is generally used for land preparation and sometimes for weeding. There is high dependence on animal manures to support cropping. Income from sales of livestock is primarily used to support crop production. For example, this income allows for purchases of seed and fertilizer and provides economic security if crops fail due to low rainfall or pests.

The sedentary ranching subsystem and the pastoral system are often outwardly similiar (having range livestock production), but they have radically different management practices. The ranching subsystem is labor extensive and focuses on managing one or two livestock species to produce marketable commodities—mainly animals for slaughter, but in some instances for wool and milk. The function of livestock is to generate cash income; thus the operations are commercial or semicommercial. Livestock graze within fixed boundaries on land improved by such capital investments as fencing and watering points; purchased minerals or other supplements are used for animal nutrition. The ranches are not always private property; some are group or peasant cooperatives established with capital provided by governments and donor agencies (Behnke 1984). In a number of countries cattle are the dominant species used in ranching. But sheep ranching for skins or pelts (karakul) and wool occurs in some of the dry areas, particularly in Southern Africa.

The landless subsystem is a system in which land is markedly less important than it is in the systems described so far. This subsystem primarily refers to the situation of livestock that are not highly dependent on grazing—i.e., swine and poultry raised in confinement and cattle fed to achieve slaughter weight in confinement. This subsystem exists in all but the arid and semiarid areas. It incorporates situations in which swine and poultry obtain their feed as scavengers about the household, consuming household waste and scraps such as maize and sorghum bran from meal preparations. This subsystem shows how landless people can still be productive; they can purchase feed from commercial sources as a substitute for owning land.

In addition to the livestock sector, Africa's wild game population—the world's largest—contributes to the economy. In several countries the viewing of game, hunting, and photography are large generators of foreign exchange. Not a single country currently has any organized harvest system for their game animals, despite game meat being of some importance as a source of human food. In a few countries large tracts of land have been set aside for meat production from game, but harvest and transport costs have made these operations uneconomical. In areas where game roam freely, there are a larger number of predators and thus higher risks for herding goats and sheep. Even though there are these problems, game and cattle complement each other by making the best use of rangeland forage and browse, leading to a higher total production of meat per area of land. We conclude that more effort should be made to increase the contribution made by game animals to African food supplies (McDowell et al. 1983; see McGlothlen in this volume).

· CONSTRAINTS, PROBLEMS, AND PROSPECTS FOR LIVESTOCK PRODUCTION ·

Seasonal shortages of water for plant growth and for animals are the major ecological constraints to increasing livestock production in Sub-Saharan Africa. Over 70 percent of Sub-Saharan Africa is located in areas with less than 1,000 millimeters of rainfall per year, i.e., lands classed as arid, semiarid, and subhumid. Annual fluctuations in rainfall of more than 50 percent in these areas further accentuate problems of inconsistent feed resources. Livestock are widely found in arid areas and have been accused of being the major contributor to increased desertification. It is important to note the influence of drought cycles and many other factors in the fragile environment of the Sahelian region (see Nicholson in this volume). For instance, crop production and cutting trees to fuel furnaces for iron making during precolonial times were important destructive forces in Ghana and possibly many other localities (Haaland 1979). An alternate view is that animals have actually slowed desertification. Many of the plants that have survived in the more arid areas produce hard-coated seeds. When these seeds are ingested and passed by animals, the outer coat can be more easily broken down, making the seeds responsive to rainfall.

The tsetse fly infests over two thirds of the subhumid zone (600 to 1100 millimeters of rainfall per year), an area covering about 4.9 million square kilometers or 22 percent of all tropical Africa. This infestation is a serious obstacle for ruminant livestock production since the tsetse fly transmits the disease trypanosomiasis, for which there is still no effective control. Only 1.6 million square kilometers of this zone are tsetse free. Nevertheless, the subhumid zone harbors important livestock populations, including 33 million cattle or 22 percent of the total cattle population of Sub-Saharan Africa. There are also 14 million sheep or 14 percent of Africa's total and 16 million goats or 16 percent of the total (ILCA 1985).

Another problem in the subhumid zone is rapid human population growth due to both natural population increase and high rates of immigration. The considerable untapped potential of the area attracts people from neighboring semiarid and humid zones, both for cropping and livestock development (Jahnke 1982). High population growth compounds other problems that also obstruct development and require further attention. One unresolved problem is that livestock in the subhumid zone have the lowest productivity of livestock anywhere in Sub-Saharan Africa. Furthermore, the conventional long-term fallow necessary to maintain land fertility has declined with rising human population. It must be concluded, from both a land conservation and a potential livestock production standpoint, that research on crop-and-livestock systems that maintain land in continuous production should be a high priority (R. E. McDowell 1984).

Genetic improvement in livestock is frequently given a high priority because animals themselves are so visible, even to the casual observer. Not all genetic development efforts have been successful. Attempts to improve stocks and semen to produce crossbreeds and upgrade stock have often failed or, at best, have met with limited success because imported livestock could not survive in conventional systems. Frequently, disenchantment with the use of improved breeds resulted because attempts at genetic improvement were introduced as a single rather than plural phase of technological intervention. The single phase technology approach led to rapid expansion in animal numbers without due consideration to feed resources and other inputs for sustained animal production. The focus on importing stocks and semen was based on the assumption that new stocks or crossbreeds would be more efficient than native types in using locally available resources. Failure to effectively utilize improved breeds will continue until feed resources are more stable, their quality raised, and better management available (McDowell 1985).

Africa's livestock industry is also plagued with periodic outbreaks of epizootic diseases such as East Coast fever and rinderpest. East Coast fever is yet without an effective vaccine, but this is one of the two diseases being researched by the International Livestock Research Centre for Animal Diseases (ILRAD) in Nairobi, Kenya. In the 1950s and 1960s, national and international agencies collaborated to eradicate rinderpest. Control was effective for a time, but countries did not allocate adequate resources to maintain a vaccination program. The result was a major widespread outbreak in the early 1980s that will take years to control.

In spite of the real constraints to productivity already noted, certain allegations concerning the low productivity of African livestock are unfounded. African pastoralists are as rational and productive as their counterparts elsewhere, given the economic and natural environment within which they operate (de Leeuw and Konandreas 1982; Shapiro 1979). For example, the output per head of cattle in Africa is about $30 per annum or 15 percent of the purchase price, while the U.S.

output is estimated at $126 per head per year or approximately 13 percent of the purchase price (ILCA 1983). Increased output with lower production costs is needed, but this will take time and resources. Over the 1965 to 1980 period, donors channeled around $600 million into livestock programs in Africa based on the assumption that direct transfer of technology was appropriate. Results have been disappointing because much of that technology was inappropriate, especially given pricing patterns and social constraints.

During colonial times, Africa had a large commercial cattle industry and a considerable export market. Now governments in most countries have instituted controlled meat prices at low levels to placate urban populations or, at least, to prevent social unrest in the short term. Productivity per head of livestock has hardly increased since colonial times and in many areas it has decreased. At the same time, there has been an expansion of cropping into former grazing lands, resulting in commercial meat production becoming almost nonexistent except in Southern Africa. It must be recognized that higher prices to producers are a requirement to bring about increased meat production, but it is difficult to determine the extent to which prices should increase in the short and intermediate terms as part of national economic development strategies.

The complexity of livestock systems in Sub-Saharan Africa is difficult for Westerners to fathom, mainly because of extensive—yet often very subtle—cultural relationships in ownership, tenure, peer evaluation, prestige, trade, and so forth (Horowitz 1979). All of these infringe upon "improvement" or at least inhibit change at the level of individual herders and their herds. There are spatial aspects of traditional herd movements that must be taken into account in any planning exercise, along with all of the physical and economic variables (Little 1984). Terms of trade for livestock producers must be carefully weighed regarding the desire for cash and short-term wants versus long-term wants. Many of the vast host of variables exogenous to livestock production and marketing per se are covered in other parts of this volume.

A large percentage of livestock in Sub-Saharan Africa is grazed on "communally owned" land, which compounds management problems. The social organization that regulates the use of communal grazing lands and the ownership of livestock is difficult for outsiders to perceive and understand, even though input by anthropologists and economists is becoming ever more helpful (Sullivan et al. 1985; Horowitz 1979). For instance, it has become apparent that pastoralists need to maintain large herds for survival under harsh ecological conditions (Simpson and Sullivan 1984). Thus, much of the argument about increased livestock as "greed rather than need" is unfounded. There is also widespread agreement that livestock support a number of social, ritual, and economic functions; the relative ranking in importance of these functions varies depending upon ethnic groups, country, and environmental constraints (Schneider 1984). Decisions by herders that were viewed a few years ago as ultraconservative are now deemed prudent. The problem is failure to recognize that livestock development in Sub-Saharan Africa must be based on promotion and proper stimulus for two sectors—commercial and traditional—and that each has its own requirements, needs, and barriers to development.

Numerous additional constraints could be identified, but enough have been presented to point out the need for well-developed programs that take a multitude of factors into consideration rather than single phase technology transfers. Recognition of the multitude of factors is especially important as overcoming one constraint such as genetic improvement often leads to more ready identification of other constraints. Finally, although opportunities to increase livestock production are restricted, the livestock sector has done as well as or better than cropping (Brumby et al. 1984). Increases in meat and milk production in Sub-Saharan Africa from the 1969–1971 period to the 1979–1981 period were considerably greater than the increases in cereal production on the average, even in the eight countries with the worst production records. In the top eight countries in terms of production increases, outputs of all commodities rose, suggesting that the challenge of overcoming these constraints to livestock production may be met.

Just as a multitude of problem areas exist, so do solutions. There is no single universal solution, but rather each one depends on a complex series of factors, at least including ecological differences, social conditions, government policies, demand and supply situations, and type of systems. Most importantly, each solution depends on a country's long- and short-term objectives.

· SUGGESTED FURTHER READINGS ·

Dahl, G., and A. Hjort. 1976. *Having Herds: Pastoral Herd Growth and Household Economy*. Stockholm: Department of Social Anthropology, University of Stockholm.

Galaty, J. G., D. Aaranson, P. C. Salzman, and A. Chouinard, eds. 1981. *The Future of Pastoral Peoples: Proceedings of a Conference held in Nairobi, Kenya, 4th–8th August 1981*. Ottawa: International Development Centre.

Horowitz, Michael M. 1979. *The Sociology of Pastoralism and African Livestock Projects*. USAID Program Evaluation Discussion Paper No. 6. Washington, D.C.: United States Agency for International Development.

ILCA (International Livestock Centre for Africa) *Bulletin*. Addis Ababa, Ethiopia: ILCA.

Monod, T., ed. 1975. *Pastoralism in Tropical Africa*. London: Oxford University Press for the International African Institute.

Pratt, David, and M. D. Gwynne. 1977. *Rangeland Management and Ecology in East Africa*. London: Hodder and Stoughton.

Sandford, Stefen. 1983. *Management of Pastoral Development in the Third World*. London: Overseas Development Institute.

Shapiro, Kenneth H., ed. 1979. *Livestock Production and Marketing in the Entente States of West Africa: Summary Report*. Ann Arbor: University of Michigan, Center for Research on Economic Development.

Simpson, James R., and Phylo Evangelou. 1984. *Livestock Development in Sub-Saharan Africa: Constraints, Prospects, Policies*. Boulder, Colorado: Westview Press.

Simpson, James R., and Gregory M. Sullivan. 1985. On Institutional Change in Utilization in African Common Property Range Resources. *African Studies Review* 27:4:61–78.

Wilson, R. Trevor. 1984. *The Camel*. New York: Longman.

·14·

Undomesticated Animals and Plants

MICHAEL E. McGLOTHLEN
PAUL GOLDSMITH
CHARLES FOX

Undomesticated animals and plants are important sources of food in rural African systems, but that importance often goes unrecognized in discussions of food and development. For most rural Africans, undomesticated animals and plants provide foodstuffs, energy, monetary income, and useful materials that complement cultivated crops and livestock. Fish and game are the major sources of animal protein in large areas and probably for the majority of people in Sub-Saharan Africa. The Food and Agriculture Organization/International Union for Conservation of Nature and Natural Resources (FAO/IUCN) special project on African wildlife (Riney 1967; Riney and Hill 1967a, 1967b) estimated game constitutes 80 percent of fresh meat eaten in Ghana and 50 percent in Congo. This amount is probably typical in Sub-Saharan Africa, since heavily populated Nigeria gets 60 percent of its animal protein from fish, 19 percent from game, and 21 percent from livestock, i.e., 48 percent of fresh meat (game and livestock) comes from game. Even Botswana, a mainly pastoral country, gets 80 percent of its animal protein from game (Butynski and von Richter 1974). Livestock, especially cattle, are usually more important as sources of byproduct foods (milk, eggs), draft power, and manure and as economic investments and savings than as sources of meat (see Simpson and McDowell in this volume). Undomesticated trees are the major source of rural and urban household energy, since firewood and charcoal are the main cooking fuels of Africa (see Webley in this volume). Undomesticated plants, including trees, are used in construction and the manufacture of utensils, implements, medicines, and fishing and hunting poisons. Rural people also exploit undomesticated animals, plants, and products such as wild honey for cash income; the ultimate purchasers and consumers of some of these foods and materials live in urban areas.

222

• INDIGENOUS ANIMALS EXCLUDING FISH (MICHAEL E. McGLOTHLEN) •

Indigenous animals have a much more prominent role in the economy and diet of Africa than they do in Europe or North America. At present, more game meat than domestic meat is consumed in most of Sub-Saharan Africa (Riney 1967; Riney and Hill 1967a, 1967b; Pullan 1981; von Richter 1979; Roth 1966; Pollock 1974; Asibey 1974; Charter 1971). Increasing use of indigenous animals with improved management is required if the nutritional needs, especially for protein, of Africa's expanding human population are to be met. Strategies include: (1) increasing supplemental use with livestock, (2) game ranches, and (3) continuing to domesticate more species. A mixture of several species of indigenous animals can use the vegetation in a balanced nondestructive manner and produce much greater quantities of meat than can domestic animals. Meat production from these animals may be greatly expanded in a permanent manner, whereas the traditional domestic animals are already exceeding the maximum carrying capacity in many areas. To increase production of animal protein and to stop ecological damage such as desertification, in many cases domestic animals must be replaced or, at least, supplemented with indigenous animals.

Present Importance and Utilization

Exact data on the extent of present utilization of indigenous animals are hard to find (Riney 1967). After fish, game meat is the main source of animal protein in Sub-Saharan Africa, followed by milk and meat from domestic livestock (Asibey 1974; Ajayi 1971, 1983). Most of the meat is obtained from small animals that are not controlled by government agencies. Even for larger animals, much meat is consumed that does not pass through formal markets where it can be measured. Studies on specific cities and countries are the best present source of information (Riney and Hill 1967a, 1967b). In Botswana, for instance, which has a lot of cattle and is usually thought of as a pastoral economy, people get about 80 percent of their meat from game and the rest from domestic stock (Butynski and von Richter 1974; von Richter 1979). More meat is harvested from larger game animals covered by hunting licenses than from cattle, but the main source of animal protein in Botswana is the springhare, a large rodent not covered by the license. Over seven million pounds of springhare meat are consumed every year (Butynski 1973). From a nutritional viewpoint, springhares are more important than cattle. In the forest zone of West Africa, the most important meat animal is another rodent, the grasscutter, or cane rat (Asibey 1974). The grasscutter and the African giant rat have been domesticated in Nigeria and Ghana and are productive enough to repay their feed costs twice over at present market prices (Ajayi 1975, 1983). About one hundred seventy thousand pounds of grasscutter meat a year are sold in Accra, the capital of Ghana, constituting more than 70 percent of all bush meat sold there

(Asibey 1974).

In Nigeria, the most populous country in Africa and where comparatively little wildlife still exists, game meat accounts for 19 percent of consumed animal protein, compared with 21 percent from domestic animals and 60 percent from fish (Charter 1971). In one year, Charter estimated that six hundred seventeen thousand tons of bushmeat were consumed. In Zambia a similar pattern is noted; fish are the largest single source of animal protein, but cattle, wildlife, and poultry are all significant (Pullan 1981). Beef is only available in the cities and certain rural areas because of nagana, or trypanosomiasis. For much of the population, fish and game meat are the only sources of animal protein. Legal hunting of controlled animals, not including small mammals such as hares and springhares and birds such as guinea fowl and francolins, yields some four thousand tons of meat; there is much illegal poaching as well (Pullan 1981). The cropping of elephants in the Luangwa Valley National Park was estimated to have provided half of the meat in Zambia's Eastern Province in the late fifties (Darling 1960a). Most of the meat from larger animals is dried to make biltong (jerky) in Zambia, as elsewhere in Southern and East Africa. Four pounds of fresh meat dries to one pound of biltong.

Invertebrates are also a very important food source, and their contribution is hard to quantify. Termites are widely eaten in Africa and provide protein for many people. Although humans do not possess the enzyme that enables some animals to digest chitin, termite alates are a valuable source of protein and fat (Redford and Dorea 1984). In Zambia the alates come out in very large numbers early in the rainy season and are easy to collect. An added advantage is that they do not require cooking as they are quite tasty raw. Termites perform some useful functions such as disposing of dead leaves and grass and creating fertile soil. With the aid of intestinal microflora, they can digest structural carbohydrates even more thoroughly than can ruminants and can produce large quantities of valuable food from otherwise useless material (Nielsen and Josens 1978). Unfortunately, some types of termites are very destructive of crops (Malaka 1983). Caterpillars are also a popular food. In northwestern Zambia, the Luvale are able to eat caterpillars throughout the year by using different species (White 1967).

Utilization of animals for food is influenced by custom and by religion, regardless of whether or not the animals are domesticated. Members of a particular clan avoid eating the totem of their clan, and in some cases, an animal may not be killed at all because of clan pressure (de Vos 1977). Norris Dembetembe stated that many Shona in Zimbabwe do not approve of the domestication and use of eland by white farmers because it is the most popular totem animal (Dembetembe 1984, personal communication). Muslims will not eat suids or rats; many other people also will not eat pork. Antoon De Vos (1977) cites many examples of animals that are not supposed to be eaten by certain people; for instance, many animals are only supposed to be eaten by men. The Bisa of Zambia will not kill striped animals such as the zebra and eland, even though this restricts the supply of available meat (Marks 1973). Traditional beliefs also give special importance and value to certain wildlife products. The meat of certain animals or even certain parts of an animal may be thought to have medical properties, especially regarding fertility and virility as with, for example, the rhinoceros horn. In another example, house rats, which are not commonly eaten in Ghana, are given to children with whooping cough (Asibey 1974).

Commercial exploitation of wildlife as food is still rather limited, and little game meat is exported from Africa (Krostitz 1979). Game ranching and supplementing domestic stock with indigenous animals are still on an experimental basis in Africa, except in the Transvaal, Republic of South Africa, and in Zimbabwe. Many white farmers there have supplemented cattle with various antelope, and a few have converted to game ranching completely. In Zimbabwe in 1964, 1,145 tons of game meat were produced by commercial cropping, compared with 1,460 tons from licensed hunting (Roth 1966). H. H. Roth stated that twice as much would have been cropped except for a partial ban on hunting to control hoof and mouth disease. Hunting small animals, which do not require licenses, probably provides more meat to the rural population, but commercial production is important. Production of game meat by private farms in the Transvaal was reported to be over five million pounds in 1959 (Riney 1963). This was mostly from farms where the animals had been reintroduced specifically for meat production and brush control. Kudu and impala were the most important, but blesbuck, bushbuck, springbuck, wildebeest, zebra, francolin, guinea fowl, and ostrich all contributed significantly. Some farms eliminated cattle and stocked only indigenous animals, but more had both (Riney and Kettlitz 1964).

Game Parks, Tourism, and Cropping

Most commercial exploitation of African game animals has been through tourism, which has been widely proclaimed as the reason for preserving wildlife. But it is a remarkably poor argument from an African perspective: large tracts of land are to be set aside forever for the entertainment of foreigners with the wealth to enjoy it, while little or no benefit comes to local people (Myers 1981). Hotels, restaurants, tour companies, and so forth are mostly foreign owned—the profits leave Africa and all that is provided to Africans is employment for a few. In most cases, the cost to African countries of providing protection for game animals and tourists far exceeds the income from tourism. The failure of tourism to make any substantial contribution to land-hungry local people reinforces Norman Myer's contention that game parks will soon be lost unless they are given value by cropping the animals to provide food. Cropping is essential to give the animals themselves value, so they will be protected from poaching that can destroy needed breeding stock as well as the harvestable surplus (Darling 1960b).

In game management, commercial hunting and culling are ways of conserving wildlife. If the harvestable surplus is taken from a population, remaining animals will be healthier and better fed. Since reproduction usually reaches its maximum at about one half of carrying capacity, many animals may be harvested from most populations with a subsequent increase in productivity. Culling animals to preserve their habitat is frequently necessary. Thousands of elephants have died in the drought in Kenya in recent years. Since they were not harvested for human use, many tons of meat were allowed to rot (Myers 1981). Elephants and hippopotami are particularly damaging to their habitat or to farmers' crops when there are too many of them or when they are in the wrong place. Both are valuable sources of meat where culling programs are in operation; hippopotami are also of special value because they are the only local source of lard.

Ecological Considerations

Mixed indigenous animals can utilize more of the vegetation than domestic stock because different species eat different plants or different levels of the vegetation (Darling 1960a, 1960b). Different species may even prefer different parts of the same plants. When grazing on the same grass, wildebeest tend to prefer the leaves, topi the sheaths, and zebra the stems (Gwynne and Bell 1968); therefore, these animals tend to graze together in joint herds, in a somewhat serial manner. The advantage of using a variety of animals that occupy different ecological niches is widely accepted. When only one type of animal is using the vegetation, the composition can change as desirable plants are removed, leaving undesirable ones to reproduce. A mixed stock can use vegetation in a balanced, nondestructive manner. Many studies have shown that the carrying capacity (on unimproved, poor quality range) for game is at least three times that for cattle or even for a mixed stock of domestic animals (Talbot et al. 1965). If the money, chemicals, water, and machinery are available, improved pasture can be maintained so cattle will be as productive as mixed game. However, lack of capital and a climate with seasonal rains preclude this type of management in most of Africa.

Meat Production Using Indigenous Animals

There are several ways of using game animals for meat production: (1) to supplement and facilitate livestock production, (2) through game ranches that replace livestock, and (3) by continuing domestication. The most widely adopted of these practices at present is supplementing and facilitating cattle production. For example, various antelope can remove brush cover and improve the grazing for cattle. This practice is common in the Transvaal, where commercial farmers now widely accept that these indigenous animals are superior to sheep and goats for stocking in bush and undeveloped range (Riney 1963). Such a utilization of browsing animals may be profitably extended to any range cattle operation where there is some brush cover, as shown by kudu in Texas, United States (Teer 1974).

Since a mix of indigenous grazers can use the grass more completely and less destructively than cattle, in some places domestic animals have been completely replaced with wildlife. This is termed "game ranching" if the animals are allowed to wander freely over the range with little handling. It has been especially successful in the Transvaal, where transport to market is easy and the government is cooperative with commercial utilization of wildlife (Deane and Feely 1974). On an experimental game ranch in Zimbabwe, R. F. Dasmann (1964) and A. S. Mossman (1963) found that the income from game meat was the same as that previously provided by cattle ranching; higher productivity of the indigenous animals was offset by lower unit prices for game meat. However, the profits from game ranching were much higher than those from cattle ranching because of lower overhead costs for game animals. Indigenous animals do not require the veterinary care, supplemental feeding, and close management needed for cattle.

The third way to utilize indigenous animals is through domestication, in which animals are tamed and managed like traditional domestic animals (Ajayi 1971, 1983). Domestication has been done in several places with the eland, which is as large as domestic cattle and very easy to tame and handle (Posselt 1963). Eland form common herds with cattle and by browsing help clear land for cattle. They can be sprayed for ticks, vaccinated for various diseases, and even castrated just like cattle in the same facilities (Lightfoot and Posselt 1977). A domestic herd of eland kept in the Ukraine, USSR, since the turn of the century is being selected for milk production—eland milk makes excellent cheese (Treus and Kravchenko 1968).

The African buffalo has a reputation for being dangerous. It is powerful and can do a great deal of harm, but it is probably no more dangerous than a Jersey or Brahman bull (Myers 1982). Buffalo have even been used as draft animals in Zimbabwe recently. This animal is of special interest because of its greater ability, compared to cattle, to recycle nitrogen; thus buffaloes utilize poor forage that would not sustain cattle. All ruminants excrete some urea in their saliva. Buffalo combine this urea with carbohydrates by the rumen bacteria to make protein that can then be used by the animal. The buffalo recycles more of its own nitrogen than most ruminants (Sinclair 1977)—cattle recycle a moderate portion and the eland, very little. Browsers such as the eland tend to select high protein vegetation such as mopani and acacia, so they do not need to save much nitrogen.

Some animals are being domesticated for use in semidesert areas, where cattle are dying in the drought and where the grazing of domestic animals is extending the desert by permanently destroying fragile vegetation. The eland is being domesticated for use here, as it needs much less water than cattle or goats. It is able to withstand heat without such a great energy expenditure and water loss because it can allow its body temperature to rise several degrees without any adverse results. The oryx and addax are even more desert adapted; in addition to having this same thermoregulatory ability, they can survive on metabolic water produced from their feed without drinking at all (Hopcraft 1970). At the Galana ranch in eastern Kenya, fairly large herds of eland and oryx have been kept and handled successfully as domestic animals for some time (King and Heath 1975; King et al. 1977). The oryx can be profitably used as a domestic animal by itself under dry conditions

(Thresher 1980). If cattle had been replaced with oryx in the Sahel and Horn of Africa, the losses of stock due to drought would have been much less severe.

Many birds such as guinea fowl and francolins are also easy to domesticate and are highly productive. Guinea fowl and francolins have been kept for many years in Africa. When their eggs are found in the bush, they are put under a domestic hen to hatch. Now there is increased interest in their domestic production; they have been shown to breed well in captivity (Ayeni and Ajayi 1983). The ostrich was originally domesticated for its plumage, which is no longer so valuable, but domestic flocks are still kept in some areas for meat.

Prospects for Future Utilization

Hunting is threatened by the destruction of wildlife habitat as more land is cleared for agriculture. As human population pressure increases, larger wildlife may be kept only where they are the most efficient means of producing food or monetary income. There are many places where this is true today, and as this becomes recognized, game management may increasingly replace pastoralism. Domestic stock damage rangeland. This destruction is minimal if livestock numbers are kept within the capacity of the range, but during periods of drought, the carrying capacity is greatly reduced and a fairly small number of livestock permanently destroy vegetation. Indigenous animals are much less destructive at the same level of production. In some countries, there are now government destocking programs instituted for range conservation, and pastoralists are being forced to sell some of their cattle. This situation indicates the need for national governments to intervene to encourage long-term, sustainable food production systems.

In addition to utilizing drought-stricken and overgrazed areas for production with game ranching, marginal land that is not suitable at any time for livestock can be utilized in this way. Such marginal lands include large tracts in Africa where nagana carried by tsetse flies kills livestock. Better-adapted indigenous animals are resistant to many diseases and do not require the medicines and supplementary feed that cattle or goats need. These characteristics, coupled with their balanced, nondestructive use of vegetation, make indigenous animals the method of choice for producing food in large areas of Africa (Darling 1960b; Talbot et al. 1965). Because of this potential, it is important to start now to develop stocks of different types of indigenous herbivores. Not only each species but also local ecotypes with special adaptations need to be preserved. Otherwise, valuable genetic resources that can help to feed a hungry world will be lost forever (Ajayi 1971; Frankel 1963; Riney 1967; Surujbally 1977). For instance, as trypanosomiasis spreads over South America, importation of African wildlife may become important there.

If game ranching is more efficient and better adapted than ranching domesticated animals, and if the need to use less-destructive animals has been recognized widely for over twenty years, the question must arise as to why game ranching has not been widely adopted. Of course, it has been accepted with enthusiasm by some white farmers in the Transvaal and Zimbabwe, but it has had little impact north of the Zambezi. The cultural value of cattle is undoubtedly the main reason, but not the only one. Some game-ranching projects have been abandoned because of financial problems. In some cases, production of meat (and income) was lower because the selection of animals was limited to those already present or to those that appealed to cattlemen because they most resembled cattle. This limited selection left gaps in vegetation usage and lowered the carrying capacity of the land. Expensive imported fencing also may increase the cost greatly (McDowell et al. 1983). This fencing is not needed to keep the animals in for harvesting but may be needed to keep the animals from eating neighboring crops or to keep poachers out. In some places, the price paid for game meat was a small fraction of that for beef. This situation may be changed by government intervention. For example, the Zambian government solved a crisis in corn production by paying more for corn than they sold the cornmeal for in the cities. Since the costs of game ranching are largely labor costs paid in local currency, these costs should not be compared to commercial animal production costs, which include many imported medicines, herbicides, pesticides, and feed supplements that must be purchased with scarce foreign currency. If the primary concern is feeding people, and given that game can produce three times the meat that cattle can from the same land, then surely some intervention to encourage game production is justified.

Like many other innovations in agriculture, game ranching projects are likely to fail because of inadequate infrastructure such as transport to market or lack of planning and extension to enable local people to master new techniques. Uma Lele (1975) showed that complete package programs such as the Swedish programs in Ethiopia are able to continue working, whereas those programs that ignore infrastructure and ongoing extension always fail. The experiences in the Transvaal and Texas showed how African indigenous animals can contribute greatly to commercial meat production. If these methods spread over Africa, much more meat could be produced with much less environmental destruction. What is required to implement this quickly—the food crisis and range destruction demand speed—is providing complete programs with efforts directed toward marketing, transportation, and extension as well as increased production.

• FISH (PAUL GOLDSMITH) •

Fish have a more significant nutritional role than livestock in large areas of Sub-Saharan Africa, even though fish and fishing are less visible and have less symbolic significance. Fish make an important contribution to protein-poor diets; they provide high quality protein, vitamins, minerals, and free amino acids that compare favorably with those supplied by beef and eggs (see Table 12.3) (Deestra et al. 1974). The average annual consumption of fish in Sub-Saharan Africa is estimated to be more than nine kilograms per capita. Fish contribute 23 percent of all animal protein worldwide, and according to FAO data on thirty-four Sub-Saharan

African countries, fish provided more than 40 percent of the animal protein consumed in twelve of these countries, between 20 and 40 percent in another thirteen, and less than 20 percent in nine (Eicher and Baker 1982).

Traditional fishing is a variation of the hunting and gathering mode of subsistence and predates both agriculture and pastoralism. Early African fishermen exploited shallows of lakes, estuaries, floodplains, and rivers using a variety of ingenious devices. Later, fishing, hunting, and gathering were combined with pastoralism and agriculture in the subsistence strategies of various groups (see McGee in this volume), and the consumption of fish spread to nonfishing peoples as fish were dried and exchanged (Jackson 1971:37). In most areas of Africa today, fish are localized resources that are exploited on a seasonal basis. Given the ease with which fish can be smoked and dried, they represent a major source of storable protein. Extensive trade networks based on dried fish have developed throughout Africa including, for example, Fante women traders in Ghana (Gladwin 1975) and the central African trade in dagaa, or dried minnows (Libaba 1983).

African fisheries fall into two main categories: artesanal and industrial. Artesanal fisheries are small-scale fisheries that do not depend on expensive equipment and inputs. Most African fishing falls into this category, and it is even estimated that as much as 95 percent of fish harvested in Africa are taken by artesanal fishermen (Eicher and Baker 1982). Industrial fisheries are a relatively new development in Africa and require expensive mechanized equipment and modern vessels in addition to organizational efficiency to operate at a profit (Luna 1983). Some African countries have attempted to establish industrial fleets in their efforts to promote national economic development. The development of modern fleets entails the export of at least part of the harvest in order to finance capital inputs or repay loans and, in general, does not aim at making fish available at low prices for the African population. In contrast, almost all the fish caught by artesanal fishermen are consumed locally.

Traditional Fisheries

The fishermen of the East African Great Lakes use a number of different methods that are representative of traditional fishing technology (Jackson 1971). Their equipment includes hooks and lines, harpoons and lances, nonreturn traps that catch fish with barriers and mazes, baskets, and movable fences constructed out of papyrus. Poison is used to stun or kill fish in small pools left by receding floods (Jackson 1971). Traditional boats range from rafts made from logs or reeds to wooden dugouts and reed canoes. Recent developments include adding planking and strakes to a dugout keel. The use of twine nets and seines is believed to have resulted from contacts with Arabs and coastal traders who pushed into the interior during the nineteenth century.

The Nuer of southern Sudan look down upon their neighbors, the Shilluk, who subsist on fishing and hippopotamus hunting. Nevertheless, the Nuer rely on fishing and hunting to offset shortfalls resulting from crop failures and outbreaks of disease among their cattle. During periods of famine, these people rely exclusively on fish. Disdaining traps, the Nuer spear the fish, which are located in murky water by subtle movement of the surface or clumps of grass or weeds. They also construct a device of shell and rope that attracts fish and betrays their presence by bobbing (Evans-Pritchard 1940).

In Southern Benin, fishermen dig pools in the floodplains or excavate channels to modify natural pools. Fish parks are then created using clumps of aquatic vegetation that are later replaced with terrestrial bushes. Variations on these fish parks are constructed in lakes and shallow areas of rivers. Fish enter the parks seeking food and shelter. To harvest the fish, the fishermen surround the park with nets or fences constructed from palm fronds, remove the vegetation, and then constrict the circle until the fish can be caught in baskets and handnets. Larger parks may be exploited by fishing different sections throughout the year, and some parks are constructed with a reserved central area where the fish are allowed to breed. As in many other variations of traditional fishing, the harvests are controlled to safeguard the fish population on a long-term basis (Welcomme 1971).

The Swahili-speaking peoples of the East African coast have a long and highly developed maritime tradition. The Bajuni subgroup of the Swahili are skilled mariners and captain many of the dhows that carry goods to and from India and Arabia. The original Bajuni vessel, the mtepe, was a sailboat sewn together with coir rope and fastened with wooden pegs; it used a sail woven from thin strips of palm leaves (Prins 1965). The mtepe today has iron nails and canvas sails. Traditional twine nets and lines made from the bark of the baobab have given way to monofilament and machine-woven nets. The Bajuni developed a unique and curious technique for capturing two of their preferred catches, the dugong and seaturtles. First, remoras are caught alive and quartered in wooden enclosures on the shoreline, where their owners feed and care for them. When they fish for turtles or the elusive dugong, fishermen take the remoras along as living harpoons. Released in the sea with a rope attached, a remora seeks out its quarry and fastens to it with its suction disc. The fishermen then gingerly pull the remora back to the boat with its prize in tow. An expert at the task dives into the water and dispatches the dugong or turtle in proper Islamic fashion, and the remora is fed and returned to its enclosure until needed again.

Other coastal peoples fish the ocean, especially in West Africa, but unlike the Swahili fishermen, they do not indulge in deep-sea fishing, which has become the province of industrial fleets. They only work the shoreline and lagoons with seine nets. The Fante and Ewe of Ghana use large, fine-meshed nets to catch sardines and mackerel along the coast. Larger and more expensive nets are purchased through traditional cooperatives such as the "apapa" system of the Ewe (Kaplan et al. 1971).

Taboos

Some Africans are reluctant to eat fish. In some instances this avoidance may be due to simple unfamiliarity, but there do exist localized traditional sanctions or taboos against the consumption of various food items such as fish, poultry, eggs, etc. These food taboos are especially common among Nilotic and Cushitic pastoralists in East Africa. Maasai, for example, do not eat fish or poultry and only resort to hunting in times of extreme necessity.

Environmental conditions may be the basis for much of this cultural refusal to utilize all available food supplies. The pastoral mode of production is found in dry savanna areas, where the costs and benefits of expending human energy in fishing might make this activity impractical. Marvin Harris (1979) demonstrated how environmental factors may become codified in such cases into sanctions and taboos that express the cost-benefit relationship within a cultural context. These cultural expressions or traditions do not necessarily continue to constrain the utilization of fish as food when circumstances force pastoralists into a different economic mode, as evidenced by recent projects that have converted famine-stricken herdsmen into fishermen (Haakonsen 1983).

Taboos against eating fish may also act as a manifestation of social distinctions. The Katwa clan of the Siyu Swahili do not eat fish, despite the fact that they live directly on the ocean. The Katwa explain that this taboo resulted from the time when the son of a former sultan choked to death on a fishbone. Because the Katwa are a royal clan and have easy access to beef and poultry, the injunction against fish may be a dramatic way of expressing their wealth and social status.

Development of African Fisheries

The food crisis in Africa emphasizes the need to develop fisheries. The nutritional value of fish and its low price compared to meat make it an attractive source of protein. The development of this underexploited resource offers additional benefits in domestic employment opportunities and potential foreign-exchange earnings, especially in light of the declaration of 200-mile exclusive economic zones (EEZs). Policy options open to African countries are wide (Carroz 1984), and development strategies vary among the three contrasting areas of artesanal fisheries, industrial fisheries, and aquaculture.

If the main intent is to meet the food needs of African populations, development emphasis should be on artesanal fisheries. Although they are small scale and local in nature, artesanal fisheries provide most of the fish consumed in Africa. They are often located in remote areas where communications and social services are poor, and they provide employment and supplemental income for many people.

Some interventions that would benefit the artesanal sector include: (1) constructing and providing more efficient boats, (2) providing motors for existing boats, (3) providing credit so fishermen can upgrade their equipment, (4) constructing and operating facilities that can maintain boats and motors, and (5) constructing cold storage and better drying facilities. Better roads and marketing are also essential, as are making more readily available such necessities as fuel, potable water, and improved medical and social services (Ba 1983). And, as the level of production increases, management and research become more important.

Some of the world's richest fishing grounds lie off the coast of Africa, West Africa in particular, and are largely exploited not by Africans but by fishing fleets from Japan, South Korea, the USSR, and several European countries. The FAO estimated that foreign vessels net 65 percent of the coastal catch from Morocco to Zaire (FAO 1983a). Thus, most of this food is not consumed in Africa, but some returns to Africa in the form of canned and processed fish with the profits accruing to other countries. Establishing 200-mile EEZs partially ameliorates this situation (Brown 1985), but declaring these EEZs does not benefit African countries unless they are able to control and utilize the area, and this requires fishing vessels and naval forces. Recently, a few African countries have obtained mechanized fleets. Tanzania has established a government-owned operation to harvest deep water stocks of species for use in animal feeds and to harvest the popular dagaa, a freshwater sardine, for distribution in fresh and cured forms. Problems with the maintenance of boats and purse seines have plagued the operation, however, and plans for expansion have been cancelled (Libaba 1983).

African universities and development planners attach increasing importance to aquaculture, the controlled cultivation of fish. In a sense, aquaculture is domesticating fish, managing them in ponds rather than hunting them as a wild resource. The expansion of human populations and more complete utilization of natural fisheries make aquaculture an attractive venture. It is well developed in China and Japan, where it can be combined with paddy rice production. In Africa, the cost of constructing and managing ponds is a serious barrier. Aquaculture requires a relatively high level of technical management and competes with agriculture for water and land resources. In most of Africa for the foreseeable future, aquaculture is likely to lag behind the increased exploitation of fish stocks in natural waters.

Successful utilization of fish depends as much on marketing and distribution as on production. G. K. Libaba (1983) used Tanzania to illustrate the way that fish consumption may vary within a single country: although the national average annual consumption of sixteen kilograms per capita is well above the continental average, local consumption varies from fifty kilograms on the shore of Lake Tanganyika to one kilogram in Dodoma, the capital city, distant from both lake and ocean. To date there has been relatively little research on fish marketing and the impact of different policy interventions, price controls, and relative prices on distribution and production patterns.

• UNDOMESTICATED PLANTS AS FOOD (CHARLES FOX) •

Only a few studies mention the extent or significance of the use of undomesticated plants as food in Sub-Saharan Africa, although the importance of trees for fuel is noted (see Webley in this volume). The absence of data does not mean that these plants are unimportant as sources of food for rural Africans, but it does show the lack of scientific attention that these foods have received. Almost all of the available studies are by anthropologists, who have noted medicinal and religious uses as well as dietary information. Much of this data refers to hunting and gathering societies, which represent less than 1 percent of Africa's population (Lee and DeVore 1968; see McGee in this volume). More information about indigenous and undomesticated plants is needed before any definitive statements may be made about their significance today throughout Sub-Saharan Africa.

For hunting and gathering groups these plants represent the major source of daily calories (Allan 1965; Schneider 1981). Research on the Dobe !Kung people in the Kalahari shows that an average of 60 percent of daily caloric intake and many essential vitamins are derived from plants gathered by women; these foods include fruits, nuts, berries, gums, roots, and bulbs (Lee 1979). Hunting is the main food production activity for men, and game meat provides most of the protein in the !Kung diet.

Undomesticated plants are important to the diets of most agriculturalists and pastoralists even though they rely on undomesticated plants for smaller percentages of their daily caloric intake than do hunters and gatherers. Thayer Scudder (1971) noted that gathered plants represent an essential source of vitamins and minerals in the daily diet (especially during periods of agricultural shortages) of the Gwembe Tonga, who are Zambian agriculturalists. Patrick Fleuret and Anne Fleuret (1980) cited a similar use of undomesticated plants among non-hunter-gatherer groups in East, West, and Southern Africa and note that many groups employ a wide variety of plant types.

Richard Lee (1979) compared the gathering patterns of the Dobe !Kung and the Gwembe Tonga and found that even though the !Kung rely solely on gathered plants for their vegetable foodstuffs, the Gwembe Tonga utilize more plant species, consuming at least 131 types of wild plants (Scudder 1971). It is true that there is more plant diversity in the Tonga area, principally due to rainfall patterns, but the Tonga utilize some species that are available in !Kung areas that the !Kung do not consider to be food. Lee characterized Tonga foraging as intensive and !Kung foraging as extensive, noting that the population density of the agricultural Tonga is "approximately 100 times that of the Dobe !Kung" (Lee 1979).

The propagation of undomesticated plants may be increased by humans. Many plants grow more efficiently or in greater numbers in the ecosystems that are created by agricultural processes (Fleuret and Fleuret 1980). For example, wild grasses that are relatively uncommon in certain areas of Africa appear in large numbers in fallowed agricultural fields (Scudder 1971). Thus the disruption of natural ecosystems by agriculture does not necessarily mean that undomesticated plants will become unavailable as foods. Farming may enhance the variety and number of wild plants available for human consumption.

Categories of Food Use

Undomesticated plants that are gathered as food may be categorized according to their use. Four principal categories are: (1) relishes, or side dishes that accompany the staple food in typical meals, (2) snacks that are consumed between meals, (3) short-term staple substitutes, and (4) famine foods. It is important to remember that these categories are not static. Instead, they are flexible and depend largely on such factors as the relative availability of other types of food (domesticated or undomesticated) and local custom.

The diet of the Gwembe Tonga illustrates these four uses (Scudder 1962, 1971). During the rainy season, fresh leaves are gathered from numerous varieties of trees, local bushes, and herbs growing in cultivated and fallow fields. The leaves are deveined, pounded, and cooked into a thick souplike relish that accompanies the staple porridge. Other leaves are dried and stored for use during the dry season, when standing leaves may not be abundant or have the desired flavor. Various herbs, amaranths, and jutes are the plants most commonly used.

The snacks category consists of a number of different items, of which the most popular are fruits. Numerous different fruits from undomesticated trees and plants are eaten in season. Although fruits are generally popular among all ages, the highest recorded consumption is among children. Honey is a desirable snack and an important source of caloric energy for many people. Honey is often a rich source of insect protein because the combs frequently contain bee larvae and pupae (Bodenheimer 1951).

A variety of plants are used as short-term substitutes for staple crops in the diet during the "hungry months," the period just before the harvest when stored supplies of grain from the previous harvest are exhausted (Richards 1939). These alternative staples include roots, fruits, and grasses that are normally used as dietary supplements and are more heavily relied on during times of hardship.

Famine foods are those that are only utilized during periods of extreme food deprivation. Foods in this category are not generally used as dietary supplements when other foods are available because of prohibitive cooking procedures, low digestibility, or a combination of the two factors. For example, the beans of Acacia albida, a famine food, frequently cause intestinal disturbance and require long soakings in water, a long cooking time (about a full day), at least three changes of cooking water, and treatment in an ash-and-water solution before they are rendered edible (Scudder 1971).

Gathered wild plants may also be used in the household production of salt. The ashes of certain plants are high in salt content. Frequently the ashes of these plants are mixed into cooking water, or water is filtered through the ashes prior to cooking.

The examples cited in this section are by no means exhaustive of the gathered food inventories present in many African homes, but merely suggest the diversity and importance of such foods in the diets of many Africans. Foods gathered as nutritional supplements may also be used as trading commodities. The Hadza highly value honey as a food source, but it is also readily traded with neighbors who use it to make beer (Woodburn 1968). Mushrooms are commonly collected and sold along roads and in markets as well as eaten as subsidiary foods, but they have little nutritional value (Richards 1939). Refugee populations and others who are alienated from their normal food supply may utilize caterpillars, termites, honey, etc. as part of their diet and may devote their time to collecting these to sell as a way to procure their basic subsistence. Such a pattern has been noted for Angolan refugees living in Zambia (Hansen 1981). Collecting wood, reeds, and grasses to sell for fuel and as construction materials are other refugee livelihoods that use undomesticated plants.

• SUMMARY •

Indigenous undomesticated animals including fish are extremely important in the African diet and contribute more of the animal protein that is consumed than do domestic livestock. This importance in the diet is not matched by the amount of attention these food sources receive in discussions of food in Africa. It is intriguing to speculate about the possible reasons for this lack of public notice: (1) livestock are more visible than game animals or fish; (2) urban Africans and foreigners, including agricultural and development experts, associate game animals with tourism rather than with a meat supply; (3) urban elites and foreigners share "European" tastes for tender, domestic meat; (4) governments are land based and oriented toward the interior (or the airport) rather than being maritime powers oriented toward the ocean; and (5) domesticated animals are more controlled and, thus, more amenable to development programs, while game animals and fish are "uncaptured"—this is similar to a governmental bias toward totally controlled agricultural schemes rather than working with the "uncaptured peasants" (Hyden 1980).

Indigenous plants are also important in the diet, but much less information is available about the uses made of them and the extent of that usage. Leaves from undomesticated and domesticated plants are prepared as the most common relish, making the staple porridge palatable and providing essential vitamins and minerals for people who cannot regularly afford fish or meat—a large proportion of the African population even in urban areas. Fuelwood is obviously a critical resource (see Webley in this volume), and the great majority of all fuelwood comes from indigenous trees that are not grown in managed plantations or groves. Fruit, mushrooms, medicinal plants, wood, and charcoal are sold even in urban markets; thus undomesticated plants are a source of food and fuel to urban areas as well as a source of monetary income for the rural areas. Care must be taken to preserve valuable undomesticated plants while crop and firewood production are increasing.

Indigenous animals can be used as a supplement to cattle, in game ranching, or as domesticated livestock. Cropping the animals in game parks and supplementing cattle with antelope that help remove bush cover and improve pasture will produce a lot of meat with little cost or political opposition. Destocking rangeland and implementing game ranching would stop the destruction of vegetation by cattle and allow the production of much more meat from the same land, but would obviously be very unpopular with pastoralists. Indigenous animals must be used to increase animal protein production as much as politically possible, and it is essential that the productive potential of these animals not be lost by allowing valuable types to become extinct.

Fishing productivity can be greatly increased by providing some needs of the artesanal sector at modest cost. This intervention is probably the most cost effective of any intervention to improve nutrition in Africa. With modern fishing fleets and naval forces to protect African waters, many coastal countries could reap considerable fish crops from the sea, but this involves large capital investment and technological expertise.

• SUGGESTED FURTHER READINGS •

Bodenheimer, F. S. 1951. *Insects as Human Food: A Chapter of the Ecology of Man.* The Hague: Dr. W. Junk Publications.

Christensen, James B. 1982. Problems Resulting From Technological Change: The Case of Fanti Fisherman in Ghana. In *Modernization and Marine Fisheries Policy.* John R. Maiolo and Michael K. Orbach, eds. Pp. 249–274. Ann Arbor, Michigan: Ann Arbor Science Publishers.

Darling, F. F. 1960. Wildlife Husbandry in Africa. *Scientific American* 203:5:123–128.

Dasmann, R. F. 1964. *African Game Ranching.* Oxford: Pergamon Press.

Fleuret, Patrick, and Anne Fleuret. 1980. Nutrition, Consumption and Agricultural Change. *Human Organization* 39:3:250–260.

Gibbs, David. 1984. The Politics of Economic Development: The Case of the Mauretanian Fishing Industry. *African Studies Review* 27:4:79–93.

Hopcraft, David. 1970. East Africa: The Advantages of Farming Game. *SPAN* 13:1:29–32.

Jackson, P. B. N. 1971. The African Great Lakes Fisheries: Past, Present, and Future. *African Journal of Tropical Hydrobiology and Fisheries* 1:1:35–48.

Lee, Richard B. 1979. *The !Kung San: Men, Women, and Work in a Foraging Society.* Cambridge: Cambridge University Press.

King, J. M., and B. R. Heath. 1975. Game Domestication for Animal Production in Africa: Experiences at the Galana Ranch. *World Animal Review* 16:23–30.

Mann, M. J. 1975. Freshwater Fisheries. In *East Africa: Its Peoples and Resources.* W. T. W. Morgan, ed. Pp. 229–242. Nairobi: Oxford University Press.

Pollnac, Richard B. 1981. *Sociocultural Aspects of Developing Small-Scale Fisheries: Delivering Services to the Poor.* World Bank Staff Working Paper No. 490. Washington, D.C.: The World Bank.

Prins, A. H. J. 1965. *Sailing from Lamu: A Study of Maritime Cultures in Islamic East*

Africa. Assen, Netherlands: Van Gorcum.

Riney, T., and W. L. Kettlitz. 1964. Management of Large Mammals in the Transvaal. *Mammalia* 28:189–248.

Scudder, Thayer. 1971. *Gathering Among African Woodland Savannah Cultivators.* Zambian Papers No. 4. Manchester: Manchester University Press.

Talbot, L. M., W. J. A. Payne, H. P. Ledger, L. D. Verdcourt, and M. H. Talbot. 1965. *The Meat Production Potential of Wild Animals in Africa.* Farnham Royal, Buckshire, England: Commonwealth Agricultural Bureau.

·15·

Postharvest Considerations in the Food Chain

ROBERT P. BATES

The Council on Environmental Quality (1980) forecasted malnutrition to increase 160 percent, from affecting 0.5 billion persons in 1975 to 1.3 billion by 2000, despite a 90 percent increase in food production. They projected global population to increase 60 percent during this time (from 4 to 6.4 billion) and be accompanied by chronic shortages of potable water, arable land, and energy in poorer nations due to deforestation and overly intensive agriculture. Unpredictable changes in climate and inevitable environmental deterioration could make this worse. Some countermeasures must be taken to forestall or lessen the impact of this threatening malnutrition.

In the sequence of activities from plant and animal breeding and propagation to human food consumption (actual ingestion), the postharvest chain—the segment from harvest to ingestion—has received comparatively little global attention. This lack of attention is particularly true for Africa where many countries lack the infrastructure necessary to effectively transport, store, refine, preserve, distribute, and market foodstuffs (J. McDowell 1984). Consequently, postharvest food losses range from 20 percent to more than 50 percent (May 1977; National Academy of Sciences [NAS] 1978). These are dramatic and tragic losses since all of the care, labor, and agricultural inputs that went into producing and handling the food are lost upon spoilage. Moreover, such waste elevates food prices and causes shortages—burdens inevitably borne by the poor who economically and nutritionally can least afford more problems.

This chapter is a revised version of an earlier article by the author entitled "Appropriate Technologies for Increasing Food Utilization," in *Malnutrition: Determinants and Consequences,* ed. Philip L. White and Nancy Selvey, (New York: Alan R. Liss, 1984), pp. 355–364. Used by permission of the publisher.

• A BALANCED STRATEGY •

Any strategy designed to overcome limitations in the quantity and quality of food and associated resources requires five distinct but highly interrelated components: conservation, conversion, complementation, innovation, and implementation. Before elaborating on these five components, the concept of interrelationships warrants some emphasis because food handling and preservation (a critical postharvest activity) is only one important link in the food chain.

Bourne's (1978) classic pipeline metaphor clearly illustrates the linkages in the food chain (see Figure 15.1). Unbalanced attention to any one element is apt to exacerbate bottlenecks in others. For example, enhanced production efficiencies cannot be fully exploited, even when combined with improvement in food preservation, if other factors such as packaging, transportation, and marketing are not improved concurrently. Although these interrelationships are logical, almost self evident, it is remarkable how frequently inadequate attention is paid to the *whole* while dedicated capable individuals devote considerable efforts to the *parts*.

Within the context of the need for balanced or appropriate applications of technology, this chapter emphasizes important features of the postharvest food chain, outlines food loss mechanisms, and suggests technologies and application strategies to ameliorate the situation.

• CONSERVATION •

Postharvest loss prevention encompasses the major conservation strategy worldwide (Herzka 1980). Wasted food reflects a loss of critically needed nutrients and vital, costly auxiliary inputs throughout the food chain such as seed, feed, labor, fertilizer, herbicides, pesticides, irrigation capital, water, land, packaging, transportation, storage facilities, and energy. Furthermore, if spoiled food is consumed, serious human or animal illnesses can result.

From one-fifth to one-half of the harvest is estimated to be lost in some less-developed countries (May 1977; NAS 1978). Since this loss can accompany low production yields and preharvest losses due to environmental constraints (vagaries of weather, poor soils, rapacious insects and pests, and persistent plant disease), the consumable food supply is often a pathetically small fraction of the total potential.

Postharvest food conservation occupies a high priority within the international technical assistance community (NAS 1978). Goals consist of (1) recovering efficiently and economically the greatest amount of edible food from a harvest, catch, or slaughter and (2) protecting this harvest from spoilage throughout the food chain (Lindblad and Druben 1980; Reusse 1976). A variety of food processing techniques are applicable, but efforts to make the most of available food resources are complicated by the perishable nature of foods (see Table 15.1).

FIGURE 15.1. Postharvest Food Pipelines

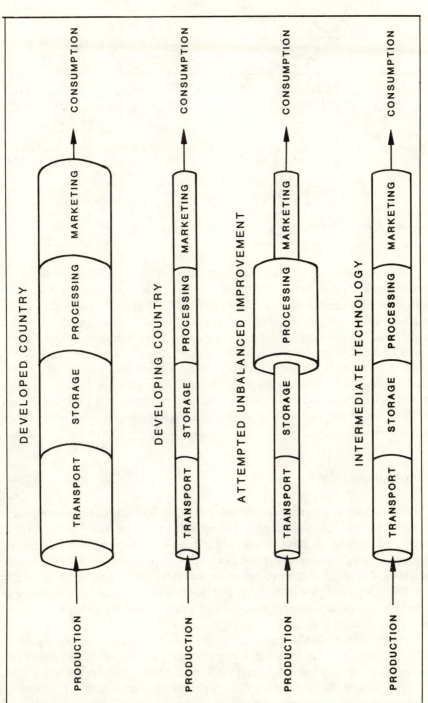

Source: M. C. Bourne. 1978. What is Appropriate/Intermediate Food Technology? *Food Technology* 32:4:77–78, 80.

TABLE 15.1. Food Spoilage Categories

Type	Durables	Semi-perishables	Perishables
Example	Cereals and and oilseeds	Roots and tubers	Vegetables and Meats
Stabilizing Feature	Low moisture, protective hull	Low, balanced metabolism	Low temperature rapid preservation
Deterioration	Insects, vermin, mold	Injury, metabolic imbalance	Microbial, enzymatic
Storage Life	Months-years	Days-months	Hours-days

Tactics required to stabilize foods depend upon the type; handling history; intrinsic physical, chemical, and biological characteristics; and extrinsic interaction with the environment (Bourne 1977). In more-developed countries, food preservation methods are largely based on sophisticated capital and energy intensive practices, although increasingly subject to resource and environmental constraints. Less-developed countries use many of these practices on a smaller scale, sometimes restricted to the major cities; they can afford only the most straightforward preservation alternatives for the majority of their populations, and even these techniques are severely hampered by resource limitations (Brown and Pariser 1975). A few of the potentially most useful methods for that majority are presented in this chapter.

Dehydration

The bulk of food staples are in the durable category. For millenia the most practical preservation was accomplished by "letting nature take its course" in the form of sunny, dry weather at harvest time. Natural solar drying simplified harvest and storage, although unseasonable rains or excessive humidity often raised havoc. Mechanical drying and other preservation methods evolved to overcome climatic constraints to sun drying (Szulmayer 1971). The need to reduce crop moisture to about 13 percent, depending upon commodity, and keep it dry and protected from insects and pests is still a major challenge.

Solar drying methods range from simply spreading the food out during sunny days to elaborate double-walled structures that serve as both solar collectors/dryers and food storage facilities (Midwest Plan Service 1980). There are many examples of drying systems suitable for durables; some are even applicable to higher moisture semiperishables and perishables under more humid conditions (Clark 1976; Moody 1980). These involve indigenous construction materials, supplemented by industrial materials (glass, plastic sheets, screening, and aluminum foil) when economically and logistically practical (Coleman et al. 1980; Doe et al. 1977; Darrow and Pam 1976). Even indirect absorption drying is used in some systems (Srinivas et al. 1976).

Once the food is dry, storage facilities can be constructed from local materials such as bamboo, mud, plant fibers, ceramics, etc. Sound construction and design are necessary to protect the stored food from flooding, driving rains, larger predators, and insect contamination (Majumder 1980; Anandaswam and Iyengar 1980; Dichter 1980). In Africa a common inexpensive solution is a simple, well-constructed thatched hut. At greater expense, ferrocement is a durable alternative (NAS 1973). Simple protection such as the coating of dry legumes with about 0.5 percent vegetable oil (League for International Food Education [LIFE] 1979) and the use of small amounts of inorganic powders are promising approaches to counteract insect infestation, though additional alternatives based upon local resources are needed.

Semiperishables and perishables represent a more difficult drying problem. Since deterioration is more rapid at the higher moisture contents characterizing these foods, more extensive drying is required for them. Auxiliary preservation steps such as salting, smoking, and use of chemicals often accompany dehydration. Any combination of salt, pH reduction, and smoke helps to retard microbial growth (Labuza 1978). Indigenous methods for producing reasonably pure salt are in need of development (NAS 1974), as are other curing compounds and substances that reduce the water activity of foods (Flink 1978). Water activity refers to establishing an equilibrium between the relative humidity of the food and the relative humidity of the atmosphere and is related to the moisture content of the food.

Intermediate moisture foods—moist enough to be eaten out of the hand, yet dry enough to resist microbial growth—are a useful preservation category. Dried fruits, prunes, raisins, jams, jellies, other sugar confections, and certain cheeses are examples (Gee et al. 1977). High concentrations of sugar, salt, or acid are the preservation agents involved. Water activity reducing substances such as glycerol, corn syrup, and other palatable humectants are effective, if available.

Wet Preservation

To deal with perishable foods in the moist state, methods such as thermal processing, fermentation, and chemical stabilization apply. Canning is hampered by the expense and scarcity of hermetic containers (NAS 1974). In the United States, home and community canning are practical processes that now rely more on reusable glass canning jars than on metal cans. In less-developed countries, community canning with canning jars and lids would function on an institutional or small, cottage industry scale (Jackson and Mehrer 1978). The concept of a local canning center may be extended to other food preservation practices. A well-designed food preservation center could serve for both training and utilization research, involving a variety of foods and processes including canning in a realistic local setting. The moderate expense of a small, versatile facility is a more logical step in exploring and demonstrating food preservation alternatives than a turnkey processing plant—many turnkey plants now stand in less-developed countries as rusting monuments to poor planning.

Fermentation is such an appropriate preservation method that there are few cultures that have not developed some type of indigenous fermentation (Beuchat 1978; Hesseltine 1979; Eka 1980). Lactic and acetic acid fermentations lower pH and thereby extend shelf life (Pontecorvo and Bourne 1978; Rao et al. 1978). These fermentations also simplify canning by reducing both process temperature and time (Worgan 1977; Anand 1975).

Properly controlled proteolytic processes can change fish, a highly perishable commodity, into a fairly stable, nourishing, and flavorful product. Specifically, under high salt and anaerobic conditions the digestive enzymes of small fish reduce the flesh to a semifluid paste. Although the product is salty and strongly flavored by Western standards, the process is inexpensive and could make an important contribution to bland, high-carbohydrate diets (Burkholder et al. 1968). Similar fermentations have potential in many countries. The vegetable process analogous to autolysis is the sprouting process by which the enzymatic activity of viable seeds can be exploited (Fordham et al. 1975).

The preservation agent need not be generated from the food. It may be added from another source to promote chemical stabilization. Using cassava leaves to wrap cassava roots apparently decreases the rate of deterioration, presumably due to the cyanogens present in the leaves (Aiyer et al. 1978). Natural products also may contribute other functional substances such as antioxidants (Hudson and Mahgoub 1980). The use of added acid in quick pickling, added sulfur dioxide to perishables (Green 1976), high sugar concentration in conserves, and the many curing recipes for animal products—all are applications of chemicals to aid preservation. Discarded materials such as banana peels or vegetable refuse may be ready sources of acids for preservation (Adams 1978; Bates 1971). There is a rather impressive inventory of preservatives available for food use (Robach 1980), although due to cost, availability, or safety considerations only a few are applicable or affordable for nonindustrial uses in less-developed countries. Salt is one of the most ubiquitous chemicals and has important uses in food drying, fermentation, and curing to restrict undesirable microbial growth. It is particularly valuable in the preservation of highly perishable animal products such as meat (Thomas 1975) and fish. To overcome penetration problems, salt may be thoroughly mixed with fish to produce a range of stable intermediate moisture foods that may be desalted and reconstituted for consumption (Mendelsohn 1974).

Acid is a very useful and easily obtained preservative. It is used synergistically with heat in canning, and sulfur dioxide and acid may be combined to stabilize foods for reasonably long periods without the need for extensive heating (Rizvi 1978). Of course, the misuse of chemicals may be dangerous, so they should be handled and applied with care, and chemical preservatives should never be a substitute for proper food sanitation and handling practices.

Cold preservation, a method of considerable value, is restricted in its use because of the cost and logistics associated with mechanical refrigeration. Electric refrigerators are usually only found in Africa in cities and in specially favored locations, but kerosene refrigerators are more widespread. Nevertheless, it is possible to maintain food at modest subambient temperatures by taking advantage of natural or constructed shade, prevailing winds, cool water, or earth, and by timing harvesting and handling operations to coincide with the minimum daily temperature (Rickard and Coursey 1979). In arid regions with adequate water, evaporative cooling can lower the storage temperature (Volunteers in International Technical Assistance [VITA] 1970). High temperature abuse of food is more difficult to avoid in the tropics due to warmer heat sinks, but steps toward cool, dark, dry storage should be taken when possible.

Resources

Scarcities of fossil fuels have vast implications for the food chain that are currently reflected in food shortages and high costs. The unavailability and high cost of high grade energy sources such as electricity or kerosene have had an unfortunate trickle-down effect. Former users have turned to charcoal and wood. Increased demand has increased price and scarcity of these fuels, putting them beyond the economic means of some poor people; increased demand has also caused irreversible depletion of forest resources (Eckholm 1975). This depletion can have grave environmental consequences as deforestation affects soil fertility, the water shed, and, ultimately, climate. Competition for cooking wood requires a great expenditure in time and labor, primarily by women, detracting from other essential tasks such as food production, child care, and income generation (O'Kelley 1977; Carr 1978). As firewood becomes more expensive, the expense also affects cooking procedures, resulting in less cooking and in rejection of foods requiring extensive heating. These changes may adversely influence food sanitation and dietary nutritive value. For these reasons, fuel conservation in food processing and preparation has a very high priority. One response has been a number of simple, inexpensive cooking stove designs (Openshaw 1980; Gubbins 1980).

Water is another resource that may be limiting if too abundant—causing flooding, erosion, and food spoilage—or if inadequate in quantity or quality—resulting in crop failure and insanitary conditions. When water scarcity makes it impractical to wash food, prevention of initial food contamination by careful handling, efficient dry cleaning, and minimum water use must be stressed.

Packaging is essential since food must be protected from the environment all the way from bulk storage down to single serving containers. The cost and unavailability of hermetic containers has already been cited as a serious disincentive to thermal processing, although a small-scale can fabrication line may make on-site manufacture more practical (Leppington 1980). Packaging similarly limits the handling and storage associated with other food preservation operations. Any mechanism that promotes safe repetitive use of food containers and packaging material reduces unit cost and promotes preservation technology (Mahdeviah 1970). The retortable pouch is increasing in commercial importance (Mermelstein 1978). Pouch fabrication is simple, requiring only roll stock and an impulse sealer, but the retort system required for low acid foods is expensive and sophisticated. Nevertheless, the pouch processing system for high acid foods may be much simpler. If the pouch stock is rugged and reasonably impermeable to oxygen, inexpensive small-scale pouch processing appears practical (Gomez et al. 1980).

The high value of industrial containers—glass jars, metal cans, and plastic packaging material—to the poor in many countries is evident by the way all sound containers are carefully salvaged and used in many household applications. In contrast, the United States is a particularly poor example of packaging conservation (evidence abounds in any domestic trash dump), although New Zealand is setting a good example of glass reuse and recycling, thereby conserving both energy and raw materials (McC. Webber 1977).

A valuable feature of food and resource conservation efforts is that they may be practiced at many stages from production through consumption, often without appreciable cost, and result in significant overall savings. Unfortunately, the most frugal and needy—those at and below subsistence level—have usually already been forced to initiate the few conservation measures available to them. A major goal of technical assistance is to provide the poor with more and better conservation alternatives.

• CONVERSION •

Agriculture converts diffuse resources such as sunlight, water, soil nutrients, and the genetic potential of plants and animals into a reliable food supply. Similarly, the change from simple collection and direct consumption of wild grass seeds to the fabrication of nutritious, appetizing baked products derived from domesticated progeny (cereal grains) of those same seeds is a remarkable conversion accomplishment. The development of cooking, which gave humans access to foods hitherto toxic in the raw state, may have been a response to limited food supplies (Leopold and Ardrey 1972). Food preparation methods can stabilize foods and convert them to more valuable and convenient forms. Most fermentations; the processes by which milk becomes refined dairy products; sugar cane, sugar; grains, baked goods; other staples, formulated foods—all these are techniques for converting perishables to semiperishables or durables, amorphous substances to textured form, or unpalatable constituents to desirable, functional foods.

The feeding of inedible crop residues, food waste, and forage to animals that in turn form meat, milk, and valuable byproducts (Satterlee 1975), illustrates a significant leverage or multiplier effect in converting low value or even undesirable substances to important items of agriculture and commerce. Another conversion activity is resource upgrading: converting dangerous unpotable water into sanitary water; biomass into bioenergy; sewage into methane, feed, or fertilizer; and crude fiber and minerals into valuable consumer products.

Effective utilization of solar energy, either directly by capture of the sun's rays (geometric concentration of solar energy) or indirectly by recovery of biomass energy (biological concentration of solar energy), illustrates both conservation, or sparing of other energy resources, and conversion. Appealing features of solar energy are the comparative abundance and reliability of the source and the potential low cost of conversion techniques (NAS 1976; Brown and Howe 1978). When process interruption is not acceptable—e.g., during cooking or when sunset or overcast conditions interfere with drying of a highly perishable food—a backup system must be provided. This may be as simple as providing a fire for drying (Bialostacki 1977). The use of stored heat in the form of solar-generated hot water or rocks, dry desiccants, and phase change chemicals provides a more continuous backup (Merrill and Gage 1978), but stored heat is comparatively expensive and complicated in circumstances in which cost and simplicity are primary concerns.

Fortunately, solar energy stored in biomass provides an intriguing source for uninterrupted processing (De Lucia and Lesser 1980). When direct combustion and pyrolysis are unfeasible due to low biomass production, high moisture content, or environmental limitations, then agricultural, industrial, and community wastes can produce methane through anaerobic digestion (Garg et al. 1980). This process has been well exploited in China as a means for producing biogas for household and community use as well as for producing feed and fertilizer (Lovejoy 1980). When properly designed and operated, biogas generation provides a sanitary means of waste disposal at reasonable community cost.

Charcoal and wood are common fuels in Africa today. Charcoal is more versatile, energy dense, cleaner burning, and compact and convenient than wood, and is used extensively. Unfortunately, traditional charcoal manufacturing wastes the pyrolysis gases formed and uses scarce forest resources (Hall 1979). A recently developed charcoal production process has the capability of capturing these combustible gases, primarily carbon monoxide and hydrogen, and may be adapted to producing charcoal from other materials such as plant fiber and nut husks (Breag and Harker 1979).

Approaching economic feasibility in industrialized countries is the technology for converting that most ubiquitous biopolymer, cellulose, to glucose by enzymatic or acidic hydrolysis or both (Lipinsky 1978; Hall 1980) and then to versatile ingredients such as fructose, alcohol, and single-cell protein. Such a conversion directly addresses the need for integrating food and energy systems, but this conversion is beyond the reach of the majority of people in less-developed countries.

From an awareness of the limitations of some technology has grown the concept of appropriate technology, well articulated by Schumacher (1973) in his classic book *Small is Beautiful: Economics as if People Mattered*. The concept is now a global endeavor of high international priority (Wakefield and Stafford 1977). Many international organizations interested in using appropriate technology for refining conversion processes as tools in increasing food and energy self-sufficiency are listed at the end of this chapter.

• COMPLEMENTATION •

Combining several materials in mutually complementary proportions is an effective strategy to overcome food and resource limitations. The use of a single dietary staple, particularly when in short supply, has serious nutritional implications, but if the single staple is combined with modest quantities of foods that provide complementary nutrients, a more complete utilization of all nutrients is accomplished. Legumes, small quantities of animal products, leafy greens, or less conventional ingredients may significantly upgrade the nutritional value of cereal, tuber, and other starch-based diets (Swaminathan 1980; Bressani and Elias 1968; see Hiebsch and O'Hair in this volume).

Developing foods and dietary regimes based upon indigenous food complementation is a sound nutrition strategy in any country (Rajalakshmi and Ramakrishnan 1977; Pellett and Mamarbachi 1979). Diverse culture-specific culinary arts attest to the importance of complementation in both nutrition and sensory appeal. The use of functional foods and food ingredients to enhance texture, flavor, appearance, storage durability, convenience, and overall commercial value is central to food technology and essential to the food industry. However unappreciated, it also upgrades the food supply and enhances food self-sufficiency.

Complementation further suggests combining raw materials, refined products, and even waste substances to optimize their collective usefulness. If not removed, excess heat that is generated in a stationary internal combustion engine will destroy the engine. This same heat as hot exhaust may be used in a heat exchanger to heat air or water for process applications. Animal manure high in nitrogen may be combined with high-carbon waste vegetation to provide a more ideal carbon-to-nitrogen ratio for methane production than either source provides independently (Chittenden et al. 1980). Pollution has been defined as a resource out of place, and excellent industrial and rural nonindustrial models exist for combining mutually complementary waste streams for food, feed, fuel, or fertilizer applications (Wolverton and McDonald 1979; Lipinsky 1978). When used for fuel, bagasse from sugar cane and hulls, husks, and pits from crops complement the attendant crop refining processes.

A proper balance of complementary inputs insures that none of the components are in excess or are limiting factors in the total system. Therefore, complementation promotes conservation.

• INNOVATION •

The mechanism for accomplishing better food and resource conservation, conversion, and complementation is innovation—i.e., the application of ingenuity and diligence to solve difficult problems. Scientific knowledge and technical mastery of a subject contribute importantly to innovation; practical experience, insight, and common sense are essential to it. Some of the best examples of innovation involve the application of well-known principles in straightforward ways—or applying old ideas to new problems. These innovations are often deceptively simple and may consist of devices (machinery) or techniques (Brown and Pariser 1975). As the driving force of appropriate technology, innovation often consists of a blend of traditional and modern technology that takes advantage of nature (Clay 1980).

Innovative devices reduce tedious, time-consuming, raw material-consuming manual operations. Unfortunately, mechanization often makes a "quantum jump" from tedious manual operations to mechanical devices that replace many people (Ahmad and Jenkins 1980). A delicate challenge for innovation is the need to make human labor more efficient without either excessive employment displacement or undue reliance upon expensive, complicated, usually imported electric or fossil fuel dependent machines. Hand-powered devices can be used to accomplish more efficiently some food refining tasks such as extracting oils (Boatwright 1979; Donkor 1979) and grinding staples (Makanjula 1974). Hand-powered and pedal-powered devices (William 1975; Ghosh 1978) are interesting on-farm or small-scale alternatives that are receiving attention even in the United States (Branch 1978). A hand-held corn sheller developed by the Tropical Products Institute, now the Tropical Development and Research Institute, is probably the simplest example (Pinson 1977). For more or continuous operations, animal-driven linkages may be fabricated (Scott 1975).

The journal *Rural Technology Guides* (1977 to present) covers a number of practical devices for increasing the efficiency of home or small-scale industrial operations. Similarly, each issue of *Appropriate Technology* (1974 to present) deals with innovative solutions to development problems in less-developed countries and provides an excellent communication forum for field workers and technical experts. In addition, there are a number of private and governmental international assistance agencies whose commitment to overcoming food and resource constraints involves useful on-site and laboratory activities (United Nations Industrial Development Organization [UNIDO] 1979); some of these agencies and their mailing addresses are listed at the end of this chapter.

Resource utilization innovations consist of techniques and devices for accomplishing more with less. For example, the Lorena mud stove, which improves the efficiency and safety of wood cooking, and the Family Cooker, which achieves very high wood combustion efficiencies (Evans and Wharton 1977; Small Industry Development Network [SIDN] 1979), are welcome responses to cooking fuel scarcities. Pyrolytic gasification offers the opportunity to power spark ignition engines in the absence of liquid fuels. Ferrocement construction for crop and water storage and even fishing boats is a good substitute for imported materials (NAS 1973). Where metal is unavailable, plant fibers may have reinforcement value for construction (Watt 1976).

The ubiquitous nature of solar energy has prompted many practical dryer and cooker designs (Darrow and Pam 1976). Development of solar refrigeration is a little further off, since improvements in system reliability and equipment costs are needed before this ideal match between solar radiation intensity and food cooling requirements may be widely applied. The photovoltaic cell promises to be an eventual, but currently expensive, means of converting solar energy to electricity at remote locations (Kelly 1978).

Other energy-saving food preparation practices are minimum water cooking, pressure cooking, and the use of soaking solutions to reduce the cooking time of refractory foods such as grain legumes. For example, chemicals (Narasunha and Desikachar 1978; Rockland et al. 1979; Silva et al. 1981) or natural substances (Ankra and Dovlo 1978) significantly reduce cooking requirements for beans, thus increasing the convenience and economy of these nutritive foods. The legume storage regime, however, must be nonabusive to take advantage of soaking solutions (Molina et al. 1976).

Some high priority innovations in food processing and utilization that could help enhance food self-sufficiency are listed in Table 15.2. These are primarily, but not exclusively, oriented toward less-developed countries.

• IMPLEMENTATION •

No matter how sound the technology, urgent the need, or favorable the politics for enhancing local self-reliance in food and related resources, unless technology designers, practitioners, and recipients pay particular attention to the human factor, the results of their efforts are apt to be minimal or even counterproductive. Many failures are the antecedents of appropriate technology, the hopeful antonym of inappropriate technology (Harrison 1976) that eliminated jobs, weakened sociocultural linkages, discouraged or impeded self-sufficiency, and diminished the quality of life.

Added to these disruptive consequences of the implementation of inappropriate technology are now the serious environmental consequences of overexploitation of limited resources (Council on Environmental Quality [CEQ] 1980). There is a disturbing parallel between England's "Tragedy of the Commons" (Hardin

TABLE 15.2. Some Key Appropriate Food Technology Needs

1. Cement-like substances for protective storage

2. Safe indigenous chemicals that eliminate/discourage insect and pests

3. Dessicants to extend solar heating

4. Phase change chemicals to store and generate heat/cold

5. Inorganic and organic acids and salts as synergists in food preservation

6. Simple salt refining techniques

7. Sulfur dioxide generation as gas, liquid and soluble salts

8. Effective, safe preservatives/synergists from indigenous botanicals

9. Solvents for oil/protein extraction

10. Plant, animal, microbial enzyme systems/processes

11. Palatable humectants for intermediate moisture foods

12. Plastics/glass/ceramics from indigenous raw materials

13. Antioxidants and absorbants for lipid refining and stabilization

14. Surfactants/emulsifier for baking and formulations

15. Indigenous pharmaceuticals for therapeutic applications

16. Sanitation aids for water purification and food/utensil cleaning

17. Techniques for eliminating natural toxins

18. Small pressure vessels for safely generating steam (10 PSI)

19. Can cutter/reflanger machinery

20. Jar lid regasketing substances/techniques

21. Efficient conversion of indigenous resources into heat, electricity, mechanical power and steam

22. Biomass energy linkages with solar devices for dryers and cookers

23. Simple, inexpensive food refining and preparation tools such as mills, grinders and shellers

1968) and the current firewood crisis in Africa (see Webley in this volume). Development of inexpensive, efficient, wood-burning or charcoal-burning cooking devices in a region suffering intense deforestation might alleviate the problem or merely provide an incentive for more people to use (an increased demand for) already scarce wood.

Air quality improves when smoky open fires inside dwellings are replaced by efficient vented stoves, which consequently may result in unprecedented indoor insect infestation and reduced preservation of foods previously exposed to the smoke (VITA 1980). Increased access to commercial or indigenous infant foods may have a negative influence upon desirable breast feeding practices, unless accompanied by an education effort. Efficient mechanically powered (wind, water, animal) or human-powered processes appear to be desirable innovations, but they are desirable only if attention is given to alternate livelihoods for those workers who might be replaced. The disruptive effect of many such changes upon women's status has only recently been acknowledged (Ahmad and Jenkins 1980). Wheat and other donated or subsidized imported foods may be more functional, nutritious, and acceptable to people than traditional staples. But if the imports are impractical to produce locally, this commodity substitution may be counterproductive with potentially disastrous consequences for local agricultural incentives (Muller 1974).

People with few material resources may not be able to initiate some promising but risky endeavors. If they expend scarce resources in a failing effort, their very survival may be jeopardized. They cannot afford the luxury of making the mistakes that are inevitable in the application and refining of new practices. They do not have the time and economic margin necessary to take chances, make errors, correct mistakes, and move confidently into unpredictable situations. The conservatism that characterizes those in the lower economic strata has positive survival value: the adage "If at first you don't succeed, try, try again" has little logic if the penalty for initial failure is starvation. The potential of unforeseen, undesirable side effects is inherent in any technical innovation. More effort must be devoted toward understanding the total consequences of change in order to eliminate or minimize serious disruptions (Dahl 1979; Tyler 1979; Kassapu 1979; Wood and Schmink 1978).

From appropriate technology implementation has emerged a concept that is both simple in principle and difficult in practice—the village dialogue approach. This approach emphasizes the patient, continual involvement of potential beneficiaries all the way from problem identification to solution (Anonymous 1977). Technical assistance agencies are giving more attention to the prospect that those facing food and resource restrictions, if carefully provided with external inputs such as technical information, management skills, and examples of successful activities elsewhere, can use their insights and talents to achieve greater self-reliance. This entails a greater respect for traditional practices and a more open dialogue between practitioners and recipients.

A lot has been written regarding conservation, conversion, complementation, and innovation. Implementation is the most difficult and least clearly delineated. The patience, dedication, and time required of agents, beneficiaries, and administrators are hard to quantify or describe. It is uncommon for new or unfamiliar laboratory experiments to work the first time, even with the benefit of training, proper equipment, and comprehensive literature. To have the experiment function routinely in the field in the hands of less skilled practitioners is even more unlikely. Nevertheless, experiments do eventually work—not necessarily exactly as described in the literature nor as planned—and they ultimately improve our understanding of and control over natural phenomena.

The conservation, conversion, complementation, innovation, and even implementation strategies suggested here have positive value in overcoming Africa's food and resource limitations. These strategies are certainly not "quick fixes" and require that far more time and attention be paid to the human factor than to technical matters—but they must work. What other alternative is there for Africa?

• SUGGESTED FURTHER READINGS •

Intermediate Technology News (monthly). In Appropriate Technology, Intermediate Technology Development Group (ITDG), 9 King Street, London WC2E 8HN, England.

LIFE Newsletter (monthly). League for International Food Education, 915 15 Street, N.W., Washington, D.C. 20005, USA.

PIP News (quarterly). Postharvest Institute for Perishables, University of Idaho, Moscow, ID 83843.

Small Industry Development Network (quarterly). Office of International Programs, Engineering Experiment Station, Georgia Institute of Technology, Atlanta, GA 30332, USA.

TAICH News (quarterly). Technical Assistance Information Clearing House, 200 Park Avenue, New York, 10003, USA.

TDRI Newsletter (quarterly). Tropical Development and Research, 127 Clerkenwell Road, London, EC1R 5DB, England.

TRANET Newsletter Directory (quarterly). Transnational Network for Appropriate/Alternate Technology, P.O. Box 567, Rangely, ME 04970, USA.

UNICEF News (quarterly). United Nations Children's Fund, United Nations, NY 10017, USA.

UNU Newsletter (quarterly). The United Nations University, Toho Seimi Bldg., 15-1, Shibuya 2-chome, Shibuya Ku, Tokyo 150, Japan.

VITA News (quarterly). Volunteers in Technical Assistance, 1815 North Lynn Street, Arlington VA 22209, USA.

·16·

Fuelwood

OLIVIA WEBLEY

Fuelwood is an essential link between food production and food consumption, since almost all foodstuffs are cooked before they are eaten. Fuelwood is also another major product supplied by rural woodlands and savannas to the growing urban areas and industrial sectors of developing countries. It is estimated that about 80 percent of the wood cut in developing countries is burned for energy (Arnold 1978). Traditional development theory presumed that, as economic development took place, people would gradually shift from wood to commercial energy sources such as petroleum products, natural gas, and electricity. It is increasingly obvious, however, that commercial energy sources are not readily available for most of the people in Sub-Saharan Africa, and fuelwood will continue to be the major source of energy for many years to come (see Table 16.1). Africa's woodlands and savannas also supply many products besides fuelwood. These products include timber and twine for construction, as well as food and animal fodder from leaves, nuts, and fruits (see Fox in this volume). Trees also harbor foods such as honey and caterpillars. In general, wooded areas are not managed to sustain or improve production of any of these products. They are still perceived by many people to be "free" items in plentiful supply that require only harvest labor.

Nonetheless, in 1980 some 50 million people in Sub-Saharan Africa experienced fuelwood shortages and were unable to meet their basic fuelwood requirements (Pickstock 1983). Another 130 million Africans obtained their minimum fuelwood requirements through excessive exploitation of wood resources. With projected population growth, these numbers may triple by the year 2000. Certain areas are more severely affected by fuelwood shortages than others (see Figure 16.1). High and centralized fuelwood demands from urban and industrial areas put further stress on rural areas. When transportation networks are improved, the cutting of wood inevitably increases (Brokensha et al. 1983). Studies have shown that fuelwood supplies for some cities are commonly transported over distances of up

254

TABLE 16.1. Fuelwood Dependency in Selected Countries of Sub-Saharan Africa

Country	Fuelwood As Percent of Total Energy Consumption	Country	Fuelwood as Percent of Total Energy Consumption
Benin	86	Kenya	74
Burkina Faso	94	Malawi	82
Burundi	89	Mozambique	74
Cameroon	82	Mali	97
Central African Republic	91	Niger	87
Chad	94	Nigeria	91
Congo	80	Rwanda	96
Ethiopia	93	Somalia	90
Ghana	74	Sudan	81
Guinea Bissau	87	Tanzania	94

Source: Hall, D.O., G.W. Barnard and P.A. Moss. 1982. Biomass for Energy in the Developing Countries. New York: Pergamon Press.

to 100 kilometers (Ki-Zerbo 1981; Whitlow 1980). This transportation costs money, and in some urban areas as much as 40 percent of the recorded household income may be used to purchase wood (Ki-Zerbo 1981).

· IMPACT ON AGRICULTURE ·

On-Farm Interactions

As fuelwood becomes increasingly scarce, the use of crop residues and cow dung as fuel competes with their use as fodder and fertilizer. It is estimated that the current worldwide amount of nutrients lost to the soil by burning dung as fuel would produce food for 100 million people if the dung were returned to the soil as fertilizer (Grainger 1982). In Africa, sorghum stalks and maize cobs are increasingly relied upon as supplementary fuel sources (Ki-Zerbo 1981; Whitlow 1980). Fuelwood scarcity may also increase the workload of farmers, especially that of women farmers because fuel collection is usually their responsibility. In Burkina Faso, women sometimes walk four to six hours three times a week to collect fuelwood; another study showed that in Tanzania a total of 300 person-days of labor are needed to provide the average-size family with fuelwood for a single year (Grainger 1982). Research in Benin showed farmers walk fifteen to twenty kilometers to collect fuelwood every four days (Worou and Van Nao 1982). This allocation of labor to fuel collection may cause problems during periods of peak demand for farm labor. To minimize the conflicting labor demands, many women stockpile fuelwood toward the end of the dry season (Whitlow 1980).

The scarcity of fuelwood may even affect nutrition. A study in Benin found that food may be badly cooked or not cooked at all due to lack of fuel (Worou and Van Nao 1982), and women in Burkina Faso reported that, as wood became scarcer, they were forced to reduce their cooking from two hot meals a day to one hot meal every other day (Hoskins 1980). The diversity of the average diet may

FIGURE 16.1.   Fuelwood Scarcity in Africa

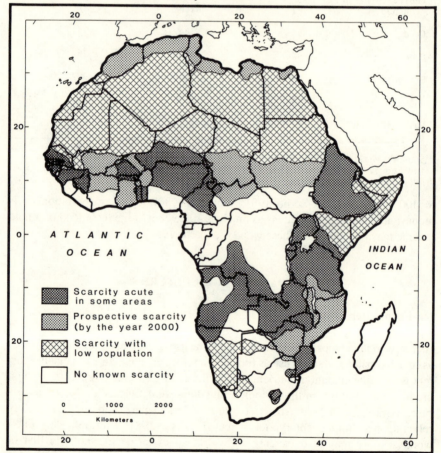

Source: Revised from Food and Agriculture Organization. 1981. Map of the Fuelwood Situation in the Developing Countries. *Supplement to Unasylva*. Rome: Food and Agriculture Organization.

also diminish due to a reduction in edible forest byproducts such as nuts, leaves, fruits, and native wildlife (Hoskins 1980).

Off-Farm Interactions

Deforestation may occur for many reasons but is seldom due to fuelwood collection alone, unless it is to supply urban and industrial needs (Foley and Barnard 1984). Loss of trees, for whatever reason, can decrease on-farm food production. One mechanism for this decrease is increasing surface runoff, which increases watershed drainage rates, resulting in decreased dry season river flow and, consequently, decreased on-farm food production. Proper watershed management, which entails maintaining year-round vegetative cover, can prolong river flows further into the dry season (Russell 1981). Under forest cover, soil erosion may be almost negligible, 0.2 tons per hectare (t/ha) per year, but under cultivation it may increase to between 600 and 1200 t/ha per year (Lal 1981). Forest cover can reduce soil erosion by increasing raindrop interception, thereby maintaining soil aggregate stability and enhancing rain infiltration (Sanchez 1976). Trees can also decrease wind erosion by reducing wind velocity.

If managed appropriately, trees can maintain or increase soil fertility through tree litter deposition, atmospheric nitrogen fixation, and nutrient storage in tree biomass (Nair 1982). Tree cover can exert a moderating effect on soil reactions and temperature regimes, which is particularly important in tropical ecosystems. As trees are cut, these ameliorating effects on the soil are lost. Deforestation is also a major cause of manmade desertification, which can affect agricultural productivity by creating deserts on cultivated lands and by desert encroachment. For example, fertile agricultural lands in Sudan have been buried by the progressive infringement of sand dunes, resulting in crop damage and blocked irrigation canals (Kunkle and Dye 1981).

• REMEDYING THE SITUATION •

Innovative systems are required to grow trees to satisfy demand for forest products, promote food production, and maintain ecosystem stability. To create these systems, it is necessary to bring forestry into a farming context. There are two major concepts that may be used in the design of appropriate forestry systems: (1) Community or Social Forestry—large numbers of people are mobilized to plant and protect trees, either on village or private lands, with the aim of producing wood and other products mainly for village rather than commercial uses; and (2) Farm Forestry or Agroforestry—forestry is blended with agriculture in such a way that tree crops are planted to enhance rather than displace crop production or livestock production or both.

The categories of tree species that may be used in either system include fast-growing fuelwood species from genera such as *Eucalyptus*; fast growing leguminous species from genera such as *Leuceana, Gliricidia, Acacia,* and *Prosopsis*; and perennial agricultural tree crops such as oilpalm, rubber, and coconut. Trees are seldom planted for fuelwood alone (Brokensha et al. 1983); preferred species are those that provide farmers with a variety of products.

There are a range of possibilities in farm and community forestry that vary tremendously from country to country and may be applied in various ways (Foley and Barnard 1984). Tree windbreaks were established in Sudan to protect fields against desertification; to supply fuelwood, construction timber, and animal fodder; and to provide new sources of rural income (Kunkle and Dye 1981). Alley cropping, growing maize and other food crops in alleys between strips of trees, is being used successfully in Nigeria (Kang et al. 1981). Research has suggested that intercropping nitrogen-fixing Acacia with millet may add the equivalent nutrients of fifty to sixty tons of manure per hectare (Kunkle and Dye 1981). Acacia planted twenty trees per hectare quadrupled millet and sorghum yields at one research site in Burkina Faso (National Research Council [NRC] 1983). A traditional system of agroforestry and livestock management, illustrating many of the principles discussed here, is found in parts of Sudan, Chad, and Niger. In this system, gum arabic is interplanted with millet. In three to five years it is no longer possible to grow millet due to shading, and instead animals are grazed under the trees. After ten years the trees are harvested, and the rotation begins again (NRC 1983).

Efforts to decrease fuelwood scarcity must also consider cookstove technology. The traditional open three stone fire loses between 92 and 95 percent of the energy produced by fuelwood combustion (Foley et al. 1984). Innovative stove designs save wood by more-efficient utilization of the energy produced from burning wood.

In summary, there is a growing recognition in many parts of Africa that it is more costly in terms of time, labor, and cash to heat the pot than to fill it. Trees may play an important role in creating sustainable cropping systems. Policymakers concerned with improving the nutritional status and living standards of rural Africans must address fuelwood issues.

· SUGGESTED FURTHER READINGS ·

Allan, William. 1965. *The African Husbandman*. Westport, Connecticut: Greenwood Press.
Food and Agriculture Organization (FAO). 1983. *Wood Fuel Surveys*. FAO/SIDA Forestry for Local Community Development Programme. Rome: Food and Agriculture Organization.
Foley, G., and G. Barnard. 1984. *Farm and Community Forestry*. Earthscan Energy Information Program. Washington, D.C.: International Institute for Environment and Development.
Hall, D. O., G. W. Barnard, and P. A. Moss. 1982. *Biomass for Energy in the Developing*

Countries. New York: Pergamon Press.

Montalembert, M. R. de, and J. Clement. 1983. *Fuelwood Supplies in the Developing Countries*. FAO Forestry. Rome: Food and Agriculture Organization.

Unasylva, A Journal of Forestry and Forest Products. 1981. Wood Energy Special Editions 1 and 2. Vol. 33:131 and 132. Rome: Food and Agriculture Organization.

United Nations. 1981. *Proceedings of Workshop on Energy, Forestry and Environment*. Nairobi. Vols. 1, 2, and 3. Washington, D.C.: Bureau for Africa, United States Agency for International Development.

·17·

Distribution of Resources and Products in Mossi Households

DELLA E. McMILLAN

A recurrent theme throughout this volume is the multifaceted nature of development planning that is needed to improve the performance of African food systems. To increase the productivity of scarce resources obviously requires new technology, but development planning must consider more than just food production. This chapter addresses another essential dimension: the distribution of resources and products.

The increasingly numerous urban population depends almost entirely on imported food from rural food-producing areas or other countries. To people in cities and towns, children in boarding schools, workers in the mines, and many others, food distribution is a critical dimension of African food systems. Less obvious but equally important is the distribution of resources and products among people in rural food producing areas. Productive resources such as land, labor, livestock, cash, credit, skills, and information are never evenly distributed. Access to these resources is restricted, as is the access to food and other products that result from the management and employment of resources. Some resources and many products may be bought and sold for money, and the chain of monetary transactions ultimately resulting in food reaching the cities works largely through markets, traders, business people, and, sometimes, government marketing bureaucracies. In most rural areas of Africa, however, the majority of productive resources and most of the food eaten by farm families and their neighbors are acquired through non-monetary exchanges or as part of the set of transactions characterizing social life. That is, rural people enjoy access to and control over resources and products through their social, political, and economic relationships with other people.

Although this complex interweaving of relationships that affect production and consumption is known to development workers, there is a tendency to gloss over the importance of the control over distribution that is exercised by the basic social units that produce (and consume) food. Development workers also tend to ignore the complexity of basic socioeconomic units. These basic units are usually assumed to be households, and households or household heads are seen as the clients or targets of development projects. This simplistic focus on households alone overlooks the existence and functioning of individuals and subhousehold and suprahousehold groupings that may be involved in independent or separate activities.

This chapter begins with a discussion of reservations about the usefulness of the concept of household as a descriptive and analytical unit. Because abstract ideas about social organization, production, and distribution may seem colorless but become vividly real when actual people and villages are observed, the chapter continues by analyzing intrahousehold organization of food production, consumption, and distribution in a village in the Central Mossi Plateau region of Burkina Faso (formerly Upper Volta).[1] Between 1975 and 1980, more than 30 families left this village to settle in a new development project in the southern part of the country. The changing patterns of intrahousehold production and interhousehold distribution of food for settlers in this project is the subject of the third section of this chapter. The research on which the chapter is based was conducted in two time periods. A baseline survey of production activities in the settlers' home area and in a project village was conducted over two agricultural seasons from 1978 to 1980. A restudy of the project village was conducted in 1983[2] (McMillan 1983, 1984).

• RESERVATIONS ABOUT THE HOUSEHOLD CONCEPT •

In general, the household, or *menage,* continues to be the primary unit used in descriptions, analyses, and predictions of the local production, distribution, and consumption of food crops and domestic animals (see Cohen in this volume). The working definition of household is a variation of the idea that a set number of people are united through their sharing a single cooking pot, a single cooking fire, or a single granary—"the social organization in which members live in the same place and share their meals" (Shaner et al. 1982) or "those who cook together as members of a pot" (Norman et al. 1982). Most economic or social surveys still use the household as the unit of study, and studies of agricultural decisionmaking or management usually focus on the household's allocative decisions and assume that each household has a single head who makes its decisions; therefore, many studies refer to the farming household or family instead of the farmer, or the studies may use the terms interchangeably (Shaner et al. 1982; Norman et al. 1982; Gilbert et al. 1980). Statistics about production or wealth report household income; statistics about per capita production are generally based on household means weighted across all households or groups of households with different characteristics in terms of social structure; access to land; physical, biological, and socioeconomic constraints; choices of production activities; management practices and goals that presumably influence both the profitability and acceptability of certain types of technological innovations or government policies.

In recent years, however, there has been a growing concern with the use of a simple household concept to describe local units of production and consumption in African food systems (Guyer 1981, 1984; Jiggins 1984; Haugerud 1982; Koenig 1982; Spring 1984); more analysts are now convinced that the conventional economic model of the household as an autonomous unit of production and consumption with a single decisionmaking locus does not apply in most parts of Africa. This complexity of African households has not gone unrecognized in the major methodological discussions of research on African agriculture. In the farming systems literature (see Poats and Fresco in this volume), a great deal of attention is now being focused on intrahousehold production and consumption patterns, particularly that women usually have some command over certain resources and make decisions on their own initiative. Nonmarket flows of labor and commodities that relate or unite households are also attracting more consideration.

In spite of these theoretical shifts, there is still a tendency for field research, policy planning, and development project design to focus at the level of the aggregate household unit. To some extent this reflects the inevitable delay between theoretical change and policy/field implementation. Other important reasons for continuing to use the simple household concept are the practical difficulties involved in collecting and quantifying information on intrahousehold labor and commodity flows (Crawford 1982). Jane Guyer noted that "almost every survey contains somewhere, in the foreword, footnotes, an appendix, the problem of defining household membership and maintaining continuous records on people with . . . high mobility rates" (1981:98).

The vast majority of the data on intrahousehold and interhousehold groupings and distribution come from intensive field research that combines quantitative and qualitative, structured and unstructured techniques, often with small samples. The following case study from Burkina Faso, an example of this intensive field research, illustrates the importance of distribution patterns in influencing production and consumption and the inadequacy of a simple household concept that assumes a central decisionmaking locus. If only that simple concept is used, important data are not collected and analyzed including the following specific areas that are easily overlooked: (1) the semiautonomous rights and obligations of different subhousehold groups, (2) how goods and labor are distributed across household frontiers, and (3) variation in the size and composition of household units over the life cycle and in response to specific types of technological innovations and outside influences.

· INTRAHOUSEHOLD ORGANIZATION OF FOOD PRODUCTION, CONSUMPTION, AND DISTRIBUTION IN THE CENTRAL MOSSI PLATEAU ·

Given this working definition of the household—a group in which members live in the same place and share their meals—then most households in the home village may be described as overlapping units of production and consumption that share a residence and work certain fields collectively, or rely on the harvest of these cooperatively worked fields, or both, for most basic food needs.

Distribution of Land

Land that is farmed by a particular household group in the home village is acquired through a combination of inherited, customary, and borrowed rights. Inherited fields are referred to as *mam pasago* or *mam solem* ("my right"); these are clan fields that have become identified with a particular household through inheritance from father to son. Other tracts of clan land cannot be inherited and are described as lands of customary right. These are associated with certain kinship and political offices such as elder of the clan or chief of the village. Land that has come to be associated with different households through inheritance and customary right may be redistributed to people outside the household through a system of institutionalized borrowing. If a household member has proprietorship over fields that are not being cultivated by anyone in the household, then any member of the proprietor's extended family may ask to farm a portion of the "surplus" land. This type of reallocation takes the form of a loan: the proprietor retains permanent rights to the land and the borrower obtains temporary rights of usage. No rent money is paid nor is any interest charged. Although first priority in the granting of a land loan is usually given to members of the extended family or clan, a loan may be made to someone outside the patrilineal kinship group, usually loaning to someone who is related through marriage or personal friendship. Approximately 19 percent of the total land area planted in the home village in 1979 was acquired through inherited right, 25 percent through customary right, and 56 percent through borrowing[3] (see Figure 17.1).

Cooperative and Private Fields

The total area of borrowed, customary, and inherited land that a household cultivates is subdivided into cooperatively and privately worked fields. Cooperatively worked fields are cultivated by the entire household. The head of household dictates what crops are to be cultivated on these fields, timing of operations, and use of the products. For example, grain produced on cooperatively worked fields is usually allocated to feed the household for most of the year. Any monetary income

FIGURE 17.1.   Land Tenure in Home Village, 1979—Percentage of Land
Acquired for Cultivation Using Various Rights

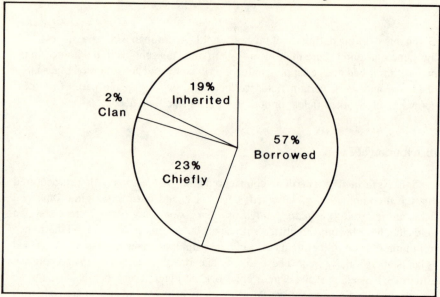

FIGURE 17.2.   Land Allocation to Various Groups and Individuals and
Labor Allocation to Cooperative and Private Fields in
Home Village, 1979

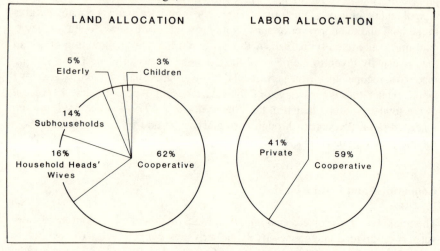

from the sale of food or cash crops from the cooperatively worked fields is controlled by the male or female household head.

All individuals in a household have the right to cultivate a certain amount of land for their own personal needs. Wives have the right to farm at least one plot of food grain, one or two plots of peanuts (groundnuts) or ground peas, and at least one vegetable patch. Unmarried children usually farm one parcel of grain or a cash crop such as peanuts or cotton. Subhousehold groups are composed of married sons or brothers and their families, and these groups also farm a certain amount of food and cash crops apart from the main cooperative fields. Any crops or money income produced on a private field are under the private control of the person responsible for its cultivation, and these crops are stored separately.

Approximately 62 percent of the land planted in 1979 in the home village was farmed cooperatively. The 38 percent privately farmed was subdivided as follows: an estimated 16 percent by the wives affiliated with the household, 3 percent by unmarried children, 14 percent by subhousehold family groups led by married sons or brothers, and 5 percent by elderly men and women who hardly participate in cooperative work activities (see Figure 17.2)[4]. Labor allocation patterns between cooperative and private fields are roughly equivalent to land allocation patterns. Of total hours spent working in agriculture, 59 percent was spent on cooperative fields (62 percent of cultivated land) and 41 percent on private fields (38 percent of cultivated land).

Each year the household head determines where the members of his family are allowed to plant their private parcels of specific crops. Certain times are specified for individuals and subhousehold groups to cultivate their private fields, usually an hour or two in the early morning before going to the cooperative fields and an hour or two in the late afternoon before returning home. Occasionally a household head may designate one or two days after the main cooperative fields are planted for planting private fields. The amount of time an individual allocates to the cultivation of cooperatively versus privately worked fields varies enormously over the person's life cycle in response to a variety of factors including the total size of the household and the individual's relationships. The amount of time a married woman devotes to her private production activities is related to her childbearing responsibilities, age, health, as well as the number, sex, and age of her older resident children. Her position is also affected by the presence and relative status of any co-wives and whether or not she retains any rights to the inherited fields of a deceased husband.

Subhousehold Groups

While a married son or brother, his wife or wives, and their children collectively cultivate the private fields controlled by that man, he may still owe a major portion of his and his subhousehold's labor to the household's cooperatively worked fields. These private subhousehold holdings change location less frequently than do other private fields and represent the first stage of the son or brother becoming the proprietor of a portion of the household's inherited land. The ideal for most Mossi families is to form as large a household as possible, but in practice it is difficult to acquire enough land to satisfy the cooperative and private needs of large households and to achieve an equitable distribution of household land through inheritance and subdivided cultivation rights. As a man's sons marry and start families of their own, the sons slowly increase the size of their private holdings and the amount of time devoted to them. Although the father gradually increases his household's access to clan and lineage lands as he becomes older, these increases do not usually keep up with the growing size of his household. Over time there is inevitably less inherited land per person, and one of the sons receives less than an even share.

The individual who receives less may acquire additional land through alternative patterns of residency and work such as borrowing land from other households, affiliation with the mother's patrilineage in a neighboring village, resettling some portion of the household in a less-populated area, or plantation wage labor in the adjacent country of Ivory Coast. At times a man who left the village returns once he has access to larger holdings at home. This new access may occur because of a death in the family or as a result of the emigration of other household members. A change in individual status such as a man's succession to the office of clan elder or village chief, positions with entitlements to customary right fields, might also influence a decision to return.

Land needs may increase in the early stages of the growth cycle of a household and decrease in the later stages. As a father ages he has fewer dependent children and thus needs fewer fields under his direct supervision. At the same time, the eldest son usually expands the size of the private fields cultivated by his own subhousehold until he supervises work on the cooperative fields and until the father and the father's wives are incorporated as semiautonomous production and consumption subunits within the son's household. When a father dies, his sons usually split the inherited fields and granaries and cease to farm the same cooperative fields, although they usually continue to live in the same residential compound. The brothers' households may continue to help one another during peak labor periods and through lending equipment. It must be emphasized that subdivision and composition of household and subhousehold units are quite fluid—households may split, and they may unite in response to the death of a family member, a new crop package, immigration, illness, or other factors affecting family needs and goals.

Distribution of Production and Income

The division of cultivated land into cooperative and private fields is associated with choices regarding which crops and varieties to plant in which fields. Sorghum and millet are the only important crops that are evenly distributed in both kinds of fields: 38 percent of cultivated land is in private fields, and approximately 40 percent of the land devoted to sorghum and millet is in private fields. Cotton and corn (maize) are less commonly planted in private fields than in cooperative fields—only 26 and 14 percent respectively of each crop is grown in private fields. Rice, peanuts, and vegetables are disproportionately common in private fields—51, 74, and 91 percent respectively of each crop is grown in private fields. More rapid maturing (short term) crops and varieties tend to be found in private fields since these fields are generally planted later than the cooperative ones. This factor is extremely important in determining crop rotations and the geographical relationship of fields. For example, the wives' private fields tend to be planted in areas alongside the cooperatively worked fields in order to reduce the amount of time involved in commuting from one field to the other. The use of new technology such as animal traction and fertilizer tends to be more extensive on the cooperative fields supervised by male household heads because they are the focus of most government extension programs. Crops and monetary income produced from cultivating private fields give individuals and subhousehold groups a certain amount of autonomy from the household head. Some food may be stored for later use. For example, during the time of year when the man or woman supervising the cooperatively worked fields reduces rations to one meal a day, many wives use the grain from their private stores to provide an extra meal each day for their children. The cash income that a woman earns from the sale of privately grown peanuts, groundpeas, sesame, cotton, and dried vegetables is used to meet her own needs and the needs of her children, including childrens' school fees and supplies when these are not paid by the husband. In addition, it is the wife's responsibility to provide basic condiments such as spices, meat, and fish for the daily sauces that flavor the sorghum porridge. Under the best of circumstances, a woman is able to invest her money by purchasing livestock with cash earned from selling her privately produced crops and from nonagricultural activities such as spinning and petty trade. In fact, very few village women have sufficient income to do so on their own. Almost all purchases of small livestock are made with cash gifts from returning labor migrants or from gifts a woman receives when she is married. In contrast, food and cash crops produced by unmarried sons and daughters on their private fields tend to be sold in local markets immediately after harvest. The cash income they derive is usually used for personal needs such as clothes, bicycle repairs, and petty trade.

Cotton and other cash crops produced on the cooperatively worked fields are sold immediately after harvest. Money from the sale is used to meet cash needs of the family and of the household head. Preferably, food grains are not sold until after the first weeding of the next crop when clear evidence of a good prospective harvest reduces risks in selling extra grain; furthermore, at this time grain prices are the highest due to grain shortages.[5] Some of the poorer farmers with smaller reserves sell small quantities of grain immediately after harvest in order to meet specific cash needs. Grain has other uses as well: in exchange for hired labor, as barter for other goods and services, as food to host people invited for weeding and threshing and to host marriage and naming celebrations, and as part of the economic and social alliances that are associated with the exchange of wives between extended families.

• CHANGING PATTERNS IN A SETTLEMENT PROJECT •

A large number of people from the home village moved in 1975 to a new land settlement project, the Volta Valley Authority (AVV), in the south of Burkina Faso. There was little consideration of private cultivation rights in the original design of the project. In contrast to conditions in the settlers' home village, the project assumes that each household farms all fields cooperatively under the leadership of an adult male recognized as the official household head. This designated household head is considered to represent the entire household group in extension programs and in contractual dealings with the project for insurance, equipment purchases, credit, and sales. Although this concept of an autonomous household unit with a single decisionmaking locus was a fairly accurate reflection of intrahousehold production when the project started in 1975, the organization of production had changed by the fifth cropping season (1979).

During the early years of the project, settler households were small and were involved in the heavy work of clearing fields. There was little time or money for noncrop activities such as livestock and trade. By the fifth year, households had accumulated large stores of reserve grain, had earned much higher cash and total incomes than typically earned in the home village, and had paid off all or most of their initial debts to the project. Moreover, most households had increased substantially in household size due to the immigration of additional family members. In 1975 each household received a fixed amount of land to farm, ten or twenty hectares, but later, due to the increased household size, settlers increased the area planted in the food grain (sorghum), reduced the area planted in the cash crop (cotton), and invested time and money in noncrop activities such as livestock and trade. Most households by 1979 had established a small area of private fields for the wives and unmarried and married children. By 1983 the absolute acreage cultivated by each household was greater, although the relative proportions planted by each category of family member remained much the same as in 1979 (see Figure 17.3).[6]

To compensate women and other household members for loss of personal income due to reduced size of private fields, the designated male household head makes cash gifts to family members after selling the cooperatively produced cotton. Settlers have reinstated a system of private harvest gifts whereby the male household head gives twenty to thirty dried ears of corn to wives of close friends and allies in the project. During the harvest, a woman may receive 100 to 200 kilograms of such gift corn that she may use as she wishes. In contrast to the home village, almost all of the women's grain in the AVV is sold rather than used for

FIGURE 17.3. Percentage of Land Cultivated by Various Groups and Individuals in Home Village, 1979, and in Project Village, 1983

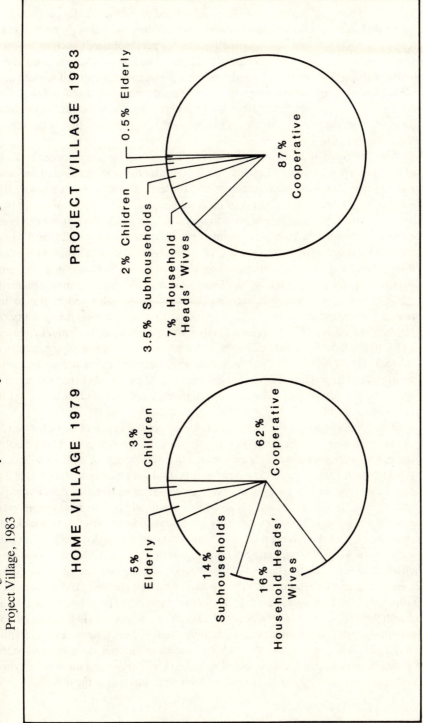

family consumption, and the male household head is responsible for purchases of sauce condiments, school materials, and clothing. Income that AVV women earn from cash payments and sales is usually used for personal needs such as jewelry, travel, clothes, and gifts or to purchase trade goods and livestock. One of the most dramatic changes between 1979 and 1983 was the large-scale entry of women into livestock production, which seems to be related to their desire for semiautonomous sources of income. In 1979 very few AVV women had animals, but in 1983 several of the older wives had large herds of twenty to thirty goats, and two of the senior wives owned cattle.

Most of the marketed grain that is produced on cooperatively worked fields is sold in single lots of several hundred kilograms after the first weeding of the next crop. By that time food prices are high and settlers are able to guess whether the next crop will be successful. Other grain is sold in smaller quantities of one or two tins (17 to 36 kilograms) in response to specific cash needs throughout the year. Settlers continually increase the amount of grain they sell while residing in the project. 1983 showed a slight increase in grain sales over 1979, both in absolute terms and as a percentage of recorded sales of agricultural products. However, actual production increased to a greater degree. There was an overall increase in area planted, and settlers had accumulated large grain stores. Grain sales underestimate increased production because of alternative distribution patterns—the quantity of grain exchanged as gifts, for reciprocal labor arrangements, and in barter increased substantially. One important example of barter is the exchange of sorghum for livestock. By 1979, the fifth year in the project, the majority of settlers had sold the original oxen purchased from the project and used the money to pay off remaining debts. Usually replacement oxen are bartered from local Fulani herdsmen in exchange for grain.

There are five major types of gift exchange between project households: (1) gifts of grain to new settlers moving into the area, (2) harvest gifts, (3) symbolic gifts in recognition of historic or anticipated ties of marriage or political alliance, (4) joking relationships, and (5) religious gifts. Gifts of grain to new settlers is the largest category. In 1983 a growing number of settler households directly sponsored new settlers; new settlers received this aid in addition to food rations provided by the project. Sponsors typically gave several hundred-kilogram sacks of grain, the estimated equivalent of 30 to 50 percent of the recorded 1982 harvest for many sponsoring households. Sponsorship sometimes doubles a sponsoring household's food needs. By far the major motivation to become sponsors is the desire to affirm, strengthen, and in many cases create ties between older and newer settler families. Typically, new settlers claim some form of prior lineage or affinal tie with their sponsor. A small amount of food aid is also given to indigenous inhabitants of a project area to create new community ties. Project villages are geographically isolated and resented by non-AVV residents of the area, so settlers consider the socioeconomic ties between sponsors and new settlers important in solidifying their new communities and insuring their long-term survival in the region.

• SUMMARY AND CONCLUSIONS •

In sum, this analysis of Mossi settlers in a traditional home village and an agricultural settlement project shows the interrelationship of production and distribution and some of the complexities of distributing resources and products in food-producing areas. First, farmland is an essential productive resource, and access to it is affected by kinship, political office, personal life cycles, marriage, and other social relationships. Second, this land is subdivided into fields either cooperatively or privately worked. Agricultural products produced on cooperatively worked fields are used to meet the needs of the entire family group. In contrast, agricultural products produced on privately worked fields are stored apart and under control of the individual responsible for their cultivation. Third, the decision to sell a certain quantity of a crop, as opposed to eating or storing it, is not the only option individuals within a farming household have for the disposition of food crops. Other choices include the distribution of food products through barter for livestock, in payment for hired labor, for cooperative labor arrangements with nonhousehold groups, and as part of the wider social and political relationships that unite families.

This study also shows that a failure to recognize the complex patterning of distribution rights within and between households may limit our understanding of the constraints to increasing food production and raising nutritional standards. For instance, if we fail to recognize the disproportional access of certain clans, household, and subhousehold groups to inherited fields, we are likely to overlook one of the most important factors affecting the level of family food and total income. Similarly, if we focus on the household as a single decisionmaking unit in the home village with regard to the distribution of food products, we are likely to overlook the importance of private production in meeting basic food needs of women and children and the need to increase private production. Similarly, reliance only on recorded grain sale totals to assess the impact of the development project on food supplies is inadequate because it excludes large areas of exchange such as gifts and barter.

A second set of conclusions relates more specifically to the use of household as a descriptive and analytical concept. Although members of a household group may function as a unit with a single decisionmaking locus at times, at other times they may not. The case study of households in the home village shows the existence of overlapping semiautonomous units with regard to the allocation and management of land, labor, and capital and the distribution of food products. Moreover, research on the households that moved to the development project suggests that this subdivision of household rights, obligations, and activities is not fixed but can be expected to change over the life cycle of a family and to change in response to variations in the economic, political, institutional, and social conditions of development. In addition to these intrahousehold activities, boundaries between households are crossed by a number of socially and economically important nonmarket exchanges that unite household units, one example being food aid to new settlers and indigenous inhabitants of a project area to create new community ties.

This research points up a tremendous need for researchers and policymakers to consider the distribution of food products in the design of government programs and policies to increase production, reduce food losses, and raise nutritional standards. In particular, researchers and policymakers need to examine and understand the following:

1. The quantitative significance of independent production and consumption activities within households and the exchange of food products between households

2. Economic and social effects of independent food production activities for the internal organization of farm families

3. Economic and social consequences of nonmarketed exchange of food products between households

4. Patterns of interhousehold exchange for privately versus cooperatively produced products

5. The many ways these overlapping production and consumption units may affect distribution of adequate nutrition for specific subhousehold groups, design of new farm technology and extension programs to increase food production and distribution of adequate nutrition to rural households, and government policies and extension programs to direct the sale of marketed foodstuffs.

• NOTES •

1. The Mossi ethnic group constitutes approximately half the population of Burkina Faso. In precolonial times the Mossi lived in a number of related kingdoms and subkingdoms that formed a major cultural, economic, and political force in the Sahelian area.

2. The research (April 1978 to April 1980) on which the present study is based was part of a four country survey of Sahelian farming systems funded by the United States Agency for International Development (USAID) through the Department of Agricultural Economics at Purdue University (AFR-C-1247 and AFR-C-1258). Trained enumerators gathered information on crop and noncrop production activities and income in the AVV village and the traditional home village. The two sites are separated by 120 kilometers, 200 kilometers by main roads. A short, two-month restudy of the settlers was conducted during the summer of 1983 through a Technical Assistance Grant from the South-East Consortium for International Development (SECID), Center for Women in Development.

3. Figure 17.1 is based on the percentage of total area planted in 1979 for fifteen defined household units that were included in the survey of the home village. Two other villages in the area of the home village were included in the survey but are not discussed here.

4. Land figures are based on the percentage of total area planted in 1979 for the fif-

teen sampled households in the home village. Labor figures are based on total recorded labor hours for these fifteen households.

5. For a more comprehensive examination of grain marketing behavior in a grain surplus region of Burkina Faso see Jackie Sherman (1984).

6. The 1983 figures are based on the percentage of total area planted for the ten households in the project village that were surveyed in both 1979 and 1983.

• SUGGESTED FURTHER READINGS •

Boutillier, J. L. 1964. Les Structures Foncières en Haute-Volta. *Etudes Voltaïques* (nouvelle serie) 5:84–94.

Broekhuyse, J. T. 1974. *Développement du Nord des Plateaux Mossi*. 4 Volumes. Amsterdam: Département de Recherches Social, Institut Royal des Tropiques.

Guyer, J. 1981. Household and Community in African Studies. *The African Studies Review* 34:2/3:87–138.

Hammond, P. 1966. *Yatenga: Technology in the Culture of a West African Kingdom*. New York: The Free Press.

Lallemand, S. 1977. Une Famille Mossi. *Recherches Voltaïques* 17.

Murphy, J., and L. Sprey. 1980. *The Volta Valley Authority: Socio-Economic Evaluation of a Resettlement Project in Upper Volta*. West Lafayette, Indiana: Department of Agricultural Economics, Purdue University.

Saul, M. 1983. Work Parties, Wages and Accumulation in a Voltaic Village. *American Ethnologist* 10:1:77–96.

Scudder, T. 1984. *The Development Potential of New Lands Settlement in the Tropics and Subtropics: A Global State-Of-The-Art Evaluation with Specific Emphasis on Policy Implications*. Executive Summary. A. I. D. Discussion Paper No. 21. Washington: United States Agency for International Development. PN-AAL-039.

Sherman, J. 1984. *Grain Markets and the Marketing Behavior of Farmers: A Case Study of Manga, Upper Volta*. Ann Arbor, Michigan: Center for Research on Economic Development.

Yanagisako, S. J. 1979. Family and Household: The Analysis of Domestic Groups. *Annual Review of Anthropology* 8:161–205.

·18·

Meeting Human Nutritional Needs

PATRICIA A. WAGNER

Procurement of food to meet nutritional needs is basic to human survival and quality of life. Nutritional needs are universal, but human populations have adapted to a remarkable diversity in patterns of food availability. Indeed, these needs are met by thousands of different plants and animals throughout the world. Generally, nutritional needs are more likely to be met if there is diversity or variety in the spectrum of foods available rather than a very narrow range of available foods. Nutrition is fundamental to human health and functional performance. Among the consequences of nutritional deprivation are increased frequency and severity of infections, impaired mental and physical development, and reduced levels of work performance and educational achievement. Obviously other factors may contribute to these negative outcomes, but the basic importance of nutrition should be recognized and appreciated.

The concept of nutrition as a major determinant of human health and functional performance is the underlying theme of this chapter. An adequately nourished population is an essential component of economic and social development; levels of nutritional well-being both influence and reflect development. However, it is also clear that nutritional deprivation among segments of the population may persist and even increase in spite of overall economic growth and development. Sustained nutritional improvements depend upon policies and programs that enhance quality and quantity in food availability and distribution to people of all socioeconomic levels. Sound policies and programs in health, family planning, and education also contribute significantly to the nutritional well-being of the population. A goal of the World Health Organization (WHO) of the United Nations and its 150 member nations is "Health for All by the Year 2000." As defined in the 1946 WHO constitution, health is "a state of complete physical, mental and social well-being and not merely the absence of disease or infirmity." Nutritional well-being is an integral component of "Health for All" and must receive primary attention if this goal is to be achieved.

This chapter provides a foundation in the principles of human nutrition for persons seeking to learn more about food issues in Sub-Saharan Africa. The physiological and biochemical aspects of nutrition science are reviewed within the context of human dietary patterns and common health problems. Practical considerations in development of appropriate nutrition policies and programs are emphasized. This chapter begins with an examination of nutrition in relation to human health and functional performance, which is followed by a brief overview of human nutritional needs in relation to dietary patterns and standards. Issues related to nutrition policies and programs are addressed in the final section.

• NUTRITION, HEALTH, AND FUNCTIONAL PERFORMANCE •

Nutrition is a major determinant of human health and functional performance and although the need for research to further define these relationships is recognized, an appreciation of the significance of nutrition is of practical importance. A view of nutrition from this perspective is much more useful than perceptions limited to severe nutrient deficiency disorders such as blindness from vitamin A deficiency or goiter from iodine deficiency. Where nutritional deprivation exists in human populations, there is a continuum of levels of nutritional status, or relative deficiency, and the problem is rarely limited to only one nutrient. It is important to understand that human beings require—in appropriate amounts and balance—water, energy (calories), and more than forty other elements or compounds. The earliest signs of nutritional deprivation are simply reductions in amounts of nutrients stored in various tissues and cells of the body; this type of mild deficiency means that the individual has fewer reserves to call upon during times of physiological stress, illness, or injury. At intermediate or marginal levels of nutritional status, various nutrient-dependent molecular functions are reduced, perhaps impairing resistance to disease or resulting in mild anemia (reduction in circulating levels of hemoglobin) or both.

Available data suggest that marginal, or subclinical, nutritional deficiencies are widespread among people of all ages in Sub-Saharan Africa. It is also important to understand that mild to marginal deficiencies of micronutrients (vitamins and minerals) may exist in young children even when growth rates are normal. The following discussion examines basic concepts in nutrition science related to immunity and infection, reproductive function, and work performance and educational achievement.

Nutrition, Immunity, and Infection

Nutrition is basic to maintenance of host resistance to disease and infection.

Among the consequences of even mild to marginal nutritional deprivation are increased frequency and severity of infections. This concept is supported by a large body of historical and epidemiological evidence as well as by recent advances in our understanding of immunology and nutrition (Wray 1978; Scrimshaw 1983; Good et al. 1984; Solomons and Keusch 1981).

It is now clear that virtually every aspect of the body's defense system may be compromised by nutritional deprivation or imbalances. This critical interaction of nutrition with immunity raises questions as to the appropriateness and effectiveness of immunizations in undernourished children. Although research is needed to clarify the interrelationship between nutrition and immunity, provision of an adequate supply of nutrients should be viewed as the first line of defense against infection. The poorly nourished are much more susceptible to respiratory infections and diarrheal disease. J. P. Grant (1985:82) stated that "diarrheal disease is the greatest single killer of children in the developing world—and often the chief cause of childhood malnutrition," and its prevention "depends upon improvements in water supply, sanitation, and hygiene." Nutritional improvement should be added to these basic preventative measures. The current popular promotion of oral rehydration therapy is at best only a temporary solution to a very serious problem.

Generally, well-nourished individuals are better able to tolerate infections. For example, in the tropics apparently healthy people live symbiotically with large populations of intestinal parasites (worms) or with malaria parasites in the blood. However, when nutritional status declines, the infection overwhelms them. Repeated infections in individuals with marginal nutrient reserves have a negative effect on nutritional status due to several contributing factors: (1) decreased appetite commonly associated with infection; (2) cultural practices that tend to provide a less nutritious diet for the sick; (3) decreased nutrient absorption associated with gastrointestinal infections; and (4) the normal physiological response to infection involving internal redistribution of nutrients such as amino acids and zinc for synthesis of compounds that fight infection and increased excretion of nitrogen, vitamin A, vitamin C, zinc, and other essential nutrients. In environments where these cycles of infections and malnutrition persist, effective public health measures primarily focus on nutritional improvements, while emphasizing immunizations and personal hygiene.

Malnutrition is a primary or associated cause of childhood morbidity and mortality from measles, whooping cough, bronchitis, pneumonia, influenza, and gastrointestinal disease. Although nutritional deprivation has negative consequences for people of all ages, young children are especially vulnerable. Morbidity and mortality levels among children under age five are commonly accepted as indices of general malnutrition in the population. The infant mortality rate (IMR), viewed as a major indicator of nutritional and health status, refers to the annual number of deaths of infants under one year of age per 1000 live births. Historical evidence shows that IMR declines as nutrition and general living conditions improve.

Grant (1985) grouped countries of the world into four IMR categories: (1) very high, over 100 IMR; (2) high, 60 to 100 IMR; (3) middle, 26 to 50 IMR; and (4) low, 25 and less IMR. The highest IMR in 1982 was 200 in Sierra Leone, compared to the lowest IMR of 7 in Sweden and Japan. Countries listed in Table 18.1 are ranked in descending order of IMR. The table includes data for: (1) IMR, (2) death rate of children ages one to four, (3) percentage of children under age five with mild or severe protein-energy malnutrition (PEM), and (4) percentage of total population below absolute poverty. These data suggest that malnutrition is a major underlying health problem in the countries of Sub-Saharan Africa. Problems and limitations are inherent in population statistics of this type (see Berry in this volume), however they do provide a general picture of the situation.

The incidence of anemia also serves as a useful general index of malnutrition in a population. Anemia is usually directly related to insufficiencies of iron and folacin, a B vitamin, and anemia typically coexists with marginal deficiencies of several other micronutrients such as zinc and other B vitamins. As previously discussed, such marginal deficiencies of iron and other essential nutrients are associated with increased frequency and severity of infections. The available data show a high incidence of anemia among people of all ages in Sub-Saharan Africa. More is known about anemia rates for women than for other groups—Grant (1985) estimated that 40 percent of nonpregnant women and 63 percent of pregnant women were anemic.

Nutrition and Reproductive Function

The important role of nutrition in reproductive function is more widely recognized than other roles of nutrition in functional performance. The effect of maternal nutritional status on pregnancy outcome and infant development has been the primary focus of much research (Duhring 1984; Hamilton et al. 1984; Grant 1985). Reductions in IMR are directly related to improvements in maternal nutrition. Nutritional improvement is also a major factor in long-term population control. Family-planning measures are not readily accepted by parents who anticipate high death rates among their infants and children. Thus, malnutrition actually contributes to high rates of population growth and exacerbates the problem of limited food resources.

Nutrition, Work Performance, and Educational Achievement

The role of nutrition in human behavior is of great interest, nevertheless research in this area is difficult and controversial (Brozek 1984; Pollitt 1984; Solomons and Allen 1983; Pollitt and Lewis 1980; Dobbing 1984; Cravioto and Delicardie 1976). Behavior, as defined by J. Brozek (1984), is a complex system of responses in-

TABLE 18.1. Indicators of Nutritional and Health Status in Relation to Measures for Poverty Incidence in Descending Order of Infant Mortality Rate (IMR) for 32 Sub-Saharan African Countries

IMR Rank/Country[a]	IMR ages 0-1 1982	Child Death Rate ages 1-4 1982	Children under 5 with PEM 1975-1981 mild/severe[b] (Percent)	Total Population Below Absolute Poverty Level 1977-1981 urban/rural[b] (Percent)
2 Sierra Leone	200	35	24/ 3	--/65
4 Malawi	170	29	----	25/85
5 Guinea	160	50	----	----
7 Angola	150	39	----	----
8 Benin	150	23	----	--/65
10 Mali	150	27	----	27/48
12 Burkina Faso	150	36	--/40	----
14 C. African Rep.	140	23	----	----
15 Chad	140	37	----	30/56
16 Ethiopia	140	25	60/10	60/65
17 Guinea-Bissau	140	--	----	----
18 Mauritania	140	27	10/--	----
19 Niger	140	27	17/ 9	--/35
20 Senegal	140	34	----	----
21 Somalia	140	47	16/--	40/70
25 Congo	130	10	30/ 1	----
26 Cameroon	120	16	----	15/40
28 Ivory Coast	120	23	23/28	30/26
30 Nigeria	120	20	24/16	----

Rank	Country	IMR	Child Death Rate	PEM (mild/severe)	Absolute Poverty Level
33	Sudan	120	23	50/ 5	---
38	Liberia	110	24	17/ 2	23/--
39	Mozambique	110	23	---	---
41	Togo	110	25	---	42/--
43	Zaire	110	20	---	---
45	Ghana	100	15	---	--/80
51	Tanzania	100	18	43/ 7	25/--
52	Zambia	100	20	---	---
56	South Africa	90	5	---	---
58	Uganda	90	22	15/ 4	---
60	Botswana	80	--	27/--	40/55
63	Kenya	80	13	30/ 2	10/55
69	Zimbabwe	70	14	---	---
119	USA	11	<0.5	---	---

Source: J.P. Grant. 1985. The State of the World's Children, 1985. Published for United Nations International Children's Emergency Fund (UNICEF). Cambridge: Oxford University Press.

a Countries are listed in descending order of infant mortality rate (IMR). Number in first column represents IMR ranking in relation to 130 other countries for which data area available.

b Whenever possible official government data were used; otherwise figures are estimates by relevant United Nations agency or United Nations Field offices. Symbol "--" indicates data not available.

Definitions:
  Infant Mortality Rate (IMR): annual number of deaths of infants under one year of age per 1000 live births.
  Child Death Rate: annual number of deaths of children aged 1-4 years inclusive per 1000 population in the same age group.
  Child Protein-Energy-Malnutrition (PEM): percentage of children under age 5 suffering from two levels of PEM; "mild" includes "mild or moderate" and describes children who are between 60 and 80 percent of desirable weight-for-age; "severe" describes those who are less than 60 percent of desirable weight-for-age.
  Absolute Poverty Level: income level.

volved in the adaptation of organisms to changes in the external and internal environment. The effect of nutrition on work performance has practical economic implications. Nutritional improvements in workers leads to increased productivity with greater economic returns, which makes a convincing argument for investments in these nutritional improvements (Basta 1976; Solomons and Allen 1983). Interpretation of research on the role of nutrition in work output is complicated by other variables such as workers' overall physical fitness, prior experience, infections, and personal motivation. However, increased work productivity has been correlated with seasonal variation in energy intake and with blood levels of hemoglobin.

The importance of iron nutriture was demonstrated in a study of road construction workers in a coastal area of Kenya (Basta 1976). Anemia was present in 34 percent of a sample of 180 men; following four weeks of iron supplementation, work output was greater in the treatment group than in the control group. Iron deficiency, with or without anemia, is present in an estimated two thirds of the populations of most developing countries (Hallberg 1984; Grant 1985). Low bioavailability of iron from predominantly plant diets and blood loss from widespread hookworm and schistosomiasis infections are contributing factors. Even when total energy (calorie) needs are met, iron intake may be inadequate.

The vital role of iron in producing hemoglobin (the oxygen-carrying protein in blood) is well known, and when hemoglobin levels are below normal, delivery of oxygen to body tissues is impaired, leading to reduced physical capacity and work performance. This is only one of several critical functions of iron (Hallberg 1984). It is also a component of myoglobin (the oxygen-carrying protein found in muscle) and plays a key role in many biochemical reactions including enzymes (cytochromes) responsible for electron transport in energy metabolism. Anemia represents a relatively late stage in development of iron deficiency. Earlier stages without anemia also may have negative consequences such as impaired cognitive function or decreased resistance to infection. Marginal deficiencies of other micronutrients such as zinc and folacin are also likely to coexist with poor iron status.

In environments where basic energy (calorie) intake is chronically below normal, individuals adapt by eliminating activities not absolutely essential for day-to-day survival. This situation imposes severe limitations on discretionary activities necessary to bring about improvements in family and community welfare. Undernourished children in such environments are typically listless, apathetic, and tend to have limited interactions with other people and the physical environment.

Greater educational achievement is an important goal for many in the developing world. Poor nutrition tends to limit this effort (Brozek 1984; Cravioto and Delicardie 1976). The well-nourished child is more likely to achieve genetic potential in mental and physical development; the malnourished child commonly has reduced physical activity and thus receives less stimulation than needed for normal cognitive development. Food deprivation represents not only a shortage of energy and nutrients, but also a lack of sensory stimuli and social experiences associated with eating and mealtime. In the classroom, the hungry or poorly nourished child tends to be apathetic, disinterested, and irritable when confronted with new or difficult tasks. When others respond negatively to these behaviors, the child's sense of self-worth decreases, further contributing to learning failure.

Meal skipping or "short-term fasting" tends to increase chances of error in problemsolving tasks, even in generally well-nourished American children. For example, skipping breakfast has been associated with impaired problemsolving performance in late morning (Pollitt et al. 1981). These findings suggest that proper attention to regular and frequent meals may be as important as overall nutritional quality of the diet.

Research on the effect of specific micronutrient (vitamins and minerals) deficiencies on mental function is difficult to study in human populations due to: (1) limitations in methodology for measuring mental performance, (2) a general lack of accurate biochemical methods for assessing marginal nutritional status, and (3) the likely coexistence of multiple nutrient deficiencies in malnourished children. Demonstration of the role of iron nutriture in cognitive functions of young children, particularly concentration and short-term memory, represents significant progress in this complex research area (Leibel et al. 1981).

• HUMAN NUTRITIONAL NEEDS AND DIETARY PATTERNS •

Human nutritional requirements include water, energy, and more than forty other elements or compounds. The three major physiological functions of essential nutrients are listed in Table 18.2. This section provides an overview of essential nutrients and their basic biochemical functions in relation to nutrient intake standards and dietary patterns. The material is organized into three main parts: (1) macronutrients (water, carbohydrates, fats, and proteins); (2) micronutrients (vitamins and minerals); and (3) nutrient intake standards and dietary patterns.

TABLE 18.2. Three Major Functions of Nutrients

Function	Nutrients Involved
Form Body Structures	Water Proteins Lipids Minerals
Provide Energy	Carbohydrates Lipids or Fats Proteins
Regulate Body Processes	Proteins Vitamins Minerals

TABLE 18.3. Major Functions of Macronutrients

Macronutrient	Function
Water	1. A component of all body tissues; helps to form body structures
	2. Serves as a medium or solvent for biochemical reactions
	3. Participates in biochemical reactions; for example, in "hydrolysis" or chemical breakdown process in which water is one of the reacting substances
	4. Serves as a lubricant that enables solid materials to slide against each other. For example, tears, saliva and synovial fluid in joints
	5. Helps to control body temperature
Carbohydrates	1. Provide energy
	2. Spare protein for its unique physiological functions
	3. Participate in fat metabolism
	4. Provide fiber or bulk in the gastrointestinal tract
Lipids or Fats	1. Provide essential fatty acids (linoleic and linolenic)
	2. Carry fat-soluble vitamins into the body
	3. Provide energy
	4. Provide components for body structure (adipose tissue, cell membranes, nerve coverings)
	5. Insulate the body thermally
	6. Protect vital organs
Proteins	1. Provide structure as components of all cells and in skin, muscles, connective tissue and the matrix or framework of bones and teeth
	2. Provide energy in circumstances when carbohydrates and fats are insufficient to meet energy needs
	3. Regulate body processes

Source: J.L. Christian and J.L. Greger. 1985. Nutrition for Living. Menlo Park, California: The Benjamin/Cummings Publishing Company, Inc.

Macronutrients

Water

Water accounts for about half of adult body weight; percentage of water varies inversely with fat content of the body (Christian and Greger 1985). In the newborn, water is about 77 percent of body weight. Water is the most limiting nutrient (see Table 18.3 for major functions); adults can survive for several weeks without food, but only for a few days without water. A decrease of 10 to 12 percent of body weight due to water loss can be fatal; a loss of as little as 3 percent will impair performance. In contrast, the body can lose about half its protein and all of its reserves of carbohydrate (glycogen) and fat without serious consequences. Except in conditions of illness or prolonged heavy sweating, the thirst mechanism operates to maintain water homeostasis (normal balance); thirst is normally experienced prior to a loss of 1 percent body weight as water. Average daily turnover of water ranges from two to three liters. Usually a daily intake of four to six cups of water from beverages, in addition to water obtained from solid foods, is sufficient. Water content of foods ranges from 30 percent in bread to more than 90 percent in fresh vegetables and fruits.

Energy

Energy needs are supplied primarily by carbohydrate and fat; protein serves as a reserve energy source (Hegsted 1984; Briggs and Calloway 1984; Christian and Greger 1985). Alcohol also furnishes energy. Energy is measured in kilocalories; the commonly used lay term is calories. A kilocalorie is the amount of heat required to raise the temperature of one kilogram water one degree Celsius. The metric system also quantifies energy in kilojoules. Energy value of foods may be estimated from the following guide: 4 kilocalories per gram (kcal/g) carbohydrate and protein, 7 kcal/g for alcohol, and 9 kcal/g for fat. Energy needs for basal metabolism are proportional to body size in terms of lean (nonfat) body mass and are increased during the growth process. Typical ranges of daily energy needs for a "standard" 70 kg adult male are 2300 to 3100 kcal, compared with 900 to 1800 kcal for a 13 kg child, 540 to 870 kcal for a 6 kg infant, or 2100 to 3900 for a 66 kg adolescent male. Most healthy, moderately active people maintain their body weight reasonably well, in spite of large day-to-day variations in physical activity. At low levels of physical activity, normal physiological regulation of energy balance is less precise and results in overfatness, or obesity.

In general, the condition of underweight is associated with more serious health risks than overweight. A body weight more than 10 percent below the standard range for an individual's height and body build usually means reduced vigor. In healthy adults of normal weight, a loss of about 25 percent of body weight is without serious permanent damage; it is difficult, if not impossible, to recover from losses of 50 percent of body weight. The degree or severity of protein-energy malnutrition (PEM) in infants and children may be categorized according to a median weight-for-age criterion: "normal"—greater than or equal to 86 percent of normal median weight; grade I (mild PEM)—76 to 85 percent; grade II (moderate PEM)—60 to 75 percent; grade III (severe PEM)—below 60 percent. The various syndromes of chronic, severe undernutrition represent a spectrum of serious and complex medical conditions requiring careful diagnosis and treatment by skilled physicians (Golden and Jackson 1984). Terms traditionally used to describe severe PEM in children and infants are *kwashiorkor,* characterized by edema (swelling due to excess fluid in body tissues), discolored hair, scaly skin, enlarged liver, lack of appetite, extreme apathy, and *marasmus,* characterized by "wasting" (atrophied muscles) and relatively normal hair, skin, and liver functions. The marasmic child has a "wizened old man" look. Marasmus comes from the Greek word meaning "to waste away"; kwashiorkor comes from the Ga language of West Africa and means "the disease suffered by the displaced child."

Proteins

Proteins provide (1) nitrogen for synthesis of vital nitrogen-containing compounds such as nonessential amino acids and (2) essential amino acids, or those that cannot be synthesized by the body (Crim and Munro 1984; Briggs and Calloway 1984; Christian and Greger 1985). The major issue in protein intake is the quantity must be sufficient to supply adequate nitrogen. A secondary issue is protein quality, or the amounts and balance of essential amino acids. Generally animal proteins are higher quality than plant proteins. Combining plant protein foods to make up for the amino acid shortfalls of each is a common dietary practice; grains, nuts, and seeds are made more nutritionally valuable by combining them with legumes (beans, peas, and lentils).

Protein requirements are proportional to body size and are usually expressed in terms of grams protein per kilogram (g/kg) body weight; protein needs per unit body weight increase during growth, pregnancy, lactation, and illness or injury. The suggested protein intake for adults is 0.75 to 0.80 g/kg body weight; however, protein intake needs to be increased if the diet consists predominantly of coarse and fibrous plant foods, which are only 85 to 90 percent digestible. Protein needs may also be expressed as a percentage of the total energy intake. About 10 to 15 percent of total energy intake supplied by protein is sufficient in most cases—i.e., at a daily energy intake level of 3000 kcal, 10 percent or 300 kcal should be from protein, or 75 g of protein should be consumed (4 kcal per g protein). On a weight basis, starchy roots such as cassava and yams have only about one-third the amount of protein that grains have. In areas of Africa where these roots are staples, only about 5 to 8 percent of the energy intake comes from protein (see Hiebsch and O'Hair in this volume).

Micronutrients

A discussion of individual micronutrients is beyond the scope and space limitations of this chapter; a summary of physiological or biochemical functions, dietary sources, and recommended dietary allowances (RDA) is presented in Table 18.4. For state-of-the-art reviews see *Nutrition Reviews*; for basic information see J. L. Christian and J. L. Greger (1985) and G. M. Briggs and D. H. Calloway (1984).

Nutrient Intake Standards and Dietary Patterns

Standards for nutrient intake are a practical tool for dietary assessment. The wise use of such standards requires understanding their limitations and underlying assumptions (Food and Agriculture Organization [FAO] 1974; Food and Nutrition Board 1980). Nutrient intake standards, or recommended dietary allowances, are periodically reviewed and revised as more data become available. In general, these standards are intended as estimates of the amounts of nutrients necessary to meet needs of almost all (97.5 percent) healthy people in the population. In fact, these standards exceed the actual requirements of many. Differences in nutritional needs of healthy individuals are usually not known, but clearly there is a rather wide range of adequate and safe intake levels. Knowledge of nutrient composition of foods commonly consumed by the population is also basic to dietary assessment involving nutrient intake standards. Because of insufficient data, standards have not been established for several nutrients. Nutrient intake standards usually assume consumption of a varied diet consisting of foods from both plant and animal sources.

Practical recommendations take into account centuries of human dietary experience, as well as current research data on nutritional requirements and food composition. The statement of C. G. King (cited in Todhunter 1983:1683), "Eating as an art is very old, but as a science very young," reminds us to respect whatever food intake patterns have sustained various human populations in reasonably good health for generations. Any deliberate dietary modifications should be based on sound scientific and health principles. External factors, such as agricultural change or economic development, may have unintended negative effects on established dietary patterns (Fleuret and Fleuret 1980). An important concept is that food selection to meet nutritional needs is a culturally learned experience and not just a natural instinct. Conditions that result in a breakdown of cultural and family traditions may adversely influence nutritional status; attention to nutrition education may be especially important in such circumstances. Replacement of breast-feeding of infants by bottle-feeding in many Third World countries is a classic example of inappropriate dietary change. Bottle-feeding under typical conditions is not only unsafe, but prohibitively expensive. For example, according to data

TABLE 18.4. Micronutrients

Vitamin	RDA[a] for Healthy Adults		Major Dietary Sources	Major Functions
	Females	Males		
Water-soluble				
Thiamin (B-1)	1.1 mg[b]	1.5 mg	Pork, legumes, peanuts, enriched or whole grain products	Component of coenzyme used in energy metabolism
Riboflavin (B-2)	1.3 mg	1.7 mg	Dairy products, meats, eggs, enriched grain products, green leafy vegetables	Component of coenzyme used in energy metabolism
Niacin	14 niacin equivalents	19 niacin equivalents	Nuts, meats; provitamin tryptophan in most proteins	Component of coenzyme used in energy metabolism
B-6	2.0 mg	2.2 mg	High protein foods in general, bananas, some vegetables	Component of coenzyme used in amino acid metabolism
Folacin	400 µg[c]		Green vegetables, orange juice, nuts, legumes, grain products	Component of coenzyme used in DNA and RNA metabolism
B-12	3 µg		Animal products	Component of coenzyme used in DNA and RNA metabolism
Patothenic acid	4-7 mg		Widely distributed in foods	Component of coenzyme used in energy metabolism

Nutrient	RDA		Widely distributed in foods	Function
Biotin	------100-200 µg------		Widely distributed in foods	Component of coenzyme used in energy metabolism
C	------60 mg------		Fruits and vegetables, especially broccoli, cabbage, cantaloupe, cauliflower, citrus fruits, green pepper, strawberries	Maintains collagen; is an antioxidant; aids in detoxification; still under intense study
Fat-soluble				
A	800 REd 4000 IUe	1000 RE 5000 IU	Fat-containing and fortified dairy products; liver; provitamin carotene in orange and deep green produce	Component of rhodopsin (Still under intense study)
D	------5 µg (200 IU)------		Fortified and full-fat dairy products, egg yolk	Promotes absorption and use of calcium and phosphorus
E	8 alphatocopherol equivalents	10 alphatocopherol equivalents	Vegetable oils and their products; nuts, seeds; present at low levels in other foods	Antioxidant to prevent cell membrane damage; still under intense study
K	------70-140 µg------		Green leafy vegetables; meats	Aids in formation of certain proteins, especially those for blood clotting
Major minerals				
Calcium	------800 mg------		Milk, cheese, dark green vegetables, legumes	Bone and tooth formation; blood clotting; nerve transmission

cont'd.

288 · POSTHARVEST TECHNOLOGY, DISTRIBUTION, AND NUTRITION

Table 18.4 (cont'd.)

Vitamin	RDA[a] for Healthy Adults Females	Males	Major Dietary Sources	Major Functions
Major minerals				
Phosphorus	800 mg		Milk, cheese, meat, poultry, whole grains	Bone and tooth formation; acid-base balance; component of coenzymes
Magnesium	300 mg	350 mg	Whole grains, green leafy vegetables	Component of enzymes
Sulfur	Provided by sulfur amino acids		Sulfur amino acids in dietary proteins	Component of cartilage, tendon, and proteins; acid-base balance
Sodium	1100-3300 mg		Common salt, soy sauce, cured meats, pickles, canned soups, processed cheese	Body water balance; nerve function
Potassium	1875-5625 mg		Meats, milk, many fruits and vegetables, whole grains	Body water balance; nerve function
Chloride	1700-5100 mg		Common salt, many processed foods (as for sodium)	Plays a role in acid-base balance; formation of gastric juice
Trace minerals				
Iron	18 mg	10 mg	Meats, eggs legumes, whole grains, green leafy vegetables	Component of hemoglobin and enzymes
Iodine	0.15 mg		Marine fish and shellfish; dairy products; iodized salt; some breads	Component of thyroid hormones

Mineral	Amount	Source	Function
Fluoride	1.5-4.0 mg	Drinking water, tea, seafood	Maintenance of tooth (and maybe bone) structure
Zinc	15 mg	Meats, seafood, whole grains	Component of enzymes
Selenium	0.05-0/2 mg	Seafood, meat	Component of enzymes; functions in close association with vitamin E
Copper	2-3 mg	Seafood, nuts, legumes, organ meats	Component of enzymes
Cobalt	(Required as vitamin B-12)	Vitamin B-12 (animal products)	Component of vitamin B-12
Chromium	0.05-0.2 mg	Brewers' yeast, liver, seafood, meat, some vegetables	Involved in glucose and energy metabolism
Manganese	2.5-5.0 mg	Nuts, whole grains, vegetables and fruits	Component of enzymes
Molybdenum	0.15-0.5 mg	Legumes, cereals, some vegetables	Component of enzymes

Source: J.O. Christian and L.L. Greger. 1985. Nutrition for Living. Menlo Park, California:the Benjamin/Cummings Publishing Company, Inc.

a Recommended Daily Dietary Allowance
b milligrams
c micrograms
d retinol equivalents
e international units

from Kenya half the annual income of an urban family in 1983 was required to adequately bottle-feed an infant for six months (Latham 1984). Excellent reviews of dietary beliefs and practices in several countries in Sub-Saharan Africa are available in a series of publications from the International Nutrition Communication Service (Israel 1983).

• NUTRITION POLICIES AND PROGRAMS •

Attention to human nutritional needs and problems should be an integral part of national development planning (Joint FAO/WHO Expert Committee on Nutrition 1976; Winikoff 1978; Underwood 1983; Hamilton et al. 1984; Dinning 1984; Sahn et al. 1984). Policies and programs in agriculture, health, family planning, and education should be carefully examined for their present and potential effects on nutritional well-being of the population. The first step in alleviation of hunger and malnutrition is a government that, regardless of its ideological base, cares about the health and welfare of its people and allocates an adequate level of resources for this purpose. The Joint FAO/WHO Expert Committee on Nutrition (1976:22) stated that "a major objective of national development is to create conditions which enable every individual to have a diet which provides his/her nutritional requirements, to permit him/her to achieve his inherited physical and mental potential and to sustain him/her at a full level of activity."

Nutrition planning begins with identifying malnourishment in terms of who is malnourished, in what ways, in what circumstances, and why. An analysis of the existing situation should be operationally meaningful; attention must be given to both short- and long-term solutions. Nutritional surveillance should be an ongoing and integral component of intervention strategies, and it is important to maintain an appropriate balance between program implementation and surveillance (Sahn et al. 1984). From an analysis of the few national successes, B. A. Underwood (1983) has proposed several key elements of successful nutrition intervention strategies at both national and community levels including: (1) clear conceptualization of program and major objectives, (2) involvement and commitment of local community leaders, (3) adequate resources, (4) cultural and social appropriateness, (5) feasibility under local conditions, and (6) a functional structure for program development, evaluation, and maintenance. More nations need to become successful in improving their citizens' nutrition.

• SUGGESTED FURTHER READINGS •

Briggs, G. M., and D. H. Calloway. 1984. *Nutrition and Physical Fitness*. Eleventh edition. New York: CBS College Publishing, Holt, Rinehart & Winston.
Christian, J. L., and J. L. Greger. 1985. *Nutrition for Living*. Menlo Park, California: The

Benjamin/Cummings Publishing Company.

Dinning, J. S. 1984. A Commentary: The Role of the Nutritionist in Third World Agricultural Policy Planning. *Journal of Nutrition* 114:1739–40.

Fleuret, P., and A. Fleuret. 1980. Nutrition, Consumption, and Agricultural Change. *Human Organization* 39:3:250–260.

Hamilton, S., B. Popkin, and D. Spicer. 1984. *Women and Nutrition in Third World Countries*. New York: Praeger Publishers, CBS Educational and Professional Publishing.

Israel, R., ed. 1983. *Maternal and Infant Nutrition Reviews*. An International Nutrition Communication Service Publication Series, Education Development Center.

Nutrition Foundation, The, Inc. 1984. *Nutrition Reviews' Present Knowledge in Nutrition*. Fifth edition. Washington, D.C.: The Nutrition Foundation, Inc.

Sahn, D. E., R. Lockwood, and N. S. Scrimshaw. 1984. *Methods for the Evaluation of the Impact of Food and Nutrition Programs*. Tokyo: The United Nations University.

Winikoff, B., ed. 1978. *Nutrition and National Policy*. Cambridge, Massachusetts: M. I. T. Press.

·19·

The Role of International Agricultural Research Centers in Africa

DONALD L. PLUCKNETT
NIGEL J. H. SMITH
ROBERT W. HERDT

The recent famine in Ethiopia sparks another debate about the best strategies for promoting increased food production in Africa. The issue is complex, and there are no short-term solutions. More people are realizing that a solid foundation of agricultural research is needed to help nations improve and stabilize farm productivity. Other factors such as more favorable prices and credit policies are also important, but improved farming technologies are essential to upgrade and sustain agricultural productivity on the continent. This chapter focuses on the role of international agricultural research centers supported by the Consultative Group on International Agricultural Research (CGIAR), which now devotes 40 percent of its resources to Africa, in the concerted effort to improve food production on the continent. We provide a brief history of the development of CGIAR centers, describe their ongoing efforts, review their impact on the lives of farmers and consumers on the continent, and finally outline some of the issues and options facing decisionmakers in agricultural research.

· HISTORY OF CGIAR ·

The first institution to be established as an international agricultural research center was the International Rice Research Institute (IRRI), which served as a model for subsequent centers. IRRI began operations at Los Baños in the Philippines in 1960 under the sponsorship of the Rockefeller Foundation and the Ford Foundation. In collaboration with national research programs, IRRI soon produced a series of high-yielding dwarf rices that respond well to fertilizers. Subsequent rice varieties produced by IRRI resist a broad range of diseases and pests, and one variety (IR36) is the world's most widely planted rice.

The International Maize and Wheat Improvement Center, or Centro Internacional de Mejoramiento de Maíz y Trigo (CIMMYT), emerged from a Rockefeller Foundation program to assist Mexico's agriculture. The program started in 1943 and was based at El Batán, an hour's drive from Mexico City. In 1963, the Rockefeller Foundation and the Mexican government established CIMMYT to work on wheat and maize for tropical and subtropical environments. The center gained worldwide recognition in the 1960s for its development of high-yielding, short-statured wheats, and Dr. Norman Borlaug received a Nobel Prize in 1970 for his leadership in this effort. CIMMYT wheats and IRRI rices launched the Green Revolution. Wheats developed by CIMMYT were first released in Mexico in the early 1960s and now account for virtually all the wheat planted in that country (Plucknett and Smith 1982). Semidwarf wheats with CIMMYT germplasm also greatly boost food production on the Indian subcontinent and in several countries in North Africa and the Middle East.

Rapid and far-reaching payoffs of CIMMYT and IRRI soon prompted the New York-based Rockefeller and Ford foundations to provide funding for two more international agricultural research centers in 1967, one in West Africa and the other in South America. The International Institute of Tropical Agriculture (IITA) at Ibadan, Nigeria, has a mandate to develop technologies for stable farming systems for the humid and subhumid tropics and to raise yields of tropical staples such as the sweet potato (*Ipomoea batatas*), yams (*Dioscorea* sp.), cocoyam (species of *Colocasia* and *Xanthosoma*), and cowpea (*Vigna unquiculata*). In addition, IITA was assigned responsibility for developing cultivars of cassava (*Manihot esculenta*), rice, maize (*Zea mays*), and soybean (*Glycine max*) for Africa. The objective of IITA's farming systems program is to devise more productive and ecologically sound alternatives to traditional systems of bush fallow and shifting cultivation. The Centro Internacional de Agricultura Tropical (CIAT), based near Cali, Colombia, seeks to improve the productivity of cassava, rice, beans (*Phaseolus* sp.), and cattle pastures in the humid tropics of Latin America.

The Rockefeller and Ford foundations wanted to install more centers, but such a task called for a transnational framework with sizeable financial resources that would systematically analyze agricultural problems throughout the developing world and assign research priorities accordingly. Following a meeting at Bellagio, Italy, in 1971, the Food and Agriculture Organization (FAO) of the United Nations, the United Nations Development Program (UNDP), and the International Bank for Reconstruction and Development (World Bank) decided to sponsor CGIAR in 1971. With its secretariat at the World Bank in Washington, D.C., CGIAR acts on behalf of a consortium of thirty-nine donors ranging from national governments and multinational organizations to private foundations. CGIAR's basic objective is to produce technologies or technology components that increase the quantity or quality of food in developing countries. CGIAR centers avoid competing with national programs and concentrate on research—not adequately covered by other research institutions—concerning critical aspects of food production in the Third World with regional or global significance. Thirteen centers now belong to CGIAR

TABLE 19.1. Centers Supported by the Consultative Group on International Agricultural Research (CGIAR), 1985

Acronym	Center	Location	Research Programs	Geographic Focus	1985 Budget[a] ($ million)
IRRI	International Rice Research Institute	Los Banos, Philippines	Rice Rice-based cropping systems	Global Asia	21.4
CIMMYT	Centro International de Mejoramiento Maiz y Trigo	Mexico City, Mexico	Maize, Bread wheat, Durum wheat, Barley, Triticale	Global	21.0
IITA	International Institute of Tropical Agriculture	Ibadan, Nigeria	Farming systems, Maize, Rice, Cassava, Cowpea, Lima Bean, Soybean Sweet potato, Yams	Tropical Africa Global	21.2
CIAT	Centro Internacional de Agricultura Tropical	Cali, Colombia	Cassava, Field beans Rice, Tropical pastures	Global Latin America	22.9
CIP	Centro Internacional de la Papa	Lima, Peru	Potato	Global	10.4
WARDA	West African Rice Development Association	Monrovia, Liberia	Rice	West Africa	2.4
ICRISAT	International Crops Research Institute for the Semi-Arid Tropics	Hyderabad, India	Chickpea, Pigeonpea Pearl millet, Sorghum, Groundnut Farming systems	Global Semi-Arid tropics	20.4

ILRAD	International Laboratory for Research on Animal Diseases	Nairobi, Kenya	Trypanosomiasis, Theileriosis	Global	9.5
IBPGR	International Board for Plant Genetic Resources	Rome, Italy	Plant genetic resources	Global	4.3
ILCA	International Livestock Center for Africa	Addis Ababa, Ethiopia	Livestock production systems	Tropical Africa	14.0
IFPRI	International Food Policy Research Institute	Washington, D.C.	Food policy	Global	4.7
ICARDA	International Center for Agricultural Research in the Dry Areas	Aleppo, Syria	Farming systems, Wheat, Barley, Triticale, Broad bean, Lentil, Chickpea, Forage crops	Dry areas of West Asia and North Africa	19.0
ISNAR	International Service for National Agricultural Research	The Hague, Netherlands	National agricultural research	Global	3.6

aCGIAR supported core budget in USA dollars.

including CIMMYT, IRRI, IITA, and CIAT; these centers conduct research on most of the major food crops and ecological zones of the developing world (see Table 19.1). Four of the CGIAR centers—IITA, the International Livestock Center for Africa (ILCA), the International Laboratory for Research on Animal Diseases (ILRAD), and the West African Rice Development Association (WARDA)—are headquartered in Africa.

After the formation of CGIAR, nine new international agricultural research centers were inaugurated in rapid succession. WARDA was started in 1971 in Liberia to promote self-sufficient rice production in fifteen West African countries. WARDA differs from other CGIAR centers in that it is an intergovernmental association. CGIAR supports WARDA's efforts to evaluate improved rice varieties for adaptation to the region's agroclimatic and social conditions and to develop farming systems appropriate to improved rice varieties. WARDA concentrates on four systems of rice production: mangrove swamp rice in brackish waters at Rokupr, Sierra Leone; irrigated rice at a research program located at four stations in Senegal; upland rice or rice dependent on rainfall at Bouake, Ivory Coast; and deep water rice at Mopti, Mali.

The International Potato Center (CIP), or Centro Internacional de la Papa, was created in 1971 in Lima, Peru, to work on the potato (*Solanum tuberosum*), a crop of growing importance in the highland tropics. In 1972 the International Crops Research Institute for the Semi-Arid Tropics (ICRISAT) began research near Hyderabad, India, on peanut (or groundnut) (*Arachis hypogaea*), chickpea (*Cicer arietinum*), pigeonpea (*Cajanus cajan*), pearl millet (*Pennisetum typhoides*), and sorghum (*Sorghum bicolor*).

In 1974 CGIAR unveiled three more institutes. One of these, the International Livestock Center for Africa (ILCA), based at Addis Ababa, Ethiopia, explores ways of improving African pastoral and mixed-farming economies. ILCA assists national research efforts to improve livestock production and marketing systems, trains livestock specialists in Africa, and gathers documentation useful to the African livestock industry. Livestock husbandry in Africa is deeply embedded in traditional and highly complex farming cultures, and ILCA concentrates on systems analysis and management approaches and techniques rather than on individual commodities. Although cattle are the primary focus of research, sheep and goats also receive attention and ILCA conducts research in arid, subhumid, humid, and highland areas. ILCA's humid-zone program is based at IITA in Ibadan, Nigeria, and the two centers cooperate in farming systems research.

A sister institute based in Nairobi, Kenya, the International Laboratory for Research on Animal Diseases (ILRAD), was also established in 1974. Researchers there are studying theileriosis (East Coast fever) and trypanosomiasis, two livestock diseases that severely limit productivity of beef, dairy, and goat herds in over fifty developing countries. These two debilitating diseases reduce meat and milk yields, production of leather, wool, and fertilizer, as well as animal power for agricultural work. Both diseases are provoked by parasites transmitted by insects;

tsetse flies carry trypanosomes and ticks carry the parasite that causes East Coast fever. ILRAD's research emphasizes identifying disease control methods based on immunological responses of livestock breeds that resist or tolerate the parasites.

The International Board for Plant Genetic Resources (IBPGR) was the third center established in 1974. Based in Rome, Italy, IBPGR promotes the conservation of crop genetic diversity by sponsoring an international network of germplasm collections (Plucknett et al. 1983). The board also helps establish priorities for collecting missions and assists national programs to establish genetic resource conservation programs.

In 1976 the International Center for Agricultural Research in Dry Areas (ICARDA) joined the CGIAR system to examine the potential for boosting food production in dry subtropical and warm temperate areas, particularly in North Africa and the Middle East. ICARDA and ICRISAT thus cover the most important crops of the drought-prone regions of the developing world. Based near Aleppo, Syria, ICARDA scientists are developing new strains of bread and durum wheats, barley, triticale (wheat crossed with rye), lentil (*Lens esculenta*), faba bean (or field or broad bean) (*Vicia faba*), and forage plants, particularly medics (*Medicago* sp.). ICARDA collaborates with CIMMYT in cereal work; ICRISAT assists ICARDA in the chickpea program.

The International Food Policy Research Institute (IFPRI) was founded in Washington, D.C., in 1975 to analyze strategies for meeting world food needs. By monitoring food production in developing countries as well as world trade in cereals and pulses, IFPRI provides information for policymakers drawing up priorities for research and development. IFPRI joined the CGIAR system in 1979. In the same year, the International Service for National Agricultural Research (ISNAR) was started in The Hague, Netherlands, to help strengthen national agricultural programs, so that research results benefit inhabitants of developing countries. ISNAR advises developing countries on ways to start or upgrade their agricultural research and extension services.

Many initiatives have been undertaken by CGIAR to help increase food production in the Third World. Over 750 senior staff from many countries are engaged in this effort (see Table 19.2). CGIAR centers provide modern laboratory and field equipment, well-stocked libraries, and reliable funding for travel to the field, international conferences, and to meet with collaborating scientists at other institutions. Many CGIAR centers offer a wide range of technical courses for Third World nationals, collaborate with national programs, and help improve germplasm collections. Whenever possible, international agricultural research centers leave the final selection and naming of crop varieties to national programs.

• CURRENT WORK IN AFRICA •

Africa figures prominently in the current work programs in the CGIAR centers. In

TABLE 19.2. Number of International Agricultural Research Center (IARC) Senior Staff, Visiting Scientists and Staff on Deputation, Posted in Each Region in 1984[a]

Country	Total	Scientists[b]	CIAT	CIMMYT	CIP	IBPGR	ICARDA	ICRISAT	IFPRI	IITA	ILCA	ILRAD	ISNAR	IRRI	WARDA
Total Senior Staff	757	231	81	66	62	15	46	79	31	105	53	30	28	92	68
West Africa	199	99	--	5	--	1	--	18	--	92	12	--	1	3	68
East & South Africa	114	39	3	6	5	2	--	7	--	5	41	41	3	1	--
Asia	171	26	1	12	7	3	--	49	2	1	--	--	--	96	--
Latin America	199	29	61	71	58	1	--	2	--	4	--	--	1	1	--
North Africa & Middle East	53	11	--	1	2	1	46	2	--	--	--	--	--	3	--
Others	65	--	--	1	1	9	--	--	28	--	--	--	26	--	--

[a]These are 1983 statistics for ICARDA, IFPRI and IITA and 1982 figures for WARDA.

[b]Not in their Center's Host Country.

addition to the four centers headquartered in Africa, seven other centers have staff stationed in Africa engaged in a variety of outreach activities in cooperation with national and international research institutions. As of 1984, over 300 of the 750 senior staff at CGIAR centers worldwide were stationed in Sub-Saharan Africa; 109 of these scientists lived in Ethiopia, Kenya, Liberia, and Nigeria, the four countries hosting CGIAR centers on the continent (see Table 19.2).

ICRISAT is headquartered in India, but much of its work is applicable to or conducted in the semi-arid regions of Africa. ICRISAT scientists work in Burkina Faso, Kenya, Malawi, Mali, Niger, Nigeria, Senegal, Sudan, and Zimbabwe. IC-RISAT is responsible for two major cereal crops, sorghum and pearl millet, that are major staples in West Africa, and it is responsible for peanut, or groundnut, an important crop in many parts of the continent. ICRISAT's work in West Africa is largely designed to facilitate technology transfer from India; however, the varieties of sorghum and pearl millet widely accepted in India are not adapted to the ecological conditions and farm family needs of West Africa. Thus ICRISAT recently established a research subcenter near Niamey, Niger, to improve agricultural productivity in the region. ICRISAT also has a regional team at Bulawayo, Zimbabwe, and another team in Kenya. Between 1974 and 1983, ICRISAT provided in-service training to 210 researchers from West Africa, 103 from East Africa, and 51 from southern Africa; another 31 researchers from Africa were ICRISAT research fellows or research scholars.

CIAT, based in Colombia, is responsible for the world germplasm collection of cassava and, with IITA, supplies cassava material to African national programs. CIAT conducts similar work with the common bean in East Africa and is now building up a nine-member team to work on bean improvement in humid and subhumid Africa. CIAT's large tropical pastures program in Latin America is developing cooperative research efforts in Africa, particularly with ILCA.

CIMMYT, based in Mexico, has several ongoing outreach programs in Africa, some of which are funded by bilateral donors. Most of these programs are run jointly with national agricultural research and extension agencies. Staff in CIM-MYT's maize program work in the national programs of Ghana, Tanzania, and Zaire, and there is a joint African maize program with IITA at Ibadan, Nigeria. CIMMYT's wheat program has staff assigned to an East African regional project spanning seventeen countries from Ethiopia in the north to Lesotho in the south. In addition, a CIMMYT economist is stationed at ILRAD in Nairobi to coordinate the East African economics program that involves national research organizations in Kenya, Tanzania, Malawi, and Zambia. Training is an important part of CIM-MYT's contribution to African agriculture; 187 individuals from Sub-Saharan Africa attended CIMMYT maize in-service training between 1971 and 1983, and 96 trainees were involved in their in-service wheat training between 1966 and 1983. CIMMYT also uses its headquarters and research sites in Mexico for training African scientists.

Potatoes are not widely grown in most African countries, but the importance of that root crop is growing. CIP maintains several staff members in Africa for cooperative research and training activities. A regional scientist is located at ILRAD's headquarters in Nairobi, two staff members reside in Rwanda, and one lives in Burundi; other regional representatives are stationed in Egypt and Tunisia. The Peru-based center also supports local scientists in Ethiopia and Kenya. A regional network, Programe Regional d'Amélioration de la Culture de Pomme de Terre en Afrique Centrale (PRAPAC), was established in 1982 to improve potato productivity in Burundi, Rwanda, and Zaire.

Philippines-based IRRI has a liaison scientist for Africa based at IITA who works closely with IITA, WARDA, and national institutions. Two IRRI scientists are posted in Egypt, and the center is exploring the need for similar arrangements elsewhere in Africa. Through the International Rice Testing Program, a network for testing rice germplasm that embraces eight hundred scientists in some seventy-five countries (Plucknett and Smith 1984), IRRI makes advanced rice-breeding lines available to WARDA and to various interested national institutions. IRRI has recently initiated an outreach program in Madagascar, where rice production systems are similar in many respects to those in Asia.

ICARDA, located in Syria, is working with national researchers in Egypt and Sudan to evaluate new production technologies for faba beans. A research team is now in Tunisia to work on barley and legumes in North Africa, and ICARDA is beginning with ILCA to work on the integration of livestock and crop production. Rome-based IBPGR has periodically stationed staff in Africa for extended periods to assist in crop germplasm conservation and collection and has sponsored a number of collecting missions, particularly to West Africa. IBPGR coordinators for East and West Africa reside in their respective regions to stimulate germplasm conservation work. The board has also helped IITA set up storage facilities for the long-term preservation of cowpea, Bambarra groundnut, and African rice (*Oryza glaberrima*).

Two other CGIAR centers conduct research in Africa without having staff stationed there. Netherlands-based ISNAR is surveying the strengths and weaknesses of several national research systems in Africa and has completed assessments of Burkina Faso, Ivory Coast, Kenya, Madagascar, Malawi, Rwanda, and Somalia. Washington-based IFPRI now devotes about 33 percent of its research to Africa-related projects, compared with about 18 percent over the past ten years. As part of its work on policy issues, IFPRI has published monographs on such topics as food security in the Sahel, agricultural research policy in Nigeria, and growth linkages of Nigerian and Kenyan agricultural exports. An IFPRI-sponsored conference on accelerating growth in Sub-Saharan Africa is being prepared for publication.

• IMPACT ON AFRICAN FOOD PRODUCTION •

Improved maize lines from CIMMYT help raise yields in Zaire and Tanzania.

IITA-developed maize lines resist streak virus, a virulent pathogen that has spread throughout large areas of Nigeria and Cameroon. These improved maize varieties now cover some five hundred thousand hectares in Africa. To enable farmers to grow their customary varieties while ensuring that they are protected against the devastating streak virus, CIMMYT and IITA are working together to transfer streak resistance to local African maize cultivars.

In cooperation with national research organizations, CIP has released potato varieties that yield well in farm conditions found in Burundi, Ethiopia, Kenya, and Rwanda. Small-scale farmers in these countries now plant over ten thousand hectares in improved varieties. ILCA and CIP have obtained potato yields of eighty tons per hectare in the highlands of Ethiopia. Such yields show the potential for dramatic increases in farm income and improved nutrition in areas where the crop is cultivated and consumed. WARDA has tested and released a number of improved rice varieties for its West African member countries.

IITA, in cooperation with Zaire's national program, has made significant progress in developing high-yielding cassava varieties that resist cassava mosaic virus and other pathogens as well as insects that attack the crop in Central and West Africa. Biological control of cassava mealybug and green spider mites is also progressing, and test sites in Nigeria indicate control of mealybugs is possible by releasing certain wasps imported from South America. Mealybugs were accidentally introduced to Africa from South America in the early 1970s. IITA will help raise cassava mealybug parasites and predators for eventual release in several African countries. Release of these predators and parasites and dissemination of resistant cultivars promise to restore some of the estimated $2 billion annual loss in cassava production caused by the pests in Africa. In addition, IITA has developed sweet potato lines that genetically resist attack by the sweet potato weevil, a major cause of postharvest losses; insecticides are not required for control of the pest on these resistant lines.

IITA and ILCA have worked to develop and improve alley cropping, a form of agroforestry in which food crops are grown between rows of perennial tree crops that can be used for fodder, wood fuel, and green manure (see Webley in this volume). Such agroforestry programs could help ameliorate the deteriorating environment in many parts of Africa and elsewhere by better protecting soil and water resources (Brown et al. 1984; Smith 1985). Several alley-cropping patterns will soon be ready for further testing in farmers' fields. The International Center for Research on Agroforestry (ICRAF), based in Nairobi, serves as an information clearing house for work on the integration of tree and other crops. ICRAF, an international research center operating outside of CGIAR, collects and disseminates information on various agroforestry schemes and monitors agroforestry projects in various parts of the world.

The work of several CGIAR centers on livestock trypanosomiasis is also approaching a payoff. A network approach, typical of much work in international centers, is used to tackle this widespread livestock disease. The Trypanotolerance

Network, coordinated by ILCA, unites twenty scientists of the ILCA center in Addis Ababa with two centers in Nairobi—ILRAD and a non-CGIAR center, the International Center for Insect Physiology and Ecology (ICIPE)—and nine national programs in Central and West Africa. In 1981 members of this team began to informally coordinate research on the potential of trypanotolerant cattle breeds, particularly the N'Dama and West African Shorthorn. Network researchers have demonstrated that N'Dama produce more meat and milk than the tall Zebu in areas of low trypanosomiasis transmission and significantly outperform susceptible breeds in regions with high trypanosomiasis transmission (Murray et al. 1981, 1982, 1983).

Scientists in the Trypanotolerance Network have confirmed that trypanotolerance is genetic and not merely a localized condition as previously thought. N'Dama and West African Shorthorn regulate the growth of the etiological agents and their red blood cells resist destruction by the parasites. ILRAD is shipping frozen N'Dama embryos to Kenya for further study and possible transfer of resistance to susceptible breeds.

Apart from the Trypanotolerance Network, ILCA is helping Africa improve its pastoral and mixed-farming economies in other ways. An oxen-drawn metal scoop has been developed that can create water reservoirs without using expensive machinery or fossil fuels. The Ethiopian government is interested in promoting the use of these locally made scoops throughout the country to retain water for livestock, irrigation, and aquaculture.

ILCA's Selective Dissemination of Information service (SDI) keeps livestock researchers in Africa abreast of the latest publications in their fields. Each scientist in the information network receives a monthly printout containing citations and abstracts of relevant journals and books generated from tapes of the Commonwealth Agricultural Bureau and the International Information Systems for Agricultural Sciences and Technology. Within six months of SDI's inception in 1983, 250 researchers had applied for the free service. SDI is being integrated with another service of ILCA's library—the microfiche collection of unpublished documents on agriculture from African government agencies. Previously, these documents were virtually inaccessible; now they are assembled by ILCA staff who visit agricultural agencies to copy documents. In return for supplying documents to be copied, cooperating governments receive microfiche copies of materials from their own agencies as well as from those in other cooperating countries.

· OUTLOOK ·

The CGIAR centers are clearly committed to improving agricultural productivity in Africa. The CGIAR system is small, however, and plays only a part in the difficult and long-term process of generating more food from African lands. The 1985 CGIAR budget was under $200 million, compared with an estimated $1.3 billion spent by developing countries on agricultural research (Picciotto 1985). The cost of three new Boeing 767 airplanes would exhaust the CGIAR annual operating budget, and Brazil spends about that much every year just on its cacao research and extension program, Comissão Executiva do Plano da Lavoura Cacaueira (CEPLAC).

The Green Revolution that swept Mexico, the Indian subcontinent, and large parts of Southeast Asia is unlikely to sweep Africa, at least in the near future. Substantial irrigated areas, fertile soils, and strong national research programs were in place or were quickly developed in areas where the Green Revolution's semidwarf rice and wheats were adopted; these advantageous conditions do not exist in Sub-Saharan Africa. Furthermore, most African governments are not firmly committed to agricultural growth (Walsh 1984a). Given that most of Africa's farmlands are not irrigated and are spread over a vast range of environments, no single crop genotype is likely to be widely appropriate. Progress will come through tailoring high-yielding genotypes to local conditions and tastes, wider use of fertilizers and integrated pest-management systems, and more favorable prices for farm products.

Agricultural research authorities and development experts stress the need for African governments to give higher priority to agriculture in their development strategies and to collaborate more fully (York 1984a, 1984b). Since population growth is outpacing per capita food production on the continent, agricultural output must increase (Mellor 1985). To increase agricultural output it is preferable to improve production on existing farmlands rather than open new areas for farming, which increases pressure on marginal environments and fragile ecosystems.

Each African country needs to develop viable technologies (through research) and create effective extension and information services to help farmers increase productivity. International centers can be a valuable resource for national institutions in this effort; international centers are more useful if linked with strong national research and extension programs. CGIAR centers help strengthen national institutions, but other international and bilateral organizations must provide financial and technical assistance. The World Bank has recently identified national agricultural research as an area that requires more investment in most developing countries (Walsh 1984b). Prior to 1980, for example, the World Bank and its affiliate, the International Development Association, provided virtually no support for agricultural research, but since then these donor institutions have disbursed $1 billion for agricultural research. Other multilateral and bilateral organizations are also giving increased attention to this need.

• SUGGESTED FURTHER READINGS •

Cock, James H. 1985. *Cassava: New Potential for a Neglected Crop.* Boulder, Colorado: Westview Press.

International Service for National Agricultural Research (ISNAR). 1985. *Serving National Agricultural Research Systems: Lessons from Country Experiences, 1980–84*. The Hague: International Service for National Agricultural Research.

Jahnke, Hans E. 1982. *Livestock Production Systems and Livestock Development in Tropical Africa*. Kiel, West Germany: Kieler Wissenschaftsverlag Vauk.

Kang, B. T., G. F. Wilson, and T. L. Lawson. 1984. *Alley Cropping: A Stable Alternative to Shifting Cultivation*. Ibadan, Nigeria: International Institute of Tropical Agriculture.

Mosher, Arthur T. 1966. *Getting Agriculture Moving*. New York: Praeger.

Office of Technology Assessment (OTA). 1984. *Africa Tomorrow: Issues in Technology, Agriculture and U.S. Foreign Aid*. Washington, D.C.: Office of Technology Assessment, Congress of the United States.

Pinstrup-Anderson, Per. 1982. *Agricultural Research and Technology in Economic Development*. London: Longman.

Ruttan, Vernon W. 1982. *Agricultural Research Policy*. Minneapolis: University of Minnesota Press.

Weiss, Charles, and Nicolas Jequier. 1984. *Technology, Finance and Development: An Analysis of the World Bank as a Technological Institution*. Toronto: Lexington Books.

·20·

Farming Systems Research and Extension: An Approach to Solving Food Problems in Africa

LOUISE O. FRESCO
SUSAN V. POATS

Y ields of food crops per hectare have been stagnating in most of Africa and have been declining on a per capita basis (World Bank 1981; U.S. Department of Agriculture [USDA] 1981). Although these figures are open to questions (see Berry in this volume), there can be no doubt that yields must be raised. There are many reasons for Africa's low performance in food production, such as deficiencies in marketing, infrastructure, price incentives, and general agricultural policies. The low yields have also been attributed to the nature of African soils and climate. All of these reasons are important; yet it must also be recognized that there are considerable differences in productivity among different areas in Africa. Maize yields in Zimbabwe and intensive cropping systems in parts of Cameroon are examples of high productivity. Nonetheless, there is obviously room for improvement in most of Africa, even though ecological limits appear to have been reached in some areas such as the Sahelian belt.

It is also clear that most agricultural research conducted thus far has not produced many results that can be applied by subsistence farmers in communities in which labor is relatively scarce. The real breakthroughs in world agricultural production have been achieved in irrigated wheat and rice, and to some extent in maize, but not in any of the major African food crops such as sorghum, millet, and roots and tubers. Furthermore, most current agricultural innovations are not adapted to the rainfed shifting and fallow systems that are characteristic of most farming in Sub-Saharan Africa.

Therefore, there is an obvious need for a reorientation of agricultural research in two respects. First is the need for an inventory of small farmers' constraints that takes into account the great variability and location-specificity of African farming systems, with a view to formulating more relevant research problems. Second is the need for adaptive research procedures whereby existing innovations may be tested and adapted to the specific and localized needs of farmers. Although some general problems and solutions are known, such as the maintenance of soil fertility through tied ridging, mulching, and manuring, these are not always translated into the terms that fit specific farming systems.

Farming Systems Research and Extension (FSR/E) provides a framework for this reorientation. Although this framework is still in many ways struggling to define its mandate and methodology, it has broad appeal among researchers, extension workers, and policymakers, as well as farmers. However, any research program or technology will have only a limited impact if other things remain equal. FSR/E is not a panacea; it is no more than a tool or an approach that may help African countries and farmers to increase food production.

The purpose of this chapter is to explore FSR/E and its use and suitability as a method for generating technology for agricultural development in Africa. A definition that includes an overview of the basic concepts, methods, and stages of activities begins the chapter, then the historical development of FSR/E in Africa is outlined. This historical perspective provides the basis for an exploration of how the approach, as it has evolved, may contribute to solving Africa's food problems. Despite a fairly widespread belief in the appropriateness of this approach in Africa, there are still a number of problems confronting its implementation in many countries. In this chapter examples from current projects and programs that illustrate these obstacles have been provided. Notwithstanding these problems, FSR/E is being institutionalized now in some national agricultural research and extension systems, and examples of such systems are included. Finally, in the last section the possible future and limitations of FSR/E in Africa are explored.

· GENERAL CONCEPTS AND FEATURES ·

FSR/E has rapidly become a popular "catch word" in agricultural and rural development programming during the past decade.[1] Although by no means a new concept, since many of its principles have been used for more than a generation, it combines different earlier approaches for the dual purpose of (1) understanding limited-resource farmers and their interactions with the biological, social, and economic environment and (2) providing procedures for the adaptation of technology to the needs and constraints of these limited-resource farmers. The combination developed as a result of growing concern over the difference in yields on research stations and yields by actual farmers, the unintended negative side effects of the large scale diffusion of new agricultural technology during the Green Revolution, and the low rates of adoption of new technology by farmers, particularly those identified as small or resource limited (Simmonds 1984). FSR/E provides an orientation for commodity research and perhaps also for rural development policy. It is not, however, a development strategy by itself. It is complementary to other research and extension approaches, not a substitute for them. It is also important to recognize that there is inherent tension between systemic interdisciplinary approaches to problemsolving, such as FSR/E, and approaches that follow a more singular or disciplinary line, such as commodity and component approaches.[2]

Because FSR/E is a relatively new approach that is still taking shape, and because its name is applied as a descriptive generic label to a variety of ongoing activities known by an assortment of titles, there is still some disagreement over terminology and methodology. Most practitioners, however, seem inclined to take a pragmatic view of the field, focusing on common features and concepts, rather than arguing for a common definition and methodology. This pragmatic view allows for the development and inclusion of a wider range of research-extension projects, greater diversity of applications, and greater experimentation in methods for solving problems, all of which should promote further growth and development of the approach. Most of these practitioners agree that a farming system is a

> reasonably stable arrangement of farming enterprises that the household manages according to well-defined practices in response to the physical, biological, and socioeconomic environments and in accordance with the household's goals, preferences, and resources. These factors combine to influence output and production methods. . . . The farming system is part of larger systems—e.g., the local community—and can be divided into subsystems—e.g., cropping [or livestock] systems (Shaner et al. 1982:16).

The same authors define FSR/E as an approach aimed at "increasing the productivity of farming systems by generating technologies for particular groups of farmers and by developing greater insight into which technologies fit where and why" (Shaner et al. 1982:13).

Although other definitions exist and considerable discussion still takes place over their relative merits, there is general consensus on the basic assumptions, objectives, and methodologies of the approach. Regarding assumptions on the nature of farmers, farms, and farm households, FSR/E holds that farmers are rational and make decisions based on their understanding of their farming system and the environmental, social, and economic constraints that they face. The farm is viewed as a holistic system with all subsystems interconnected. A change in one subsystem initiates changes in the linkages within other subsystems and ultimately in the whole farming system. Research and extension improve as researchers and extension workers stop dealing with individual crop and livestock enterprises as if they were isolated and start treating farms as systems. Finally, farm households have multiple objective functions. Farmers do not necessarily seek technical optima or even optimal economic returns from a single crop or livestock enterprise, and farm level production constraints may be cultural, as well as technical and economic. Thus, FSR/E involves action-oriented research with a high degree of location specificity, usually directed toward more than one crop or farm enterprise. The primary objective is to increase the supply and stability of farmers' food as a basis for the improvement of the welfare of farmers.

The nature of FSR/E methodology is interdisciplinary, involving biological, technical, and socioeconomic scientists. It requires complementary on-farm and on-station research, and its success depends to a great extent on the linkages with component and commodity research.[2] FSR/E's starting point is the whole farm, including livestock and off-farm employment, and farmer participation in the research process becomes both a means and an end in itself. Finally, FSR/E is iterative and practical, incorporating methods of knowledge generation that include two principal elements: informal diagnostic surveys and on-farm experimentation based on the results of agricultural research and farmers' experiences. As a result, FSR/E shows a new appreciation of traditional farming techniques (for example, mixed cropping or combinations of upland and valley plots) and of traditional risk averting crops and practices (for example, the use of drought-resistant but usually low-yielding cereals such as bullrush and finger millet). Further, this approach pays attention to the need to reduce variations in total farm output and to ensure household food security.

FSR/E generally proposes five steps in the development of technical improvements for limited-resource farmers: diagnosis, design, testing and evaluation, dissemination, and referral and evaluation. These steps may occur cyclically or simultaneously, depending on the nature of the research program; in most cases they are continuous activities.

Diagnosis usually consists of two steps. The first is an inventory of agricultural production systems, existing research results and recommendations, and input delivery structures in a given region, which is usually defined as the project area. The second is the determination of production constraints or problems for groups of farmers—each group consists of farmers with similar production systems. These groups are often referred to as recommendation domains for the development and testing of specific technological innovations. In both steps various methods of informal and formal, quantitative and qualitative data collection by an interdisciplinary team are used. The simple and effective diagnostic procedure, developed in Central America, known as the *sondeo* (Hildebrand 1981) and the rapid rural appraisal (Chambers 1981), similar to the sondeo, are effective diagnostic tools that may be used to distinguish groups of farmers and their production constraints. In some areas farmer groups are not easily distinguished initially, and group definitions are refined as on-farm work progresses and greater information is collected concerning the features of specific farming systems and farmer constraints. Diagnosis has often included more formalized surveys for data gathering; however, the trend is toward informal methods with complementary focused formal surveys to verify informal results or to explore in greater detail some particular aspect of the farming system. It is important to note that diagnosis does not take place only at the start of FSR/E work, but is continuously carried out to monitor on-farm experimentation, gather new information, assess impact, or generate new research directions. In the same fashion farmer groups or recommendation domains are not fixed; they are redefined as more understanding of the farming system is reached (Hildebrand et al. 1985).

In the design step the results of diagnosis are used to develop strategies to overcome the identified constraints and technological innovations involving on-station and on-farm experimentation. FSR/E, in principle, introduces changes only at the farm level. Often food production is constrained by factors at other levels, for example, transportation systems or pricing structures. Following design, the testing, monitoring, and evaluation of proposed innovations are conducted in farmers' fields with varying levels of supervision from researchers, or extension agents, or both, and under varying levels of farmer management.

The fourth step, dissemination, involves the adaptation and transfer of successful innovations to other farmers in the same recommendation domain via extension systems. The development process does not end here. The fifth step, referral and evaluation, addresses unsolved problems and the evaluation of reasons for farmer adoption or rejection of the new technology, which must be communicated to relevant component and commodity researchers, as well as to policymakers.

Broadly speaking, at present most FSR/E practitioners throughout the world agree upon these five steps. Nonetheless, the historical development of the approach and the actual application of the methodological steps differ considerably from region to region, as well as from project to project. In the remainder of this chapter the history of FSR/E in Africa and its application within the sub-regions of Africa are explored.

• HISTORICAL ROOTS AND DEVELOPMENT IN AFRICA •

FSR/E is rapidly gaining a place in agricultural research and extension programs today in Africa. Though it has only recently attracted the attention and funding of foreign aid donors, it is not a new approach to agricultural research in Africa. Carl Eicher and Doyle Baker (1982:161) described an "invisible literature on FSR in Africa which can provide a perspective on current FSR programs" (1982:161). In particular, they cited the experiences of the Cotton Research Corporation in Uganda during the 1950s, the Uboma study in eastern Nigeria during the 1960s, and the Experimental Units in Senegal's groundnut basin of the early 1970s as predating contemporary FSR/E programs. In addition to these were the many multilocational testing programs instituted by various African research institutes that were valuable in identifying the potential of recommended varieties and techniques in particular agro-ecological zones. As Eicher and Baker pointed out, these early experiences demonstrated that on-farm research is not a luxury but a necessity in shaping national research programs, that multidisciplinary teams incorporating social scientists are essential to agricultural research, and that farmer testing of technological innovations is needed prior to dissemination of new technology through extension systems.

Since the early 1970s, the development of FSR/E in Africa has been largely supported by the efforts of several of the International Agricultural Research Centers (IARCs) that are sponsored by the Consultative Group on International Agricultural Research (CGIAR) (see Plucknett et al. in this volume). These efforts are detailed later in this chapter. Foreign donor agencies have also entered the picture—notable examples include the French efforts in Senegal, Burkina Faso, Algeria, Tunisia, Mali, Niger, Cameroon, and Ivory Coast; the Dutch aid to the FSR programs in Sikasso, Mali, and in Burkina Faso; and the Canadian International Development Research Center's (IDRC) extensive support to cropping systems research activities throughout Africa. U.S. Agency for International Development (USAID) support has come largely during the 1980s and primarily through its funding of the CIMMYT East African Programme and through bilateral contracts in Senegal, Malawi, Gambia, Zambia, Lesotho, Sudan, Botswana, Swaziland, and Tanzania.

Important also in this historical development were several conferences that served as turning points in the evolution of FSR/E in Africa (Eicher and Baker 1982:160). For example, the need to consider indigenous farm practices such as intercropping, rather than automatic promotion of Western practices, was revealed at an intercropping conference in 1976 in Tanzania. A conceptual framework for FSR was spelled out at a conference in 1977 at the Institut d'Economie Rurale in Mali. In 1977 a symposium on the Experimental Unit approach in Senegal highlighted the importance of on-farm experimentation. And in 1979, at a conference organized by the Office de la Recherche Scientifique et Technique Outre-Mer (ORSTOM) in Ouagadougou, occurred a major synthesis of social, economic, geographical, and technical perspectives on farm-level studies in Africa. Roughly half the countries in Africa had initiated FSR projects by 1981 (Eicher and Baker 1982:161).

Generally, most of the FSR/E efforts in Africa can be categorized into two groups. One group comprises studies that largely describe existing farming systems in a holistic way, with a view to understanding the relationships of the components of the system (for example see Ruthenberg 1980). This group is rarely directly related to applied developmental efforts. The second group consists of those efforts that are actively developmental, those that seek changes in the production system. Efforts in this latter category may be further divided into (1) efforts that view on-farm research as a complement to ongoing station research, usually focus on one crop or commodity system, and assume that production increases result from stepwise iterative changes in selected components of the farming system and (2) efforts that attempt to develop new farming systems under the assumption that a radical restructuring of the entire system is required, such as replacing shifting with permanent cultivation in the humid tropics or introducing farming systems based on animal traction as opposed to hoe cultivation. These categories help to structure the understanding and analysis of the development of FSR/E in Africa. To this end it is equally important to trace the roots of two sometimes conflictive, sometimes complementary FSR/E perspectives in Africa: the Francophone and Anglophone perspectives.

Francophone refers to the approaches utilized by the French during the 1960s and 1970s in the former French-speaking colonies in Africa and to the systems approaches to agricultural production that evolved in the 1950s in the former Belgian colonies. Anglophone refers loosely to the FSR/E and cropping systems research that evolved at the IARCs, in some U.S. universities, and in certain national programs around the world. Though these two terms may seem exceptionally broad and subject to overgeneralization, this simplistic dichotomy is justified because

(1) the similarities among the different Francophone approaches are far greater than their differences, as is also the case among Anglophone approaches, and (2) there seem to be some theoretical differences in perspective between the Francophone and Anglophone traditions. These differing traditions teach us something about the strengths and weaknesses of FSR/E and the ways a FSR/E approach may fit within national research programs. It should be noted that recent exchanges among national programs that are inspired by Francophone or Anglophone traditions have become more frequent, and many national programs are developing their own special blend of FSR/E. The comparison of Francophone and Anglophone approaches to FSR/E is drawn from a comparative study conducted by Louise Fresco (1984) and is summarized here to highlight some of the general issues confronting FSR/E in Africa today, with particular respect to its institutionalization and the extension of its results.

· FRANCOPHONE APPROACHES IN AFRICA ·

French Initiatives

The development of French research on tropical agriculture was dominated by a commodity/sector approach that was reflected in its organization. Beginning in 1924, eight research institutes were created, one for each of the following: livestock; oil crops; textiles and fibers; timber and forestry; coffee, cocoa, and other stimulants; rubber products and plastics; agricultural machinery; and food crops. Each of the institutes created its own field program both at home and abroad, resulting in the organization of agricultural research along commodity lines in many of the former French colonies in Africa. The institute for food crops, Institut de Recherches Agronomiques Tropicales et des Cultures Vivrières (IRAT), developed a concern for a systems approach to integrate the results of component research programs in field projects. A brief look at the development of the Experimental Units, or Unités Expérimentales (UE), in Senegal provides insights into the evolution of the French approach.[3]

Up until 1960, agricultural research in Senegal, mainly at the peanut (groundnut) research station at Bambey, had been nearly exclusively component or commodity oriented and focused on cash crops. Little work on food crops had been conducted. Detailed studies of specific climatological and natural constraints, as well as large-scale soil surveys, were part of a concentrated effort to overcome technical constraints to production. Development programs centered on introduction of animal traction and ploughs, breeding of heavier oxen, detailed recommendations on cultivation techniques, and the dissemination of improved varieties. During the 1960s, many development programs failed and questions regarding the role and methods of agricultural research were raised. Of the new insights gained during this period, the following laid the basis for a systems approach (Tourte 1971):

1. Agricultural production is carried out by farmers who seek production systems that best fulfill their needs given the socioeconomic and ecological environment.

2. Research priorities must be defined with an understanding of the rural environment and national objectives.

3. The transfer of research results through the extension service is inadequate, and results developed in the artificial context of research stations are inappropriate.

4. The combination and application of technologies, as well as the development of integrated production systems, must be studied; production systems must be adapted to the technical and socioeconomic environment.

5. Integrated systems must be field tested in order to identify constraints in their application.

In 1968, two Unités Expérimentales (UE) were created within the National Agricultural Research Institute (Institut Sénégalais de Recherches Agricoles, or ISRA). A UE is a geographical and social unit in which the results of agricultural research are tested on a real scale to develop and refine production systems that take into account the interactions between physical and human environments. ISRA was based at Bambey and the UEs were located in the Sine Saloum region of Senegal. The two UEs covered 6,000 hectares with 2,200 inhabitants and 4,500 hectares with 2,000 inhabitants and included several villages and hamlets that were united into cooperatives. Creation of the UEs must be considered a milestone in the history of FSR/E in Africa because for the first time production systems became not only the subject of research but their study was institutionalized within the existing research structure. At the same time, the UEs were considered as a pilot project in which technically sound interventions were tested for economic and social feasibility.

With the creation and use of UEs and the attempt to involve farmers in the formulation of new technologies, a distinction became drawn between light innovations (*thèmes légers*) and more fundamental innovations (*thèmes lourds*). Light or classical innovations include improvements to the traditional production system such as new varieties, additional fertilizers or changes in their application, or light equipment that do not alter the system's basic structure. Fundamental innovations, however, are a coherent package aimed at an overall intensification and a profound transformation of the traditional production systems. These would include efforts such as land improvement and reorganization of land holdings in order to allow permanent cultivation or the introduction of animal traction and tractorization. The two sets of innovations are not diametrically opposed but complementary, and both are viewed as essential to the development of the full agricultural potential of Senegal. Therefore, restricting research to the development of improvements in the traditional production systems limits economic growth.

It is not possible to detail fully the development of the UEs in Senegal; however, it is necessary to highlight three new features introduced into agricultural research in Africa as a result of the UEs. (1) Detailed procedures for data collection outside the research station throughout the process of technology formulation were introduced—namely, case studies, focused followup thematic surveys, surveys on themes new to agricultural technology innovation such as nutrition and demography, and the use of group and individual interviews. (2) Explicit linkages were established between research and development organizations—namely, the use of experimental areas of realistic scale, continuous interaction of agricultural researchers and extension workers, direct feedback into research through field trials, and the combination of short term (*thèmes légers*) and longer term (*thèmes lourds*) development goals. (3) The production system in all its complexities was accepted as a unit of analysis, leading to a decentralization and location-specificity of research and to the recognition that evaluation criteria include farmers' motivations and national development goals, as well as agronomic criteria.

Several features of the UE experience were also prominent in other French agricultural development activities in Mali, Tunisia, Burkina Faso, Algeria, Ivory Coast, Niger, and Cameroon. All these have added to the development of what can be loosely defined as a Francophone approach to FSR/E. There is no single Francophone approach; yet some key concepts common to most French programs may be identified. Central among these key concepts is that of *recherche-développement,* which refers to the essential linkage between agricultural research and rural development. Récherche-développement is the study of the application, on the basis of tests conducted under real physical and socioeconomic conditions, of technical and social changes, in particular the intensification of production and the creation of producer organizations and delivery or extension systems. Recherche-développement concentrates mainly on innovations or packages for labor (input and skills), types and quantities of agricultural inputs (seeds, fertilizer, tools, and machinery), and the organization and management of production systems. The approach rarely tests economic innovations in marketing, price policies, agricultural wages, credit, or agrarian reform in general. Recherche-développement comprises three complementary activities: (1) studying the conditions of application of production systems that have been developed in agricultural research stations, in particular through field tests; (2) identifying the principal factors that limit agricultural production and choosing and testing solutions to overcome these constraints; and (3) developing policies and methods to improve the socioeconomic conditions of production (Billaz and Dufumier 1980:19).

That all three of the above activities are pursued in concert tends to give the Francophone approach a rather broad mandate to integrate the results of component research aimed at solving technical problems, while assessing economic feasibility and practicality at farm level. In conducting research activities, recherche-développement operates at four levels of observation to which four units of analysis correspond. From the specific to the general the levels are: the field/plot, the farm, the village, and the subregion (see Table 20.1).

TABLE 20.1. Levels and Units of Analysis in the R-D (Recherche-Developpement) Approach to Farming Systems Research

Level	Unit of analysis	Study of:
Field/plot	a. cropping system (systeme de culture) b. livestock system	a. soils, agro-ecological history, crop/weed/insect populations, micro-climate b. also: herds, grazing conditions
Farm	farming system (systeme de production)	means and methods of production, including non-agricultural work; recent history, past change in capital and technology utilization; labor profiles; household budgets
Village	village production systems (systeme agraire/terroir)	management of natural resources, land evaluation, climate, vegetation, morphology, etc., (social) control of natural resources and water
Subregion	subregional production system (systeme agraire/petite region)	Same as above but on a scale of 10,000 hectares and over

Source: E. de Miranda and R. Billaz. 1980. Methodes de Recherche en millieu sahelien: Les approches ecologiques et agronomiques d'une demarche pluridisciplinaire: l'exemple de Maradi au Niger. Agronomie Tropicale XXXV:4:357-373.

One may interpret Table 20.1 as representing a certain hierarchy of systems, much as Robert Hart and Antonio Pinchinat (1980) have discussed elsewhere. The major contribution of this distinction of levels of activity and corresponding units of analysis is that it explicitly carries the results of field-level testing to the regional policy levels, and vice-versa, and it effectively demonstrates the necessary linkage of on-farm research to extension, natural resource management, and policy formulation. Although it is possible to distinguish six phases in recherche-développement, in practice these phases are not necessarily conducted chronologically—that is, the phases may occur simultaneously or as problems emerge in the research process (Ramond 1970; Billaz and Dufumier 1980; Tourte and Billaz 1982). The six phases are as follows:

1. Observation and analysis of constraints to rural and agricultural development that require a multidisciplinary effort and rely on various types of surveys that lead to a zonage (homogeneous units based largely on agro-biological and technical criteria) and to a typology of farm enterprises

2. Formulation of farm models or new farming systems formulated in a quantitative way and comprising the hypotheses to be tested

3. Definition of multilocational trials on substations, on farms, and in test villages

FIGURE 20.1.   Communication Among Researchers, Farmers, and Development Workers

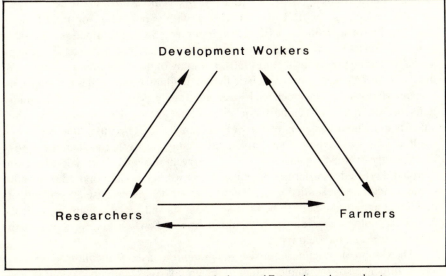

Source: Louise O. Fresco. 1984. Comparing Anglophone and Francophone Approaches to Farming Systems Research and Extension. Farming Systems Support Project Networking Paper No. 1.

4. Evaluation and interpretation of trial results

5. Proposals for and discussions with development programs

6. Definitions of new hypotheses for further research

Concerning these phases, great attention is placed on the classification of farms according to their size, number of people employed, and annual per capita income. Several different socioeconomic types of farms may be found within a single agro-ecological zone. Additionally, farm models are proposed combinations of improved or new technologies.

To summarize, recherche-développement is an integrated attempt to define the sequence of technical and socioeconomic changes and pathways required for a farming system to reach optimal production levels. To achieve this result, there must be an ongoing, functional partnership among research, farmers, and development (see Figure 20.1). This triangular relationship allows researchers to learn from farmers how they manage their existing farming systems and allows farmers to try innovations proposed by researchers. The role of development is one of a long-term iterative process between researcher and farmer that leads to the diffusion of innovations.

Belgian Contributions

Though there are many examples worthy of note, this section focuses on only two Belgian contributions to FSR/E in Africa: the first is the work of Pierre de Schlippe and the second is the INEAC experience with *paysannats,* or resettlement schemes. Pierre de Schlippe, a Belgian agronomist, must be regarded as one of the founding fathers of farming systems; yet his work in Central Africa has been neglected for a long time. During the 1950s, his study of the traditional agriculture of the Zande in Zaire led him to conclude that agricultural technologies developed in research stations must be preceded by a detailed analysis of local agricultural traditions and the rationale behind them (de Schlippe 1956). He proposed that this analysis must involve agronomy as well as anthropology because "traditional agriculture is at once both a human activity and a natural process" (de Schlippe 1956). De Schlippe warned against promoting interventions that were not based on thorough knowledge of farmer practices and constraints. He proposed that traditional agriculture be studied by agricultural anthropology because all students of traditional agriculture need to be both agronomists and social scientists. Agricultural anthropology, according to de Schlippe, is based on two concepts: the system of agriculture and the field type.

The system of agriculture consists of agricultural as well as cultural elements, and is influenced by the whole culture of the group. Agricultural behaviour is governed by social norms and values and by knowledge of the environment. This knowledge is extremely detailed, covering the criteria for relative fertility of each soil-vegetation pattern, the exact timing of every operation in the process of raising each variety of every crop, and the utilization of all sorts of fruits, seeds, leaves, wood, and barks for every kind of food and utensil. This knowledge is shared by the community, and its practice is codified by rules that govern behavioral patterns.

The field type is both an agronomic term and a sociological one. In the sociological sense, a field type is a cluster of behavioral constraints that rigidly define the way fields are to be cultivated and the obligations of the cultivator of a field toward others. In the agronomic sense, a field type consists of an association or sequence of crops, or both, with the following characteristics: (1) prescribed combination of crops and varieties, (2) a determined ecological environment, and (3) a fixed succession of cultivation practices throughout the season to take place at predetermined moments in time (de Schlippe 1957:12–13).

De Schlippe used illustrations from the Zande to show that a combination of field types allows a population to make the best use of its natural environment and labor resources. He demonstrated that field types change over generations. Farmers do conduct experiments, and the results of successful experiments can lead to new field types. Changes also occur as a result of the process of incorporation and the introduction of innovations such as cash crops. New varieties of existing crops such as short cycle groundnuts may induce new field types and a better use of fields. De Schlippe stated that observation and interviewing are key tools in agricultural anthropology, but cautioned that interviews often give idealized pictures of reality. He makes no mention of on-farm experimentation in his work, but he contributed much to the understanding of agriculture as a cultural-agronomic phenomenon, rather than as solely an agronomic or solely an economic activity, especially regarding subsistence production.

A second important contribution comes from the experience of the Institut National pour l'Etude Agronomique du Congo Belge (INEAC) in Zaire. Created in 1933, INEAC succeeded in creating one of the best basic research organizations in tropical Africa. Among its other duties, INEAC assisted the government in implementing its 1917 legislation to enforce compulsory cultivation of predetermined acreages in order to encourage food production. Paysannats (resettlement schemes) were a feature of this project, and INEAC assisted in developing the technical features of the resettlement policy. Paysannats were primarily formed to develop and disseminate improved farming methods. The main feature was the spatial reorganization of agriculture to make optimal use of and improve the physical resources. In each ecological region, the exact location and the necessary improvements were determined for the spatial units—namely, the village, the fields under cultivation, the fallows, the rotations, the pastures, the perennial plantations, firewood lots, fish ponds, and roads. Fields and fallows were laid out in *couloirs,* or corridors, one hundred meters wide and laid east to west to gain maximum daylight. The length of the couloirs depended on the number of farmers; the number of the couloirs equalled the total number of years in the cultivation and fallow cycle so that alternating couloirs could be opened annually. This system was modified to suit each ecological and social setting. The objective was not only to encourage modern farming techniques, including the use of machinery, fertilizer, and pesticides, but to facilitate supervision by the administration. At the same time, the couloir system mimicked the Bantu traditional system of farming.

The couloir system was far from successful everywhere; expected breakthroughs in productivity did not materialize, and a large gap remained between research station results and average farmer yields. The paysannats remained a colonial invention and have been severely criticized for their paternalistic and authoritarian features (Dumont 1962). However, many concepts underlying the paysannat strategy—the holistic approach,the detailed study of agro-biological and socioeconomic aspects of the environment, and the gradual introduction of appropriate technical innovations—cannot be ignored in an analysis of the roots of FSR/E.

· ANGLOPHONE APPROACHES IN AFRICA ·

In contrast to the Francophone approaches in Africa, which largely may be traced to efforts initiated by France and Belgium in areas of former colonial influence, the various Anglophone approaches found in Africa have their roots in a wide variety of development efforts.[4] Though diversity is great, two general sources of influences can be identified. One source is the several International Agricultural Research Centers (IARCs) active on the continent. The other source is characterized by bilateral donor intervention and national initiatives. These two Anglophone influences often overlap a great deal, and within each influence distinct and often differing philosophical and methodological underpinnings exist.

David Norman and Michael Collinson offer another useful perspective on the characterization of the different FSR/E approaches by distinguishing among "in the large," "in the small," and "with a pre-determined focus." FSR/E in the large "treats all system parameters as potentially variable in a wide ranging search for improvement" (Norman and Collinson 1985). In this instance the emphasis is placed on the development of optimal new farming systems that take advantage of state-of-the-art technology applied to existing ecological conditions. This concept parallels that of thèmes lourds, introduced earlier. FSR/E in the small and FSR/E with a predetermined focus recognize that

> small farmers evolve from their existing situation in steps. The content and scale of these steps must necessarily be compatible with farmer resource endowments, their risk ceilings and their management capabilities. Both seek a focus within the system which identifies potential development steps. Because both recognise the step by step development process in small farming and both seek to identify steps in technology there has been confusion between the two. The difference is that FSR "in the small" arrives at a focus within the system in the course of diagnosis, while FSR "with a predetermined focus" moves into the system to research an enterprise, or one facet of an enterprise, looking for improvements within that focus, which are compatible with the whole farming system. The two approaches

have different implications for the level of leverage obtained in the system and for institutionalization (1985:6).

Using the above criteria for categorization, in the following sections the major Anglophone FSR/E efforts are outlined, providing some insight as to their different methodological frameworks and the directions in which they are evolving. FSR/E efforts that were influenced by the International Agricultural Research Centers are discussed first, followed by discussion of the efforts that developed through bilateral or national initiatives.

CIMMYT Initiatives

The International Center for Maize and Wheat Improvement (CIMMYT), headquartered in Mexico, has probably inspired greater FSR/E activity in Africa than any other single entity. Their Eastern and Southern African Economics Program (CIMMYT/ESA) established a base in Nairobi and posted Michael Collinson, a farm economist, there in 1976 to begin on-farm research work with a focus on maize. In 1983 he was joined by two other farm economists, one as a training officer based in Nairobi and the other based in Mbane, Swaziland, to work with the Southern African countries. In 1985 four agronomists were appointed to the CIMMYT African maize and wheat program, two to focus on on-farm research development in national programs. As CIMMYT gained experience in on-farm research, primarily in maize, a more holistic perspective was incorporated and the label on-farm research in a farming systems perspective (OFR/FSP) was adopted to identify the FSR/E orientation.[5]

CIMMYT's overall objectives in OFR/FSP are: (1) to improve the capacity of national agricultural research services to develop appropriate technologies by establishing the routine use of OFR/FSP as an agricultural research tool, (2) to improve the procedures of OFR/FSP through the experiences of the national programs, and (3) to help national programs be even more precise in reflecting germplasm needs of farmers so that CIMMYT can be even more responsive to those needs. There are four methods to pursue these overall objectives: (1) demonstration of OFR/FSP procedures and direct participation in national agricultural program field research work, (2) training of national research staff in OFR/FSP procedures, (3) networking through a newsletter and a series of workshops on technical and management issues, and (4) institutionalization of OFR/FSP through counseling on ways to create linkages among research, extension, planning, and OFR/FSP.

CIMMYT/ESA proposes that OFR/FSP may play several important roles in national agricultural research programs (Collinson n.d.). First, OFR/FSP allows for testing technical research findings in appropriate farming systems. It also enables national programs to better identify farmers' priority problems and the unsolved technical questions in these problems and then channel this information to propriate specialist researchers. Finally, the approach encourages researchers, extension workers, and farmers to cooperate in the selection and adaptation of agricultural technology to farmer situations.

Collinson argued that adaptive research and on-farm experimentation are not novel techniques, but that OFR/FSP provides these procedures with new perspectives. Among these perspectives is the view that social and economic circumstances, not just agro-ecological ones, dictate farmer decisionmaking on potential new technology. Therefore, innovations should be exposed to farmers and extension staff as part of the technology development process to weed out nonviable options before making recommendations. Of equal importance is the realization that farmers operate multiactivity systems that demand compromises on technical perfection in any one activity in the interests of the whole system. New technology packages that are not accepted by farmers may not be inherently bad but may prove unacceptable if they were developed without consideration of these OFR/FSP perspectives. The procedures followed in OFR/FSP are the same as those listed previously (diagnosis, design, testing and evaluation, dissemination, and referral) with only slight modifications in application. The essential linkage between on-farm and on-station work in conducting effective research is explicit in OFR/FSP procedures (see Figure 20.2).

With the CIMMYT mandate focused on maize and wheat, their FSR/E activities could easily have the predetermined focus described earlier in this section. However, it is clear that the CIMMYT/ESA program promotes FSR/E in the small as the more appropriate alternative in the long-term effort to institutionalize the process (Norman and Collinson 1985). FSR/E in the small may be seen in the countries with which they are currently working, primarily because these countries want to use OFR/FSP as a basis for the total agricultural research and extension effort, not just for the improvement of maize and wheat. These national programs may be grouped as follows: (1) There are three countries (Zambia, Malawi, and Zimbabwe) in which the national agricultural research and extension system has been reorganized to accommodate OFR/FSP and its linkages among farmers, researchers, and extension personnel through regionally deployed teams of on-farm researchers, each team a mix of technical and social scientists. (2) Ten countries have OFR/FSP-type programs and are actively debating how these may be best integrated with technical component research and extension (Botswana, Ethiopia, Kenya, Lesotho, Sudan, Swaziland, Tanzania, Zimbabwe, Rwanda, and Burundi). (3) Three countries (Mozambique, Uganda, and Somalia) have initiated or will shortly initiate pilot programs in OFR/FSP.

In each country within each group, some initial leverage may have been gained through a commodity program entry (predetermined focus), since it is usually easier to begin on-farm research when a priority commodity or problem has already been determined before the diagnostic process begins. For CIMMYT, maize as a priority commodity provides an advantage because they are able to draw upon their store of maize technology in proposing potential solutions for maize problems. However, the perspectives and methods of the institutions in most of

FIGURE 20.2.   Interactions Between Station-Based Technical Research
and On-farm Adaptive Research

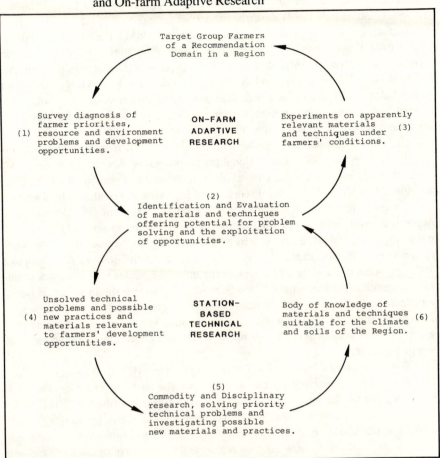

Source: Michael P. Collinson. 1982. *Farming Systems Research in Eastern Africa: The Experience of CIMMYT and Some National Agricultural Research Services, 1976–81.* MSU International Development Paper No. 3. Department of Agricultural Economics. East Lansing: Michigan State University.

these countries are emphasizing FSR/E in the small in order to address the total agricultural system.

Other IARC Initiatives

Though not active in as many locations as CIMMYT, the International Potato Center (CIP) has been engaged in FSR/E for several years in those regions of Africa most appropriate for white potato (*Solanum tuberosum*) production. Their work has a pre-determined focus on potatoes, but the underlying principles and philosophy are quite similar to CIMMYT. The "farmer back to farmer model" (Rhoades and Booth 1982) describes the FSR/E approach used by CIP. Three points distinguish this approach from that used by CIMMYT/ESA: (1) CIP often begins exploring a technical problem with an on-farm trial, which engages the farmer in active interaction with researchers to determine the nature of the problem before them. (2) The whole food system is considered to be the target area, and researchable problems include technical and management issues in postharvest storage, processing, consumption, and marketing. (3) CIP often works with existing farmer groups or social organizations as the locus for on-farm trials.

CIP views national programs as the home for FSR/E and pursues the institutionalization of FSR/E into national potato programs. Activities are most visible in Rwanda and, to a lesser extent, in Burundi, and a "Francophone Office" is maintained in Tunis to service French-speaking African countries. In Rwanda, CIP's work with the National Potato Improvement Program (PNAP) has been quite successful. FSR/E is an integral part of the PNAP program, and there is evidence that the methods employed by PNAP have had a "spread effect" to other commodity and agricultural development projects in the country (Bicamupaka 1985: personal communication). One of the interesting sides to CIP's work in on-farm research in Africa is that CIP has been implementing programs, largely based on previous Anglophone experiences or concepts generated in Latin America, in French-speaking African countries. It will be interesting to observe, as these programs mature, to what extent Anglophone and Francophone concepts and methods merge together.

The International Institute for Tropical Agriculture (IITA), located in Ibadan, Nigeria, has had a farming systems program for the past fifteen years. This program, at least for the initial twelve years, could best be described as FSR/E in the large or as having a thème lourd focus. The objectives of the program were (1) the environmental characterization and analysis of humid and subhumid farming systems in the West and Central African region and (2) the development of crop and soil management technologies suited to these areas. This work, though officially titled Farming Systems Research, was done largely on-station and resulted in a considerable body of information and technology that should now be tested under farmer conditions. IITA's program today is expansive, with on-station efforts at the main campus and FSR/E extending through the outreach program across a variety of ecological conditions through cooperative efforts with national programs.

IITA's FSR/E activities follow stages that are similar to the programs described earlier (diagnosis, design, experimentation and recommendation, and extension). The program emphasizes that far greater efforts have been placed on diagnosis than on experimentation, especially in West and Central Africa (where the bulk of IITA work is conducted). For this reason IITA now pushes hard for more rapid initiation of on-farm trials in their FSR/E-supported programs. The Institute has also recently placed more attention on gender issues in FSR/E and is increasing the consideration of gender variance to ensure equitable access, appropriateness, and benefits for new technology. Like the other IARCs, IITA is engaged in the institutionalization of FSR/E into national programs. IITA has been very effective in assisting the organization of a Nigerian network of FSR/E and has been supporting a similar effort in Ivory Coast. Malik Ashraf et al. (1985) discussed IITA's FSR/E activities in cooperation with Nigerian institutions in their report on the Bida project. These national networks have come about largely as a result of training efforts and collaborative on-farm diagnosis and experimentation. IITA is also expanding its cooperation with national programs in Cameroon, Zaire, Benin, Sierra Leone, Tanzania, and Rwanda. In several of these situations, IITA appears to be merging concepts and methods from both the Francophone and Anglophone experience. A more explicit effort to promote exchange between these two bodies of experience is IITA's part in the efforts to develop the West African Farming Systems Research Network (WAFSRN). This network is coordinated from Amadu Bello University in Nigeria and includes sixteen West and Central African countries. Though slow to get started due to financial and organizational problems, WAFSRN has the potential to become a vehicle for expanded communication within the region and should promote greater interaction between researchers following a largely Francophone tradition and researchers connected to the Anglophone experiences.

The West African Rice Development Association (WARDA), headquartered in Monrovia, Liberia, does not use the FSR/E or OFR/FSP terminology; nonetheless, it conducts on-farm interdisciplinary research and extension within its Technology Assessment and Transfer (TAT) program (Levasseur et al. 1981). WARDA operates with a predetermined focus on rice and uses an ecological perspective in defining four systems of rice production within the West African region: the mangrove swamp system, the floating rice system, the upland rice system, and the irrigated rice system. WARDA has based interdisciplinary TAT teams at four research stations designated to focus on each of the rice production systems. One of the important results from the on-farm work is the discovery that many of the improved rice varieties developed in other regions of the world do not perform better than existing West African varieties in the upland system. These results indicate the need for locally developed varieties rather than the simple transfer of existing varieties and help to reorient WARDA's program.

Three other IARCs active in African FSR/E are: the International Center for Tropical Agriculture (CIAT), the International Center for Research for the Semi-Arid Tropics (ICRISAT), and the International Livestock Center for Africa (ILCA). CIAT's FSR/E activities in Africa have only begun recently and are focused on the Great Lakes Region of East Africa, including Rwanda, Burundi, and eastern Zaire. CIAT works with a pre-determined focus in FSR/E in Africa— beans, in this case. CIAT's methodological stages are similar to those of CIMMYT and other Anglophone FSR/E projects. The CIAT bean program in the Great Lakes Region has focused initially on the question of bean varieties, and much of their initial diagnostic efforts have been toward understanding traditional bean variety systems, varietal characteristics desired by farmers for beans, and bean production systems. On-farm research is still in the exploratory trial stage (Voss 1985: personal communication).

ICRISAT's FSR/E activities in Africa have been concentrated primarily in the Sahelian regions of West Africa, principally in Burkina Faso and Niger, and are grounded firmly in a village studies framework that relies heavily on baseline surveys and other formal survey tools. Farmer tests are an integral part of the approach, and ICRISAT enumerators live in the villages to monitor the tests and continue the companion baseline studies. ICRISAT's FSR/E may be described as having a predetermined focus on sorghum and millet production. The primary audience for the results of the on-farm tests is the ICRISAT scientists. "The tests are designed not only to examine technologies that are in a final stage of development but also to examine the concepts and objectives on which the technologies are based. Results are intended to help scientists appreciate the conditions that technologies must satisfy if they are to be widely adopted" (Matlon 1983).

Major differences exist between FSR/E as practiced by ICRISAT and the other IARCs previously described. That the major client for the results is ICRISAT scientists has meant that less attention is paid to developing the concepts and practices of FSR/E within national programs. Less attention is paid to the merits and effectiveness of informal surveys for diagnosis, and the extensive formal surveys used by ICRISAT are less readily transferable to national program management. The existing extension system is virtually excluded from the FSR/E activity, a situation more common in Francophone countries than in Anglophone ones. Finally, ICRISAT uses FSR/E to see if developed technology fits within existing farming systems, rather than turning the process around to develop technology that satisfies farmer priorities and existing farmer conditions.

ILCA is the only IARC in Africa to focus FSR/E on livestock systems. FSR/E as a whole has devoted very little time to the problems of diagnosis and on-farm experimentation with animals. ILCA focuses on ruminant livestock due to their prevalence in African farming systems and has placed priority on the development and testing of FSR/E methodologies appropriate for the African setting. ILCA FSR/E activities follow stages similar to those followed by the other IARCs (diagnosis, design, testing, and extension). Somewhat different than the other international centers, ILCA has research farms at the station in which trials are conducted that are researcher managed and farmer executed. This research seems to be a cross between on-station and on-farm research. At the same time, ILCA runs on-farm trials within the traditional farming systems surrounding the station. Within this setting, ILCA is conducting on-farm research on animal traction with Ethiopian farmers and reports some success in adapting single ox plowing within the traditional plowing system (Gryseels 1984).

Unfortunately, there are relatively few examples in which an IARC has combined technological solutions from different centers for testing on-farm; however, in Nigeria ILCA is using IITA's alley-cropping technology as a basis for the integration of crops and small ruminants. ILCA is also using FSR/E methods with other types of livestock producers such as agropastoralists, highland pastoralists, and pastoralists in arid and semiarid zones. In these research endeavors, they are working with national livestock programs in Kenya, Botswana, Ethiopia, Niger, and Mali.

Though it is difficult to summarize the efforts of the various IARCs involved in FSR/E in Africa, it is possible to see common methodological threads. All of the centers identify the same or almost the same procedural stages in OFR or FSR/E. Differences appear in the interpretation of the actual implementation of these stages. There is still little consensus on the appropriate methods for diagnosis, and each center promotes differently the usage of informal and formal diagnostic tools. Most of the IARC-influenced FSR/E falls within the category of having a predetermined focus. Though this is not recognized as a major initial problem, it poses a challenge to national agricultural research and extension systems if each commodity has a different IARC backstop or collaborator with a different set of jargon and specific methods to be followed. Institutionalization of FSR/E within any national system requires an agreement on FSR/E among the different commodity programs and a national approach shaped to fit national needs. Better inter-center cooperation and collaboration among the IARCs will help this process.

National Initiatives in FSR/E

Strong, well-developed, national agricultural research and development programs are essential. Although the appropriate role of the IARCs is to support national programs, less has been written about national initiatives in Anglophone African countries to develop FSR/E than about those initiatives supported by the IARCs. In East and Southern Africa, it is safe to say that most FSR/E efforts have the support of an IARC either through training, networking, and technical assistance or through direct financial or personnel support. Even where there are bilateral contracts for FSR/E projects or projects with FSR/E components there has been considerable IARC collaboration. This is especially true of the relationship between the United States Agency for International Development (USAID) and CIMMYT/ESA, since the latter receives funding from USAID to provide substantial support to USAID-funded FSR/E projects in East and Southern Africa.

Since 1979, USAID has taken a strong interest in supporting the development of FSR/E in African agricultural programs, and large projects have been funded in Zambia, Malawi, Lesotho, Botswana, and Sudan, as well as in several Francophone countries including Senegal and Burkina Faso. These project contracts have been directed largely by U.S. agricultural land grant universities. One important result of having universities involved in the development of FSR/E bilateral projects has been the growing institutionalization of the approach within the home campuses. Though resistance was initially strong, continued contact with FSR/E practitioners has gradually pushed the acceptance and legitimization of the approach within academic departments and, more recently, the agricultural professional societies. USAID further encouraged the growth of FSR/E with the creation in 1982 of the Farming Systems Support Project (FSSP), managed by the University of Florida, which provides technical assistance, training, and networking support to many FSR/E projects in Africa. New USAID-funded projects with strong FSR/E components are being implemented in Rwanda, Burundi, Mali, Mauritania, Zaire, and Gambia. British assistance to FSR/E has not been as large as that of USAID; it has concentrated on placing skilled individuals within national agricultural programs in which they have been able to assist in the development of FSR/E skills and projects. Examples of their efforts include the assignments of two agricultural economists, one to Gambia and one to Zambia—both have played catalytic roles in encouraging FSR/E.

Outside donor funding has played a major role in the development of FSR/E activities in national programs, and there are relatively few examples of FSR/E activities initiated without donor funding. Those that do exist are unique and should be highlighted. A number of African universities have initiated FSR/E projects, often with limited funding, as a way of conducting on-farm research to complement academic research and introducing students to the concepts of FSR/E. Njala University in Sierra Leone is one such program. With a small grant from the Canadian International Development Research Centre (IDRC), Njala has been conducting a FSR/E project in several chieftancies near the university. On-farm experimentation has included work on root and tuber crops and has incorporated a nutrition and consumption component. Another example comes from Nigeria: several universities there are engaged in on-farm research, and professors from the universities, as well as researchers from government agricultural agencies, participate in the Nigerian FSR Network. Though supported in part by CIMMYT, the University of Zimbabwe has taken a lead in incorporating FSR/E through on-farm projects conducted by university faculty and students.

It is important to note the role IDRC has played in national initiatives in FSR/E. In contrast to IARCs and most bilateral donor projects, IDRC has placed its emphasis on funding national researchers to conduct projects. The funding level is considerably lower than with most donor projects in agriculture, primarily because there is no reliance on expatriate teams. IDRC-funded FSR/E projects have been linked with IARC initiatives, but most of the planning and implementation of the projects is done with national researchers and a regional project officer (Kirkby 1984). Occasionally, IDRC has funded an expatriate adviser; yet national leadership is being developed and the projects retain a strong national identity, rather than a donor identity. Examples of IDRC national projects include the highland maize project in Burundi, the Tanzanian projects based out of Morogoro University, the efforts in southern Mali, and the work at Njala University previously mentioned.

Other national initiatives exist and are not fully elaborated here. It is obvious, however, that the major thrust behind FSR/E in the Anglophone efforts comes from external donors and IARCs. It is difficult to say whether national programs have no interest in or knowledge of FSR/E until the IARCs or bilateral donors get involved, or whether the cost of getting started and maintaining FSR/E is too high for national research and extension systems to undertake on their own. However, despite strong external support, FSR/E will not become institutionalized within national research and extension programs without strong national commitment and management of the FSR/E activities.

• MAJOR OBSTACLES TO IMPLEMENTATION IN AFRICA •

Five major obstacles to FSR/E implementation in Africa can be identified: (1) a technical shortfall, (2) the institutional separation of research and extension, (3) the lack of human resource capability, (4) the lack of necessary infrastructural support, and (5) actual versus perceived holism. Each of these contribute to difficulties in getting started with FSR/E or even in making an initial commitment to the concept.

Technical Shortfall

Technical shortfall refers to the general lack of what is called "shelf technology" for many agricultural problems in Africa. Unlike other regions of the world, less investment has been made in basic agricultural research in Africa. Therefore, when researchers attempt on-farm activities, little technology is available to test immediately. In other areas of the world, FSR/E made initial headway with technology that was available already in the area and required only minor adaptation. In contrast, there have been no clear technological breakthroughs with sorghum and millet, the design of improvements for low external input, rainfed systems is still in its infancy (Fresco 1985), and African root crops are only beginning to draw attention from geneticists and agronomists. West and Central Africa suffer more from the technological shortfall than do East and Southern Africa where prior maize research provides a substantial database. If FSR/E is to overcome the technical shortfall, there will have to be far greater cooperation between systems research and commodity research, as well as between on-farm and on-station activities, in order to set priorities for research based on farmer priority needs.

Institutional Separation of Research and Extension

To function, FSR/E requires involvement of both research and extension from the beginning. Extension personnel cannot be tacked on to the last stage of the process and be expected to achieve successful mass dissemination. Planning for eventual dissemination and diffusion of technology through the extension service should begin before on-farm trials are designed. Extension personnel should be members of FSR/E from diagnosis forwards. The unités expérimentales in Senegal are an example of an attempt to link research and extension within a project framework.

The desire to have extension and research engaged in on-farm research is hindered when the two are located institutionally within different ministries. It is logistically difficult to manage FSR/E teams if staff members are not responsible to the same institution. The duties of extension personnel often include jobs related more to the monitoring of government credit or cooperative programs, land tenure decisions, or distribution of inputs. None of these duties provide a base for building farmer collaboration in most developing countries. Extension is further hampered by its lower status, compared to research. The existence of these agricultural hierarchies increases the difficulty in fostering interdisciplinary relationships between research and extension.

Lack of Trained Human Resource Capability

The lack of trained and available personnel in agricultural research is a serious problem for FSR/E implementation. Too often researchers who wish to engage in FSR/E are also responsible for major commodity programs, manage research stations, handle large-scale multilocational trials, and are already involved in other donor-assisted agricultural development projects. It is possible that lower-level field technicians and extension workers could be the better target as team members than highly qualified researchers, especially for field-level FSR/E work. In-country, in-service FSR/E training, which could proceed in step with the unfolding stages of field-level activity, has the potential for relieving the lack of human resources. For this to take place, training would have to begin in the very early stages of the project, and the time frame for on-farm experimental results and dissemination would have to be lengthened. However, such an approach could engage the national senior researchers as part-time members of FSR/E teams, interacting with several locally deployed teams on a regular but discontinuous basis. It is obvious that FSR/E in Africa will not be able to contribute to solving Africa's food problems without specific steps to train a larger number of people, both men and women.

Lack of Necessary Infrastructural Support

Two key problems are embodied within this topic. The first relates to the fact that FSR/E means getting out to see and talk with farmers, which cannot take place if team members have no mobility beyond the research station fence. Transportation of some practical nature is an absolute requirement, and this requires its own support system, particularly maintenance and gasoline. Many of the frustrations in trying to deal with on-farm research come from trying to gain access to transportation. Some of the problem is alleviated with locally deployed teams within walking or bicycle distance; however, team leaders need to meet with field teams, and interaction between FSR/E and commodity research can only occur with adequate transportation. For successful implementation of FSR/E, the transportation issue must be worked out in advance of any plans to begin diagnostic or other field-level activity. A second infrastructural issue regards financial flexibility. FSR/E usually requires readily accessible funds to purchase necessary inputs for trials and other needs on a timely basis to coincide with normal farmer production activities, which is difficult to achieve if the research-funding system is highly centralized.

Real Versus Perceived Holism

Viewing the farming system with a holistic perspective is a basic concept in all of the FSR/E approaches described in this chapter. One would assume from this perspective that both males and females would be considered equally. Unfortunately, very few FSR/E initiatives anywhere in Africa actively seek to uncover any gender considerations in the on-farm generation of new agricultural technology. In a world region where women are documented as performing up to 80 percent of agricultural production in many countries, it is a serious oversight to neglect women farmers. If FSR/E is to serve the needs of Africa's small farmer majority, it will have to adopt a perspective that encompasses both male and female farmers and their respective constraints and potentials.

• THE FUTURE OF FSR/E IN AFRICA: IS IT AN APPROPRIATE SOLUTION? •

It is the obvious bias of the authors that FSR/E can be appropriate and important in future agricultural development in Africa. The challenge before us now as we close this chapter is to explore what shape and responsibilities this future will have. If one looks generally at FSR/E projects to date, particularly in Africa, by far the greater proportion of time has been spent in diagnosis. Testing and evaluation, in many projects, has only gotten underway during the past four years. In the future, far greater attention must be placed on the testing and analysis of proposed solutions on-farm. For most projects, linkages with extension systems to initiate dissemination of successful innovations have been very weak and ineffective. Little if any development of referral systems has taken place, and adoption studies are few. Consequently, it is too early to judge the impact of FSR/E on food production in Africa. Much greater attention will have to be placed on evaluations of the FSR/E approach—both procedures and results. FSR/E may be able to provide a sound framework for better analysis of farmer constraints, but there is still the risk that too much emphasis will be placed on diagnosis.

FSR/E will not solve all nor even a large part of Africa's agricultural problems, and it should not be burdened with the responsibility to achieve results beyond its capabilities. The approach on its own will not radically alter the level of infrastructural development, the degree of institutional proximity of research and extension, the rate of improving the human-resource capacity, nor the wider political and economic issues. FSR/E is not a development strategy by itself but must be part of a broad development plan. For FSR/E methods and concepts to be of practical value, they must become part of the whole research and extension system and not remain only in pilot projects. Once fully integrated, FSR/E is likely to vanish in name, but the principles will remain, just as some of its principles were already in use before the name was applied. Future research procedures will likely be a composite of the various approaches detailed in this chapter.

In summary, FSR/E offers three concrete measures for the future of agricultural development in Africa. First, if FSR/E is functionally linked to basic research, it helps set priorities for basic research. With scarce national funds available for basic research, national systems need to set priorities based on the most pressing needs of the majority of the farmers. FSR/E will be a key tool in determining these priorities. Second, FSR/E offers the potential for success in extending new technology because FSR/E provides far greater assurance that the new technology is appropriate to the needs of the client farmer group. Finally, if FSR/E can achieve true holism in its diagnosis, design, experimentation, and dissemination stages, it will be able to overcome many of the gender biases inherent in most other agricultural development projects. This potential alone gives FSR/E sound footing in the future of agricultural development in Africa.

• NOTES •

1. Readers of the growing literature find a profusion of acronyms. Farming Systems Research (FSR) has probably been the most widely used label in the past. Concern over the apparent exclusion of the extension function encouraged the addition of "/E" in order to highlight the fact that effective FSR only occurs when research and extension are engaged simultaneously in the process. As part of the dynamic development of the approach, FSR/E has been further refined as micro-level activity involving diagnosis and experimentation both on-farm and on-station. A new label, Farming Systems Infrastructure and Policy (FSIP), is used to describe the macro-level activity that provides an orientation for agricultural research and agricultural sector policy. FSR/E and FSIP are often collectively covered by Farming Systems Research and Development (FSR&D), although many simply use the FSR acronym as a collective label. Complementary to these terms is OFR/FSP, or On Farm Research with a Farming Systems Perspective, which is widely used in East and Southern Africa, particularly in those programs influenced by the technical assistance and training conducted by CIMMYT. OFR/FSP and FSR/E are being used more and more interchangeably, particularly in those regions. Because of the perceived need to actively integrate research and extension in the technology generation process, especially in areas where these two functions have been historically separated, this chapter will use the FSR/E label.

2. Commodity research refers to work focused on one specific crop or animal within the farming system. Component research refers to work on a specific input to the farming system, such as fertilizers.

3. In the French agricultural research institutes, as well as in the Francophone West and Central African institutions, a distinction is made between basic research (*recherche*

fondamentale) and adaptive research (*recherche d' accompagnement*) that is undertaken in the context of a development program. In 1974 the eight French sector institutes were centralized into the Groupe d'Etudes et de Recherches pour le Développement de l'Agronomie Tropicale (GERDAT) to promote better coordination. The integration of the institutes was completed in 1984 with the creation of the Centre International de Recherche pour l'Agriculture et le Développement (CIRAD). In addition to the eight institutes mentioned above, which have become departments of CIRAD, two more departments were created, one of which, the Département Systèmes Agraires (DSA), is concerned with farming systems research. The farming systems approach embodied in DSA is drawn largely from agricultural research and development experiences in Francophone Africa.

4. One of the few unifying characteristics of the Anglophone approaches is that information concerning their results is published in English. Additionally, some contributions to the collective Anglophone approach in Africa come from reports in English on activities conducted in French-speaking countries.

5. Though initially there were differences between FSR/E and OFR/FSP, they are currently converging upon a common definition. The term OFR/FSP will be used in conjunction with CIMMYT activities, and FSR/E will be used in all other instances.

• SUGGESTED FURTHER READINGS •

Collinson, Michael P. 1982. Farming Systems Research in Eastern Africa: The Experience of CIMMYT and Some National Agricultural Research Services, 1976–1981. East Lansing: Michigan State University, International Development Paper No. 3.

Gilbert, Elon H., David W. Norman, and F. E. Winch. 1980. Farming Systems Research: A Critical Appraisal. East Lansing: Michigan State University, Rural Development Paper No. 6.

Hildebrand, Peter E. and Federico Poey. 1985. On-Farm Agronomic Trials in Farming Systems Research and Extension. Boulder, Colorado: Lynne Rienner Publishers.

Norman, David W., Emmy B. Simmons, and Henry M. Hays. 1982. *Farming Systems in the Nigerian Savanna*. Boulder, Colorado: Westview Press.

Shaner, W. W., P. F. Philipp, and W. R. Schmehl. 1982. Farming Systems Research and Development: Guidelines for Developing Countries. Boulder, Colorado: Westview Press.

———, eds. 1982. Readings in Farming Systems Research and Development. Boulder, Colorado: Westview Press.

Simmons, N. W. 1985. Farming Systems Research: A Review. Technical Paper No. 43. Washington, D.C.: World Bank.

Whyte, William F. 1981. Participatory Approaches to Agricultural Research and Development: A State of the Art Paper. Ithaca, New York: Cornell University, Rural Development Committee.

·21·

Women Farmers
and Food in Africa: Some
Considerations
and Suggested Solutions

ANITA SPRING

This one they call 'farmer'; send in teachers to teach him to farm (while I'm out growing the food); lend him the money for tractors and tillers (while I'm out growing the food); promise him fortunes if he'd only raise cotton (while I'm out growing the food); buy our land from him to add to your ranches (while I'm out growing the food). . . . No, I daren't stop working . . . to make sure my children have food in their bellies (Taylor, quoted in Office of Technology Assessment 1984:46).

· AFRICAN WOMEN ARE FARMERS ·

W**hy does recognizing the importance of women in agriculture and including them in research and extension activities improve the ability of African countries to produce food? Because rural African women are farmers. Some families want their daughters to do tasks other than farming (Spring and Hansen 1982), but most rural women will continue to be farmers for several generations to come. Although technicians and governments may perceive or prefer women to be at home or to work as secretaries and nurses, rural African women are particularly important in the food chain. Women cultivate crops, care for livestock, and process and prepare food for all rural families; they are involved in food distribution at the family, local, and regional levels. Crops must be produced and this production entails preparing the land, planting, weeding, harvesting, and other operations. Next, farm products must be carried from the fields, processed to store or to cook, and then prepared into food for consumption. Some households work family farms to produce only enough for their own subsistence; others earn wages as agricultural laborers. In some households farm production supplements the family income; in others the farm is a commercial enterprise. Women participate in a variety of farm activities with other family members or on their own. Some aspects of their work are better recognized and accounted for than others.

332

Ester Boserup, the Danish economist, pinpointed the importance of women in African agriculture in *Women's Role in Economic Development* (1970). Using official government statistics and case materials, she showed that in several parts of the world women are the main cultivators on family farms or work as agricultural wage laborers. Sub-Saharan Africa is one area where farming is part of the definition of women's role in society. African women contribute 60 to 80 percent of the labor and management in food production in most places; however, in some regions their contribution is only 30 to 50 percent. It is estimated that a third of rural African households are headed by women (typically, there are no resident adult men in households headed by women) and women in the position of head of the household are farm managers. In the households headed by men, women do much of the farm work. Most women focus on food crops; because cereal and other food crops are often grown for both food and cash, these women might also be involved in cash enterprises. In households that produce for the market, women's participation is usually much greater than many observers have realized (Clark 1975; Guyer 1984).

Boserup distinguished between male and female systems of farming and identified the features of each. In Europe, the Middle East, and some Latin American societies, male systems of farming predominate; in Africa and some parts of Southeast Asia, female systems or male-assisted female systems predominate. The first European colonialists to encounter African farming thought that African men were lazy and underemployed because they did so little farm work (although the African men were involved in other tasks). Boserup documented how colonial powers, followed by the newly independent governments, dismissed the female system of farming as unimportant. Cash crops and new technologies were and continue to be introduced to men, while women were and continue to be discouraged or bypassed in agricultural training, credit, extension, and land-reform programs. Research focused and continues to focus on extractive agricultural enterprises rather than on local food. Although some women have moved into commercial production, most women farmers responsible for their family's food supply were and continue to be disadvantaged in many ways. Boserup noted that

> economic and social development unavoidably entails the disintegration of the division of labour among the two sexes . . . [and that] with modernization of agriculture and migration to towns, a new sex pattern of productive work must emerge. . . . The obvious danger . . . is that in the course of this transition, women will be deprived of their productive functions and the whole process of growth will be retarded (Boserup 1970:5).

The argument espoused in this chapter is that the exclusion of women from new technologies and capital schemes has negatively affected women's productivity, and this reduced productivity is a major contributor to the current food crisis in Africa.

Over the past fifteen years, researchers have extended Boserup's work by documenting African women's contributions to food production, distribution, processing, and preparation (Bukh 1979; Butler 1982; Clark 1975; Dey 1981, 1984; Due et al. 1985; Fortmann 1978, 1984; Gladwin et al. 1984; Guyer 1984; Spring et al. 1983). In addition, the ways in which development strategies include or bypass women have been studied (Brain 1976; Due and Summary 1982; Fortmann 1981; Palmer 1985; Rogers 1980; Staudt 1975–76). This chapter briefly reviews some of the major aspects of African women's involvement with food production and then offers some suggestions for solutions to improve the participation of women, especially their participation in smallholder agriculture.

• THE SEXUAL DIVISION OF LABOR •

In aggregate terms, women's agricultural labor in the smallholder sector is comparable to or greater than men's and has been increasing since the colonial period. Agricultural development projects often increase the amount of agricultural work, in terms of hours per day and days per year, for both men and women (Clark 1975; Food and Agriculture Organization [FAO] 1983b). Many studies have shown that women spend as much time on farm work as they do on domestic activities (Boserup 1970; Clark 1975; FAO 1983b). The sexual division of labor (certain tasks assigned to women and other tasks to men) varies within Africa, and any prior sexual division of labor has given way to expediency in many places. Women work on both food and cash crops and perform many farm operations such as cotton spraying and tobacco nursery planting that are commonly believed to be done only by men (Clark 1975; Spring et al. 1983). Women are involved in all aspects of farming—land clearing, plowing, applying fertilizer, etc.—routinely or when male labor is unavailable.

Standard descriptions of the sexual division of labor in African agriculture usually state that men clear and prepare the land and plow (if the society uses the plow) and women plant, weed, harvest, process, and store the crops. However, careful studies have shown that a variety of labor and cultivation patterns exist, and that these patterns have been changing in the past fifty to one hundred years. For example, the following five work patterns have been identified in Africa: (1) men and women cultivate similar crops on separate plots of land or have separate livestock holdings, or both, (2) men and women cultivate different crops, (3) women and men perform different farming operations on the same plots or with the same animals ("standard" sexual division of labor), (4) men and women perform the same farm operations on the same plots (no sexual division of labor), and (5) in households headed by women, women are responsible for all agricultural production.

In Malawi all of these work patterns vary by area and by household (Agro-Economic Surveys 1968–1983; National Statistical Office [NSO] 1982). Women in Malawi contribute the majority of labor in smallholder agriculture, and they make agricultural decisions in many rural households (Spring et al. 1983; Spring 1985). Although labor and cropping patterns vary, most women are involved in all aspects of farming. Maize is the staple crop in most areas, and cassava and rice are staples in others. Women have the responsibility for food crop production and have the greatest labor input in subsistence areas. Women work with a variety of cropping patterns including mixed subsistence farming and farming cash crops such as peanut (groundnut), rice, tobacco, cotton, and smallholder production of coffee and tea. In some groundnut-growing areas men and women work similar amounts of time but do different tasks, while in other areas groundnuts are considered a "women's crop," and women do most of the work. In some rice-producing areas men are responsible for rice cultivation, while women only assist with rice production because they must work on other food crops. Tobacco is largely considered a crop that men grow even though women and children often help in tobacco farm operations. However, there are some areas in which a female household head is responsible for rice or tobacco crops. In male-headed households, labor on oriental tobacco is distributed evenly between men and women. Everywhere men are in charge of the cotton crop, but women contribute significantly to various operations in its cultivation, and in some areas cotton growing would not be possible without adult female labor. In smallholder coffee and tea production, men are responsible for pruning, but many tasks are shared by both men and women. When tasks associated with cash crops become particularly labor intensive, women's labor in certain tasks increases to a greater extent than does men's labor (Agro-Economic Surveys 1968–1983; Spring et al. 1983; Spring 1985).

In pastoral societies or those with mixed agricultural systems, men usually care for the larger animals and women may be responsible for small ruminants and poultry. Men generally obtain the income from sales, and women control the allocation of milk between the needs of the herd and the family. Other patterns may exist out of expediency with women and men sharing livestock care, doing different tasks, or with all the care falling to women in men's absence. In some areas, women are beginning to own cattle, and as the care of large animals moves from the range to the village, as in stall-feeding projects, women become more important in cattle production (Spring 1986a).

Various researchers are now pointing to the need to understand the diverse types of African households, the intrahousehold dynamics, and the effects of these on farming systems. Christina Gladwin, Kathleen Staudt, and Della McMillan (1984) showed that neither monogamous nor polygynous African households are homogeneous and unified decisionmaking units. The Western concept of the "family farm," a husband-wife unit that maximizes utility functions and shares goals, does not apply in Africa (also see McMillan in this volume). Men and women in African families may have separate incomes and expenditures, and men's and women's involvement in the family farm may be understood only by breaking the farm into its various components in terms of land tenure, crop and livestock enterprises, and investments. These authors cited examples of husbands and wives lending each other money at "rates only slightly less usurious than the prevailing market rate," of selling each other animals for family feasts, and of husbands selling firewood to their wives (Gladwin, Staudt, and McMillan 1984:4). Moreover, these authors stated that farming households in Africa may be characterized as "overlapping but semi-autonomous production and consumption units" and that women are not simply embedded within a household but are semiautonomous persons who often have a great deal of economic independence in terms of food production and distribution.

Furthermore, various researchers have argued that smallholder agriculture is becoming more feminized (Chaney and Lewis 1980; Guyer 1984; Kydd 1982; Rogers 1980). Women are taking an even greater responsibility for farming because men are only farming part-time or have left farming entirely due to migration or other local employment. In rural areas of many countries there are more working-age women than men, and the numbers and proportion of female headed households are increasing. In some areas of Zimbabwe there are special programs to intensify rural male participation to counteract rural male out-migration. Approximately one-third of rural households in Malawi and two-thirds in Lesotho are now headed by women (NSO 1982; Butler 1982). There are six basic types of female-headed households: (1) those in which the household head never married (with variation between self-supporting women and those residing with their own relatives who take care of them), (2) married women whose husbands are away for long or short times, (3) married women who have been abandoned by their husbands, (4) separated women, (5) divorced women, and (6) widows. Each type has unique consequences for production and distribution. Households headed by women, especially those that do not receive remittances, are likely to be associated with labor constraints, simpler farming systems, food deficits, and the lack of agricultural services (Due and White n.d.; Spring 1984; Spring et al. 1983). Households in which absent husbands send remittances or return at intervals, or both, are more similar in their farming systems to comparable male headed households.

Barbara Rogers (1980) asked "where have all the young men gone?" and how has the sexual division of labor in agriculture been affected? Boserup noted that men's smaller contribution and women's self-sufficiency in female systems of agriculture mean that men may easily leave their families in the rural areas to seek employment on plantations, in mines, or in the urban sector. By contrast, in areas with male systems of farming, the entire family must move together because women are unable to provide food for themselves and their children. Extensive male migration occurred in Africa initially because of the colonial imposition of taxes; this migration continues because of a variety of factors such as the desire to obtain consumer goods, poor agricultural conditions, and drought. Wars and military recruitment also contribute to rural male out-migration. Women cannot leave the rural areas as easily as men because there are few urban jobs for women other than prostitution or petty trade. In addition, land is under continuous cultivation in many parts of Africa and there is no new land to clear; therefore, the typically male agricultural tasks of clearing and preparing land are no longer needed, making it easier for men to leave their families in the rural areas and to leave the farming to women.

Researchers studying the people left in rural areas report that with a high rate of labor out-migration the sexual division of labor in farming systems is often modified and accentuated. Women do their usual work and the men's work as well. Men rarely do any of the "women's work." At the same time, women are more bound to the homestead, sometimes waiting for remittances that never come or are too little or too late (to buy fertilizer or hire labor) for the agricultural season. Children may be in school and unable to assist, and men may only return home at harvest time to collect payments or bags of food to take to the city. The result is that men and boys help very little with the harvest, transportation, or processing of crops. Rogers noted that

> the absence of younger men or their refusal to work under the old system of obligations to the extended family means a sudden rise in the dependency ratio for the family concerned; there are the same number of dependants . . . being supported by fewer able-bodied adults. If the men actually consume more of the household production than they generate . . . they actually add to the number of dependents to be supported by women (Rogers 1980:169).

• HOUSEHOLD INCOME AND FOOD SUPPLY •

A time allocation survey in Ivory Coast (FAO 1983b) showed that men are absent more than women, women do 66 percent of the agricultural work, and 20 percent of agricultural production is carried out by children (especially by girls) and by the elderly. Women only bring in 17 percent of the total outside cash earnings through crop sales or petty trade and spend 80 percent of this money on food purchases. The important food items are mostly produced at home; women cultivate 44 to 82 percent of all food grown and use their cash income to pay for 32 to 45 percent of all food purchases (see Table 21.1). Women also bring home 93 percent of the water and 95 percent of the firewood. There is significant local variation in women's contributions; therefore, basic local research should be conducted before making any conclusions about the extent of male or female contributions in a particular locality.

Women's responsibility for the household food supply is being acknowledged in studies of intrahousehold dynamics of the farming system as well as in research on time allocations. Della McMillan (1984 and in this volume) showed that men and women are both important in farming in Burkina Faso. Women work on their husband's fields, but they also cultivate their own private fields on which they grow 13 percent of the total production of basic food grains (millet, sorghum, and maize), 16 percent of the rice, 66 percent of the groundnuts and ground beans, and 100 percent of the vegetables. Although women's separate contributions to the family food supply account for only 20 to 25 percent of the total food produced, McMillan argued that this food is vital to the survival of the extended (polygynous) family; these privately produced foodstuffs are used to feed women and their children in the dry season when food supplies from the cooperative fields are depleted. Undoubtedly, women's contribution to food supplies has implications for food security in the event of drought.

TABLE 21.1. Contribution of Ivory Coast Women to Food Supply
(Percentage of Total Calories Provided by Women for Each Food Group for Foods Grown-G and Purchased-P)

Crops	National Mean G	National Mean P	East Forest G	East Forest P	West Forest G	West Forest P	Savannah G	Savannah P
Cereals & Grains	56	35	48	40	88	25	40	38
Starchy roots & tubers	56	38	58	37	88	39	42	42
Pulses & Seeds	64	54	57	59	64	45	90	54
Vegetables & Leaves	96	48	97	41	98	40	99	59
Fruits	54	66	40	--	79	--	79	61
Sugar & Sugar Products	--	31	--	39	--	34	--	9
Meat & Poultry	12	26	23	29	7	12	2	23
Fish & Shellfish	--	39	--	36	--	27	--	68
Milk & Eggs	1	19	98	10	--	23	--	24
Fat	99	64	8	50	--	82	95	58
Drinks	5	13	--	11	--	15	--	12
Condiments	79	55	--	63	75	45	--	58
TOTAL: ALL FOOD	58	38	57	37	82	32	44	45

Source: Food and Agriculture Organization (FAO), Food Policy and Nutrition Division. 1983. Time Allocation Survey:
A Tool for Anthropologists, Economists and Nutritionists. Rome: FAO. ESA: WIFP/83/17. Pg. 28 b-c.

Analyzing intrahousehold allocation of resources and the decisionmaking process sheds more light on women's role in food production. In many Western countries, farm income or family food expenditures are aggregated at the household level, and household members are expected to pool resources and share the benefits. This type of household structure and process is not universal; in societies "where a woman's active economic participation is common and accepted . . . the decision-making process within the family can be markedly different" (Charlton 1984:49). Disaggregation of household income between husbands and wives is necessary to understand production and consumption patterns. In most of Sub-Saharan Africa wives control income they earn and are responsible for purchasing some of the food, the kitchen utensils, their own and their children's clothes, and for paying the school fees. Husbands use their own income for taxes, consumer goods, productive investments, entertainment, and "only occasionally to help their wives with cash for food in case of emergencies" (Charlton 1984:50). Household income is not aggregated in these societies. Studies have shown that the mother's income rather than the overall household income is the significant factor in the status of child nutrition (Charlton 1984). Rural development projects in Benin, Cameroon, Kenya, and the Gambia that intensified the production of cash crops, but did not safeguard women's income, saw either a loss of women's labor or a decline in general family welfare (Hanger and Moris 1973; Charlton 1984).

Jane Guyer (1984) has provided a case study of the changing nature over thirty-five years of men's and women's income sources and expenditures and the impact of these on family food supply in southern Cameroon. Men's expenses were financed in the 1950s by growing cocoa, and they spent 17 percent of their money on clothing, 11 percent on food, 8 percent on housing, and 3 percent on alcoholic drinks. In the 1960s, men's expenditures on housing fell, food and drink rose to 23 percent of their expenditures, and clothing rose to 23 percent. During that time women began producing food crops commercially for the urban market, increasing their incomes, and responsibility for purchased food shifted from men to women. The main categories of expenditures for women that developed were food (74 percent), transport (16 percent), and clothes (10 percent) (see Table 21.2). Guyer noted that many have agreed that the recent diet is less varied than ones in the past and that "the diet has been 'feminized' in cultural terms" as the foods grown by men have disappeared or been replaced (Guyer 1984:109). Procurement of the diet is also feminized, and in general, women cannot count on regular support from men who have independent incomes and expenses, and even an increase in men's incomes will not necessarily help their wives and children, falsifying the assumption that male-female incomes and relationships are complementary. It has been noted in some areas that if men increase income from agricultural production, they use this additional income for their needs and not for food for their families. Wives have to use a "variety of means to tap into men's incomes" and maintain a standard of living for themselves and their children (Guyer 1984:112).

In some areas as households increase sales of foodstuffs or production of non-food crops, then less food or lower quality foodstuffs are available for home con-

TABLE 21.2.   Cash Income and Expenditures of Married and Unmarried Cameroonian Women (Percentages)

Source	Income	
	Married	Unmarried
Sales of Own Produce	35	45
Trade	7	23
Cocoa Work	6	8
Subtotal	48	76
Transfers From:		
Husbands	40	0
Other Men	3	17
Women	9	7
Subtotal	52	24
GRAND TOTAL	100	100

Category	Cash Expenditures	
	Married	Unmarried
Food and Household	76	71
Transport	14	21
Clothes	10	8
TOTAL	100	100

Source: Guyer, Jane. 1984. Family and Farm in Southern Cameroon. African Research Series No. 15. Boston: Boston University, African Studies Center. Pp. 112-113.

sumption. A frightening indicator of this is the increase in family, especially child, malnutrition. A recent article from Zaire showed that malnutrition is increasing among children in high-production areas ("New Policies Bring Mixed Results," in *Washington Post,* May 22, 1985). Jette Bukh (1979) outlined a classic example concerning cocoa production in Ghana. When men, assisted by women, began growing this new cash crop, yam production became increasingly the women's responsibility, which increased their workload. Therefore, over the years women shifted to cassava production, which requires less labor. Compared with yams, cassava is less nutritious, depletes the soil more quickly, and is less capable of being intercropped. There are other, similar examples: (1) In northwestern Zambia, fishermen intensified sales to urban areas to obtain more cash, thereby reducing the amount of fish available for local and family consumption (Art Hansen 1985: personal communication). (2) In Malawi where rural meal frequency was only 1.6 meals per day, grain was sold to urban and international markets. (3) Although commercial rice cropping on a development scheme in Kenya increased income for men, women had less food (maize) for the family after inception of the project (Hanger and Moris 1973).

• NEW TECHNOLOGIES BYPASS WOMEN •

Barbara Rogers, in *The Domestication of Women: Discrimination in Developing Societies* (1980), argued that Western stereotypes about women's "natural" place in society influence the design of development undertakings. Consequently, programs developed for women focus on embroidery, sewing, cooking, crafts, and hygiene, and women become accustomed to seeing this type of curriculum for themselves. All over Africa, the development curriculum for boys and girls and for men and women is gender-specific. Women are often considered gardeners, instead of farmers, so women's agricultural extension curriculum includes only instruction in small-scale poultry and vegetable production rather than in major staple crops and large livestock. Extension advice and loans for mechanization (plows and tractors) and inputs (seeds and fertilizers) are given to men. Plows and tractors allow more land to be cleared; as a result some women have more land to plant or weed. Mechanization of women's work either in the field or in food processing lags far behind. Similarly, whether programs are for reallocation of land or registration of titles to land, new varieties or breeds, cash or export commodities, or credit or input programs, men as heads of households are the only people targeted for involvement in the programs, and it is assumed that all household members will benefit. Few development plans understand the economic semiautonomy of many African household members, or recognize that approximately a third of all rural households are headed by women. Few planners realize that increased income and leisure often benefit men much more than women, as shown by research in the Central African Republic where men average two hours more rest and sleep a day than do women (see Table 21.3). The efficiency of agricultural intensification is jeopardized by this failure to appreciate women's needs and interests.

Sometimes women learn about new technologies in spite of the lack of formal instruction, then purchase any necessary inputs with cash (since women are typically excluded from extension and credit programs) (Moock 1976; Guyer 1984). In other situations involving new technologies women become more dependent on men, as in the Gambia where a rice scheme allocated all the land and inputs to men

(Dey 1981). Women reacted to a similar situation in Senegal by simply stopping growing onions; in Kenya women left a rice scheme when husbands collected the income from their labor (Hanger and Moris 1973). Various studies have shown that many women are interested in new technologies and want to take advantage of development services and that women are handicapped by the way training or other programs are established. In spite of the lack of services for women, in some places women's agricultural productivity outstrips men's (Moock 1976; Staudt 1975–76). Information from various parts of the continent shows that when women are given the opportunity to receive credit, agricultural training, and inputs, their agricultural performance is similar to the better male farmers in the area (Spring et al. 1983; Dey 1984).

Another major aspect of project efficiency is that programs meant to increase production and food supply must reach the right people to be effective. Many programs are addressed to adult men in areas where food production is the responsibility of women. A paper entitled "Time allocation Survey: A Tool for Anthropologists, Economists and Nutritionists," commissioned by the Food and Agriculture Organization (FAO) of the United Nations (1983b), noted the undesired effects of development on household food supply when development projects change time-allocation patterns of people and do not account for the various contributions to the food supply of different members of the household. A survey conducted in the Central African Republic showed the large amount of time that women expend in producing food and cash crops (see Table 21.3); in fact, these women provide most of the food supply—the cash income men collect from the cotton crop does not go to purchase food. Increased production is impossible in that area unless men increase their time spent in agriculture and women are relieved of part of their workload. Yet planners do not take women's work into account in their plans to increase production, and, indeed, production has not increased (FAO 1983b).

• WORKING TOWARD SOLUTIONS •

Africa's food crisis will not be solved solely by increased production in the smallholder sector, but there are a variety of activities and changes in policy that may be carried out to enhance rural African women's ability to produce food for their families and for sale. Given the near crisis situation in terms of food in Africa, it is worthwhile to focus on women farmers. First and foremost, policymakers, project planners, and decisionmakers must recognize that many rural women are real farmers; many people, men and women alike, do not see the need to address the issue, or they do not want to give "special consideration or preference" to women. Second, policy recommendations to include women in development projects are needed from the top, from planners and project managers, ministries of agriculture, donor agencies, and international centers, to pave the way for change. The following solutions are suggested as means to incorporate female food producers into ongoing activities and to redirect research, extension services, and policy

TABLE 21.3. Time Allocation by Sex and Village in the Central African Republic (Average Time Spent in Hours and Minutes per Day over a Year)

| | Village 1 | | | | Village 2 | | | |
| | Men | | Women | | Men | | Women | |
Activity or Crop	hrs	min	hrs	min	hrs	min	hrs	min
Cotton	2	0	2	0	2	26	2	8
Food Crops	0	23	1	54	0	39	1	5
Other Crops	0	5	0	3	0	12	0	4
Subtotal Agricultural Activities	(2)	(28)	(3)	(57)	(2)	(17)	(3)	(17)
Domestic Activities	0	17	3	37	0	10	3	40
Other Work Activities	2	44	0	36	2	5	0	44
Non-Work	3	18	2	9	2	52	2	28
Rest and Sleep	15	13	13	41	15	36	13	51
Total	24	0	24	0	24	0	24	0

Source: Food and Agriculture Organization (FAO), Food Policy and Nutrition Division. 1983. Time Allocation Survey: A Tool for Anthropologists, Economists and Nutritionists. Rome: FAO: ESA: WIFP/83/17. Pp. 5 1-b.

planning so that they focus on aspects of production that will increase food production by women:

1. Disaggregate data by sex to remove women's invisibility

2. Recognize intrahousehold dynamics in farming systems research

3. Use data about women's roles to guide the development of new technologies

4. Reorient training and extension programs to target women

5. Focus women's income generation on agricultural productivity rather than on minor methods of income generation such as crafts or cooked foods

6. Involve women in capital intensification and credit schemes

7. Involve women in land reallocation and registration schemes

8. Research "women's crops," food crops, and livestock, especially low-moisture varieties and smaller, domesticated animals

Disaggregated Data

Women's contribution to agriculture has been described as invisible. Data on farm enterprises and development services must be collected and analyzed by sex and by type of household in order to demonstrate that women are important in food production, distribution, and processing and that women have been handicapped by lack of access to new technologies and capital-intensive schemes. This change in procedures proved surprisingly easy to implement in Malawi (Spring et al. 1983; Spring 1986a, 1986b). Survey enumerators usually know the participants in a program and the people involved in various food-generating activities and they can record the gender of the farmers. The analysis of data is increasingly being carried out by computers. It becomes a relatively simple procedure to design surveys, questionnaires, and data-reporting forms to record and analyze the answers of farmers by their gender and household affiliation. As part of development project monitoring, data may also be collected and analyzed by gender on all participants in land allocation schemes, credit programs, training courses, livestock programs, and the like. The collection and analysis of sex-disaggregated data will provide a sound basis for understanding gender similarities and differences in agriculture. Furthermore, patterns and problems related to farmers as a group will be discernable from those specific to one gender or to one type of household.

Farming Systems Research and Intrahousehold Dynamics

Farming systems research has pinpointed the need to look at the farm as a system, but often existing relationships are not properly considered in constructing the system and it is not realized that family members may belong to more than one system simultaneously. Up until recently, gender issues and intrahousehold dynamics have been ignored in most farming systems research. Descriptions of farming systems often do not include the structure and process of work patterns, capital accumulation and investment, off-farm employment, delegation of responsibilities, and household status. A methodology that considers the specifics of intrahousehold dynamics such as who does which farm tasks, who has access to particular resources, and who makes decisions at each step is necessary. Assessment of needs by gender will be more accurate when gender issues in the data-collecting phases as well as in the design, testing, and acceptance of technologies are considered. Women must participate in farming systems research trials and the dissemination of new technologies; women's problems as well as those of other household members must be considered in research and extension efforts (Spring 1986b).

Development of New Technologies

As part of the U.S. Agency for International Development (USAID) Bean/Cowpea Collaborative Research Support Program, Anne Ferguson and Nancy Horn (1985) asked what kinds of technologies would result from a recognition of women's needs in farming. They showed how the description and analysis of the major themes concerning women's role in agriculture in Botswana and Cameroon are useful in project advisement and, in particular, "allow entomologists, plant breeders, and others to design innovations for small farmers and women that keep present and future needs in mind" (Ferguson and Horn 1985:85–86). Projects often try to breed improved, high-yielding, and pest-resistant varieties, but small producers have different production problems than large producers. Gender and wealth constraints have to be considered. Ferguson and Horn have suggested to production researchers that they incorporate the following concerns into breeding strategies: (1) a focus on stability of yield rather than on quantity of yield, (2) technologies that decrease rather than increase market dependence, and (3) multipurpose varieties that fulfill a number of the household's requirements. Women's needs as processors and food preparers also have to be considered. Problems of storage, processing, and cooking must consider local conditions and other work women must do. These authors argued that "crops with synchronous maturity" pose problems for smallholder farmers in terms of storage and market glut. Consumer preferences also have to be considered. For example, high protein is important, but digestibility needs to be a specification of the breeding program, especially if the food is to be given to children as a weaning food. New varieties that require additional labor for weeding or pest control will affect women's workload and will meet with resistance.

Training and Extension Programs

In Malawi male extension staff were redirected to work with female farmers (Ministry of Agriculture 1983; Spring 1985, 1986a, 1986b). First, a careful study was made of the extension system and the extension workers' interactions with farmers so that culturally acceptable ways of training and interaction could be devised. Techniques to help male extensionists to work with women farmers include using male leaders and husbands to recruit women for courses and input programs, using the group approach for meetings and visits, and having male and female extension workers share teaching and program responsibilities. Most importantly, the directives, mandate, and techniques that legitimized the male extension staff's work with women farmers came as recommendations from the Ministry of Agriculture (MOA) in the form of an extension circular (MOA 1983). Most African countries believe that only women extension agents are able to work with rural women. Yet there are few women extension agents and compared with the better trained male staff, they are poorly equipped to deal with agriculture. Curriculum for female staff needs revamping to include training in the agriculturally productive aspects of women's work.

Income-Generation Projects

Few programs directed toward men enjoin them to participate in group income-generating projects that realize meager profits. Yet women are often encouraged to participate in small-scale enterprises such as making crafts or preparing food. Usually the markets for these minor enterprises are few or nonexistent, and the profits are paltry—it is no wonder that many women lose interest in or drop out of the projects (Dhamija 1981). Some of the income-generation activities for women are really income-preservation activities valued (really overvalued) because the family does not have to buy what the woman can make. By contrast, male farmers are encouraged as individuals to generate more substantial incomes through crop and livestock production. The types and scale of income-generation projects for women have to be rethought in order to make a real impact on women's incomes and on the food supply.

Capital Intensification Schemes

Women's production is often constrained because they lack capital for improved seed, inputs, and mechanization. There may be problems in giving credit to women using current lending criteria because women often lack the typical requirements of collateral, tenure to the land, and sufficient scale of farming in terms of acreage (hectarage) and commodities produced. A pilot project in a food-deficient area of Malawi allows women who have no collateral to be deemed "credit worthy" on the recommendation of male village leaders; these credit worthy women receive input packages for maize that are half the size and cost of standard credit packages. The program recognizes that women are not going to be able to repay their input loans with sales because they need the increased production in order to feed their families. In fact, the women devise strategies for obtaining small sums of cash from beer brewing and the like to pay off their loans before the harvest (Evans 1983). Near an urban area in Cameroon, women expand production of vegetables by making use of traditional informal saving associations common in that region (Guyer 1977, 1984). Formal lending would assist them even further.

Land Reallocation and Registration Schemes

Following planned resettlement (e.g., resettlement due to dams or the formation of ujamaa villages) or forced relocation (e.g., resettlement due to wars or drought) women in married households tend to lose access to independently held plots or livestock that formerly provided them with food or income (Colson 1971). Female heads of households are not given any land or livestock in these resettlement projects. Sometimes women are even forced to move from projects when they divorce or become widows (Brain 1976). Planned resettlement, land registration, or livestock replenishment programs should not omit men's or women's traditional and modern claims.

Research on "Women's Crops," Food Crops, and Small Ruminants

Millet, sorghum, groundnuts, beans, pumpkins, melons, squash, and green leafy vegetables are some examples of traditional food crops that are mostly grown by women and that generally have received little or no attention by research institutions. These crops often are intercropped in fields and used mostly for home consumption or for local sale. African food supplies will increase if more research focuses on these crops and leads to improvements in varieties (especially in dwarf and low-moisture requirements), cultivation techniques, farm management, and marketing. Currently, livestock research tends to focus on cattle and to ignore sheep and goats, the animals women often own and manage; domestic food supplies will improve if more research is directed toward sheep and goat production.

• CONCLUSION •

The majority of African farmers are women, and the majority of rural African women are farmers, working with men or on their own to produce food and cash crops and livestock. Women farmers do not constitute a homogeneous group. Some are modern growers using scientific methods and commercial procedures; most are not very efficient and are constrained by the lack of knowledge and access to resources, as well as by labor burdens. There is a food crisis and environmental dessication in many parts of Africa. To ameliorate this situation, development plans must consider local conditions and they must target women as farmers, sellers, processors, and preparers of food. African and foreign planners and program implementors must put aside their stereotypic notions of the place of women in society in order to enhance the development of new strategies that will assist women to become more productive agriculturalists.

• SUGGESTED FURTHER READINGS •

Boserup, Ester. 1970. *Women's Role in Economic Development*. New York: St. Martin's Press.

Chaney, Elsa, and Martha W. Lewis. 1980. *Women, Migration and the Decline of Smallholder Agriculture*. Washington, D.C.: Office of Women in Development, United States Agency for International Development.

Charlton, Sue Ellen. 1984. *Women in Third World Development*. Boulder, Colorado: Westview Press.

Dixon, Ruth. 1980. *Assessing the Impact of Development Projects on Women*. AID Program Evaluation Discussion Paper No. 8, Washington, D.C.: United States Agency for International Development.

————. 1985. Seeing the Invisible Women Farmers in Africa: Improving Research and Data Collection Methods. In *Women as Food Producers in Developing Countries*, J. Monson and M. Kalb, eds. Pp. 19–36. Los Angeles: UCLA African Studies Center and African Studies Association.

Gallin, Rita, and Anita Spring, eds. 1985. *Women Creating Wealth: Transforming Economic Development*. Washington, D.C.: Association for Women in Development.

Palmer, Ingrid. 1985. *The Nemow Case: Case Studies of the Impact of Large Scale Development Projects on Women: A Series for Planners*. International Programs, Working Paper No. 7. Washington, D.C.: U.S. Agency for International Development (1979). Reprinted in 1985. West Hartford, Connecticut: Kumarian Press.

Rogers, Barbara. 1980. *The Domestication of Women: Discrimination in Developing Societies*. London: Tavistock.

Spring, Anita, and Art Hansen. 1985. The Underside of Development: Agricultural Development and Women in Zambia. *Agriculture and Human Values* 2:1:60–67.

·22·

Prospects for Long-Term African Change: The Lagos Plan of Action Versus the Berg Report

ROBERT S. BROWNE
ROBERT J. CUMMINGS

T he economic stress that characterized Africa in the latter half of the 1970s provided the stimulus for two highly significant documents published at the beginning of this decade: *The Lagos Plan of Action,* which sets forth the African perspective on what steps need to be taken to put the continent on a proper development path (Organization of African Unity 1981), and *Accelerated Development in Sub-Saharan Africa: An Agenda for Action,* the World Bank report popularly known as the Berg Report after Elliot Berg, the principal author (World Bank 1981). The Berg Report identifies some problem areas in the economies of Africa and offers a number of corrective policy prescriptions. Because the Lagos Plan of Action (LPA) bears the signatures of the African heads of state, it constitutes a significant official statement of African aspirations and is a major international document. Because the Berg Report expresses developmental views of the World Bank, which typifies the international capital-supply community to which Africa will continue to depend on for vast, constant financial inflows for decades to come, the Berg Report is an important document. Taken together, these two documents constitute a compendium of the most influential perspectives on Africa's economic plight and how it should be addressed. Both documents merit the earnest attention of all who are seriously interested in African economic development.

• BACKGROUND •

The impetus for the preparation of both documents was the economic deterioration that most African countries experienced in the latter half of the 1970s. This economic distress extended to virtually every aspect of the economy on the continent. Decline in per capita food production and associated famine conditions were the most publicized facets of the crisis; other prominent manifestations included burgeoning payments imbalances, escalating debt burdens, declining export vol-

349

umes, unfavorable terms of trade, stagnating industrial sectors, and shortages of foreign exchange needed to maintain supplies of essential imports.

Propelled by the World Bank's global publicity apparatus, the Berg Report burst upon the international development scene in 1981 with great fanfare and continues to attract attention from every quarter. Its complaints about the policies of many African governments have been widely repeated and have become the newest economic development wisdom. In contrast, the earlier adoption of the LPA in 1980 went virtually unnoticed outside of Africa, and even within Africa little attention was paid to it until the Berg Report appeared. The lack of publicity of the LPA may be in part the fault of its overseers, the Economic Commission for Africa (ECA) and the Organization of African Unity (OAU), who have proclaimed the absolute necessity for popularizing the LPA among the African population, but have restrained from actually carrying out such an effort. Regardless of one's views about the Berg Report, one must admit that its publication helped publicize the LPA, whose existence had been largely unnoticed outside a small circle within Africa.

The linkage of the two documents may mislead many persons to believe that both exist at the same level and address the same problem, which in fact, they do not. The LPA is a far more fundamental document than is the Berg Report. The LPA sketches a strategy that Africa might use for its long-term development. It is not a conventional development plan; it is a plan that attempts to galvanize African countries into creating national development plans that are coordinated toward a collective goal, to be eventually followed by subregional plans and ultimately by a regional plan. The Berg Report, on the other hand, is more of a tactical program that Africa is urged to adopt to ward off an immediate, presumably temporary crisis.

For the authors of the Berg Report, Africa's niche in the global economic scheme is already determined. These authors identify Africa's rich endowment of mineral resources, tropical climate well suited to grow certain crops, and enormous technological disadvantage relative to the industrialized world. They concur with orthodox liberal economic theory regarding Africa—i.e., that Africa enjoys comparative advantages in extractive industries, including tropical agriculture, and comparative disadvantages in advanced technology areas. Consequently, they define Africa's role in the global scheme as an exporter of raw materials and importer of sophisticated manufactured goods.

Unlike the Berg Report's prescription to put Africa back on an efficient, export-led growth path, the LPA exhorts its constituency to break away from this discredited path and strike out in a new direction—not in 1990 or 2000, but right now—in the hope that major goals will be achieved by the year 2000. Authors of the LPA do not see Africa as destined to be a raw materials exporter and a sophisticated goods importer. The LPA is not restrained by a static theory of comparative advantage but is clearly eager to experiment with new relationships, structures, and institutions. Authors of the LPA move in such new directions because they think that the present growth path is not taking African countries where they want to go and global economic trends suggest that a continuation of the current path offers more risk than hope.

For its part, the World Bank presumably thinks that no new strategy is required, or perhaps that none is possible. The Berg Report charts no new path for Africa, breaks no new ground, and offers no new perspectives. In the face of all the gloomy projections for Africa at the close of the 1970s, the World Bank is content to restrict its recommendations to a discussion of ways by which Africa might do better the things that it was already attempting to do. If there were no LPA, no one would question the Berg Report's exclusive attention to policy analysis and prescription within the existing development strategy. But the LPA does exist. The Berg Report authors have chosen to ignore it, despite making several references to it; nonetheless, the LPA represents an alternative proposal for the development of Africa, one endorsed by the highest possible echelons of African authority.

· POLICY ANALYSES AND PRESCRIPTIONS ·

Although most of the formal responses to the Berg Report have been negative, most of the Berg Report's major criticisms of national policy are probably not challenged by its critics. The bulk of criticism centers around the validity of Berg Report policy analyses and prescriptions for modifying Africa's operational practices. Most critics agree with such basic Berg Report complaints as Africa's inadequate incentives for farmers, inadequate provision of basic services, and the gross inefficiency of parastatal organizations. At the same time, most critics generally dismiss Berg Report recommendations for exchange rate devaluation, user charges, and an expanded private sector as ineffective, counterproductive, or not feasible. Nevertheless, some Berg Report policy prescriptions are fully endorsed by critics, and the Berg Report contains many statements that might easily have come from the Lagos Plan.

Differences between the Berg Report and the LPA are often more a matter of emphasis than of substance. Much of both documents is devoted to identifying grave problems or needs confronting Africa, and many designated problem areas are shared by both documents, with occasional disagreements on details. Examples of these "consensus" topics are: manpower constraints; urbanization; data inadequacies; depletion of forest land; inadequate agricultural research, transportation, and communications infrastructure; deforestation and fuelwood; energy sources; and the need for clean water. A number of other issues are treated at length in one document and not mentioned or mentioned only cursorily in the other. Listing some of the more prominent topics in this category provides additional insight into the differing perspectives of the two documents. The Berg Report focuses heavily on policy issues and administrative practices; the LPA focuses heavily on intrasectoral and intersectoral African relationships and on reducing all forms of dependency (see Table 22.1).

Other topics are discussed at some length in both documents, but with little

TABLE 22.1. Comparison of Topics in Berg Report and Lagos Plan

Berg Report Topics	Lagos Plan Topics
Public vs. Private sector roles	institution building
user costs	interAfrican linkages
policy reforms	intersectoral linkages
agricultural marketing practices	expanding the usage of local currencies
pricing policies	food losses and food security
tax policies	appropriate technology
donor policies	patents, licensing and technology transfer
wage rates	role of multinational corporations, banking, insurance and shipping costs
exchange rates	
investment climate	

agreement. Protectionism is a good example. The Berg Report assails at great length the protectionist policies prevalent in many African industrial sectors. These policies are said to result in unnecessarily high costs and inefficient management in the protected industries, thereby hurting the continent's efforts to build a viable industrial export sector and imposing higher costs on domestic customers, including the agricultural sector. The LPA, however, treats protectionism as an internal policy helpful to the development of the industrial sector and as an external policy used by industrialized countries with harmful effects on less-developed African countries.

The contrast in treatment of regionalism is more subtle. The Berg Report recognizes the importance of regional integration to the industrial development of Africa. In two separate discussions, the Berg Report analyzes the need for and difficulty of achieving meaningful regional integration and suggests it will be a long time coming. In the LPA, regionalism is discussed in nearly every chapter. Regionalism constitutes an integral condition for implementation of the LPA. Without regional integration, the LPA collapses as a concept; so the LPA does not allow for failure in achieving regional integration. The strikingly different treatment afforded this topic evokes the classic contrast between the disinterested spectator and the besieged activist; in a sense, this contrast symbolizes the difference between the two documents.

Table 22.2 displays a more comprehensive comparison of some of the more salient features of both documents. Some oversimplification is necessary to conform to this abbreviated format and it is hoped that there are no serious distortions of position. The table, like both documents, inevitably suffers from overgeneralization. There are forty-four countries plus the colony of Namibia in Sub-Saharan Africa and another five countries in North Africa. These countries have extremely varied economies, and statements and recommendations about the continent are not meant to be applicable to every country and instance.

The most significant conflict between the two documents, as shown in the table, is in strategy, which is not surprising in view of the differing objectives and time frames. The LPA has the longer time frame—the year 2000 is the target date for achievement of the plan—and this target date is certainly not realistic. The LPA is more of a dynamic concept than a static plan; consequently, its achievement will not be a discrete occurrence on a specific day. Only two goals are targeted for completion by the year 2000: the creation of an African Economic Community and the achievement by Africa of a modest 2 percent of world industrial production. Self-sufficiency in food, building materials, clothing, and energy have target dates before the year 2000, but most programs have no specific completion dates and the LPA merely exhorts member states to start implementation.

Although neither document attempts to place a price tag or cost on its program, the Berg Report does suggest the magnitude of Overseas Development Assistance (ODA) required to fulfill the program envisaged. Unfortunately, the minimum projected ODA level of $89 billion has been invalidated by the recession in industrialized countries, the parsimony of the current U.S. administration, which strongly influences the volume of ODA offered by other donors, and the subsequent reneging by the United States on its commitment to the sixth replenishment of the International Development Association (IDA).[1] The LPA provides no indication of its cost of implementation other than some partial figures in the agriculture, transportation, and communication sectors. Implementation of the LPA requires such extensive restructuring of relationships and institutions that meaningful cost estimates are difficult to project in some crucial sectors. Nevertheless, the costs of some programs could have been estimated. Even more useful would have been some clearer indication of probable sources for the funds needed to implement the plan.

The LPA provides a growth projection target of 7 percent for the decade of the 1980s (see Table 22.2). The LPA does not disclose how this figure is determined or any underlying assumptions used in its calculation. In the LPA preamble, the average annual growth rate for the continent is given as only 4.8 percent for the period from 1960 to 1980, with 7 percent for the oil exporters. The LPA's surprising 7 percent projection for the decade of the 1980s is 40 percent greater than the Berg Report's highest growth projection and nearly 300 percent of its lowest growth projection. Even these lower Berg Report projections, based on data through 1979, are generally viewed as high because the global recession went deeper and extended further into the 1980s than had been expected at the time the Berg Report

TABLE 22.2. A Comparison of Some Highlights of the Berg Report and the Lagos Plan

Item	Berg Report	Lagos Plan
Objectives	To enable the African countries to reduce their balance of payments deficits. To enable the African countries to enjoy a positive per capita growth rate during the decade of the 1980s and to maintain and expand their existing infrastructure.	To lay a durable foundation for internally generated, self-sustained processes of development and economic growth based on the twin principles of national and collective self-reliance. To bring about self-sufficiency in food and a diminishing dependence on exports and on expatriate technical assistance. To create an African Economic Community--i.e., an economically unified Africa.
Strategy	Export of primary products and import of manufactured goods, food, and technology, build infrastructures using multilateral and bilateral aid. Attract private investment for developing the mining and industrial sectors.	Collective self-reliance via a partial delinkage of Africa from the global trading system and enlarged emphasis on intra-African trading rather than on exports, (although production for export remains an important secondary focus). Interactive agricultural and industrial development within a network of strong sub-regional frameworks. Multilateral and bilateral aid to assist in the building of infrastructure and the improvement of agricultural efficiency. Private investment (including foreign) permitted to participate in development of mining and heavy industrial sectors but with African self-interest definitely paramount.
Time Frame	The decade of the 1980s	From 1980 until the year 2000
Cost, and Source of Funds	ODA of $89-120 billion (current dollars), Private loans and investments and domestic costs not available.	Cost not available. For agriculture, $22 billion for 1980-85 (1979 dollars) of which at least half coming from domestic sources. For transportation and communications, $9 billion is required to fund those

Cost, and Source of Funds (cont'd.)

projects which are already prepared for implementation.
ODA; private loans and investments, both foreign and domestic.

Growth projections 1980-1990 (Average Annual)

GDP	2.4 percent to 5.0 percent (oil importers)	7.0 percent
Exports	2.6 percent to 5.2 percent (oil importers)	7.0 percent
Imports	0.7 percent to 3.9 percent (oil importers)	less than 8.0 percent
Agriculture	2.3 percent to 3.8 percent (oil importers)	4.0 percent
Manufacturing	Not available	9.5 percent

Assumptions External

A slowly expanding demand for Africa's nonfuel commodity exports.
Terms of trade moving not too seriously against primary commodities producers.
Capital available to Africa to meet a substantial portion of development needs and to refinance existing unpayable loans.
ODA falling somewhere between $89-120 billion for the decade.
Most of the technology which Africa needs must be imported.

A continuation of ODA.
A cooperative attitude on the part of multi-national corporations in terms of investment, credit, and technology transference. The decision to delink will not provoke retaliation by North on a scale sufficient to destabilize the effort.
Africa can retain its financial credibility in world capital markets so as to enable it to borrow short and long term funds at near market rates.
Africa has a considerable store of indigenous expertise which can be adapted to serve Africa production requirements.

Assumptions Domestic

African governments will accept conditionality for development financing and can institute the policy reforms called for without experiencing so negative a response as to undermine the program.
Comparative advantages for Africa are in the production and sale of certain primary commodities.

African leadership will genuinely embrace regional cooperation and integration.
African leaders will be willing to impose the necessary austerity entailed by delinkage, and to live with the discontent precipitated thereby. The African public will accept this austerity and will rally to the call.

cont'd.

Table 22.2.(cont'd.)

Item	Berg Report	Lagos Plan
Assumptions Domestic (cont'd.)		Africa is able to produce a viable plan for the Continent, and the anticipated linkages and complementarities (inter-country and inter-sectoral) are in fact realizable. Africa's comparative advantages are yet to be determined. Adequate indigenous management and technological expertise will be forthcoming to carry out the bulk of the LPA without excessive reliance on expatriates.
Some Key Issues		
Agriculture	Farmers should be given strong cash incentives to produce. Small holders should be favored over large scale developments although larger farmers may sometimes be afforded leadership opportunities. Production of cash crops (export crops) should have priority over food crops. The marketing of farm products should be placed primarily in private hands or in cooperatives to render them more efficient.	Farmers should be given strong cash incentives to produce. Although clearly stated, small-holders appear to be favored over large planters. Support for farmers cooperatives and integrated rural development approaches. Food self-sufficiency is first priority. Food imports should be mainly eliminated and the production and consumption of local foods encouraged. Agricultural sector is to provide the necessary imputs to the processing industries as well as markets for the products of the domestic industrial sector.
Administration	Given existing manpower restraints, the public sector is greatly overextended and should be cut back.	Africa faces a tremendous shortage of trained manpower in all areas and must afford a high priority to over-coming this deficiency.

Industry	Terminate the existing biases against exports and in favor of industrial assembly operations. Develop industry largely as a support to agri-culture. Heavy capital-intensive type industries are generally unsuited to the small African market size. Export processing, import substitutions and regional projects are all valid if they do not impose burdens on agriculture.	Initially, resource-based industries to be devel-oped as a support to agriculture through the supplying of necessary agricultural inputs. To insure that basic industries can operate at an efficient scale, sub-regional marketing agree-ments must be negotiated. Industry priorities are food and agro-industries; construction materials; raw materials processing; textiles; energy development; intermediate and capital goods industries, including metal-lurgical, mechanical, chemical, electrical and electronic industries.
Protection for Industry	Eliminate protection; it fosters inefficiency and raises costs in other sectors.	Protect local industry until it becomes competi-tive. (Developed countries should eliminate protectionist measures against Third World goods).
Import Controls	Eliminate them; they introduce distortions, encourage corruption and absorb scarce admini-strative skills.	The local market should carry mainly goods to satisfy basic needs. Non-essential and other imports should be restricted, so as to conserve foreign exchange and reduce inventory costs.
Population Growth	Crucial to take steps now to reduce fertility.	The current levels of fertility and mortality are of concern.
Education	General, rather than technical education should be expanded.	Scientific and technical training is the educa-tional priority.
Public or Private Sector	Curtail parastatal activity in favor of private entreneurship. Parastatals must be relieved of conflicting goals.	Neutral, but considers that opportunities for expanding the private domestic sector are extremely limited.

projections were made. Actual growth figures for black Africa for the years 1980 to 1982 appear to have been only about 2.5 percent. Achievement of a 7 percent overall rate for the decade requires a rate of 9 percent from 1983 to 1989. Thus, the LPA's projected 7 percent average annual growth rate for the decade has to be viewed as highly optimistic within the current strategy of African development. To be sure, the LPA proposes a radically different strategy of development for Africa, but since it is unlikely that any major changes in strategy will be in place during most of the 1980s, there is no basis for assuming a radical upward discontinuity in the growth rate before the end of the decade. Even if the 7 percent average growth were attained, it is dubious that this achievement would generate surplus for investment that approaches the magnitudes required for financing any significant portion of the LPA's necessary physical infrastructure. If the LPA is to be treated seriously, its sponsors must pay urgent attention to financing the plan so that some reasonable assessment of its financial feasibility may begin.

· ASSUMPTIONS UNDERLYING BOTH DOCUMENTS ·

This discussion of costs is linked to the full range of assumptions that underlie both documents (see Table 22.2). Clearly, all persons seriously interested in the LPA await more concrete analyses of the intercountry and intersectoral linkages that provide the backbone for the plan.

The LPA states that the primary user of Africa's natural resources should be Africa itself; exports should be limited to whatever surplus production remains after Africa's needs are met. Years, if not decades, are required for Africa to develop the capability to utilize its raw materials. Because Africa is currently drowning in balance-of-payments deficits, exports remain a major and vital African concern for the foreseeable future, which is why the Berg Report has great short-term relevance. The absorption within Africa of its raw materials—iron ore, bauxite, manganese, chromite, sodium, phosphates, food and fiber crops, etc.—and the transformation of these materials into the consumer and capital goods that the continent requires are tasks of massive proportions. Training of every imaginable sort, industrial experience, management experience, research, and technology adaptation—these are just a few of the necessary inputs that must be vastly expanded within Africa for an effective program of collective self-reliance.

Having set forth the vision, the LPA devotes most of its text to describing what the member states must do to bring themselves and the continent to a position where such a program is feasible. In particular, the LPA extensively exhorts member states to acquire training and skill, to prepare resource inventories, to adapt technology to African capabilities, to facilitate communications within the continent, and to intensify and expand research and subregional and regional cooperation efforts.

Economic realities must be addressed, however, and the ECA needs to provide preliminary analyses of how some of these LPA linkages might be implemented.

Some tentative idea is needed of what Africa's production profile (in commodity-specific and country-specific terms) might be some years from now when the LPA will approach full implementation. The data may already be available to make preliminary calculations of some of the financial, economic, and social costs entailed in a preliminary implementation of an expanded regional trading effort. Abolition of customs duties between neighboring countries, for example, may result in serious declines in tax revenues if the countries involved depend heavily on customs duties as revenue generators. Among the questions requiring answers are these two: which countries are likely to have this problem? and how serious a problem is this?

There is a host of such problems that existing subregional organizations are beginning to face, and their experience is valuable for the LPA. Achieving the transformation of African economies that the LPA envisions will also require the squeezing of savings from already meager African economies on an unprecedented scale, even under optimistic assumptions regarding ODA, which implies the coercion of a substantial surplus for investment from a poverty-stricken population. This challenge is perhaps comparable to China's problem in the 1950s, but Africa does not have the same political and social means. China was a unified state directed by an invincible totalitarian government astride a relatively homogeneous population. How this surplus is to be amassed in Africa is a missing chapter in the LPA.

Where Africa will fit into the global economy of the 21st century is another unexamined avenue. Massive shifts are taking place within the world with regard to industrial locations. Newly industrializing countries (NICs) such as Hong Kong, Singapore, Korea, Taiwan, Brazil, Mexico, Spain, and India are rapidly replacing the traditionally industrialized nations of Western Europe, the United States, Canada, and Japan in the production of consumer appliances, such capital-intensive items as autos and ships, and some basic processing industries such as steel. Low-wage industries such as clothing, footwear, toys, and simple electronic assembly are now being taken over by countries such as Malaysia, Thailand, Sri Lanka, and the Philippines, where the average wage is about $25 per month.

African wages are generally higher than wages in other developing areas. Is Africa better advised to (1) move toward capital-intensive production methods to raise labor productivity and be more competitive internationally or (2) pay greater attention to maximizing employment via labor-intensive production (and turn out products that may be undersold by other Third World countries)? Africa is the actual producer of many necessary raw-material inputs. Does this counteract the labor cost differential? Definitive answers to such questions are not now possible, and it is a heroic assumption by the drafters of the LPA that Africa will transform its raw materials into intermediate and final goods and capital equipment with sufficient efficiency to make it an economically attractive strategy for supplying even an exclusively internal market. Preliminary structuring of internally consistent subregional plans must be undertaken as promptly as possible so that the feasibility of this assumption may be evaluated.

If the LPA's assumptions seem to be heroic, the Berg Report's seem to be dubious, especially the financial and commercial assumptions. The entire Berg Report strategy is built upon expanding export earnings, but the volume of Africa's trade, and of international trade in general, has declined further since the publication of the 1981 report; and the deterioration in Africa's terms of trade, already emerging in the 1979 data upon which the report is based, continued past 1981.[2] Capital availability is scarcer now than either document anticipated it would be, both in terms of ODA concessional funds and commercial loans, the latter having retreated in the face of the shaky global debt situation.

· PRAGMATISM, FEASIBILITY, AND APPROPRIATENESS OF THE DOCUMENTS ·

The short-term outlook for Africa is inescapably grim, regardless of which development strategy or policy prescriptions are pursued. Actual options available to Africa are frighteningly limited. As an immediate strategy option, delinkage is not really feasible. Africa's intimate linkages with the industrialized nations cannot be abruptly severed without inflicting unacceptable pain upon the continent's fragile economies; Africa's dependency is all-embracing for food, consumer imports, capital goods, technology, technicians, and training. Cultural dependency is also evident because the foreign-educated African elite has become so indoctrinated with non-African cultural artifacts and lifestyles that it is unlikely to relinquish them easily. Despite these affinities, the harsh economic realities of the 1980s are that Africa can no longer pay the bill for satisfying its Western tastes. Either the West will pay, for political reasons, or the linkages will begin to weaken. The message of the LPA is that most of these linkages should be drastically pared, at least until an interdependence of equals can be established.

Sorting out these conflicting aims and realities is Africa's agenda for the 1980s. The Berg Report is clearly out of step with the LPA, but the extent to which this is a serious disservice to Africa depends on the extent to which the LPA is truly an expression of African thinking. At the moment, it appears likely that the LPA is more the avant garde of African thought than a popular expression, and the Berg Report may be right in focusing exclusively on urgent short-term survival issues and in stressing enhanced efficiency and productivity.

Many Berg Report recommendations are correct under all circumstances. For example, African governments are doing Africa a disservice by deliberately expanding the mass demand for rice and wheat by setting artificially low prices for these imports. Rice and wheat do not grow easily in most of Africa; increasing demand for these imported basic foods insures dependency. Aside from discouraging tastes for imports, African governments also need to encourage agricultural and food technology research to improve yields of African staples such as cassava, sorghum, and millet and to process these staples into bread and other convenient foods. The Berg Report's call for Africa to diversify her agricultural and industrial production is not challenged by anyone, but more information is needed about how to do this.

Other Berg Report recommendations are correct within the short term to maintain Africa's present role as supplier of raw materials and importer of finished goods, although the recommendations may be incorrect within a longer-term strategy. It makes sense for African countries to provide incentives to farmers to increase production of existing export crops. Foreign exchange is badly needed, and the capital structures are already in place. In the longer run, it may be better for these countries to shift resources used in these export crops into a different crop or sector to be consumed at home or processed into a higher value export, as advocated by the LPA.

Finally, some Berg Report prescriptions appear to be manifestly erroneous. Three examples of such misdirection are the recommendations on general education, industry protection, and food self-sufficiency. The Berg Report warns against mismatches "between types of schooling offered and social demand" (1981:83). This warning refers to a tendency to establish technical secondary schools when people are demanding general secondary schools. Career prospects are alleged to be better from the general schools. Even without the LPA, it seems clear that Africa is suffering from inadequate numbers of technically trained personnel whereas, in some places at least, Africa may have a surplus of graduates with general diplomas. The problem may lie with a tendency for technical jobs to be less remunerative or to have lower social rank than clerical jobs, especially when government is the employer. If so, then the recommendation should be for governments to institute more rational pay scales, so as not to misdirect the educational system from satisfying national needs.

Berg Report opposition to protectionism for African industry is based on general liberal abhorrence of any obstacles to free trading and, more specifically, on the belief that protection insures that African industry will remain costly and uncompetitive. This fear is valid, with some empirical basis in fact. To remove all protection for nascent African industrial efforts, however, is to insure that they will be stillborn or destroyed by cheaper imports. Where the market is made large enough, for instance by utilizing regional cooperation, local competition might be permitted as a means of increasing efficiency. Where a monopoly is unavoidable, a means for monitoring and controlling costs might be established, perhaps tied to a system of benchmark pricing based on costs of comparable imports. Certainly the West's experience with public utility pricing has some relevance here.

The Berg Report is hostile toward the top African priority of self-sufficiency in food, which contrasts sharply with the LPA that strongly emphasizes it. The Berg Report stand on this issue is difficult to understand. On strictly economic criteria it may make sense; however, the political unacceptability of an entire continent being dependent on external sources for its food supply is self-evident. People who cannot feed themselves are people who are not in control of their destiny, and the history of humankind is replete with demonstrations of the importance of food self-sufficiency. In this area strictly economic criteria must yield to other considerations, as in the U.S. policy regarding shipping and other industries where the United States has low relative efficiency but chooses not to be totally dependent and subsidizes these industries.

Despite its own policy of subsidizing economically nonviable industries for political reasons, the United States is unwilling to concede the wisdom of such a policy for Africa. The U.S. assistant secretary of state for African affairs in 1983 roundly condemned the LPA's call for self-sufficiency in food production when he declared that "some old shibboleths badly need reexamination, including the notion that a country must physically produce its own food supplies, when in some cases it may be more efficient—and no less self-sufficient—to concentrate on cash crops and buy food with the money thus earned" (Crocker 1983).[3]

The most remarkable misdirection of the Berg Report, however, is that it reinforces the impression that Africa's future is necessarily the continuing expansion of its present export mix rather than some more promising initiative. Although the Berg Report reveals on several occasions uneasiness about the long run viability of the present export-led policy, no alternative to its continuation is offered, leaving the impression that there are no alternatives. Perhaps in the short run there are none, but the LPA exists and challenges the existing strategy with an alternative. The authors of the Berg Report should have either rejected the LPA as an inappropriate strategy for Africa to pursue or else endorsed it and suggested how implementation of the LPA should proceed. The decision to withold making any judgment was clearly a triumph of political timidity. The Berg Report missed an excellent if not unique opportunity to make a major contribution to a vital dialogue about Africa's long-term economic prospects.

· NOTES AND ACKNOWLEDGMENTS ·

This chapter is based on a longer monograph by the two authors (Browne and Cummings 1984), entitled *The Lagos Plan of Action vs. The Berg Report: Contemporary Issues in African Economic Development,* which was published in 1984 as part of the Monograph and Occasional Paper Series of the African Studies and Research Program, Howard University, Washington, D.C.

1. The International Development Association (IDA) is the concessional lending window of the World Bank and the major source of development capital for Africa. In 1981, the United States refused to fully honor its share of the global contribution to replenish this program from 1981 to 1983, thereby reducing IDA's commitment authority by more than $500 million in 1981–1982, with the likelihood of the decrease going considerably higher had other donor countries not rallied to the plight of less-developed countries and released funds to restrain the reduction (World Bank 1982:15–16). This trend was further exacerbated in 1983 when the United States, in the face of near unanimous objections of the other major donor countries, forced a 25 percent reduction in the seventh IDA replenishment. In the U.S. administration's 1986 federal budget submission, no funds whatsoever are projected for the eighth IDA replenishment.

2. According to an article in the *Economist* magazine (June 11, 1983:79), "UNC-TAD's index of non fuel commodity prices fell by 16% in 1981 and by a further 15% last year. Poor countries' terms of trade (the ratio of their exports to import prices) worsened by 27% in 1978–80 and 12% in 1981."

3. Chester Crocker said this at a March 1983 seminar on the African Economic Crisis held at Georgetown University, Washington, D.C.

• SUGGESTED FURTHER READINGS •

Adedeji, Adebayo. 1984. The African Economic and Social Crisis: An Agenda for Action by Africa and the International Community. Statement delivered at the 1984 Second Regular Session of the Economic and Social Council of the United Nations at Geneva. Addis Ababa, Ethiopia: Economic Commission for Africa.

Adedeji, Adebayo, and Timothy Shaw, eds. 1985. *Economic Crisis in Africa: African Perspectives on Development Problems and Principles*. Boulder, Colorado: Lynne Rienner Publishers.

Browne, Robert S., and Robert J. Cummings. 1984. *The Lagos Plan vs. the Berg Report*. Washington, D.C.: African Studies and Research Program, Howard University. Republished in 1985. 2nd ed. Lawrenceville, Virginia: Brunswick Publishing. *Development* 7:1/2.

Economic Commission for Africa (ECA). 1983. *ECA and Africa's Development, 1983–2008: A Preliminary Perspective Study*. ECA Document No. E/ECA/CM 9/23. 6 April.

Institute of Development Studies. 1983. *What Agendas for Action?* Bulletin Vol. 14, No. 2. Sussex, England: Institute of Development Studies.

Organization of African Unity. 1981. *The Lagos Plan of Action for the Economic Development of Africa 1980–2000*. Geneva: International Institute for Labor Studies.

World Bank. 1981. *Accelerated Development in Sub-Saharan Africa*. Washington, D.C.: World Bank.

———. 1983. *Sub-Saharan Africa: Progress Report on Development Prospects and Programs*. Washington, D.C.: World Bank.

———. 1984. Toward Sustained Development in Sub-Saharan Africa. Washington, D.C.: World Bank.

References

Adams, Dale W., and Douglas H. Graham. 1984. A Critique of Traditional Agricultural Credit Projects and Policies. In *Agricultural Development in the Third World*. Carl K. Eicher and John M. Staatz, eds. Pp. 313–328. Baltimore: Johns Hopkins University Press.

Adams, M. R. 1978. Small-Scale Vinegar Production from Bananas. *Tropical Science* 20:11–19.

Adelman, Irma. 1975. Development Economics—A Reassessment of Goals. *American Economic Review* 55:2:302–9.

Adelman, Irma, and Cynthia Taft Morris. 1973. *Economic Growth and Social Equity in Developing Countries*. Stanford: Stanford University Press.

Agro-Economic Surveys (AES) 1968–1983 (51 reports). Lilongwe, Malawi: Ministry of Agriculture.

Ahmad, M., and A. Jenkins. 1980. Traditional Paddy Husking—An Appropriate Technology Under Pressure. *Appropriate Technology* 7:2:28–30.

Aiyer, R. S., P. G. Nair, and L. Prema. 1978. No-Cost Method for Preserving Fresh Cassava Roots. *Cassava Newsletter* No. 4:8–9. Cali, Columbia: Centro Internacional de Agricultura Tropical.

Ajayi, S. S. 1971. Wildlife as a Source of Protein in Nigeria: Some Priorities for Development. *The Nigerian Field* 36:115–127.

———. 1975. Observations on the Biology, Domestication and Reproductive Performance of the African Giant Rat (*Cricetomys gambianus*) Waterhouse in Nigeria. *Mammalia* 39:355–364.

———. 1983. Domestication of Mammals in Africa. *The Nigerian Field* 47:145–155.

Allan, William. 1965. *The African Husbandman*. Edinburgh: Oliver and Boyd.

Amat, Soegent. 1982. Promoting National Food Security: The Indonesia Experience. In *Food Security: Theory, Policy, and Perspectives from Asia and the Pacific Rim*. Anthony H. Chisolm and Rodney Tyres, eds. Pp. 145–170. Lexington, Massachusetts: Lexington Books.

Amin, Samir. 1965. *Trois expériences Africaines de développement: le Mali, la Guinée et le Ghana*. Paris: Presses Universitaires de France.

———. 1971. *L'Afrique de l'ouest bloquée: l'économie politique de la colonisation (1880–1970)*. Paris: Les Editions de Minuit.

———. 1973. Transnational Phases in Sub-Saharan Africa. *Monthly Review* 25:5:52–57.

———. 1974a. *Modern Migrations in West Africa*. London: Oxford University Press.

———. 1974b. *Accumulation on a World Scale: A Critique of the Theory of Underdevelopment*. New York: Monthly Review Press.

———. 1976. *Unequal Development: An Essay on the Social Formations of Peripheral Capitalism*. New York: Monthly Review Press.

Anandaswam, B., and N. V. R. Iyengar. 1980. Food Packaging Research and Development in India. *Journal of Food Science and Technology* 17:59–65.

Ancey, G. 1975. *Niveaux de décision et fonctions objectifs en milieu africain.* AMIRA, No. 3 Paris: INSEE.

Andreae, Bernd. 1980. The Economics of Tropical Agriculture. Slough, England: Commonwealth Agriculture Bureau.

Ankra, E. K., and F. E. Dovlo. 1978. The Properties of Trona and its Effect on the Cooking Time of Cowpeas. *Journal of Science, Food and Agriculture* 29:950–952.

Appropriate Technology for Grain Storage. 1977. Community Development Trust Fund of Tanzania.

Anand, J. C. 1975. Development of Appropriate Technology for a Breakthrough in Fruit and Vegetable Processing Industry. *Industrial Food Packer* 29:6:31–35.

Arnold, J. E. M. 1978. *Wood Energy and Rural Communities.* Position Paper, Eighth World Forestry Congress, Jakarta. Rome: Food and Agriculture Organization (FAO), Forestry Department.

Arrighi, G. 1970. Labour Supplies in Historical Perspective: A Study of the Proletarianization of the African Peasantry in Rhodesia. *Journal of Development Studies* 6:3:197–234.

Asante, S. K. B. 1984. Planning to Feed West Africa: ECOWAS and the Lagos Plan of Action. *West Africa* November 19.

———. 1985. *The Political Economy of Regionalism in Africa: The Case of the Economic Community of West African States.* New York: Praeger Publishers.

———. 1986. Development and Regional Integration Since 1980. In *Economic Crisis in Africa: African Perspectives on Development Problems and Potentials.* Adebayo Adedeji and Timothy M. Shaw, eds. Boulder, Colorado: Lynne Rienner Publishers.

Ashraf, M., P. Balogun, and A. Jibrin. 1985. *A Case Study of On-Farm Adaptive Research in the Bida Agricultural Development Project—Nigeria.* On-Farm Research Bulletin No. 1. Ibadan, Nigeria: International Institute of Tropical Agriculture (IITA).

Asibey, E. O. A. 1974. Wildlife as a Source of Protein in Africa South of the Sahara. *Biological Conservation* 6:32–39.

Axline, W. Andrew. 1979. *Caribbean Integration: The Politics of Regionalism.* London: Frances Pinter. New York: Nichols Publishing Co.

Ayeni, J. S. O., and S. S. Ajayi. 1983. Wildlife Protein: Guineafowl (*Numida meleagris galeata Pallas*) as Animal Protein Supplement. *The Nigerian Field* 47:156–166.

Aykroyd, Joyce D., and Ann Walker. 1982. *Legumes in Human Nutrition.* FAO Food and Nutrition Paper No. 20. P. 104. Rome: Food and Agriculture Organization (FAO).

Ba, Mbaye. 1983. *The Role of Artesianal Fisheries Within the Framework of Policies, Strategies and Programmes for Fisheries Development: The Case of Western and Central Africa.* Food and Agriculture Organization (FAO) Fisheries Report No. 295. Rome: Food and Agriculture Organization (FAO).

Baier, S. 1980. *An Economic History of Central Niger.* Oxford: Clarendon Press.

Baran, Paul A. 1952. On the Political Economy of Backwardness. *Manchester School of Economic and Social Studies* 20:66–84.

Barraclough, Geoffrey. 1967. *An Introduction to Contemporary History.* Harmondsworth, England: Penguin Books.

Barraclough, Solon. 1973. *Agrarian Structure in Latin America.* Lexington, Massachusetts: Lexington Books.

Basta, S. S. 1976. Iron Deficiency, Anemia and Labour Productivity. *Food Nutrition* 15–17.

Bates, R. P. 1971. Lactic Fermentation of Florida Vegetables. *Proceedings of the Florida State Horticulture Society* 84:253–257.

Bates, Robert H. 1979. The Commercialization of Agriculture and the Rise of Rural Political Protest in Black Africa. In *Food, Politics and Agricultural Development: Case*

Studies in the Public Policy of Rural Modernization. Raymond F. Hopkins, Donald J. Pachula, and Ross Talbot, eds. Pp. 227–259. Boulder, Colorado: Westview Press.

————. 1981. *The Markets and States in Tropical Africa: The Political Basis of Agricultural Policies*. Berkeley: University of California Press.

————. 1984. Appropriate Technologies for Increasing Food Utilization. In *Malnutrition: Determinants and Consequences*. Philip L. White and Nancy Selvey, eds. pp. 355–364. New York: Alan R. Liss.

————. 1984. Some Conventional Orthodoxies in the Study of Agrarian Change. *World Politics* 36:2:234–254.

Beckman, B. 1978. *Organizing the Farmers*. Uppsala: Scandinavian Institute of African Studies.

Beer, C., and G. Williams. 1975. The Politics of the Ibadan Peasantry. *The African Review* 5:3:235–56.

Behnke, Roy H., Jr. 1984. Fenced and Open Range Ranching: The Commercialization of Pastoral Land and Livestock in Africa. In *Livestock Development in Subsaharan Africa*. James R. Simpson and Phylo Evangelou, eds. Pp. 261–284. Boulder, Colorado: Westview Press, Inc.

Behrman, Jere R. 1968. *Supply Response in Underdeveloped Agriculture*. Amsterdam: North-Holland Publishing Co.

Benoit-Cattin, M., and J. Faye. 1982. *L'exploitation agricole en Afrique Soudano-Sahélienne PUF*. Paris: Agence de Cooperation Culturelle et Technique.

Berg, Alan. 1973. *The Nutrition Factor: Its Role in National Development*. Washington, D.C.: Brookings Institution.

Berg, E. 1965. The Economics of the Migrant Labor System. In *Urbanization and Migration in West Africa*. H. Kuper, ed. Pp. 160–184. Berkeley: University of California Press.

Berman, B., and J. Lonsdale. 1980. Crises of Accumulation, Coercion and the Colonial State: The Development of the Labor Control System in Kenya, 1919–1939. *Canadian Journal of African Studies* 14:1:55–82.

Bernal, V. 1985. Household Agricultural Production and Off-Farm Work in a Sudan Village. Ph.D. dissertation, Anthropology Department, Northwestern University.

Berry, R. Albert. 1975. Special Problems of Policy Making in a Technologically Heterogeneous Agriculture: Columbia. In *Agriculture and Development Theory*. Lloyd G. Reynolds, ed. New Haven, Connecticut: Yale University Press.

Berry, R. Albert, and William F. Cline. 1979. *Agrarian Structure and Productivity in Developing Countries*. Baltimore: Johns Hopkins University Press.

Berry, R. Albert, and R. H. Sabot. 1978. Labour Market Performance in Developing Countries: A Survey. *World Development* 6:1199–1242.

Berry, Sara. 1975. *Cocoa, Custom, and Socio-economic Change in Rural Western Nigeria*. Oxford: Clarendon Press.

————. 1984. The Food Crisis and Agrarian Change in Africa: A Review Essay. *African Studies Review* 27:2:59–112.

————. 1985. *Fathers Work for Their Sons: Accumulation, Mobility and Class Formation in an Extended Yoruba Community*. Berkeley: University of California Press.

Best, Allan C. G., and Harm J. de Blij. 1977. *African Survey*. New York: John Wiley and Sons.

Beuchat, L. R. 1978. Microbial Alterations of Grains, Legumes and Oilseeds. *Food Technology* 32:5:193–198.

Bialostacki, S. J. 1977. A Low Cost Wood Fired Grain Drier. *Appropriate Technology* 4:1:20–23.

Billaz, R., and M. Dufumier. 1980. *Recherche et Développement en Agriculture*, PUF. Paris: PUF.

Binswanger, Hans P., and Vernon W. Ruttan. 1978. *Induced Innovation: Technology, Institutions and Development*. Baltimore: Johns Hopkins University Press.

Boahen, Adu, et al. 1971. *Horizon History of Africa*. New York: American Heritage Publishing Company.

Boatwright, J. H. 1979. A Wedge Press for Oil Extraction. *Appropriate Technology* 6:2:24–25.

Bodenheimer, F. S. 1951. *Insects as Human Food: A Chapter of the Ecology of Man*. The Hague: Dr. W. Junk Publishers.

Boserup, Ester. 1965. *The Conditions of Agricultural Growth*. Chicago: Aldine.

———. 1970. *Women's Role in Economic Development*. New York: St. Martin's Press.

Bourne, M. C. 1977. Post Harvest Food Losses—The Neglected Dimensions in Increasing the World Food Supply. Cornell International Agriculture Mimeograph 53. Geneva, New York: New York State Agricultural Experiment Station.

———. 1978. What is Appropriate Intermediate Food Technology? *Food Technology* 32:4:77–78, 80.

Brain, James. 1976. Less than Second-Class: Women in Rural Settlement Schemes in Tanzania. In *Women in Africa*. N. Hafkin and E. Bay, eds. Pp. 265–84. Stanford, California: Stanford University Press.

Branch, D. 1978. Tools for Small-Scale Grain Raising. *Organic Gardening and Farming* 25:4:88–93.

Bratton, M. 1985. Drought, Food Production and the Social Organization of Small Farmers in Zimbabwe. Paper presented at the National Center for Atmospheric Research, Boulder, Colorado, August 14–16.

Breag, G. R., and P. A. Harker. 1979. *The Utilization of Waste Heat Produced During the Manufacture of Coconut Shell Charcoal for the Centralized Production of Copra*. Report G127. London: Tropical Products Institute.

Brelsford, W. V. 1946. *The Fishermen of the Bangweulu Swamps*. Manchester: Manchester University Press.

Bremaud, O., and J. Pagot. 1968. Grazing Lands, Nomadism and Transhumance in the Sahel. *UNESCO Arid Zone Research* 18:311–334.

Bressani, R., and L. G. Elias. 1968. Processed Vegetable Protein Mixtures for Human Consumption in Developing Countries. *Advanced Food Research* 16:1–103.

Briggs, G. M., and D. H. Calloway. 1984. *Nutrition and Physical Fitness*. 11th ed. New York: Holt, Rinehart & Winston.

Brokensha, D. W., B. W. Riley, and A. P. Castro. 1983. *Fuelwood Use in Rural Kenya: Impacts of Deforestation*. Binghampton, New York: Institute for Development Anthropology.

Brown, Lester R. 1970. *Seeds of Change*. New York: Praeger Publishers.

———. 1985. Maintaining World Fisheries. In *State of the World*. Lester R. Brown, et al., eds. Pp. 73–96. Ontario: Worldwatch Institute.

Brown, L. R., W. Chandler, S. Postel, L. Starke, and W. Wolfe. 1984. *State of the World: A Worldwatch Institute Report on Progress Toward a Sustainable Society*. New York: W. W. Norton.

Brown, Lester R., and Edward C. Wolf. 1985. *Worldwatch Paper 65: Reversing Africa's Decline*. Washington, D.C.: Worldwatch Institute.

Brown, N. L., and J. W. Howe. 1978. Solar Energy for Village Development. *Science* 199:651–657.

Brown, N. L., and E. R. Pariser. 1975. Food Science in Developing Countries. *Science* 188: 589–593.

Brown, Robert S., and Robert J. Cummings. 1984. *The Lagos Plan of Action vs. The Berg Report*. Washington, D.C.: The African Studies and Research Program, Howard University.

Brozek, J. 1984. Malnutrition and Human Behavior. In *Nutrition Reviews' Present Knowledge in Nutrition*. 5th ed. Pp. 682–692. Washington, D.C.: The Nutrition Foundation.

Brumby, P. J., G. Gryseels, and R. A. Stewart. 1984. *ILCA: Objectives and Achievements*. Addis Ababa, Ethiopia: International Livestock Center for Africa.

Bukh, Jette. 1979. *The Village Woman in Ghana*. Uppsala: Scandinavian Institute of African Studies.

Bukharin, N., and E. Preobrazhensky. 1922. *The ABC of Communism*. London: Communist Party of Great Britain.

Bundy, Colin. 1979. *The Rise and Fall of the South African Peasantry*. Berkeley: University of California Press.

Burkholder, L., P. R. Burkholder, A. Chu, N. Kostyk, and O. A. Roels. 1968. Fish Fermentation. *Food Technology* 22:1278–1284.

Butler, Lorna. 1982. *Review of Social and Cultural Documents and Annotated Bibliography*. Maseru, Lesotho: Ministry of Agriculture.

———. 1983. Lesotho Farming Systems: A Closer Look at Women Farm Managers and the Problems of Subsistence Production. Paper Presented at the 11th International Congress of Anthropological and Ethnographical Sciences. Vancouver, Canada. Mimeograph.

Butynski, T. M. 1973. Life History and Economic Value of the Springhare (*Pedetes capensis*) in Botswana. *Botswana Notes and Records* 5:209–213.

Butynski, T. M., and W. von Richter. 1974. In Botswana Most of the Meat is Wild. *Unasylva* 26:106:24–29.

Byerlee, Derek, Carl K. Eicher, Carl Liedholm, and Dunstan S. C. Spencer. 1983. Employment-Output Conflicts, Factor Price Distortions and Choice of Technique: Empirical Results from Sierra Leone. *Economic Development and Cultural Change* 31:2:315–36.

Caldwell, J. S. 1983. *An Overview of Farming Systems Research and Development: Origins, Applications and Issues*. Paper for the 3rd Annual Conference on Farming Systems Research, Manhatten, Kansas. Manhatten: Kansas State University.

Calvocoressi, Peter. 1985. *Independent Africa and the World*. New York: Longman.

Cardoso, F. H., and E. Falleto. 1979. *Dependency and Development in Latin America*. Berkeley: University of California Press.

Carr, M. 1978. Appropriate Technology for Women. *Appropriate Technology* 5:1:4–6.

Carroll, Thomas F. 1961. The Land Reform Issue in Latin America. In *Latin American Issues: Essays and Comments*. Albert O. Hirschman, ed. Pp. 161–201. New York: Twentieth Century Fund.

Carroz, J. E. 1984. World Fisheries Face Change and Challenges. *Mazingira* 8:2:17–28.

Chambers, R. 1981. Rapid Rural Appraisal: Rationale and Repertoire. *Public Administration and Development* 1:95–106.

Chaney, Elsa, and Martha W. Lewis. 1980. *Women, Migration and the Decline of Smallholder Agriculture*. Washington, D.C.: Office of Women in Development, United States Agency for International Development.

Charlton, Sue Ellen. 1984. *Women in Third World Development*. Boulder, Colorado: Westview Press.

Charney, J. G. 1975. Dynamics of Deserts and Drought in the Sahel. *Quarterly Journal of the Royal Meteorological Society* 101:193–202.

Charter, J. R. 1971. *Nigeria's Wildlife, a Forgotten National Asset*. Morges, Switzerland: International Union for the Conservation of Nature and Natural Resources.

Chauveau, J. P., J. P. Dozon, and J. Richard. 1981. Histoire de Riz, Histoires d'Igname: Le Cas de la Moyenne Côte d'Ivoire. *Africa* 51:2:621–658.

Chayanov, A. V. 1966. *The Theory of the Peasant Economy*. D. Thorner, B. Kerblay, and R. Smith, eds. Homewood, Illinois: Richard D. Irwin.

Cheater, A. 1981. Women and Their Participation in Commercial Agricultural Production: The Case of Medium-Scale Freehold in Zimbabwe. *Development and Change* 12:3:349–378.

———. 1983. Formal and Informal Rights to Land in Zimbabwe's Black Freehold Areas: A Case Study from Msengezi. In *Past and Present in Zimbabwe*. J. D. Y. Peel and T. O. Ranger, eds. Pp. 77–91. Manchester, England: Manchester University Press.

Chenery, H. B., M. S. Ahluwalia, C. L. G. Bell, J. H. Duloy, and R. Jolly, eds. 1974. *Redistribution with Growth*. London: Oxford University Press.

Chittenden, A. E., S. W. Head, and G. Breag. 1980. *Anaerobic Digesters for Small-Scale Vegetable Processing Plants*. Report G139. London: Tropical Products Institute.

Christian, J. L., and J. L. Greger. 1985. *Nutrition for Living*. Menlo Park, California: The Benjamin Cummings Publishing Company.

Chuta, Enyinna, and Carl Liedholm. 1984. Rural Small-Scale Industry: Empirical Evidence and Policy Issues. In *Agricultural Development in the Third World*. Carl K. Eicher and John M. Staatz, eds. Pp. 296–312. Baltimore: Johns Hopkins University Press.

CIMMYT Economics Staff. 1984. The Farming Systems Perspective and Farmer Participation in the Development of Appropriate Technology. In *Agricultural Development in the Third World*. Carl K. Eicher and John M. Staatz, eds. Pp. 326–77.

Clarence-Smith, G. 1985. Thou Shalt Not Articulate Modes of Production. *Canadian Journal of African Studies* 19:1:19–22.

Clark, Barbara. 1975. The Work Done by Rural Women in Malawi. *Eastern Journal of Rural Development* 8:2:80–91.

Clark, C. S. 1976. Village Food Technology: Solar Drying of Vegetables. *League for International Food Education (LIFE) Newsletter*, April. Pp. 1–3.

Clay, E. 1980. The Economics of the Bamboo Tube Well. *Ceres* 13:3:43–47.

Cleave, J. 1974. *African Farmers*. New York: Praeger Publishers.

Clute, Robert E. 1982. The Role of Agriculture in African Development. *African Studies Review* 25:4:1–20.

Cohen, A. 1969. *Custom and Politics in Urban Africa*. Berkeley: University of California Press.

Cohen, Ronald. 1967. *The Kanuri of Bornu*. New York: Holt, Rinehart & Winston.

———. 1970. Traditional Society in Africa. In *The African Experience*. Vol. 1. John N. Paden and Edward W. Soja, eds. Pp. 37–60. Evanston, Illinois: Northwestern University Press.

———. 1984. Production Systems in Borno: A Comparison. Lecture delivered at Cambridge University, Nov. 1984.

Cohen, Ronald, and John Middleton, eds. 1970. *From Tribe to Nation in Africa*. San Francisco: Chandler.

Coleman, R. L., C. J. Wagner, Jr., R. E. Berry, and J. M. Miller. 1980. *Building a Low-Cost, Solar Food Dryer Incorporating a Solar Reflector*. Florida: United States Department of Agriculture Citrus & Subtropical Products Lab.

Collier, P., and D. Lal. 1980. *Poverty and Growth in Kenya*. World Bank Staff Working Paper No. 389. Washington, D.C.: World Bank.

Collins, J. 1976. Clandestine Movement of Groundnuts Across the Niger—Nigeria Boundary. *Canadian Journal of African Studies* 10:2:259–278.

Collinson, M. P. 1982. *Farming Systems Research in Eastern Africa: The Experience of CIMMYT and Some National Agricultural Research Services, 1976–1981*. Michigan State University International Development Paper No. 3. East Lansing: Michigan State University.

———. 1984. *Farming Systems Research, Diagnosing the Problem*. Paper Presented at the 1984 Annual Agricultural Symposium. Washington, D.C.: World Bank.

————. n.d. On Farm Research with a Systems Perspective: Its Role in Servicing Technical Component Research in Maize and Some Examples from Eastern and Southern Africa. Unpublished manuscript.

Colson, Elizabeth. 1970. Incorporation in Tonga. In *From Tribe to Nation in Africa*. Ronald Cohen and John Middleton, eds. San Francisco: Chandler.

————. 1971. *The Social Consequences of Resettlement*. Kariba Studies IV. Manchester: Manchester University Press.

————. 1979. In Good Years and Bad: Food Strategies of Self-Reliant Societies. *Journal of Anthropological Research* 35:1:18–29.

Colvin, L., ed. 1981. *The Uprooted of the Western Sahel*. New York: Praeger Publishers.

Coulson, A. 1982. *Tanzania: A Political Economy*. London: Clarendon Press.

Council on Environmental Quality and the Department of State. 1980. *The Global 2000 Report to the President*. Vol. 2. The Technical Report. Washington, D.C.: U.S. Government Printing Office.

Cowen, M. 1983. The Commercialization of Food Production in Kenya after 1945. In *Imperialism, Colonialism and Hunger: East and Central Africa*. R. Rotberg, ed. Pp. 199–224. Lexington, Massachusetts: D. C. Heath.

Cravioto, J., and E. R. Delicardie. 1976. Malnutrition in Early Childhood and Some of its Later Effects at Individual and Community Levels. *Food Nutrition* 4.

Crawford, E. W. 1982. A Simulation Study of the Growth of Small Farms in Northern Nigeria. MSU International Development Paper No. 1. East Lansing: Michigan State University, Department of Agricultural Economics.

Crim, M. C., and H. N. Munro. 1984. Protein. In *Nutrition Reviews' Present Knowledge in Nutrition*. 5th ed. Pp. 131–146. Washington, D.C.: The Nutrition Foundation, Inc.

Crowder, Michael. 1968. *West Africa Under Colonial Rule*. Evanston, Illinois: Northwestern University Press.

Cruise O'Brien, C. 1970. *The Mourides of Senegal*. Oxford: Clarendon Press.

Dadson, J. A. 1970. Socialized Agriculture in Ghana, 1962–1965, Ph.D. Dissertation, Department of Economics, Harvard University, 1970. Cited in Bates, Robert. 1981. *The Markets and States In Tropical Africa: The Political Basis of Agricultural Policies*. Berkeley: University of California Press.

Dahl, H. A. 1979. Commentary: Factors Involved in the Development, Marketing and Financing of Appropriate Technology in Developing Countries. *Ecology Food Nutrition* 7:257–260.

Dahlberg, Frances. 1981. *Woman the Gatherer*. New Haven, Connecticut: Yale University Press.

Danaker, K. 1984. *Myths of African Hunger*. San Francisco, California: Institute for Food and Development Policy.

Darling, F. F. 1960a. *Wild Life in an African Territory*. London: Oxford University Press.

————. 1960b. Wildlife Husbandry in Africa. *Scientific American* 203:5:123–128.

Darrow, K., and R. Pam. 1976. *Appropriate Technology Sourcebook*. Stanford, California: Volunteers in Asia.

Dasmann, R. F. 1964. *African Game Ranching*. Oxford, England: Pergamon Press.

Davidson, Basil. 1969. *A History of East and Central Africa to the Late Nineteenth Century*. Garden City, New York: Anchor Doubleday.

Davis, R. Hunt, Jr. 1973. Interpreting the Colonial Period in African History. *African Affairs* 72:289:383–400.

de Janvry, Alain. 1981. *The Agrarian Question and Reformism in Latin America*. Baltimore: Johns Hopkins University Press.

————. 1984. The Role of Land Reform in Economic Development: Policies and Politics. In *Agricultural Development in the Third World*. Carl K. Eicher and John M. Staatz, eds. Pp. 263–75. Baltimore: Johns Hopkins University Press.

De Lucia, R., and M. Lesser. 1980. Energy From Organic Residues in Developing Countries: Present Use, Potentials and Observations on Feasibility. Proceedings, Bio-Energy 1980. Pp. 62–70. Washington, D.C.: Bio-Energy Council.

De Vos, Antoon. 1977. Game as Food: A Report on its Significance in Africa and Latin America. *Unasylva* 29:116:2–12.

Deane, N. N., and J. M. Feely. 1974. The Development of a South African Game Ranch. In *The Behaviour of Ungulates and Its Relationship to Management*. V. Geist and F. Walther, eds. Pp. 882–887. Morges, Switzerland: International Union for the Conservation of Nature (IUCN).

Deestra, H. A., D. White, and D. S. Wiggins. 1974. Nutritive Value of Fish of Lake Tanganyika. I. Amino Acid Composition. *African Journal of Tropical Hydrobiology and Fisheries* 3:2:161–166.

Delancey, Mark W. 1980. Cameroon National Food Policies and Organizations: The Green Revolution and Structural Proliferation. *Journal of African Studies* 7:2:109–122.

Delgado, C. 1978. *Livestock vs. Foodgrain Production in Southern Upper Volta*. Ann Arbor, Michigan: Center for Research on Economic Development.

Demment, M. W., and P. J. Van Soest. 1983. *Body Size, Digestive Capacity and Feeding Strategies of Herbivores*. Morrilton, Arkansas: Winrock International Livestock Research and Training Center.

Dey, Jennie. 1981. Gambian Women: Unequal Partners in Rice Development Projects? *Journal of Development Studies* 17:3:109–122.

———. 1984. *Women in Rice-Farming Systems: Focus: Sub-Saharan Africa*. Rome: Food and Agriculture Organization (FAO).

Dhamija, Jasleen. 1981. *Women and Handicrafts: Myth and Reality*. Seeds, a Periodic Publication. New York: Carnegie Corporation, Ford Foundation and the Population Council.

Dichter, D. 1980. Improved Mud Brick Silo for Storing Grain. *Appropriate Technology* 7:2:6–8.

Dinham, Barbara, and Colin Hines. 1984. *Agribusiness in Africa*. Trenton, New Jersey: Africa World Press.

Dinning, J. S. 1984. A Commentary: The Role of the Nutritionist in Third World Agricultural Planning. *Journal of Nutrition* 114:1739–40.

Dittch, Saa. 1981. Green Revolution or Evolution: The Case of Independent African Countries. *Africa Development* 6:3:103–105.

Dixon, Ruth. 1985. Seeing the Invisible Women Farmers in Africa: Improving Research and Data Collection Methods. In *Women as Food Producers in Developing Countries*. J. Monson and M. Kalb, eds. Pp. 19–36. Los Angeles: University of California, Los Angeles, African Studies Center and African Studies Association.

Dobbing, J. 1984. Infant Nutrition and Later Achievement. *Nutrition Reviews* 42:1–7.

Doe, P. E., M. Ahmed, M. Muslemidden, and K. Sachitnananthan. 1977. A Polyethylene Tent Drier for Improved Sun Drying of Fish. *Food Technology in Australia* 29:437–441.

Donahue, R. L., et al. 1971. *Soils: An Introduction to Soils and Plant Growth*. 3rd ed. Englewood Cliffs, New Jersey: Prentice-Hall.

Donkor, P. 1979. A Hand-Operated Screw Press for Extracting Palm Oil. *Appropriate Technology* 5:4:18–20.

Dorner, Peter, and Donald Kanel. 1971. The Economic Case for Land Reform: Employment, Income Distribution and Productivity. In *Land Reform in Latin America*. Peter Dorner, ed. Pp. 41–56. Land Economics Monograph No. 3. Madison: University of Wisconsin Land Tenure Center.

Dos Santos, T. 1970. The Structure of Dependence. *American Economic Review* 40:2:231–36.

372 · WORKING TOWARD SOLUTIONS

Dotson, Floyd, and Lillian O. Dotson. 1975. The Economic Role of Non-Indigenous
Ethnic Minorities in Colonial Africa. In *Colonialism in Africa, 1870–1960*. Vol. 4.
The Economics of Colonialism. Peter Duignan and L. H. Gann, eds. Pp. 565–613.
Cambridge: Cambridge University Press.

Dovring, Folke. 1959. The Share of Agriculture in a Growing Population *Monthly Bulletin
of Agricultural Economics and Statistics* 8 (August-September):1–11. Reprinted in
Agriculture in Economic Development, 1964. Carl K. Eicher and Lawrence W. Witt,
eds. Pp. 78–98. New York: McGraw Hill Book Co.

Drachoussoff, V. 1965. *Agricultural Change in the Belgian Congo: 1945–1960*. Stanford,
California: Stanford University Food Research Institute.

Due, Jean, and Rebecca Summary. 1982. Constraints to Women and Development in Africa. *Journal of Modern African Studies* 20:1:155–166.

Due, Jean M., and Marcia White. n.d. Female Farm Households in Zambia: Further Evidence of Poverty. Urbana-Champaign: University of Illinois, Department of Agricultural Economics. Mimeograph.

Due, Jean M., and Timothy Mudena, with Patricia Miller and Marcia White. 1985.
Women's Contributions to Farming Systems and Household Income in Zambia. WID
(Women in Development) Series Working Paper No. 85. Ann Arbor: Michigan State
University.

Duhring, J. L. 1984. Nutrition in Pregnancy. In *Nutrition Reviews' Present Knowledge in
Nutrition*. 5th edition. Washington, D.C.: The Nutrition Foundation Inc.

Duignan, Peter and L. H. Gann. 1975. Economic Achievements of the Colonizers: An Assessment. In *Colonialism in Africa, 1870–1960*. Vol. 4, *The Economics of Colonialism*. Peter Duignan and L. H. Gann, eds. Pp. 628–683. Cambridge: Cambridge University Press.

Dumont, R. 1962. *L'Afrique Noir est Mal Partie*. Paris: Editorial Du Seuil. Economic
Commission for Africa (ECA).

———. 1983. *ECA and Africa's Development 1983–2000: A Preliminary Perspective
Study*. Addis Ababa, Ethiopia: Economic Commission for Africa.

———. 1984. *Apparent Discrepancy Between Increasing Resource Allocation to Food
and Agriculture in Africa and the Declining Performance of the Sector*. Addis Ababa,
Ethiopia: Economic Division, Economic Commission for Africa, Council of Minis-
ters. (E/ECA/CM) 10/21.

Eckholm, E. P. 1975. The Firewood Crisis. *Natural History* 84:8:6–22.

ECOWAS (Economic Community of West African States). 1984. Resolution of the Authority of Heads of State and Government on Economic Recovery of West Africa.
Addis Ababa, Ethiopia: Economic Community of West African States (ECOWAS).

Eicher, Carl K. 1982. Facing Up to Africa's Food Crisis. *Foreign Affairs* 61:1:151–174.

Eicher, Carl K., and Doyle C. Baker. 1982. *Research on Agricultural Development in Sub-
Saharan Africa: A Critical Survey*. MSU International Development Paper No. 1. Department of Agricultural Economics. East Lansing: Michigan State University.

Eicher, Carl K., and John M. Staatz, eds. 1984. *Agricultural Development in the Third
World*. Baltimore: Johns Hopkins University Press.

Eicher, Carl K., and Lawrence W. Witt, eds. 1964. *Agriculture in Economic Development*.
New York: McGraw Hill Book Co.

Eicher, C. K., T. Zalla, J. Kocher, and F. Winch. 1970. *Employment Generation in African Agriculture*. East Lansing: Michigan State University, Institute of International
Agriculture.

Eka, O. U. 1980. Effect of Fermentation on the Nutrient Status of Locust Beans. *Food
Chemistry* 5:303–308.

Elloitt, H. 1977. Farming Systems Research in Francophone Africa: Methods and Results.
Ford Foundation Farming Systems Seminar. Tunis.

Enke, Stephen. 1962a. Industrialization through Greater Productivity in Agriculture. *Review of Economics and Statistics* 44:88–91.

———. 1962b. Economic Development with Limited and Unlimited Supplies of Labor. *Oxford Economic Papers* 14:158–72.

Essang, S., and A. Mabawonku. 1974. *Determinants and Impact of Rural-Urban Migration: A Case Study of Selected Communities in Western Nigeria.* East Lansing: Michigan State University, Department of Agricultural Economics.

Evans, I., and D. Wharton. 1977. The Lorena Mudstove: A Wood-Conserving Cookstove. *Appropriate Technology* 4:2:8–10.

Evans, Janis. 1983. Women's Involvement in the Seasonal Credit Programs in the Phalombe Rural Development Project. Paper presented at the National Credit Seminar. Chintheche, Malawi. Mimeograph.

Evans-Pritchard, E. E. 1940. *The Nuer.* Oxford: Oxford University Press.

FAO (Food and Agriculture Organization). 1974. *Handbook on Nutritional Requirements.* FAO Nutritional Studies, No. 28:WHO Monograph Series, No 61. Rome: Food and Agriculture Organization (FAO).

———. 1978a. Tenth FAO Regional Conference for Africa. Africa Regional Conference (ARC/785). Arusha, Tanzania: Food and Agriculture Organization (FAO).

———. 1978b. Regional Food Plan for Africa. Rome: Food and Agriculture Organization (FAO).

———. 1978c. *Report on the Agro-Ecological Zones Project.* Vol. 1. *Methodology and Results for Africa.* Rome: Food and Agriculture Organization (FAO).

———. 1981. Map of the Fuelwood Situation in the Developing Countries. *Unasylva* (Supple.). Rome: Food and Agriculture Organization (FAO).

———. 1983a. *Interim Report on Constraints on Food Production in Low-income Food Deficit Countries of Africa. Rome: Food and Agriculture Organization (FAO).* Committee on Food Security.

———. 1983b. *Time Allocation Survey: A Tool for Anthropologists, Economists and Nutritionists.* Expert Consultation on Women in Food Production, December 7–14. Rome: Food and Agriculture Organization (FAO), Food Policy and Nutrition Division. ESH: WIFP/83/17.

———. 1984. Harare Declaration on the Food Crisis in Africa Adopted by the 13th FAO Regional Conference for Africa on 25 July 1984. Rome: Food and Agriculture Organization (FAO). Mimeograph.

———. 1984. *1983 FAO Production Yearbook* 37:132–135. Rome: Food and Agriculture Organization (FAO).

———. 1985. *1984 FAO Production Yearbook.* Rome: Food and Agriculture Organization (FAO).

Fei, John C. H., Gustav Ranis, and Shirley W. Y. Kuo. 1979. *Growth with Equity: The Taiwan Case.* New York: Oxford University Press for the World Bank.

Ferguson, Anne, and Nancy Horn. 1985. Situating Agricultural Research: Class and Gender Issues in Project Advisement. In *Women Creating Wealth: Transforming Economic Development.* R. Gallin and A. Spring, eds. Pp. 85–90. Washington, D.C.: Association for Women in Development.

Fisher, S. L. 1961. Africa: Mother and Muse. *Antioch Review* 21:305–318.

Fishlow, A. 1972. Brazilian Size Distribution of Income. *Proceedings of the American Economic Review* 62:391–402.

Fleuret, Patrick, and Anne Fleuret. 1980. Nutrition, Consumption and Agricultural Change. *Human Organization* 39:3:250–260.

Flink, J. M. 1978. Intermediate Moisture Food Products in the American Marketplace. *Journal of Food Processing & Preservation* 1:324–339.

Foley, G., and G. Bernard. 1984. *Farm and Community Forestry.* Earthscan Energy Information Programme. Washington, D.C.: International Institute for Environment and Development.

Foley, G., P. Moss, and L. Timberlake. 1984. *Stoves and Trees*. An Earthscan Paperback. Washington, D.C.: International Institute for Environment and Development.

Fordham, J. R., C. E. Wells, and L. H. Chen. 1975. Sprouting of Seeds and Nutrient Composition of Seeds and Sprouts. *Journal of Food Science* 40:552–556.

Forrest, Tom. 1981. Agricultural Policies in Nigeria, 1900–78. In *Rural Development in Tropical Africa*. Judith Heyer, Pepe Roberts, and Gavin Williams, eds. Pp. 222–58. London: The Macmillan Publishing Co.

Fortes, Meyer. 1958 Introduction. In *The Development Cycle in Domestic Groups*. Cambridge Papers in Social Anthropology, No. 1. J. R. Goody, ed. Pp. 1–14. Cambridge: Cambridge University Press.

Fortmann, Louise. 1978. *Women and Tanzanian Agriculture Development*. Economic Research Bureau Paper 77.4. Dar-es-Salaam, Tanzania: Economic Research Bureau, University of Dar-es-Salaam.

———. 1981. The Plight of the Invisible Farmer: The Affect of National Agricultural Policy on the Women in Africa. In *Women and Technology Change*. R. Dauber and M. Cain, eds. Pp. 205–214. Boulder, Colorado: Westview Press and American Association for the Advancement of Science.

———. 1984. Economic Status and Women's Participation in Agriculture: A Botswana Case Study. *Rural Sociology* 49:3:452–464.

Frank, A. G. 1966. The Development of Underdevelopment. *Monthly Review* 18:4:17–31.

Franke, R., and B. Chasin. 1980. *Seeds of Famine: Ecological Destruction and the Development Dilemma in the West African Sahel*. Montclair, New Jersey: Allanheld and Osmun.

Frankel, Francine R. 1971. *India's Green Revolution: Economic Gains and Political Costs*. Princeton: Princeton University Press.

Frankel, S. H. 1963. Some Economic Aspects of the Conservation and Development of Wild Life Resources in Modern African States. In *Conservation of Nature and Natural Resources in Modern African States*. Morges, Switzerland: IUCN.

Fresco, Louise O. 1984. *Comparing Anglophone and Francophone Approaches to Farming Systems Research and Extension*. Farming Systems Support Project (FSSP) Networking Paper No. 1.

———. 1985. Food Security and Women: Implications for Agricultural Research. Paper presented at the International Workshop on Women's Role in Food Self-Sufficiency and Food Strategies. January 14–19. Paris: ORSTOM/CIE.

Freund, Bill. 1984. *The Making of Contemporary Africa*. Bloomington: Indiana University Press.

Fried, M. H. 1968. On the Concepts of "Tribe" and "Tribal Society." In *Essays on the Problem of Tribe*. American Ethnological Society Proceedings. Seattle: University of Washington Press.

Furtado, Celso. 1970. *Economic Development of Latin America: A Survey from Colonial Times to the Cuban Revolution*. Cambridge: Cambridge University Press.

Galtung, J. 1971. A Structural Theory of Imperialism. *Journal of Peace Research* 2:81–116.

Garg, H. P., P. C. Pande, and K. P. Thanvi. 1980. Designing a Suitable Biogas Plant for India. *Appropriate Technology* 7:1:29–31.

Gastellu, J. M. 1977. L'Absence de differenciation économique en Pays Serer. In *ORSTOM, 1977: Essais sur la Reproduction de Formations Sociales Dominées*. Paris: ORSTOM.

Gaury, C. 1977. Agricultural Mechanization. In *Food Crops of the Lowland Tropics*. C. Leakey and J. Wills, eds. Pp. 273–294. Oxford: Oxford University Press.

Gee, M., D. Farkas, and A. R. Rahman. 1977. Some Concepts for the Development of Intermediate Moisture Foods. *Food Technology* 31:4:58–64.

Gersowitz, Mark, Carlos F. Diaz-Alejandro, Gustav Ranis, and Mark R. Rosenweig, eds. 1982. *The Theory and Practice of Economic Development: Essays in Honor of Sir W. Arthur Lewis*. Boston: George Allen and Unwin.

Ghai, Dharam, and Samir Radwan, eds. 1983. *Agrarian Policies and Rural Poverty in Africa*. Geneva: International Labor Office.

Ghosh, B. N. 1978. A Bicycle-Operated PTO Unit for Small-Scale Farm Jobs. *World Crops* 30:222–224.

Gibbs, Jernea L., Jr. 1965. *Peoples of Africa*. New York: Holt, Rinehart & Winston.

Gilbert, E. H., D. W. Norman, and F. E. Winch. 1980. *Farming Systems Research: A Critical Appraisal*. MSU Rural Development Paper No. 6. East Lansing, Michigan: Department of Agricultural Economics, Michigan State University.

Gladwin, C. H. 1975. A Model of the Supply of Smoked Fish from Cape Coast to Kumasi. In *Formal Methods in Economic Anthropology*. S. Plattner, ed. Pp. 77–127. Washington, D.C.: American Anthropological Association.

Gladwin, Christina, Kathleen Staudt, and Della McMillan. 1984. Reaffirming the Agricultural Role of African Women: One Solution to the Food Crisis. *Proceedings of the Association of Facilities of Agriculture in Africa, Fifth General Conference on Food Security*. Manzini, Swaziland.

Glantz, M. H., ed. 1976. *The Politics of Natural Disaster*. New York: Praeger Publishers.

Golden, Michael H. N. and Alan A. Jackson. 1984. Chronic and Severe Undernutrition. In *Nutrition Reviews' Present Knowledge in Nutrition*. Pp. 57–67. Washington, D.C.: Nutrition Foundation Inc.

Goldschmidt, Walter. 1975. A National Livestock Bank: An Institutional Device for Rationalizing the Economy of Tribal Pastoralists. *International Development Review* 17:2:2–6.

Gomez, J. B., R. P. Bates, and E. M. Ahmed. 1980. Flexible Pouch Process Development and Evaluation of Pasteurized-Refrigerated Mango Slices. *Journal of Food Science* 45:1592–1594.

Good, R. A., G. Fernandes, and A. West. 1984. Nutrition and Immunity. In *Nutrition Reviews' Present Knowledge in Nutrition*. 5th ed. Pp. 693–710. Washington, D.C.: The Nutrition Foundation.

Goody, J. 1962. *Death, Property and the Ancestors*. London: Tavistock.

Grainger, A. 1982. *Desertification: How People Make Deserts, How People Can Stop, and Why They Don't*. Washington, D.C.: Earthscan, International Institute for Environment and Development.

Grant, J. P. 1985. *The State of the World's Children 1985*. Cambridge: Oxford University Press for the United Nations Children's Fund (UNICEF).

Green, L. F. 1976. Sulphur Dioxide and Food Preservation—A Review. *Food Chemistry* 1:103–124.

Griffin, Keith. 1974. *The Political Economy of Agrarian Change: An Essay on the Green Revolution*. Cambridge: Harvard University Press.

Griffiths, Ieuan. 1984. *An Atlas of African Affairs*. London: Methuen.

Gryseels, G. 1984. On-Farm Animal Traction Research: Experience in Ethiopia with the Introduction of the Use of Single Oxen for Crop Cultivation. *Proceedings of Kansas State University's 1983 Farming Systems Research Symposium*. Pp. 419–430. Farming Systems Research Paper Series No. 6. Manhatten: Kansas State University.

Gubbins, P. 1980. Improved Cooking Stoves Involving the User. *Proceedings, Bio-Energy 1980*. Pp. 259–260. Washington, D.C.: Bio-Energy Council.

Gusau, Alhaji Ibrahim. 1981. Nigeria's Green Revolution. *Africa Report* 26:4:19–22.

Guyer, Jane. 1977. *The Women's Farming System: The Lekie, Southern Cameroon*.

Yaounde, Cameroon: National Advanced School of Agriculture.

———. 1981. Household and Community in African Studies. *African Studies Review* 24:2/3:87–138.

———. 1984. *Family and Farm in Southern Cameroon*. African Research Studies. No. 15. Boston: African Studies Center, Boston University.

Gwynne, M. D., and R. H. V. Bell. 1968. Selection of Vegetation Components by Grazing Ungulates in the Serengeti National Park. *Nature* 220:390–393.

Haakonsen, Jan M. 1983. *Somalia's Fisheries Case Study*. FAO Fisheries Report No. 295, supplement. Rome: Food and Agriculture Organization (FAO).

Haaland, R. 1979. *Man's Role in the Changing Habitat of Mernas Under the Old Kingdom of Ghana*. ILCA Working Document No. 2. Addis Ababa, Ethiopia: International Livestock Center for Africa.

Hall, D. O. 1979. Plants as an Energy Source. *Nature* 278:114–117.

———. 1980. Bio-Energy—A World Perspective. *Proceedings, Bio-Energy 1980*. Pp. 259–260. Washington, D.C.: Bio-Energy Council.

Hall, D. O., G. W. Barnard, and P. A. Moss. 1982. *Biomass and Energy in the Developing Countries*. New York: Pergamon Press.

Hallberg, L. 1984. Iron. In *Nutrition Reviews' Present Knowledge in Nutrition*. 5th ed. Pp. 459–478. Washington, D.C.: The Nutrition Foundation.

Hamilton, S., B. Popkin, and D. Spicer. 1984. *Women and Nutrition in Third World Countries*. New York: Praeger Publishers, CBS Educational and Professional Publishing.

Hammond, Peter, B. 1966. *Yatenga*. New York: The Free Press.

Hanger, Jane, and Jon Moris. 1973. Women and the Household Economy. In *Mwea: An Irrigated Rice Settlement in Kenya*. R. Chambers and J. Joris, eds. Pp. 209–244. Munich: Weltforum Verlag.

Hanpongpandh, Somporn. 1982. Modeling the Impact of the ASEAN Food Security Reserve. In *Food Security: Theory, Policy and Perspectives from Asia and the Pacific Rim*. Anthony H. Chisolm and Rodney Tyres, eds. Pp. 281–306. Lexington, Massachusetts: Lexington Books.

Hanlon, J. 1984. Mozambique: *The Revolution Under Fire*. London: Zed Books.

Hansen, Art. 1981. Refugee Dynamics: Angolans in Zambia 1966 to 1972. *International Migration Review* 15:175–194.

Hansen, Art, and Anthony Oliver-Smith, eds. 1982. *Involuntary Migration and Resettlement*. Boulder, Colorado: Westview Press.

Hansen, Emmanuel. 1981. Public Policy and the Food Question in Ghana. *Africa Development* 6:3:103–105.

Hardin, G. 1968. The Tragedy of the Commons. *Science* 162:1243–1248.

Hare, F. K. 1983. *Climate and Desertification: A Revised Analysis*. WCP-44. Geneva: World Meteorological Organization (WMO) and United Nations Environment Program (UNEP).

Harris, John R., and Michael P. Todaro. 1970. Migration, Unemployment and Development: A Two Sector Analysis. *American Economic Review* 60:1:126–42.

Harris, Marvin. 1979. *Cultural Materialism*. New York: Random House.

Harrison, P. 1976. Inappropriate AT. *New Scientist* 71:236–7.

Harriss, Barbara. 1979. There Is Method in My Madness: Or Is It Vice Versa? Measuring Agricultural and Market Performance. *Food Research Institute Studies* 17:2:197–218.

Hart, K. 1982. *The Political Economy of West African Agriculture*. Cambridge: Cambridge University Press.

Hart, R. 1985. Crop/Livestock Interactions as Crop Production Determinants. Cornell International Agriculture Mimeograph 107. Ithaca, New York: Cornell University.

Hart, R., and A. Pinchinat. 1980. Integrative Agricultural Systems Research. Paper presented at the Caribbean Seminar of Farming Systems Research Methodology. Basse-

Terre, Guadeloupe.

Harwood, R. R. 1979. *Small Farm Development*. Boulder, Colorado: Westview Press.

Haugerud, A. 1982. The Limits of Household Analysis in the Study of Agricultural Production: A Central Kenya Case. Paper presented at the Annual Meeting of the American Anthropological Association, Washington, D.C., December 1982.

Haugerud, A. 1983. The Consequences of Land Tenure Reform Among Smallholders in the Kenya Highlands. *Rural Africana* 15–16 (Winter-Spring): 65–89.

Hawkesworth, D., ed. 1984. *Advancing Agricultural Production in Africa*. Farnham Royal, Buckshire, England: Commonwealth Agricultural Bureau.

Hayami, Yijiro. 1984. Assessment of the Green Revolution. In *Agricultural Development in the Third World*. Carl K. Eicher and John M. Staatz, eds. Pp. 389–90. Baltimore: Johns Hopkins University Press.

Hayami, Yujiro, and Vernon W. Ruttan. 1971. *Agricultural Development: An International Perspective*. Baltimore: Johns Hopkins University Press.

Hegsted, D. M. 1984. Energy Requirements. In *Nutrition Reviews' Present Knowledge in Nutrition*. 5th ed. Pp. 1–6. Washington, D.C.: The Nutrition Foundation, Inc.

Helleiner, G. 1975. Smallholder Decision Making: Tropical African Evidence. In *Agriculture in Development Theory*. L. Reynolds, ed. Pp. 27–52. New Haven: Yale University Press.

Herzka, A. 1980. Post-harvest Food Crop Conservation. *Progress in Food and Nutrition Science* 4:3/4:138.

Hesseltine, C. W. 1979. Some Important Fermented Foods of Mid-Asia, the Middle East, and Africa. *Journal of American Oil Chemist Society* 56:367–374.

Heyer, J. 1971. Linear Programming Analysis of Constraints on Peasant Farms in Kenya. *Food Research Institute Studies* 10:1:55–67.

Heyer, J., J. K. Maitha, and W. M. Senga, eds. 1976. *Agricultural Development in Kenya*. Nairobi: Oxford University Press.

Heyer, J., P. Roberts, and G. Williams, eds. 1981. *Rural Development in Tropical Africa*. New York: St. Martin's Press.

Hildebrand, P. E. 1981. Combining Disciplines in Rapid Appraisal: The Sondeo. *Agricultural Administration* 8:423–432.

Hildebrand, P., E. Martinez, and R. Ortiz. 1985. Generalized Organization of FSR/E Regions and Field Teams. *Farming Systems Support Project (FSSP) Newsletter* 3:2:1–3.

Hill, Polly. 1963. *Migrant Cocoa Farmers of Southern Ghana*. Cambridge: Cambridge University Press.

Hinderink, J., and J. J. Sterkenberg. 1983. Agricultural Policy and Production in Africa: The Aims, the Methods and the Means. *The Journal of Modern African Studies* 21:1:1–23.

Hirschman, Albert O. 1958. *The Strategy of Economic Development*. New Haven: Yale University Press.

———. 1977. A Generalized Linkage Approach to Development, with Special Reference to Staples. *Economic Development and Cultural Change* 25 (supp.): 67–98.

———. 1981a. The Rise and Decline of Development Economics. In *Essays in Trespassing: Economics to Politics and Beyond*. New York: Cambridge University Press.

———. 1981b. *Essays in Trespassing: Economics to Politics and Beyond*. New York: Cambridge University Press.

Hobhouse, L. T., G. C. Wheeler, and M. Ginsburg. 1915. *The Material Culture and Social Institutions of the Simpler Peoples*. London: Chapman and Hall.

Hogedorn, Jan S. 1975. Economic Initiative and African Cash Farming: Precolonial Origins and Early Colonial Developments. In *Colonialism in Africa, 1870–1960*. Vol. 4. The Economics of Colonialism. Peter Duignan and L. H. Gann, eds. Pp. 283–328. Cambridge: Cambridge University Press.

Holdcroft, Lane E. 1984. The Rise and Fall of Community Development, 1950–65: A Critical Assessment. In *Agricultural Development in the Third World*. Carl K. Eicher and John M. Staatz, eds. Pp. 46–58. Baltimore: Johns Hopkins University Press.

Hopcraft, David. 1970. East Africa: The Advantages of Farming Game. *SPAN* 13:1:29–32.

Hopkins, A. G. 1973. *An Economic History of West Africa*. London: Longman.

Hopper, W. David. 1965. Allocation Efficiency in a Traditional Indian Agriculture. *Journal of Farm Economics* 47:3:611–24.

Horowitz, Michael M. 1973. Ethnic Boundary Maintenance Among Pastoralists and Farmers in the Western Sudan (Niger). *Journal of Asian and African Studies* 7:1:106–114.

———. 1979. *The Sociology of Pastoralism and African Livestock Projects*. USAID Program Evaluation Discussion Paper No. 6. Washington, D.C.: United States Agency for International Development.

Hoskins, M. W. 1980. Community Forestry Depends on Women. *Unasylva* 32:130:27–32.

Howell, Nancy. 1979. *Demography of the Dobe !Kung*. New York: Academic Press.

Hunter, John M., and George Kwaku Ntiri. 1978. Speculations on the Future of Shifting Agriculture in Africa. *The Journal of Developing Areas* 12:183–208.

Hudson, J. F., and S. E. O. Mahgoub. 1980. Naturally-Occurring Antioxidants in Leaf Lipids. *Journal of the Science of Food and Agriculture* 31:646–650.

Hyden, G. 1980. *Beyond Ujamaa in Tanzania*. Berkeley: University of California Press.

Hyden, G. 1985. No Shortcuts to Progress. In *Bulletin de Liaison, Centre de Recherche pour l'Exchange et le Développement Universitaire (CREDU)*, Nairobi.

ILCA (International Livestock Center for Africa). 1983. *ILCA Annual Report 1982: A Year in the Service of African Livestock Improvement*. Addis Ababa, Ethiopia: International Livestock Center for Africa.

———. 1985. *ILCA Annual Report 1984*. Addis Ababa, Ethiopia: International Livestock Center for Africa (ILCA).

International Labour Office. 1970. *Towards Full Employment: A Programme for Columbia*. Geneva: International Labour Office (ILO).

———. 1971. *Matching Employment Opportunities and Expectations: A Programme of Action for Ceylon*. Geneva: International Labour Office (ILO).

———. 1972. *Employment, Incomes and Equality: A Strategy for Increasing Productive Employment in Kenya*. Geneva: International Labour Office (ILO).

———. 1974. *Sharing in Development: A Program of Employment, Equity and Growth for the Philippines*. Geneva: International Labour Office (ILO).

———. 1976a. *Employment, Growth and Basic Needs: A One-World Problem*. Geneva: International Labour Office (ILO).

———. 1976b. *Growth, Employment and Equity: A Comprehensive Strategy for the Sudan*. Geneva: International Labour Office (ILO).

Israel, R., ed. 1983. *Maternal and Infant Nutrition Reviews*. An International Nutrition Communication Service Publication Series. Newton, Massachusetts: Education Development Center.

Jabara, C., and R. Thompson. 1980. Agricultural Comparative Advantage under International Price Uncertainty: The Case of Senegal. *American Journal of Agricultural Economics* 62:2:188–198.

Jackson, J., and M. Mehrer. 1978. The Food Preservation Center: An Exercise in Appropriate Technology. *Food Technology* 32:4:83–86.

Jackson, P. B. N. 1971. The African Great Lakes Fisheries: Past Present and Future. *African Journal of Tropical Hydrobiology and Fisheries* 1:1:35–48.

Jahnke, H. E. 1982. *Livestock Production Systems and Livestock Development in Tropical Africa*. Kiel, West Germany: Kieler Wissenschaftsverlag Vauk.

Jeffries, R. 1982. Rawlings and the Political Economy of Underdevelopment in Ghana.

African Affairs 81:324:307–317.

Jiggins, J. 1984. *Farming Systems Research: Do Any of the "FSR" Models Offer a Positive Capacity for Addressing Women's Agricultural Needs?* Consultative Group in International Agricultural Research (CGIAR). Working Paper No. 4, Draft 1.

Johnny M., J. Kaimu, and P. Richards. 1981. Upland and Swamp Rice Farming Systems in Sierra Leone: The Social Context of Technological Change. *Africa* 15:2:596–620.

Johnston, Bruce F. 1970. Agriculture and Structural Transformation in Developing Countries: A Survey of Research. *Journal of Economic Literature* 3:2:369–404.

Johnston, Bruce F., and William C. Clark. 1982. *Redesigning Rural Development: A Strategic Perspective*. Baltimore: Johns Hopkins University Press.

Johnston, Bruce F., and Peter Kilby. 1975. *Agriculture and Structural Transformation: Economic Strategies in Late-Developing Countries*. New York: Oxford University Press.

Johnston, Bruce F., and John W. Mellor. 1961. The Role of Agriculture in Economic Development. American Economic Review 51:4:566–93.

Joint FAO/WHO Expert Committee on Nutrition. 1976. *Food and Nutrition Strategies in National Development*. World Health Organization (WHO) Technical Report Series No. 584. Food and Agriculture Organization (FAO) Nutrition Meetings Report Series, No. 56.

Jones, W. O. 1960. Economic Man in Africa. *Food Research Institute Studies* 1:2:107–34.

———. 1972. *Marketing Staple Foods in Tropical Africa*. Ithaca: Cornell University Press.

Jorgenson, D. W. 1961. The Development of a Dual Economy. *Economic Journal* 71:309–34.

Kamarck, A. 1976. *The Tropics and Economic Development*. Baltimore: Johns Hopkins University Press.

Kandel, R. S. 1984. *Mechanisms Governing the Climate of the Sahel: A Survey of Recent Modeling and Observational Studies*. Club du Sahel D(84) 252, CILSS. Paris: Organization for Economic Cooperation in Development (OECD).

Kang, B. T., et al. 1984. *Alley Cropping a Stable Alternative to Shifting Cultivation*. Ibadan, Nigeria: International Institute of Tropical Agriculture.

Kao, Charles H. C., Kurt R. Anschel, and Carl K. Eicher. 1964. Disguised Unemployment in Agriculture: A Survey. In *Agriculture in Economic Development*. Carl K. Eicher and Lawrence W. Witt, eds. Pp. 129–44. New York: McGraw-Hill Book Co.

Kaplan, et al. 1971. *Area Handbook for Ghana*. Washington: United States Government Printing Office.

Kassapu, S. 1979. The Impact of Alien Technology. *Ceres* 12:1:29–33.

Kelly, H. 1978. Photovoltaic Power System: A Tour Through the Alternatives. *Science* 199:634–643.

Kirkby, R., ed. 1984. *Crop Improvement in Eastern and Southern Africa: Research Objectives and On-Farm Testing*. Ottawa, Canada: International Development Research Center (IDRC).

King, F. H. 1911. *Farmers of Forty Centuries*. Madison, Wisconsin: Mrs. F. H. King.

King, J. M., and B. R. Heath. 1975. Game Domestication for Animal Production in Africa: Experience at the Galena Ranch. *World Animal Review* 16:23–30.

King, J. M., B. R. Heath, and R. E. Hill. 1977. Game Domestication for Animal Production in Kenya: Theory and Practice. *Journal of Agricultural Science,* 89:445–457.

Kitching, G. 1980. *Class and Economic Change in Kenya*. New Haven: Yale University Press.

Ki-Zerbo, J. 1981. Women and the Energy Crisis in the Sahel. *Unasylva* 33:131:24–29.

Knight, J. B., and G. Lenta. 1980. Has Capitalism Underdeveloped the Labour Reserves of South Africa? *Oxford Bulletin of Economics and Statistics* 42:3:157–201.

Koenig, D. 1982. Labor Allocation, Women's Work and Social Stratification in the Rural Malian Household. Paper presented at the Annual Meeting of the American Anthropological Association, Washington, D.C., December 1982.

Kowal, J., and A. Kassam. 1978. *Agricultural Ecology of Savannah*. Oxford: Clarendon Press.

Kravis, I. B. 1970. Trade as a Handmaiden of Growth: Similarities between the Nineteenth and Twentieth Centuries. *Economic Journal* 80:320:850–72.

Krishna, Raj. 1967. Agricultural Price Policy and Economic Development. In *Agricultural Development and Economic Growth*. Herman M. Southworth and Bruce F. Johnston, eds. Pp. 497–540. Ithaca, New York: Cornell University Press.

———. 1973. Unemployment in India. *Indian Journal of Agricultural Economics* 28:1:1–23.

Krostitz, W. 1979. The New International Market for Game Meat. *Unasylva* 31:123:32–36.

Kunkle, S. H., and A. J. Dye. 1981. The Effects of Forest Clearing on Soils and Sedimentation. In *Tropical Agricultural Hydrology*. R. Lal and E. W. Russell, eds. Pp. 99–109. New York: John Wiley & Sons.

Kwamena-Poh, Michael, John Tosh, Richerd Waller, and Michael Tidy. 1982. *African History in Maps*. London: Longman.

Kydd, Jonathan. 1982. *Measuring Peasant Differentiation for Policy Purposes: A Report on a Cluster Analysis Classification of the Population of the Lilongwe Land Development Programme, Malawi for 1970 and 1979*. Zomba, Malawi: Government Printer.

Kydd, J., and R. Christiansen. 1982. Structural Change in Malawi Since Independence: Consequences of a Development Strategy Based on Large-Scale Agriculture. *World Development* 10:5:355–376.

Labuza, T. P. 1978. The Properties of Water in Relationship to Water Binding in Foods: A Review. *Journal of Food Processing and Preservation*. 1:167–190.

Lal, R. 1981. Deforestation of the Tropical Rainforest and Hydrological Problems. In *Tropical Agricultural Hydrology*. R. Lal and E. W. Russell, eds. Pp. 131–140. New York: John Wiley & Sons.

Lal, R., and D. Greenland eds. 1979. *Soil Physical Properties and Crop Production in the Tropics*. Chichester, England: John Wiley & Sons.

Lamb, G. 1974. *Peasant Politics in Murang'a*. New York: St. Martin's Press.

Lancaster, C. 1976. Women, Horticulture and Society in Sub-Saharan Agriculture. *American Anthropologist* 78:3:539–564.

———. 1979. The Influence of Extensive Agriculture on the Study of Sociopolitical Organization and the Interpretation of History. *American Ethnologist* 6:2:329–348.

Lardy, Nicholas R. 1984. Prices, Markets, and the Chinese Peasant. In *Agricultural Development in the Third World*. Carl K. Eicher and John M. Staatz, eds. Pp. 420–35. Baltimore: Johns Hopkins University Press.

Latham, M. C. 1984. International Nutrition Problems and Policies. In *World Food Issues*. M. Drosdoff, ed. Pp. 55–64. Ithaca, New York: Center for the Analysis of World Food Issues, Program in International Agriculture, Cornell University.

Lawson, R. 1972. *Changing Economy of the Lower Volta, 1954–67*. London: Oxford University Press.

Lee, Richard B. 1979. *The !Kung San: Men, Women, and Work in a Foraging Society*. Cambridge: Cambridge University Press.

Lee, Richard B., and Irven Devore, eds. 1968. *Man the Hunter*. New York: Aldine Publishing Company.

Leeuw, P. M. de, and P. A. Konandreas. 1982. The Use of an Integer and Stochastic Model to Estimate the Productivity of Four Pastoral Production Systems in West Africa. *Proceedings of the National Beef Conference*, Kaduna, Nigeria, July.

Lefort, J. 1982. *Les recherche—développement intégrés en milieu rural*. Montpellier, France: IFARC/GERDAT.

Leibel, R. L., E. Pollit, and D. B. Greenfield. 1981. A Study of the Effects of Iron Deficiency on Cognitive Function in Children. In *Nutrition and Behavior*. S. A. Miller, ed. Pp. 299–301. Philadelphia: Franklin Institute Press.

Lele, Uma. 1975. *The Design of Rural Development: Lessons from Africa*. Baltimore: Johns Hopkins University Press for the World Bank.

———. 1977. Considerations Related to Optimum Pricing and Marketing Strategies in Rural Development. In *Decision Making and Agriculture*. T. Dams and K. Hunt, eds. Lincoln: University of Nebraska Press.

———. 1984. Rural Africa: Modernization, Equity, and Long-Term Development. In *Agricultural Development in the Third World*. Carl K. Eicher and John M. Staatz, eds. Pp. 436–452. Baltimore and London: Johns Hopkins University Press.

Lele, U. and W. Candler. 1981. Food Security: Some East African Considerations. In *Food Security for Developing Countries*. A. Valdes, ed. Pp. 102–122. Boulder, Colorado: Westview Press.

Lemarchand, R. 1981. Comparative Political Clientelism: Structure, Process and Optic. In *Political Clientalism, Patronage and Development*. S. N. Eisenstadt and R. Lemarchand, eds. Pp. 7–32. Beverly Hills, California: Sage Publications.

———. *The World Bank in Rwanda*. Occasional paper. Bloomington: University of Indiana African Studies Program, University of Indiana.

Lennihan, Louise D. 1983. The Origins and Development of Agricultural Wage Labor in Northern Nigeria: 1886–1980. Ph.D. dissertation. Department of Anthropology. New York: Columbia University.

Leopold, C. A. and R. Ardrey. 1972. Toxic Substances in Plants and the Food Habits of Early Man. *Science* 176:512–514.

Leppington, B. 1980. Simple Technology for Making Cans. *Appropriate Technology* 7:1:15–17.

Leroux, Marcel. 1983. *The Climate of Tropical Africa: Atlas*. Paris: Editions Champions.

Levasseur, J. C., D. Sanni, and D. S. C. Spencer. 1981. Orientation of the Technology and Transfer Programme. Paper presented at the Annual Rice Review Meeting, West African Rice Development Association (WARDA).

Lewis, W. Arthur. 1954. Economic Development with Unlimited Supplies of Labour. *Manchester School of Economic and Social Studies* 22:2:139–91.

———. 1955. *The Theory of Economic Growth*. London: George Allen and Unwin.

———. 1972. Reflections on Unlimited Labor. In *International Economics and Development: Essays in Honor of Raul Prebisch*. Luis Eugenio Di Marco, ed. Pp. 75–96. New York: Academic Press.

Leys, C. 1974. *Underdevelopment in Kenya*. Berkeley: University of California Press. (1975) London: Heinemann.

———. 1978. Capital Accumulation, Class Formation and Dependency: The Significance of the Kenyan Case. *The Socialist Register* 1978:241–266.

Libaba, G. K. 1983. *Tanzania's Experience on Fisheries Management and Development Case Study*. Food and Agriculture Organization (FAO) Report No. 295. Rome: Food and Agriculture Organization (FAO).

LIFE (League for International Food Education). 1979. A Practical Method for Bean Storage. *LIFE Newsletter*, May. Pp. 3–4.

Lightfoot, C. J., and J. Posselt. 1977. Eland (*Taurotragus oryx*) as a Ranching Animal Complementary to Cattle in Rhodesia: 4 Management. *Rhodesian Agricultural Journal* 74:115–120.

Lindblad, D., and L. Druben. 1980. *Small Farm Grain Storage*, 3 volumes. Mt. Rainer, Maryland: Volunteers in Technical Assistance (VITA).

Lipinsky, E. S. 1978. Fuels from Biomass: Integration with Food and Materials Systems. *Science* 199:644–651.

Lipton, Michael. 1977. *Why Poor People Stay Poor: A Study of Urban Bias in World Development*. London: Temple-Smith.

Little, I. M. D. 1982. *Economic Development: Theory, Policy and International Relations*. New York: Basic Books.

Little, Peter S. 1984. Critical Socio-Economic Variables in African Pastoral Livestock Development: Toward a Comparative Framework. In *Livestock Development in Subsaharan Africa*. James R. Simpson and Phylo Evangelou, eds. Pp. 201–214. Boulder, Colorado: Westview Press.

Lofchie, M. 1975. Political and Economic Origins of African Hunger. *Journal of Modern African Studies* 13:4:551–567.

Lofchie, M., and S. K. Commins. 1984. *Food Deficits and Agricultural Policies in Sub-Saharan Africa*. The Hunger Project Papers, No. 2.

Lonsdale, J., and B. Berman. 1979. Coping with the Contradictions: The Development of the Colonial State in Kenya, 1895–1914. *Journal of African History* 20:4:487–505.

Lovejoy, D. 1980. Biogas in China. *Proceedings, Bio-Energy 1980*. Pp. 433–434. Washington, D.C.: Bio-Energy Council.

Luna, J. 1983. *Markets for Fisheries Products*. Food and Agriculture Organization (FAO) Report No. 295. Rome: Food and Agriculture Organization (FAO).

Mafaje, Archie. 1985. Food for Security and Peace in the SADCC Region. Paper presented at the United Nations University Seminar on Peace, Development and Regional Security in Africa, Addis Ababa, Ethiopia.

Mahdeviah, M. 1970. The Alternatives to Sanitary Tin Can for Packing Food Products. *Journal of Food Science Technology* 7:3–7.

Majumder, S. K. 1980. Storage and Pest Control Strategy for Preservation of Foodgrains in India. *Journal of Food Science Technology* 17:1/2:55–58.

Makanjula, G. A. 1974. A Machine for Preparing Pounded Yam and Similar Foods in Nigeria. *Appropriate Technology* 1:4:9–10.

Malaka, S. L. O. 1983. Economic Importance of Termites: Six Case Studies in Nigeria and Ghana. *The Nigerian Field* 47:222–230.

Maley, J. 1981. *Etudes palynologiques dans le Bassin de Tchad et paléoclimatologie de l'Afrique nord-tropicale de 30.000 ans à l'époque actuelle*. Travaux et documents de l'ORSTOM, no. 129, p. 58. Paris: ORSTOM.

Mantesch, Thomas J., et al. 1971. *A Generalized Simulation Approach to Agricultural Sector Analysis with Special Reference to Nigeria*. East Lansing: Michigan State University.

Marks, S. A. 1973. Prey Selection and Annual Harvest of Game in a Rural Zambian Community. *East African Wildlife Journal* 11:113–128.

Martin, Phyllis, and Patrick O'Meara, eds. 1977. *Africa*. Bloomington: Indiana University Press.

Matlon, P. J. 1983. Farmer Participation in Technology Evaluation—Five Case Studies from ICRISAT/West Africa. Paper presented at the Workshop on Farmer's Participation on the Development and Evaluation of Agricultural Technology, ICRISAT/SAFGRAD/IRAT. Ouagadougou, Burkina Faso: ICRISAT/SAFGRAD/IRAT.

May, Clifford. 1985. The Famine Workers. *New York Times Magazine*, December 1. Pp. 60–74.

May, R. M. 1977. Food Lost to Pests. *Nature* 267:669–670.

Mayer, P., ed. 1980. *Black Villagers in an Industrial Society: Anthropological Perspectives on Labour Migration in Southern Africa*. Cape Town: Oxford University Press.

McCracken, John. 1982. Experts and Expertise in Colonial Malawi. *African Affairs* 81:322:101–16.

McDowell, J. 1984. Appropriate Action Against Malnourishment: Appropriate Food Conservation Technology. *Appropriate Technology* 10:4:25–27.

McDowell, R. E. 1977. *Ruminant Products: More Than Meat and Milk*. Morrilton, Arkansas: Winrock International Livestock Research and Training Center.

———. 1984. Livestock Nutrition in Subsaharan Africa. In *Livestock Development in Subsaharan Africa*. James R. Simpson and Phylo Evangelou, eds. Pp. 43–60. Boulder, Colorado: Westview Press.

———. 1985. Crossbreeding in Tropical Areas with Emphasis on Milk, Health and Fitness. *Journal of Dairy Science* 68.

McDowell, R. E., and P. E. Hildebrand. 1980. *Integrated Crop and Animal Production: Making the Most of Resources Available on Small Farms in Developing Countries*. Working Paper. New York: Rockefeller Foundation.

McDowell, R. E., D. G. Sisler, E. C. Schermerhorn, J. D. Reed, and R. P. Bauer. 1983. Game or Cattle for Meat Production on Kenya Rangelands? Cornell International Agriculture Mimeograph 101. Ithaca, New York: Cornell University.

McGaffey, W. 1982. The Policy of National Integration in Zaire. *Journal of Modern African Studies* 20:1:87–105.

McMillan, Della E. 1983. A Resettlement Project in Upper Volta. Ph.D. Dissertation, Anthropology Department, Northwestern University.

———. 1984. *Changing Patterns of Grain Production in a Resettlement Scheme in Upper Volta*. Washington, D.C.: Southeast Consortium for International Development. Center for Women in Development.

McNamara, Robert S. 1973. Address to the Board of Governors. Nairobi, Kenya, September 24, 1972. Washington, D.C.: World Bank.

———. 1985. The Challenges to Sub-Saharan Africa. Sir John Crawford Memorial Lecture. Nov. 1, 1985. Washington, D.C.: Consultative Group on International Agricultural Research.

McNulty, Michael L. 1986. The Contemporary Map of Africa. In *Africa*. 2nd ed. Phyllis M. Martin and Patrick O'Meara, eds. Bloomington: Indiana University.

Meier, Gerald. 1976. *Leading Issues in Economic Development*. 3rd ed. New York: Oxford University Press.

Meillassoux, C. 1981. *Maidens, Meal and Money*. Cambridge: Cambridge University Press.

Meletnlema, T. M. 1978. Tanzania: Nutrition and Government Policy—Socialism as a Solution. In *Nutrition and National Policy*. B. Winikoff, ed. Pp. 291–324. Cambridge, Massachusetts: M.I.T. Press.

Mellor, John W. 1966. *The Economics of Agricultural Development*. Ithaca, New York: Cornell University Press.

———. 1976. *The New Economics of Growth: A Strategy for India and the Developing World*. Ithaca, New York: Cornell University Press.

———. 1985. The Changing World Food Situation—A CGIAR Perspective. In *International Food Policy Research Institute: Report 1984*. Washington, D.C.: International Food Policy Research Institute (IFPRI).

Mellor, John W., and Uma Lele. 1973. Growth Linkages of the New Foodgrain Technologies. *Indian Journal of Agricultural Economics* 28:1:35–55.

Mendelsohn, J. M. 1974. Rapid Techniques for Salt-Curing Fish: A Review. *Journal of Food Science* 39:125–127.

Mermelstein, N. H. 1978. Retort Pouch Earns 1978 IFT Food Technology Industrial Achievement Award. *Food Technology* 32:6:22–32.

Merrill, R., and T. Gage. 1978. *Energy Primer*. Menlo Park, California: Portola Institute.

Midwest Plan Service. 1980. *Low Temperature and Solar Grain Drying Handbook*. Ames: Iowa State University.

Miers, Suzanne and Igor Kopytoff, eds. 1977. *Slavery in Africa*. Madison: University of Wisconsin Press.

Miracle, M. P. 1967. *Agriculture in the Congo Basin: Tradition and Change in African Rural Economies*. Madison: University of Wisconsin Press.

Miranda, E. de, and R. Billaz. 1980. Méthodes de recherche en milieu sehélian: Les approches écologiques et agronomiques d'une démarche pluridisciplinaire: L'exemple de Maradi au Niger. *Agronomie Tropicale* 34:4:357–373.

MOA (Ministry of Agriculture). 1983. *Reaching Female Farmers Through Male Extension Workers*. Extension Aids Circular 2/83. Lilwongwe, Malawi: Ministry of Agriculture.

Molina, M. R., M. A. Batin, R. A. Gomez-Bremes, K. W. King, and R. Bressani. 1976. Heat Treatment: A Process to Control the Development of the Hard-to-Cook Phenomena in Black Beans (*Phaseolus vulgaris*). *Journal of Food Science* 42:661–666.

Moock, Peter. 1976. The Efficiency of Women as Farm Managers: Kenya. *American Journal of Agricultural Economics* 58:5:831–835.

Moody, T. 1980. Drying Maize for Storage in the Humid Tropics. *Appropriate Technology* 7:1:4–6.

Morris, M. 1976. Development of Capitalism in South African Agriculture: Class Struggle in the Countryside. *Economy and Society* 5:3:292–343.

Mossman, A. S. 1963. Wildlife Ranching in Southern Rhodesia. In *Conservation of Nature and Natural Resources in Modern African States*. 2 Vols. Pp. 247–249. Morges, Switzerland: International Union for the Conservation of Natural Resources.

Mudahar, M. S. and T. P. Hignett. 1981. *Energy and Fertilizer: Policy Implications and Options for Developing Countries*. International Fertilizer Development Center IFDC-T-19.

Muller, M. 1974. Aid, Corruption and Waste. *The Futurist* 64:398–400.

Munro, J. Forbes. 1976. *Africa and the International Economy, 1800–1960*. Totowa, New Jersey: Rowman and Littlefield.

Munslow, Barry. 1984. State Intervention in Africa: The Mozambique Experience. *The Journal of Modern African Studies* 22:2:199–221.

Murdock, George P. 1959. *Africa: Its Peoples and Their Culture History*. New York: McGraw-Hill Book Co.

Murray, M., D. J. Clifford, W. F. Snow, and W. I. M. McIntyre. 1981. Susceptibility to African Trypanosomiasis of N'Dama and Zebu Cattle in an Area of *Glossina moristans submoristans* Challenge. *The Veterinary Record* 109:503–510.

Murray, M., W. I. Morrison, and D. D. Whitelaw. 1982. Host Susceptibility to African Trypanosomiasis. In *Advances in Parasitology*. Vol. 21. J. R. Baker and R. Muller, eds. Pp. 1–68. London: Academic Press.

Murray, M., J. C. M. Trail, D. A. Turner, and Y. Wissocq. 1983. *Livestock Productivity and Trypanotolerance: Network Training Manual*. Addis Ababa, Ethiopia: International Livestock Centre for Africa (ILCA).

Myers, N. 1981. A Farewell to Africa. *International Wildlife* 11:6:36–47.

―――. 1982. Cape Buffalo, Not So Mean After All. *International Wildlife* 11:6:36–47.

Nair, P. K. R. 1982. *Soils and Soil Management in Agroforestry*. Nairobi, Kenya: International Center for Research on Agroforestry (ICRAF).

Narasunha, H. V., and H. R. S. Desikachar. 1978. Simple Procedures for Reducing the Cooking Time of Split Red Gram (*Cajanus cajan*). *Journal of Food Science and Technology* 15:149–152.

NAS (National Academy of Sciences). 1974. *Food Science in Developing Countries: A Selection of Unsolved Problems*. Washington, D.C.: National Academy of Sciences.

―――. 1973. *Ferrocement: Applications in Developing Countries*. Washington, D.C.: National Academy of Sciences.

——. 1976. *Energy for Rural Development: Renewable Resources and Alternative Technologies for Developing Countries*. Washington, D.C.: National Academy of Sciences.

——. 1978. *Postharvest Food Losses in Developing Countries*. Washington, D.C.: National Academy of Sciences.

Nicholls, William H. 1964. The Place of Agriculture in Economic Development. In *Agriculture in Economic Development*. Carl K. Eicher and Lawrence W. Witt, eds. Pp. 11–44. New York: McGraw-Hill Book Co.

Nicholson, Norman K. and John D. Esseks. 1978. The Politics of Food Scarcities in Developing Countries. *International Organization* 32:3:679–719.

Nicholson, S. E. 1976. *A Climatic Chronology for Africa: Synthesis of Geological, Historical, and Meteorological Information and Data*. Ph.D. thesis. Department of Meteorology. Madison: University of Wisconsin.

——. 1978. Climatic Variations in the Sahel and Other African Regions During the Past Five Centuries. *Journal of Arid Environments* 1:3–24.

——. 1979. The Methodology of Historical Climate Reconstruction and its Application to Africa. *Journal of African History* 20:31–49.

——. 1980. Saharan Climates in Historic Times. In *The Sahara and the Nile*. M. A. J. Williams and H. Faure, eds. Pp. 173–200. Rotterdam: A. A. Balkema.

——. 1981. The Historical Climatology of Africa. In *Climate and History*. T. M. L. Wigley, M. J. Ingram, and G. Farmer, eds. Pp. 249–270. Cambridge: Cambridge University Press.

——. 1981b. Saharan Climates in Historic Times. (Published title is incorrect.) In *The Sahara: Ecological Change and Early Economic History*. J. A. Allan, ed. Pp. 35–39. London: Menas Press.

——. 1982. *The Sahel: A Climatic Perspective*. Club du Sahel D(82) 187, CILSS. Paris: Organization for Economic Cooperation in Development (OECD).

——. 1983. Subsaharan Rainfall in the Years 1976–1980: Evidence of Continued Droughts. *Monthly Weather Review* 3:1646–1654.

——. In Press. Subsaharan Rainfall 1981–1984. *Journal of Climate and Applied Meterology* 24.

Nicholson, S. E., and H. Flohn. 1980. Atmospheric Circulation Patterns of the Late Pleistocene and Holocene and their Relationship to African Climatic Changes. *Climatic Change* 2:313–348.

Nielson, M. G., and G. Josens. 1978. Production by Ants and Termites. In *Production Ecology of Ants and Termites*. M. V. Brian, ed. Pp. 45–54. New York: Cambridge University Press.

Norman, D. W. 1972. *An Economic Study of Three Villages in Zaria Province*. Zaria: Institute for Agricultural Research, Samaru, Ahmadu Bello University.

——. 1982. *The Farming Systems Approach to Research*. FSR Paper Series No. 3. Manhatten: Kansas State University.

Norman, D. W., and M. Collinson. 1985. Farming Systems Approach to Research in Theory and Practice. Paper presented at the Australian Council on International Agricultural Research (ACIAR) sponsored "Workshop on Farming Systems Research" held at Hawkesbury Agricultural College, Sidney, Australia, May 12–15.

Norman, D. W., I. Ouedraogo, and M. Newman. 1981. *The Farmer in the Semi-Arid Tropics of West Africa*. 2 vols. Hyderbad: International Crops Research Institute for the Semi-Arid Tropics.

Norman, D. W., E. V. Simmons, and H. M. Hays. 1982. *Farming Systems in the Nigerian Savanna: Research and Strategies for Development*. Boulder, Colorado: Westview Press.

N.R.C. (National Research Council). 1983. *Agroforestry in the West African Sahel*.

Washington, D.C.: National Academic Press.

NSO (National Statistical Office). 1982. *Preliminary Report of the National Sample Survey of Agriculture for Customary Land 1980/81*. Zomba, Malawi: Government Printer.

Nugent, Jeffrey B., and Pan A. Yotopoulos. 1979. What Has Orthodox Development Economics Learned from Recent Experience? *World Development* 7:541–54.

Nye, P. H. 1955. Some Soil Forming Processes in the Humid Tropics, IV. The Action of the Soil Fauna. *Journal of Soil Science* 6:73–83.

Nyerere, J. 1975. Socialism and Rural Development. In *Rural Cooperation in Tanzania*. Lionel Cliffe, ed. Dar es Salaam: Tanzanian Publishing House.

OAU (Organization of African Unity). 1981. *Lagos Plan of Action for the Economic Development of Africa 1980–2000*. Geneva: International Institute for Labor Studies.

———. 1984. Declaration on the Critical Economic Situation in Africa made by the Heads of State and Government of the Organization of African Unity at its 20th Ordinary Session held in Addis Ababa, Ethiopia, 12–15 November 1984. Addis Ababa: African Heads of Government, Declaration No. 2.

O'Hair, Stephen K. 1984. Farinaceous Crops. In *Handbook of Tropical Food Crops*. F. W. Martin, ed. Pp. 109–137. Boca Raton, Florida: CRC Press.

Ohkawa, Kazaushi. 1964. Concurrent Growth of Agriculture with Industry: A Study of the Japanese Case. In *International Explorations of Agricultural Economics*. Roger N. Dixey, ed. Pp. 201–12. Ames: Iowa State University Press.

Ohkawa, Kazushi, and Bruce F. Johnston. 1969. The Transferability of the Japanese Pattern of Modernizing Traditional Agriculture. In *The Role of Agriculture in Economic Development*. Erik Thorbecke, ed. Pp. 277–303. New York: National Bureau of Economic Research.

O'Kelly, E. 1977. Intermediate Technology as an Agent of Change. *Proceedings, World Food Conference*. Pp. 505–513. Iowa State University.

Okere, L. C. 1983. *The Anthropology of Food in Rural Igboland, Nigeria*. Lanham, Maryland: University Press of America.

Okigbo, B. N. 1984. Improved Permanent Production Systems as an Alternative to Shifting Intermittent Cultivation. In *Improved Production Systems as an Alternative to Shifting Cultivation*. Bulletin 53. Rome: Food and Agriculture Organization (FAO).

Okigbo, B. N., and B. J. Greenland. 1976. Intercropping Systems in Tropical Africa. In *Multiple Cropping*. R. I. Papendick, P. A. Sanchez and G. B. Tripless, eds. Pp. 63–101. American Society of Agronomy Special Publication No. 27. Madison: University of Wisconsin Press.

Omololu, A. 1978. Nigeria. In *Nutrition and National Policy*. B. Winikoff, ed. Pp. 109–124. Cambridge, Massachusetts: M.I.T. Press.

Onwuejeogwu, M. Angulu. 1975. *The Social Anthropology of Africa*. London: Heinemann.

Openshaw, K. 1980. Energy Requirements for Household Cooking in Africa with Existing and Improved Cooking Stoves. *Proceedings, Bio-Energy 1980*. pp. 256–258. Washington, D.C.: Bio-Energy Council.

OTA (Office of Technology Assessment, Congress of the United States). 1984. *Africa Tomorrow: Issues in Technology, Agriculture, and U.S. Foreign Aid*. Washington, D.C.: United States Government Printing Office.

Ottenberg, Simon, and Pheobe Ottenberg, eds. 1960. *Cultures and Societies of Africa*. New York: Random House.

Paden, N. John, and Edward W. Soja, eds. 1970. *The African Experience*. 2 Vols. Evanston, Illinois: Northwestern University Press.

Pallangyo, E. P., and L. A. Odero-Ogwel. 1985. The Persistence of the Food and Agriculture Crisis in Africa. In *Economic Crisis in Africa: African Perspectives on Development Problems and Potentials*. Adebayo Adedeji and Timothy M. Shaw, eds. Boulder, Colorado: Lynne Rienner Publishers.

Palmer, R., and N. Parsons, eds. 1977. *The Roots of Rural Poverty in Central and Southern Africa*. London: Heinemann.

Palmer, Ingrid. 1985. *The Nemow Case: Case Studies of the Impact of Large Scale Development Projects on Women:* A Series for Planners. International Programs, Working Paper No. 7. Washington, D.C.: United States Agency for International Development, 1979. Reprinted in West Hartford, Connecticut: Kumarian Press. 1985.

Parkin, D. 1979. *The Cultural Definition of Political Response. London:* Academic Press.

Payne, P. R. 1975. Safe Protein-Calorie Ratios in Diets: The Relative Importance of Protein and Energy Intake as Causal Factors in Malnutrition. *American Journal of Clinical Nutrition* 28:281–286.

Payne, W. J. A. 1970. *Cattle Production in the Tropics*. Vol. 1: Breeds and Breeding. Bristol, England: Longman.

Pearson, S., J. Stryker, and C. Humphreys. 1981. *Rice in West Africa: Policy and Economics*. Stanford: Stanford University Press.

Pellett, P. L., and D. Mamarbachi. 1979. Recommended Proportions of Foods in Home-Made Feeding Mixtures. *Ecology, Food and Nutrition* 7:219–228.

Perring, C. 1979. *Black Mineworkers in Central Africa*. New York: Africana Publishing Company.

Petit, Michel. 1982. Is There a French School of Agricultural Economics? *Journal of Agricultural Economics* 33:3:325–37.

Picciotto, Robert. 1985. National Agricultural Research: Testing the Feasibility of Agricultural Research Schemes in Developing Countries. *Finance and Development* 22:2:45–48.

Pickstock, M. 1983. The Fuelwood Crisis in Africa: An FAO Roundtable Discussion. *Unasylva* 35:141:22–25.

Pinckney, T., J. Cohen, and D. Leonard. 1982. *Microcomputers and Financial Management in Development Ministries: Experience from Kenya*. Harvard Institute for International Development. Discussion Paper No. 137. Cambridge, Massachusetts: Harvard University Press.

Pineiro, Martin, Eduardo Trigo, and Raul Fiorentino. 1979. Technical Change in Latin American Agriculture: A Conceptual Framework for Its Evaluation. *Food Policy* 4:3:169–77.

Pinson, G. S. 1977. *A Wooden Hand-Held Maize Sheller*. Rural Technology Guide No. 1. London: Tropical Products Institute.

Pinstrup-Anderson, Per. 1981. *Nutritional Consequences of Agricultural Projects: Conceptual Relationships and Assessment Approaches*. World Bank Staff Working Paper No. 456. Washington, D.C.: The World Bank.

Platt, B. S. 1962. *Tables of Representative Values of Foods Commonly Used in Tropical Countries*. Medical Research or Special Report 301.

Plucknett, Donald L., Nigel H. Smith, J. T. Williams, and N. Murthi Anishetty. 1983. Crop Germplasm Conservation and Developing Countries. *Science* 220:163–169.

Pollitt, E. 1984. Methods for the Behavioral Assessment of the Consequences of Malnutrition. In *Methods for the Impact of Food and Nutrition Programmes*. D. E. Sahn, R. Lockwood and N. S. Scrimshaw, eds. Pp. 179–203. Tokyo: The United Nations University.

Pollitt, E., R. L. Leibel, and D. Greenfield. 1981. Brief Fasting, Stress, and Cognition in Children. *American Journal of Clinical Nutrition* 34:1526–1533.

Pollitt, E., and N. Lewis. 1980. Nutrition and Educational Achievement, Part 1. Malnutrition and Behavioral Test Indicators. *Food and Nutrition Bulletin* 2:3:32–35. Tokyo: United Nations University.

Pollock, N. C. 1974. *Animals, Environment and Man in Africa*. Lexington, Massachusetts:

Lexington Books.

Pontecorvo, A. J., and M. C. Bourne. 1978. Simple Methods for Extending the Shelf Life of Soy Curd (tofu) in Tropical Areas. *Journal of Food Science* 43:969–972.

Popkin, S. L. 1979. *The Rational Peasant*. Berkeley: University of California Press.

Population Reference Bureau. 1984. *World Population Data Sheet*. Washington, D.C.: Population Reference Bureau.

Posselt, J. 1963. The Domestication of the Eland. *Rhodesian Journal of Agricultural Research* 1:81–87.

Plucknett, D. L., and N. J. H. Smith. 1982. Agricultural Research and Third World Food Production. *Science* 217:215–220.

————. 1984. Networking in International Agricultural Research. *Science* 225:989–993.

Pratt, D., and M. D. Gwynne. 1977. *Rangeland Management and Ecology in East Africa*. London: Holder and Stoughton.

Prebisch, Raul. 1959. Commercial Policy in the Underdeveloped Countries. *American Economic Review* 64:251–73.

————. 1981. The Latin American Periphery in the Global System of Capitalism. *CEPAL Review*, April, 143–50. Reprinted in *International Economic Policies and Their Theoretical Foundations: A Source Book*. John M. Letiche. (1982) New York: Academic Press.

Prins, A. H. J. 1965. *Sailing From Lamu: A Study of Maritime Culture in Islamic East Africa*. Assen, Netherlands: Van Gorcum.

Pritchard, John M. 1979. *Africa: A Study Geography for Advanced Students*. Revised metric edition. London: Longman.

Pullan, R. A. 1981. The Utilization of Wildlife for Food in Africa: The Zambian Experience. *Singapore Journal of Tropical Geography* 2:101–112.

Rachie, K. O., and L. M. Roberts. 1974. Grain Legumes of the Lowland Tropics. *Advances in Agronomy* 26:1–132.

Rajalakshmi, R., and C. V. Ramarkrishnan. 1977. Formulation and Evaluation of Meals Based on Locally Available Foods for Young Children. *World Review of Nutrition and Diet* 27:34–104.

Ramond, C. 1970. La démarche de l'IRAT au Sénégal. Application des résultats de la recherche à la définition des modèles d'exploitations. *Agronomie Tropicale* 25:963–972.

Ranis, Gustav. 1963. Innovation, Capital Accumulation, and Economic Development. *American Economic Review* 53:3:293–313.

————. 1964. *Development of the Labor Surplus Economy: Theory and Policy*. Homewood, Illinois: Richard D. Irwin.

Ranis, Gustav, and John C. H. Fei. 1961. A Theory of Economic Development. *American Economic Review* 51:4:533–65.

Rao, C. S., C. W. Deyoe, and D. B. Parrish. 1978. Biochemical and Nutritional Properties of Organic Acid-Treated High-Moisture Sorghum Grain. *Journal of Stored Product Research* 14:95–102.

Raup, Phillip M. 1967. Land Reform and Agricultural Development. In *Agricultural Development and Economic Growth*. Herman M. Southworth and Bruce F. Johnston, eds. Pp. 267–314. Ithaca, New York: Cornell University Press.

Read, Margaret. 1959. *Children and Their Fathers: Growing Up Among the Ngoni of Nyasaland*. London: Methuen.

Redford, K. H., and J. G. Dorea. 1984. The Nutritional Value of Invertebrates with Emphasis on Ants and Termites as Food for Mammals. *Journal of Zoology* 203:385–395.

Reusse, E. 1976. Economic and Marketing Aspects of Post-Harvest Systems in Small Farm Economics. Food and Agriculture Organization (FAO) Monthly Bulletin: *Agriculture, Economics and Statistics* 25:9:1–7 and 25:10:8–17.

Reutlinger, Shlomo, and Marcelo Selowsky. 1976. *Malnutrition and Poverty: Magnitude and Policy Options*. World Bank Occasional Staff Paper No. 23. Baltimore: Johns Hopkins University Press.

Reynolds, Lloyd G., ed. 1975. *Agriculture in Development Theory*. New Haven: Yale University Press.

Reynolds, Lloyd G. 1977. *Image and Reality in Economic Development*. New Haven: Yale University Press.

Rhoades, R., and R. Booth. 1982. Farmer-Back-to-Farmer: A Model for Generating Acceptable Agricultural Technology. *Agricultural Administration* 11:127–137.

Richards, Audrey I. 1939. *Land, Labor and Diet in Northern Rhodesia*. New York: Oxford University Press.

Richards, A. I., F. Sturrock, and J. M. Fortt. 1973. *From Subsistence to Commercial Farming in Buganda*. Cambridge: Cambridge University Press.

Richards, P. 1983a. Farming Systems and Agrarian Change in West Africa. *Progress in Human Geography* 7:1:1–39.

———. 1983b. Ecological Change and the Politics of African Land Use. *African Studies Review* 26:2.

Richard, J. E., and D. G. Coursey. 1979. The Value of Shading Perishable Produce After Harvest. *Appropriate Technology* 6:2:18–19.

Riddell, R. C. 1978. *The Land Problem in Rhodesia*. London: Mambo Press.

Riley, Harold, and John Staatz. 1981. *Food System Organization Problems in Developing Countries*. Agricultural Development Council (A/D/C) Report No. 23. New York: Agricultural Development Council.

Riney, T. 1963. Utilization of Wildlife in the Transvaal. In *Conservation of Nature and Natural Resources in Modern African States*. 2 Vols., Pp. 303–305. Morges, Switzerland: International Union for the Conservation of Nature and Natural Resources (IUCN).

———. 1967. Conservation and Management of African Wildlife. Rome: Food and Agriculture Organization (FAO).

Riney, T., and W. L. Kettlitz. 1964. Management of Large Mammals in the Transvaal. *Mammalia* 28:189–248.

Riney, T., and P. Hill. 1967a. *Conservation and Management of African Wildlife: English-Speaking Country Reports*. Rome: Food and Agriculture Organization (FAO).

———. 1967b. *Conservation and Management of African Wildlife: French-Speaking Country Reports*. Rome: Food and Agriculture Organization (FAO).

Rizvi, S. R. H. 1978. Appropriate Technology for Preservation of Food in Unsealed Covered Containers. *Pakistan Journal of Scientific and Industrial Research* 21:3/4:147–149.

Robach, M. C. 1980. Use of Preservatives to Control Micro-Organisms in Food. *Food Technology* 34:10:81.

Robson, P., and D. A. Lury, eds. 1969. *The Economies of Africa*. Evanston, Illinois: Northwestern University Press.

Rockland, L. B., E. M. Zaragosa, and R. Oracca-Tetteh. 1979. Quick-Cooking Winged Beans (*Psophocarpus tetragonolobus*). *Journal of Food Science* 44:1004–1007.

Rodney, Walter. 1972. *How Europe Underdeveloped Africa*. London: Bogle-L'Ouverture.

Rogers, Barbara. 1980. *The Domestication of Women: Discrimination in Developing Societies*. London: Tavistock.

Rogowski, R. 1985. Internal vs. External Factors in Political Development: An Evaluation of Recent Historical Research. *PS* 18:4:812–814.

Röling, E. A. 1979. *The Small Farmer and Development Cooperation*. Final Report on the Prepatory Investigations, vol. 1. Main Report. Wageningen, Netherlands: International Agricultural Centre.

Roth, H. H. 1966. Game Utilization in Rhodesia in 1964. *Mammalia* 30:397–423.

Russell, E. W. 1981. The Role of Watershed Management for Arable Land Use in the Tropics. In *Tropical Agricultural Hydrology*. R. Lal and E. W. Russell, eds. Pp. 11–16. New York: John Wiley & Sons.

Ruthenberg, H. 1980. *Farming Systems in the Tropics*. 3rd ed. London: Oxford University Press.

Ruttan, Vernon W. 1975. Integrated Rural Development: A Skeptical Perspective. *International Development Review* 17:4:9–16.

Rweyemamu, M. M. 1981. Surveillance and Control of Virus Diseases: Africa. In *Virus Diseases of Food Animals*. Vol. 1. *International Perspectives*. E. P. J. Gibbs, ed. Pp. 79–100. London: Academic Press.

SADCC (Southern African Development Coordination Conference). 1984. *Overview*. Lusaka, Zambia: Southern African Development Coordination Conference (SADCC).

Sahn, D. E., R. Lockwood, and N. S. Scrimshaw. 1984. *Methods for the Evaluation of the Impact of Food and Nutrition Programs*. Tokyo: The United Nations University.

Sanchez, P. A. 1976. *Properties and Management of Soils in the Tropics*. New York: John Wiley & Sons.

Satterlee, L.P. 1975. Improving Utilization of Animal By-Products for Human Foods—A Review. *Journal of Animal Science* 41:687–697.

Scarlett, Lynn. 1981. *Tropical Africa: Food or Famine? In Food Politics: The Regional Conflict*. David N. Balaam and Michael J. Carey, eds. Pp. 166–188. Totowa, New Jersey: Allanheld, Osum & Co.

Schatz, S. P. 1984. Pirate Capitalism and the Inert Economy of Nigeria. *Journal of Modern African Studies* 22:1:45–57.

Schlippe, P. de. 1956. *Shifting Cultivation in Africa. The Zande System of Agriculture*. London: Routledge and Keagan Paul.

———. 1957. De l'anthropologie agricole. Extrait de: *Problèmes d'Afrique centrale*. No. 33, 3e Trimèstre.

Schneider, Harold K. 1981. *The Africans: An Ethnological Account*. Englewood Cliffs, New Jersey: Prentice-Hall.

———. 1984. Livestock in African Culture and Society: A Historical Perspective. In *Livestock Development in Subsaharan Africa*. James R. Simpson and Phylo Evangelou, eds. Pp. 187–200. Boulder, Colorado: Westview Press.

Schultz, Theodore W. 1964. *Transforming Traditional Agriculture*. New Haven: Yale University Press.

———. 1978. On the Economics and Politics of Agriculture. In *Distortions of Agricultural Incentives*. Theodore W. Schultz, ed. Pp. 3–23. Bloomington: Indiana University Press.

———. 1981. *Investing in People: The Economics of Population Quality*. Berkeley: University of California Press.

Schumacher, E. F. 1973. *Small Is Beautiful. Economics as If People Mattered*. New York: Harper and Row.

Scobie, Grant M., and Rafael Posada. 1984. The Impact of Technological Change on Income Distribution: The Case of Rice in Colombia. In *Agricultural Development in the Third World*. Carl K. Eicher and John M. Staatz, eds. Pp. 278–88. Baltimore: Johns Hopkins University Press.

Scott, D. 1975. Animal Power Boosts New Crop Production. *Appropriate Technology* 2:1:7–9.

Scott, J. 1976. *The Moral Economy of the Peasant*. New Haven, Connecticut: Yale University Press.

Scrimshaw, N. S. 1983. Importance of Infection and Immunity in Nutrition Intervention

Programs and Priorities for Interventions. In *Nutrition Intervention Strategies in National Development*. B. A. Underwood, ed. Pp. 209–226. New York: Academic Press.

Scudder, Thayer. 1962. *The Ecology of the Gwembe Tonga*. Kariba Studies, vol. 2. Manchester: Manchester University Press for the Rhodes-Livingstone Institute.

——. *Gathering Among African Woodland Savannah Cultivators*. Zambian Papers #5. Manchester: Manchester University Press.

Seers, Dudley. 1970. *The Meaning of Development. Agricultural Development Council (ADC) Reprint*. New York: Agricultural Development Council.

Seidman, A. 1977. The Economics of Eliminating Rural Poverty. In *The Roots of Rural Poverty in Central and Southern Africa*. Robin Palmer and Neil Parsons, eds. Pp. 410–421. Berkeley: The University of California Press.

Sen, Amaryta. 1982. The Food Problem: Theory and Practice. *Third World Quarterly* 4:3:459.

Shaner, W. W., P. F. Philipp, and W. R. Schmehl. 1982. *Farming Systems Research and Development: Guidelines for Developing Countries*. Boulder, Colorado: Westview Press.

Shantz, H. L., and L. N. Piemeisel. 1927. The Water Requirements of Plants at Akron, Colorado. *Journal of Agricultural Research* 34:1093–1190.

Shapiro, Kenneth H., ed. 1979. *Livestock Production and Marketing in the Entente States of West Africa: Summary Report*. Ann Arbor: Center for Research on Economic Development, University of Michigan.

Shaw, Thurstan. 1976. Early Crops in Africa: A Review of the Evidence. In *Origins of African Plant Domestication*. Jack R. Halan, Jan M. J. DeWit, and Ann B. L. Stemler, eds. Pp. 107–53. The Hague: Mouton Publishers.

Shepherd, A. 1981. Agrarian Change in Northern Ghana: Public Investment, Capitalist Farming and Famine. In *Rural Development in Tropical Africa*. J. Heyer, P. Roberts, and G. Williams, eds. Pp. 168–192. New York: St. Martin's Press.

Sherman, J. 1984. *Grain Markets and Marketing Behavior of Farmers: A Case Study of Manga, Upper Volta*. Ann Arbor: Center for Research on Economic Development, University of Michigan.

Silva, C. A. B., R. P. Bates, and J. C. Deng. 1981. Influence of Soaking and Cooking Upon the Softening and Eating Quality of Black Beans. *Journal of Food Science* 46:1716–1720.

Simkins, C. 1981. Agricultural Production in the African Reserves. *Journal of Southern African Studies* 7:2:256–283.

Simmonds, N. W. 1984. *The State of the Art of Farming Systems Research*. Annual Agricultural Symposium. Washington, D.C.: The World Bank.

Simpson, James R., and Phylo Evangelou, eds. 1984. *Livestock Development in Subsaharan Africa*. Boulder, Colorado: Westview Press.

Simpson, James R., and Donald E. Farris. 1982. *The World's Beef Business*. Ames: Iowa State University Press.

Simpson, James R., and Gregory M. Sullivan. 1984. On Institutional Change in Utilization in African Common Property Range Resources. *African Studies Review* 27:4:61–78.

Sinclair, A. R. E. 1977. *The African Buffalo*. Chicago: University of Chicago Press.

Singh, Inderjit J. n.d.. *Small Farmers and the Landless in South Asia*. Washington, D.C.: The World Bank.

Singh, I. J., L. Squire, and J. Strauss, eds. n.d.. *Agricultural Household Models: Extensions, Applications and Policy*. Washington, D.C.: World Bank.

Small Industry Development Network (SIDN). 1979. AT Project Activities at Einhoven University of Technology. *Small Industry Development Network Newsletter* No. 16, Sept., 1979.

Smith, M. G. 1955. *The Economy of Hausa Communities of Zaire*. London: Her Majesty's Stationery Office.

Smith, N. 1985. Trees and Food for a Hungry World. *Food Policy* 10:1:82.

Solomons, N. W., and L. H. Allen. 1983. The Functional Assessment of Nutritional Status: Principles, Practice and Potential. *Nutrition Reviews* 41:33–50.

Solomons, N. W., and G. T. Keusch. 1981. Nutritional Implications of Parasitic Infections. *Nutrition Reviews* 39:149–161.

Southworth, Herman M., and Bruce F. Johnston, eds. 1967. *Agricultural Development and Economic Growth*. Ithaca, New York: Cornell University Press.

Spencer, Dunstan S. C. 1976. *African Women in Agricultural Development: A Case Study in Sierra Leone*. Occasional Paper No. 9. Washington, D.C.: Overseas Liaison Committee, American Council on Education.

Spring, Anita. 1984. *Profiles of Men and Women Smallholder Farmers in the Lilongwe Rural Development Project, Malawi*. Final Report. Washington, D.C.: Office of Women in Development, United States Agency for International Development.

————. 1985. The Women in an Agricultural Development Project in Malawi: Making Gender Free Development Work. In *Women Creating Wealth: Transforming Economic Development*. R. Gallin and A. Spring, eds. Pp. 71–75. Washington, D.C.: Association for Women in Development.

————. 1986a. Men and Women Participants in a Stall Feeder Livestock Program in Malawi. *Human Organization*. Forthcoming.

————. 1986b. Trials and Errors: Using Farming Systems Research in Agricultural Programs for Women. In *Farming Systems Research: The Integration of Social and Biological Approaches for Agricultural Development*. J. Jones and B. Wallace, eds. Boulder, Colorado: Westview Press. Forthcoming.

Spring, Anita, and Art Hansen. 1982. Migration and Development Survey of the Lilongwe Rural Development Project. (Unpublished data.)

————. 1985. The Underside of Development: Agricultural Development and Women in Zambia. *Agriculture and Human Values* 2:1:60–67.

Spring, Anita, Craig Smith, and Freida Kayuni. 1983. *Women Farmers in Malawi, Their Contributions to Agriculture and Participation in Development Projects*. Washington, D.C.: Office of Women in Development, United States Agency for International Development.

Srinivas, T., S. N. Raghavendra Rao, M. K. Bhashyam, and H. S. R. Desikachar. 1976. Studies on the Use of Dry Earth as a Contact Medium for Absorbing Moisture from Paddy. *Journal of Food Science and Technology* 13:142–145.

Staudt, Kathleen. 1975–1976. Women Farmers and Inequalities in Agricultural Services. In Rural Women: Development or Underdevelopment. A. Wipper, ed. *Rural Africana* 29:81–94.

Stenning, Derrick J. 1959. *Savannah Nomads: A Study of the WodaaBe Pastoral Fulani of Western Bornu Province, Northern Region, Nigeria*. London: Oxford University Press.

Stevens, Robert D., ed. 1977a. Tradition and Dynamics in Small-Farm Agriculture. Ames: Iowa State University Press.

————. 1977b. Transformation of Traditional Agriculture: Theory and Empirical Findings. In *Tradition and Dynamics in Small-Farm Agriculture*. Robert D. Stevens, ed. Ames: Iowa State University Press.

Stichter, S. 1982. *Migrant Labour and Capitalism in Kenya*. London: Longman.

Streeten, Paul. 1979. Development Ideas in Historical Perspective. In *Toward a New Strategy for Development*. Pp. 21–52. Rothko Chapel Colloquium. New York: Pergamon Press.

Streeten, Paul, with Shadid Burke, Mahbub Haq, Norman Hicks, and Frances Stewart.

1981. *First Things First: Meeting Basic Needs in Developing Countries*. New York: Oxford University Press.

Sullivan, Gregory M. 1984. Impact of Government Policies on the Performance of the Livestock Meat Subsector. In *Livestock Development in Subsaharan Africa*. James R. Simpson and Phylo Evangelou, eds. Pp. 143–159. Boulder, Colorado: Westview Press.

Sullivan, Gregory M., Donald E. Farris, and James R. Simpson. 1985. Production Effects of Improved Management Practices in East African Cattle Grazing Systems. *Quarterly Journal of International Agriculture* 24:22–37.

Sunkel, Osvaldo. 1972. Big Business and Dependencia. *Foreign Affairs* 50:755–761.

Surujbally, R. S. 1977. Game Farming Is a Reality, to Rely Only on Hunting Means the Extinction of Choice Species. *Unasylva* 29:116:13–16.

Swaminathan, M. 1980. Development of Supplementary Foods and Their Usefulness in Applied Nutrition Programs. *Journal of Food Science Technology* 17:1&2:78–81.

Szulmayer, W. 1971. From Sun-Drying to Solar Dehydration. *Food Technology in Australia* 23:440–443 and 494–501.

Talbot, L. M., W. J. A. Payne, H. P. Ledger, L. D. Verdcourt, and M. H. Talbot. 1965. *The Meat Production Potential of Wild Animals in Africa*. Farnham Royal, Buckshire, England: Commonwealth Agricultural Bureau.

Tandon, Yash. 1981. New Food Strategies and Social Transformation in East Africa. *Africa Development* 6:2:86–88.

Tarrant, John R. 1980. *Food Policies*. Chichester: John Wiley & Sons.

Tax, Sol. 1953. *Penny Capitalism*. Smithsonian Institution, Institute of Social Anthropology. Publication No. 16. Washington, D.C.: United States Government Printing Office.

Terray, E. 1974. Long-Distance Exchange and the Formation of the State: The Case of the Abron Kingdom of Gyaman. *Economy and Society* 3:3:315–345.

Terry, E., K. A. Oduro, and F. Caveness, eds. 1981. *Tropical Root Crops: Research Strategies for the 1980's*. Ottowa: International Development Research Council.

Teer, J. G. 1974. Game Ranching in Texas. In *The Behavior of Ungulates and its Relationship to Management*. V. Geist and F. Walther, eds. Pp. 893–897. Morges, Switzerland: International Union for the Conservation of Nature (IUCN).

Thomas, P. L. 1975. Dried Meat Products. *Food Research Quarterly* 35:73–78.

Thorbecke, E., and E. Stoutjesdijk. 1971. *Employment and Output—A Methodology Applied to Peru and Guatemala*. Development Center Studies, Employment Series No. 2. Paris: Development Center of Organization for Economic Cooperation and Development (OECD).

Thresher, P. 1980. The Economics of Domesticated Oryx. *World Animal Review* 36:37–43.

Timmer, C. Peter, et al. 1983. *Food Policy Analysis*. Baltimore: The Johns Hopkins University Press for the World Bank.

Tinker, Irene, and Michele Bo Bramsen, eds. 1976. *Women and World Development*. Washington, D.C.: Overseas Development Council.

Todaro, M. P. 1969. A Model of Labor Migration and Urban Unemployment in Less Developed Countries. *American Economic Review* 59:138–48.

———. 1980. International Migration in Developing Countries: A Survey. In *Population and Economic Change in Developing Countries*. R. A. Easterlin, ed. Pp. 361–402. Chicago: University of Chicago Press.

Todhunter, E. N. 1983. Reflections on Nutrition in History. *Journal of Nutrition* 113:1681–1685.

Tourte, R. 1971. Thèmes Légers—Thèmes Lourds. Systèmes Intensifs—Voies Differentes

L

Ouvertes au Développement Agricole du Sénégal. *Agronomie Tropicale* 37:3:5:632–671.

Tourte, R., and R. Billaz. 1982. Approche des systèmes agraires et fonction recherche-développement. Contribution à la mise au point d'une démarche. *Agronomie Tropicale* 37:3:223–232.

Tourte, R., and J. Moomaw. 1977. Traditional African Systems of Agriculture and their Improvement. In *Food Crops of the Lowland Tropics*. C. Leakey and J. Wills, eds. Pp. 295–311. Oxford: Oxford University Press.

Treus, V., and D. Kravchenko. 1968. Methods of Raising and Economic Utilization of Eland in the Askania-Nova Zoological Park. In *Comparative Nutrition of Wild Animals*. Symposia of the Zoological Society of London, no. 21. M. A. Crawford, ed. Pp. 395–411. London: Academic Press.

Turnbull, Colin. 1961. *The Forest People*. New York: Simon & Schuster.

Tyler, P. S. 1979. New Crop Varieties Store Up Problems. *Third World Agriculture* 1:2:18–20.

Underwood, B. A., ed. 1983. *Nutrition Intervention Strategies in National Development*. New York: Academic Press.

UNIDO (United Nations Industrial Development Organization). 1979. *Appropriate Industrial Technology for Food Storage and Processing*. Monograph on Appropriate Technology No. 7.

United Nations. 1975. Report of the World Food Conference, Rome, 5–16 November 1974. New York: United Nations.

———. 1984. *The Least Developed Countries 1984 Report*. New York: United Nations.

———. 1985. *World Population Trends, Population and Development Interrelations and Population Policies: 1983 Monitoring Report*. Department of International Economic and Social Affairs. Population Studies No. 93. New York: United Nations.

Upton, M. 1973. *Farm Management in Africa*. London: Oxford University Press.

USDA (United States Department of Agriculture). 1981. *Food Problems and Prospects in Sub-Saharan Africa*. Economic Research Service Foreign Agricultural Economic Report No. 166. Washington, D.C.: United States Government Printing Office.

———. 1984. *Sub-Saharan Africa Outlook and Situation Report*. Economic Research Service. Washington, D.C.: U.S. Department of Agriculture.

Vail, Leroy, and Landes White. 1978. Tawani, Machambero! Forced Cotton and Rice Growing on the Zambesi. *Journal of African History* 19:2:239–63.

Vansina, Jan. 1962. A Comparison of African Kingdoms. *Africa* 32:324–35.

Vaughan, James H. 1977. Environment, Population, and Traditional Society. In *Africa*. Phyllis M. Martin and Patrick O'Meara, eds. Pp. 9–23. Bloomington: Indiana University Press.

Vermeer, D. E. 1981. Collision of Climate, Cattle and Culture in Mauretania During the 1970's. *Geographical Review* 71:281–297.

VITA (Volunteers in Technical Assistance). 1970. *Village Technology Handbook*. Mt. Rainer, Maryland: Volunteers in Technical Assistance.

———. 1980. Wind, Biogas and Hydropower: Just How Well Have They Done? *VITA News*, October. Pp. 4–7, 18, 20, 22.

Von Kaufmann, R. 1982. *International Livestock Centre for Africa Subhumid Programme Annual Report*. Kaduna, Nigeria: International Livestock Center for Africa.

Richter, W. von. 1979. The Utilization of Management of Wild Animals, A Form of Land Use in Marginal Areas of Africa. *Animal Research and Development* 10:93–103.

Vries, E. de. 1931. De Cultuure—en bedrijfsontledingen in den Islandschen Landbouw. *Landbouw, Buitenzorg* 6:2:1–73.

Wakefield, R. A., and P. Stafford. 1977. Appropriate Technology: What It Is and Where

It's Going. *Futurist* 11:72–76.

Walinsky, Louis J., ed. 1977. *The Selected Papers of Wolf Ladejinsky: Agrarian Reform as Unfinished Business*. New York: Oxford University Press for the World Bank.

Walsh, John. 1984a. World Bank Puts Priority on Africa Program: Problems of How to Inject Science and Technology into Development Projects Are Acute in Sub-Sahara. *Science* 226: 148–152.

———. 1984b. Sahel Will Suffer Even If Rains Come: With Potential Population Explosion, No Green Revolution, Drought Is Only Part of the Problem Confronting the Region. *Science* 224:467–471.

Warriner, Doreen. 1955. Land Reform in Economic Development. National Bank of Egypt Fiftieth Anniversary Commemoration Lectures, Cairo. Reprinted in *Agriculture in Economic Development*. Carl K. Eicher and Lawrence W. Witt, eds. Pp. 272–98. New York: McGraw-Hill Book Co.

Watt, S. 1976. A Low-Cost Rice Storage Bin of Non-reinforced Cement Mortar for Rural Farmers. *Appropriate Technology* 3:1:4–6.

Webber, J. McC. 1977. Reclamation of Waste Glass Within New Zealand. *Appropriate Technology* 4:1:10–13.

Welcomme, R. L. 1971. A Description of Certain Indigenous Fishing Methods from Southern Dahomey. *African Journal of Hydrobiology and Fisheries* 2:1:129–139.

White, C. M. N. 1967. *A Preliminary Survey of Luvale Rural Economy*. Rhodes-Livingstone Papers No. 29. Lusaka, Zambia.

Wharton, Clifton R. ed. 1969. *Subsistence Agriculture and Economic Development*. Chicago: Aldine Publishing Co.

Whitlow, J. R. 1980. Deforestation in Zimbabwe. (Supp.) *Zambezia: The Journal of the University of Zimbabwe*. Harare.

Whyte, W. F. 1981. *Participation Approaches to Agricultural Research and Development. A State of the Art Paper*. Ithaca, New York: Rural Development Committee, Cornell University.

William, Jr., B. D. 1975. A Foot-Powered Thresher for Rice, Sorghum, Oats and Other Small Grains. *Appropriate Technology* 2:2:6–7.

Williams, Maurice J. 1983. Toward a Food Strategy for Africa. *Africa Report* 28:5:22–26.

Wilson, F. 1971. Farming, 1866–1966. In *The Oxford History of South Africa*. Vol. 2. M. Wilson and L. Thompson, eds. Pp. 104–177. Oxford: Oxford University Press.

Wilson, R. T. 1982. *Livestock Production in Central Mali*. ILCA Bulletin No. 15. Addis Ababa, Ethiopia: International Livestock Centre for Africa.

———. 1984a. Goats and Sheep in the Traditional Livestock Systems in Semi-Arid Northern Africa: Their Importance, Productivity and Constraints on Production. In *Livestock Development in Subsaharan Africa*. James R. Simpson and Phylo Evangelou, eds. Pp. 91–106. Boulder, Colorado: Westview Press.

———. 1984b. *The Camel*. New York: Longman.

Winikoff, B., ed. 1978. *Nutrition and National Policy*. Cambridge, Massachusetts: Massachusetts Institute of Technology Press.

Wolpe, H. 1972. Capitalism and Cheap Labour Power in South Africa: From Segregation to Apartheid. *Economy and Society* 1:4:425–456.

Wolverton, B. C., and R. C. McDonald. 1979. Water Hyacinth (*Eichhornia crassipes*) Productivity and Harvest Studies. *Economic Botany* 33:1–10.

Wood, C. W., and M. Schmink. 1978. *Blaming the Victim: Small Farmer Production in an Amazon Colonization Project*. Pp. 77–93. Studies in Third World Societies Publication No. 7: Changing Agriculture Systems in Latin America.

Woodburn, James. 1968. An Introduction to Hadza Ecology. In *Man the Hunter*. Richard B. Lee and Irven Devore, eds. Pp. 49–55. Chicago: Aldine Publishing Company.

Worgan, J. T. 1977. Canning and Bottling as Methods of Food Preservation in Developing

Countries. *Appropriate Technology* 4:3:15–16.

World Bank. 1978. *Ivory Coast: The Challenge of Success*. Baltimore: Johns Hopkins University Press.

———. 1981. *Accelerated Development in Sub-Saharan Africa: An Agenda for Action*. Washington, D.C.: The World Bank.

———. 1984. *Toward Sustained Development in Sub-Saharan Africa: A Joint Program of Action*. Washington, D.C.: The World Bank.

———. 1985. *World Development Report 1985*. Oxford: Oxford University Press.

World Eagle. 1983. *Africa Today: An Atlas of Reproducible Pages*. Wellesley, Massachusetts: World Eagle.

Worou, L., and T. Van Nao. 1982. Orienting Forestry Towards the Needs of the People. *Unasylva* 34:136:8–10.

Wray, J. D. 1978. Nutrition and Health Policy. In *Nutrition and National Policy*. B. Winikoff, ed. Pp. 437–450. Cambridge, Massachusetts: M.I.T. Press.

Young, C., and Thomas Turner. 1985. *The Rise and Decline of the Zairian State*. Madison: University of Wisconsin Press.

York, E. T. 1984a. A Major International Dimension for U.S. Colleges of Agriculture—An Imperative. Seaman A. Knapp Memorial Lecture presented at the Annual Meeting of the National Association of State Universities and Land-Grant Colleges, Denver, Colorado, Nov. 12. Washington, D.C.: Department of Agriculture Extension Service.

———. 1984b. Speech at the University of Florida Commencement, December 15.

Zandstra, H. G. 1982. Institutional Requirements for Cropping Systems Research. In *Cropping Systems Research in Asia*. Los Banos, Philippines: International Rice Research Institute.

Zandstra, H. G., E. C. Price, J. A. Litsinger, and R. A. Morris. 1981. *A Methodology for On-Farm Cropping Systems Research*. Los Banos, Philippines: International Rice Research Institute.

Contributors

S. K. B. Asante is visiting professor of political science and a Fulbright African area studies specialist at the University of Florida. He has taught at the University of Ghana, the University of Calabar (Nigeria), and the State University of New York at Brockport, and he serves as consultant to the United Nations Economic Commission for Africa.

Robert P. Bates is professor of food science at the University of Florida. He has participated in short- and long-term international technical assistance projects in Central America, Guyana, Brazil, Ecuador, Indonesia, and India and has authored or co-authored over forty publications in the area of food processing and utilization.

Sarah Berry is associate professor of African history and economics at Boston University. She has conducted research in western Nigeria on the long-term consequences of agricultural commercialization.

Robert S. Browne is associate fellow of the Institute for Policy Sciences at Howard University and is the former executive director of the African Development Fund (Abidjan).

Ronald Cohen is professor of anthropology at the University of Florida. He has held positions at the University of Toronto, McGill University, Northwestern University, and Ahmadu Bello University.

Robert J. Cummings is professor of economic history and director of the African Studies and Research Program at Howard University and was president of the African Studies Association (United States). His research on the Akamba of Kenya has resulted in the publication of numerous articles.

R. Hunt Davis, Jr. is professor of history and director of the Center for African Studies at the University of Florida. He is also Editor of the *African Studies Review,* the journal of the African Studies Association, and the author of *Bantu Education and the Education of Africans in South Africa*.

Carl K. Eicher is professor of agricultural economics at Michigan State University and is currently visiting professor of agricultural economics at the University of Zimbabwe.

Charles Fox is a graduate student in the Department of Anthropology at the University of Florida. He has conducted research in Florida and Latin America and is planning fieldwork in Brazil to examine African-derived religious systems and their associated medical practices.

Louise O. Fresco is a research fellow with the Department of Tropical Crop Science at the Agricultural University at Wageningen in the Netherlands. She has extensive field experience in Africa: her publications cover farming systems research, cassava production, and the role of women in agriculture.

Paul Goldsmith is a graduate student in the Department of Anthropology at the University of Florida. He also teaches Swahili at the University of Florida and has taught and conducted research on indigenous agricultural development and maritime communities in Kenya.

Charles C. Guthrie is associate professor of history at Indiana Central University. He has taught and conducted research in Zambia, Uganda, Kenya, and Tanzania, and when he was the outreach coordinator of the Center for African Studies at the University of Florida, he developed a series of teaching monographs and materials on Africa and served as editor of the *Bulletin of the Southern Association of Africanists*.

Art Hansen is associate professor and graduate coordinator of the Department of Anthropology and chairs the Steering Committee of the Food in Africa Program at the University of Florida. He has conducted research in Zambia, established the adaptive research unit within Malawi's Department of Agricultural Research, and worked in rural and community development in Bolivia and the Dominican Republic.

Robert W. Herdt is a scientific adviser to the Consultative Group on International Agricultural Research of the World Bank. He has held a faculty position in agricultural economics at the University of Illinois and has worked with the International Rice Research Institute.

Clifton Hiebsch is assistant professor of agronomy at the University of Florida. He taught agriculture and sciences in Malawi and is currently an extension agronomist for soybean production.

René Lemarchand is professor of political science at the University of Florida. He has conducted research and taught in many African countries, and he has received the Herskovits Award, an award of the African Studies Association for the best Africanist Book published during a year.

Robert E. McDowell is professor of international animal science at Cornell University and chairs the Board of Trustees of the International Livestock Center for Africa. His research and planning for livestock development includes more than fourteen years working in twenty-one countries of Asia, Africa, and Latin America.

Daniel McGee is a graduate student in the Department of Anthropology at the University of Florida. He is planning to conduct research in Tanzania.

Michael E. McGlothlen recently completed a Ph.D. in dairy science at the University of Florida. He taught for seven years in Zambia and has conducted research and published in the areas of statistical genetics, wildlife management, and the utilization of African wildlife for meat production.

Della E. McMillan is assistant professor of anthropology at the University of Kentucky, and former director of the Food in Africa Program at the University of Florida, where she was also the assistant director of the Center for African Studies. She has conducted research in northern Togo and in the onchocerciasis control region and central plateau of Burkina Faso.

Sharon E. Nicholson is associate professor of meteorology at Florida State University. She has traveled and conducted research in twenty-six African countries.

Stephen K. O'Hair is associate professor of vegetable crops at the University of Florida, stationed at the Tropical Research and Education Center in Homestead, Florida. He has worked in Kenya, Tanzania, Malawi, and Zaire and recently reviewed cassava production and marketing in the Bandundu region of Zaire for the United States Agency for International Development.

Donald L. Plucknett is a scientific adviser to the Consultative Group on International Agricultural Research of the World Bank. He has held a faculty appointment in agronomy and soil science at the University of Hawaii and served as deputy executive director of the Board for International Food and Agriculture Development and as chief of the Agriculture and Rural Development Division, Bureau for Asia, United States Agency for International Development.

Susan V. Poats is associate director of the Farming Systems Support Project, which is a collaborative agreement between the United States Agency for International Development (USAID) and the University of Florida to support USAID-funded farming systems research and extension projects. She has previously worked at the International Potato Center in Peru, which included research in Rwanda.

Hugh L. Popenoe is professor of soil science and director of International Programs and the Center for Tropical Agriculture at the University of Florida. He chairs the Board of International Food and Agricultural Development and the Advisory Committee on Technology Innovations of the National Academy of Sciences; he also serves on the Board of Directors of the International Institute for Tropical Agriculture at Ibadan, Nigeria.

James R. Simpson is professor of food and resource economics at the University of Florida. He has conducted research on livestock marketing in Asia, Latin America, and Africa, including an assignment with the International Livestock Center for Africa based in Ethiopia.

Nigel J. H. Smith is associate professor of geography at the University of Florida. He has recently worked as a consultant in Africa for the Consultative Group on International Agricultural Research of the World Bank.

Anita Spring is associate professor of anthropology, associate dean of the College of Liberal Arts and Sciences, and director of the Women in Agriculture Program at the University of Florida. She has conducted research in Zambia, directed the Women in Agricultural Development Project in Malawi for the Women in Development Office of the United States Agency for International Development, and helped plan the upgrading of the agricultural university at Dschang, Cameroon.

John M. Staatz is assistant professor of agricultural economics at Michigan State University. He has previously worked for the Centre Ivorien de Recherche Economique et Sociale (Ivory Coast) and the Center for Research on Economic Development of the University of Michigan.

Patricia A. Wagner is associate professor of human nutrition in the Home Economics Program at the University of Florida. She has conducted research and published on the nutritional aspects of human health, community nutrition program development, and integration of human nutrition concerns into international food and agricultural development programs.

Olivia Webley recently completed an M.S. in forestry at the University of Florida. She has worked on village agricultural projects in Peru and India and is currently seeking a forestry position in Africa.

Index